GOD, ALLAH, AND THE GREAT LAND GRAB:
THE MIDDLE EAST IN TURMOIL

GOD, ALLAH, AND
THE GREAT LAND GRAB:
THE MIDDLE EAST IN TURMOIL

MERRILL SIMON

With a Foreword by
BINYAMIN NETANHAYU

Edited by Judith Featherman, Ed.D.

jɒ | Jonathan David Publishers, Inc.
Middle Village, New York 11379

**GOD, ALLAH, AND THE GREAT LAND GRAB:
THE MIDDLE EAST IN TURMOIL**

Address all inquiries to:
Jonathan David Publishers, Inc.
68-22 Eliot Avenue
Middle Village, NY 11379

Library of Congress Cataloging-in-Publication Data

Simon, Merrill.
    God, Allah, and the great land grab: the Middle East in turmoil/
Merrill Simon; edited by Judith Featherman.
        P. cm.
    Includes bibliographical references.
    ISBN 0-8246-0342-7
    1. Jewish-Arab relations. 2. Israel-Arab conflicts. 3. Israel-
-Politics and government. 4. Arab countries–Politics and
government—1945- I. Title.
DS119.7.S519 1989
956.04—dc20   89-35157
                                                              CIP

        1992   1991   1990   1989
    10 9 8 7 6 5 4 3 2 1

Library of Congress Cataloging in Publication Data

Printed in the United States of America

"The world that we have made as a result of the level of thinking we have done thus far creates problems we cannot solve at the same level at which we created them."

Albert Einstein

Dedication

To my son, Melech, his wife, Devorah,
and my grandchildren, Yisroel Meir,
Esther Leah, and the latest additions to their
family, my granddaughters, Brachah and Elisheva.

To my daughter, Michal, her husband, David,
and my grandchildren, Channah Sarah, Chava Eta,
Chaim Shalom, and the latest addition to their
family, my granddaughter, Chayah Leah.

Acknowledgements

I am totally indebted for the friendship and help afforded me by my very best friend in Israel—former Air Force Colonel and, more recently, Scientist of Israeli Aircraft Industries—Joseph (Yossi) Naor. Without his invaluable and incalculable assistance in time, effort, ideas, and information over the past seven years, this book could never have been written.

I also wish to extend my profound gratitude to:

My wife, Amalia, who continues her loving support with understanding and patience, while supporting my efforts in behalf of the Jewish people and the State of Israel.

My secretary, Joan Gannett, for coordinating and preparing materials for this as well as my five previous books.

My editor, Dr. Judith Featherman, for her meticulous work.

Contents

Preface xi
Foreword xiii
Introduction..................................xv
**PART ONE: HISTORY OF THE LAND AND
PEOPLE OF PALESTINE** 1
Overview 3
Historical Overview of the Region 6
  Palestina—A Roman Name 6
  The Area Referred to as "Palestine" 6
  The Jews and Their Land 7
  The Jews in Arabia 8
  Mohammed and the Jews 9
  The Arab Conquest and Arab Rule Over Palestine ...10
  The Land and Its People 11
  Immigration During the Ottoman Empire
    (1517 to 1917) 13
  The Illegal Division of Palestine 14
  Immigration During the British Mandate
    (1918 to 1948) 15
Historical Fate of Jews in Arab Lands 19
  Yemen 19
  Aden 20
  Iraq 20
  Egypt 21
  Morocco 22
  Algeria.....................................22
  Tunisia.....................................23

Syria 24
Lebanon 25
Libya 25
Summary 26
The Palestinian-Arab Political Movement 28
The Grand *Mufti* of Jerusalem 28
The Creation of the Palestinian Liberation
    Organization (PLO) 29
The Creation of *Fatah* 35
The Creation of PLO Splinter Groups 37
The PLO and Lebanon 41
PLO Propaganda 44
The PLO and World Terrorism 44
Peace for Galilee 46
Conclusion 46
Intifada 48
"Transjordan"—the Palestinian State 48
The Current Uprising 48

PART TWO: THE NATIONS OF THE MIDDLE
EAST AND THEIR SOURCES OF CONFLICT:
IMPACT ON RELATIONS WITH ISRAEL 51
Overview 53
Israel's Bordering Nations 58
Egypt 58
Lebanon 69
Syria 78
Jordan 84
Iraq 91
The African Arab Nations 97
Libya 97
Sudan 103
The Gulf States 107
Saudi Arabia 107
Bahrain 146
United Arab Emirates (UAE) 150
Qatar 154
Oman 158
Kuwait 162

The Yemens 167
  North Yemen (Yemen Arab Republic)...........167
  South Yemen (Peoples Democratic Republic
    of Yemen) 172
The Maghreb Nations 176
  Algeria.....................................176
  Morocco 180
  Tunisia.....................................184
Iran 187

**PART THREE: NON-AMERICAN GLOBAL
POWER CENTERS AND THE MIDDLE EAST:
THEIR INTERESTS, INVOLVEMENT,
INFLUENCE, AND IMPACT** 201
  Overview 203
  Western Europe 205
    Britain 205
    France 211
    Germany 213
    Turkey....................................216
  Union of Soviet Socialist Republics 218
    Imperialism 218
    Internal Political Structure 223
    The Soviet Union and the Middle East............229
    Soviet-Israeli Relations 230
  People's Republic of China 240
    The Western Nations, the Eastern Bloc, and Israel...241
    China and Israel 244

**PART FOUR: ISRAEL'S MILITARY
DEVELOPMENT: IMPACT ON GLOBAL
INTERESTS IN THE MIDDLE EAST** 249
  Overview 251
  Impact of Technology on the Philosophy of War......254
    Historical Review 254
    Assessment of the Present 266
    The Twenty-first Century 272
  Israel—The Only Middle East Military Ally of the
    United States 277

Tactical Conventional Military Power Redefined....279
The Iraq-Iran War 282
Israel's Military Strategy and Expansion...........291
Israel's Military Initiative 292
Israel—Weapon Systems Self-sufficiency 297
The Role of Science and Technology in Measuring
a Nation's Power...........................299
Worldwide Weapons Development—History and
the Present................................300
The Effect of Technology on Tank Warfare........305
Israel's Military-Industrial Complex Meets the
Future 306
Middle East Arms Race—The Facts 308
The Israeli Military Industry 310
Summary...................................316
Impact of Weapon Sales on the Middle East 318
Israel's Arms Procurement and Manufacturing......322
Israel's Rapid Deployment Force 334
Impact of Technology on Israel Over the Next Twenty
Years 340
Areas of Impact and the Effect on the Nation 340
Prospects for Arab-Israeli Peace 345
The Camp David Peace Agreement: A Model
or Antimodel for Future Arab-Israeli Treaties 345
The Middle East By the Twenty-first Century 356
Epilogue 359
Bibliography 364
Index 372

Preface

After having been interviewed hundreds of times on scores of radio and television programs about problems concerning the Middle East, I have realized the need to clarify the complexities of the issues for the layperson. It has taken me seven years to complete this project, with much of that time spent updating all that has transpired during this period.

This book has three fundamental objectives. The first is to give a pertinent history of the Middle East. This includes the so-called Palestinian problem, the history of Jewish-Arab relations in Arab lands, and the historical relationships of the superpowers—including Europe and China—to issues germane to that troubled region. It is a critical history which analyzes the legitimacy of Palestinian claims and the wisdom of many historically acclaimed decisions. Included in this history will be a pertinent account of each individual country that has had, or will have, a role to play in the Middle East. I use the word pertinent to emphasize the pains that have been taken to relieve the reader of excessive detail in the interests of clarity and brevity. Virtual libraries of material have been sifted through for the sole purpose of making this vast subject as understandable as possible.

The second objective is to apprise the reader of the arms race, which continues to run amuck in the Middle East. This includes an analysis of the dangers that are present, given the sophistication of the weaponry and the value systems of the countries who receive them. All terms, such as balance of power, parity, and deterrence, take on new meanings in a nuclear age, but, in the

Levant, the nuances resonate to the sound of a different drummer. It has been my aim to be sensitive to that.

The third objective is to present the possible geopolitical scenarios, given all the factors which have already been stated. I have projected various alternatives which are, obviously, dependent on the whims and the whispers of a region that will continue to be in *turmoil* for many years to come. One of the major factors is the current revival of Shi'ite- and/or Sunni-Islamic fundamentalism, which threatens the basic stability of regimes that have enjoyed decades of untroubled longevity. Now, as fundamentalism rages as a transnational force, even among the intellectual community of Arab lands, one can see the danger it presents for regimes which, heretofore, have had more moderate attitudes toward the West and Western values. It is this factor that prompted the title of this book, *God, Allah, and the Great Land Grab: The Middle East in Turmoil,* for it is this development which has eclipsed the Arab-Israeli dispute and should become the focal point of concern for everyone in the Free World for years to come.

Merrill Simon

Foreword

There are those who would have the West believe that the campaign to eradicate the State of Israel has ended and that all Israel must do to achieve peace is to find some combination of reassuring words and territorial concessions. We in Israel, unfortunately, have little choice but to see the situation in a more sober light. We live with ceaseless attempts at terrorist infiltration and rocket attacks, violent disruption of civil life, the murder of Arabs willing to make peace with us, and the constant threat of renewed war.

And with all this, we must contend with a relentless campaign of disinformation which strives to convince the world that Israel is not the victim of aggression but its perpetrator and that terrorism by another name is not terrorism. Sadly, these efforts pose a greater threat to Israel's resilience than all past wars.

It is in response to this torrent of half-truths and blatant distortions about the Middle East that Merrill Simon has chosen to write what can only be described as a courageous book. He explores some of the crucial and often misunderstood aspects of the long battle to secure the survival of the Jewish State. He probes the most pressing historical and moral aspects of the Middle East in his own provocative and direct manner.

Simon pulls no punches, whether in depicting the origins of Islamic fundamentalism's antagonism toward Jews, or in describing the present machinations of the Arab States and their numerous abettors. Similarly, he leads us through the maze of inter-Arab conflicts in order to put the role of each nation in the region into sharper perspective. The threats, which have greeted others willing to view Islamic extremism with a critical eye, seem not to daunt him at all.

Simon rejects an apologetic vision of the Jewish State. He sees an Israel which has struggled for survival for more than forty years—and which has not lost sight of its aspirations and its values. It is an Israel at war with the forces of terror and totalitarianism in the Middle East. It is an Israel which has created a superb military force and which has become the West's principal strategic asset in the region. It is also an Israel which has not abandoned the dream for a secure and prosperous peace with all its Arab neighbors.

Many of Merrill Simon's ideas for the direction in which Israel must move in the coming decade make sense. We must achieve greater economic, technological, and military independence, as the pillars upon which to build our future. These aims must serve as the cornerstone of the education for the next generation of Israel's political and military leaders.

But the realization of such a future requires above all else a knowledge and an understanding of the truth—something which is increasingly difficult to come by in the Middle East. In recent years, assaults at the United Nations and a sophisticated and well-trained Arab propaganda machine have made it necessary to reestablish the basic facts of the Arab-Israeli conflict. Merrill Simon's book is an important reminder of those truths, which are so indispensable for understanding the enduring strife in the Middle East and for proposing realistic solutions to it.

Binyamin Netanyahu
Deputy Foreign Minister

Introduction

The Israeli-Arab conflict is not the world's most important issue; it is also very far from being the bloodiest struggle in the world, not even in the Middle East. And yet, listening to radio broadcasts, watching the daily news on television or reading the daily press, one would naturally be led to think that this is indeed the most terrible conflict in this century. It is easy to illustrate the distortion.

Take for example the events of this week, the week of June 1989. The U.N. Security Council met in order to discuss the expulsion by Israel of eight Arabs, convicted of instigating and directing major attacks against civilians (Jews and Arabs) and against the Israeli Defense Forces. Early in 1988, they were sentenced to be expelled from the country and then appealed to the Special Tribunal which had been set up for such purposes. Their appeal having been rejected, they appealed again, this time to the Israeli Supreme Court. The two appeals lasted a year. Finally in June 1989, the Supreme Court rejected the second appeal, and the expulsions took place. Israel was censored by the Security Council, and the United States, supposedly an ally, nevertheless did not cast its vetoing vote. The story appeared in the *New York Times* on the front page.

In the same week, Bulgaria expelled 64,000 of its citizens, ethnically Turkish. The Turks conquered Bulgaria and settled it 500 years ago. In recent times, the Muslim Turks have multiplied at a higher rate than the Christian Bulgars. One day in June, the Bulgarian cabinet decided to do something about it and started mass expulsions. The Turkish government protested. The events and the protest got a few lines in the *New York Times,* on an inside page. The television networks considered the expulsion a trivial matter and no mention was made of it in the news broadcasts.

Another example: in 1988, Iraq used chemical weapons against its Kurdish minority. About 5,000 Kurdish villagers were gassed and died in one day. The *New York Times* reported this story on an inside page. On the other hand, almost every Arab killed by Israeli troops while hurling a stone or a Molotov cocktail, makes the front page of the paper.

This is one reason for the urgent need for a book such as this one. It presents a balanced account of the realities of the Middle East. It explains the Israeli-Arab conflict while including a more complete view of the background. Simon touches upon the six wars that are still raging in the area even after the end of the bloodiest—the Iraq-Iran War. At this writing, fighting is going on in Kurdistan (in Northern Iraq), where some fifty thousand Kurds are fleeing the Iraqi massacres and crossing the border into unfriendly but at least inactive Turkey. In Lebanon, the Syrians are still shelling Christian Beirut, the Hizbullah Shiites are attacking the Amal Shiites, while both militias are trying to penetrate Israel's northern border. Between North and South Yemen, the 1986 conflict is still smouldering and tribes that relate to North Yemen are being attacked by the South Yemen army. In Sudan, the extremely bloody war in the South has already killed hundreds of thousands; a truce declared by the civilian government of Saddik el Mahdi in June 1989 has just been cancelled by the new military government after the "Putsch" in early July. In Chad, the Lybian army is again on the move, its crushing defeat of 1987 notwithstanding. In the former Spanish Sahara, the Algerian-supported "Polisario" forces are still fighting the Moroccan army. This is the background which is generally ignored when the Western media deal with the Israeli-Arab conflict. Simon's book enables the reader to preserve a sense of proportion. It is carefully constructed in a quasi-encyclopaedic form. It covers the social, demographic, economical, technological, military, and political facts. Mr. Simon's experience overlaps most of these fields and enables him to juxtapose these heterogenous elements in a balanced and interesting synthesis.

In Part I, Merrill Simon introduces the reader to the region, covering its history and in particular the history of the downtrodden Jewish communities living in their "mellahs" (ghettos) in Arab countries. The yellow patch, so symbolic in its characterization of the status of the Jews, was first introduced by Arab rulers and only later copied by Christian rulers in Europe. The impression, prevalent in the West, according to which Jews lived a free existence throughout the centuries in the Arab world is completely wrong. It is only in tenth-century Ommayad Spain that Jews indeed enjoyed relative freedom and equality; the period called "The Golden Age."

In Part II, we become acquainted with the complex network of conflicts within the Arab and Moslem Middle East.

Part III describes the effects of outside influences. With the background thus fully covered, Simon now presents Israel, its strengths and its weaknesses.

Part IV is where Merrill Simon's familiarity with the impact and potentialities of modern technology helps explain how Israel with its less than four million Jews can survive in the midst of all this turbulence.

Since November 1987, the Arab-Israeli conflict has taken a new turn. In fact, it is a return to 1920–21, 1929, 1936–39. It is described as a "popular rebellion" in which the action is carried out in great part by the youth and children. It is interesting that when in 1986–88, in the Iraq-Iran War, the Iranians used batallions of teenagers to clear the minefields in the Basra area (by sending them through the minefields), world opinion was shocked and the Iranians certainly lost the image they projected in the West. In the story of the Palestinian-Arab teenagers, we again have a distorted picture. The heroism of these children is praised instead of focusing on the parents who send their immature children to be killed. This is but another example of the double standard used by the media and press when dealing with Israel.

Let us compare the Israeli situation with the case of South Africa, a comparison often made by Israel's enemies. South Africa's popular consists of 18 million Blacks, 4 million Whites, 3 million "Coloured" (descendants of imported Malay workers and Blacks), and .5 million Indians. Recently, the South African government has extended the franchise to the Coloured and Indians, thus reaching a figure of some 7.5 million for the "rulers." At the same time, South Africa has embarked on a program of creating 10 or 11 independent countries ("homelands"), including most of the rural areas heavily populated by Blacks. In the final stage, only those Blacks that come to work in the larger South African cities would remain under South

Africa's rule, as resident aliens whose nationality would relate to their original tribal homelands.

Three such homelands have already been granted independence. In one of these, there has already even been a revolution. And yet not one country in the world has recognized the new status. World opinion says to the White rulers of South Africa: your country is indivisible. We do not accept these "gerrymanderings." There is only one acceptable solution to your situation, namely "one man, one vote." Some day you will have to accept majority rule and you will have to accustom yourselves to the status of a minority, like in Rhodesia-Zimbabwe.

Now take Israel. Between the Jordan and the Mediterranean, the Arabs make up roughtly one-third of the total population (we include both "Israeli" Arabs in Jerusalem or Galilee etc., and the Arabs of Judea, Samaria, and Gaza, indigenous or refugees), the Jews representing two-thirds. The area of Israel is about one-fiftieth of the area of South Africa (it is of about the size of Connecticut). About two-thirds of the Arabs (i.e. two-ninths of the total population) live in the three geographically disconnected districts of Judea, Samaria, and Gaza. All three together have about the area of Long Island. And yet these Arabs demand an independent state and are ready to kill and to be killed for it.

Logically, world opinion should have told these Arabs: if South Africa cannot be divided, so much more so tiny Israel. You Arabs should understand that you are a small minority in this land and you should just accept majority rule. Condition yourselves to life as a minority in a Jewish State. We shall help you get your rights, we shall help you resettle the refugees (making up one-half of the population of the three districts). But forget about that impossible Palestinian "State," and, also, do not count on Israel being some day destroyed by Arab armies.

Instead, world opinion supports the Arab demands for a twenty-second Arab state that would dismember the only existing Jewish state! As to the Jews, they are so used to suffering from these double standards that they do not even try to fight the distortions in the media. This is why books such as this one are so needed.

Dr. Yuval Ne'eman
Member of the Knesset
(Former Minister of Science)

Part One

HISTORY OF THE LAND AND PEOPLE OF PALESTINE

History of the Land and People of Palestine

Overview

Only Israel has re-emerged three times as a nation—each time after decades or centuries of occupation and destruction. Throughout the past 3,000 years, only the Jewish nation has existed continuously on the land of Palestine. Although Palestine was occupied and ruled by foreign powers, during the periods in between destruction, there was *always* a Jewish presence, and Jewish majorities were maintained in the three holy cities of Safed, Jerusalem, and Tiberias. Not until after the modern state of Israel emerged in May 1948 did the Arabs living in Palestine refer to themselves as Palestinians. Before that, they never considered Palestine nationally but, rather, as part of some other Arab entity.

Since 1948, the world has been plagued by the inability to find a solution to the Arab-Palestinian refugee problem. The entire world of Arab nations has not allowed a settlement—short of the destruction of the State of Israel. This is the case, even though until June 1967 Israel occupied less than 20 percent of the land of Palestine and since the 1967 war, approximately 25 percent of the land—all west of the Jordan River. That has left King Hussein ruling over all of eastern Palestine, inhabited by a sizable majority of Arabs who identify as Palestinians.

Since 1973 (although to some extent since 1967) the world body politic has accepted the concept that those Arabs living in

Judea, Samaria, and Gaza along with Palestinian refugees in Lebanon present not just a refugee problem but a political one requiring a political solution. For many, such a political solution calls for Palestinian self-determination.

Since the inception of the December 1987 *Intifada* (uprising) in Judea, Samaria, and Gaza and the subsequent cessation of active hostilities between Iraq and Iran, King Hussein's rule over eastern Palestine (renamed Transjordan by the British in 1922) has been, paradoxically, extremely tenuous. Iran's freedom to export her Shi'ite extremist fundamentalism throughout the Moslem world and the realization that those forces leading and organizing the *Intifada* in Israel (western Palestine) were Shi'ite Fundamentalists was one of the factors that helped convince Hussein to relinquish all claims to the "West Bank" that he had occupied until June 1967.

Hussein's problem, however, is inescapable. Not only does he occupy 75 percent of Palestine, but nearly that percentage of his subjects consider themselves Palestinians. The assertion that Jordan is not Palestine made King Hussein a steward of the West Bank unable to trade "Palestinian land" for peace with Israel. Since the Palestinians were unable to assert their nationhood in Jordan where they are a majority, the only place left was the area of Judea, Samaria, and Gaza where they were occupied and stateless. The world (including Israel) has supported the fiction that the only Palestinian problem that exists is west of the Jordan River. Along with this fiction comes the belief that once Palestinian self-determination is discussed, the majority of the East Bank inhabitants won't want to be counted.

Since Hussein is not shackled by democratic restraints, he is able to deal ruthlessly with any Palestinian *Intifada* within his boundaries. Since "Black September 1970," the Palestinian Liberation Organization (PLO) has placed Palestinian national aspirations within Jordan on a back burner. Israel has co-operated with the sham that Jordan is not Palestine, and even saved Hussein from a Palestinian takeover in 1970. That was all well and good as long as the Israelis could deal with Hussein regarding the West Bank rather than with the Palestinians; however, now that Hussein has renounced any claim to the West Bank, the situation is much different. The Jordanian charade can no longer be useful to either Israel or the Palestinian Arabs. If the issues at hand are Palestinian self-determination and Palestinian sovereignty, then they cannot be resolved or confined to negotiations about title of the West Bank and Gaza when eastern Palestine has a Palestinian majority. Hashemite suppression of a Palestinian identity on the East Bank (eastern Palestine) becomes an obstacle to a political and territorial resolution of the historic conflict between Israel and the Palestinian Arabs.

Historical Overview of the Region

PALESTINA—A ROMAN NAME

The ancient principality of Judea was renamed Palestina by the Romans to eradicate any traces that remained of Jewish civilization. This tactic was employed after the Bar-Kochba revolt in the second century. The name Palestina can be traced back to the Philistines, an agrarian people, who settled in southern Palestine in Biblical times where they founded a series of city-states. They existed as independent city-states for only a short time and, certainly, were nowhere to be found during the Roman period. The name Palestine never appears in either the Old or New Testament; the area was referred to as Judea, the name that was used continuously to as late as the fourth century.

THE AREA REFERRED TO AS "PALESTINE"

From Roman times—after the suppression of the great Bar-Kochba revolt—until the League of Nations gave Britain the mandate over the area in 1919, the land now commonly called Palestine was never a proper country and had no frontiers. There were boundaries only for administrative purposes. This territory, as it was mandated to the British, is now occupied by Israel west of the Jordan River (25 percent of the land) and by Jordan east of the Jordan River (75 percent of the land). The *same* area had been ruled by the Turks during the Ottoman Empire (A.D. 1517 to 1917), the Mamelukes (1291 to 1516), the Christians during the Crusader period (1099 to 1291), the Arab caliphates (637 to

1099), the Persians (614 to 628), the Byzantines (395 to 614), and the Romans (70 to 395).

Since Biblical days and the establishment of the first Jewish nation in 1220 B.C., *most* of that same area had been occupied during one period or another by the Jews (Hebrews). Throughout the history of this area—called Palestine since 1000 B.C.—Amman and Petra, the two major cities of modern-day Jordan, were always included. It must be noted that while any Arab presence in the area referred to as Palestine began only in A.D. 637 there has been a continuous Jewish presence since the days of the Hebrew patriarchs—Abraham, Isaac, and Jacob. No Arab nation ever adopted the name Palestine for this region prior to the establishment of the State of Israel in 1948. Even today, the Syrians consider this area to be part of greater Syria and officially refer to it as Southern Syria.

THE JEWS AND THEIR LAND

From a religious perspective, an area encompassing Palestine was promised to the Hebrews in G-d's covenant with Abraham approximately 4,000 years ago. From an historical perspective, however, the Jews' devout attachment to this area dates back to 1220 B.C., when Israel first became a nation. From that time until today, there has always been a Jewish presence on the land. Even during those periods when foreigners who ruled the land attempted to extinguish them and when Jewish settlement was diminished, return to Jerusalem was always in the prayers and thoughts of the entire Jewish people. Since the Babylonian exile until today, Jews have sung, "If I forget thee, O' Jerusalem, may my right hand lose its cunning." Throughout the centuries Diaspora Jews have observed the commandment of pilgrimage to the Holy Land.

Roman efforts to convert the Jewish nation, Judea, and her capital, Jerusalem, met with little success. Even after approximately 500,000 Jews were slain by the Romans who renamed the territory Palestine, the Jews did not abandon their land; for them, the name Judea did not disappear. And when the Romans changed Jerusalem's name to Aelia Capitolina, to the Jews it was still Jerusalem. The Jews remained loyal to their land and its capital, Jerusalem.

Before the Roman dispersion of the Jewish people in A.D. 70, there were approximately 5 million Jews living in Palestine. From that time until the Bar-Kochba revolt in 132 to 135, there still remained 3 million Jews in Palestine. At those times when the Temple was destroyed, the religious center shifted from Jerusalem to Yavne or to Tiberias in the Galilee. This demonstrated Jewish attachment to the whole area and not just to one particular city.

When the Byzantines replaced the Romans (in A.D. 395), the Jews were no longer a majority in the land; however, they were still an important element in the ethnic make-up of the area. In fact, when the Persians invaded the area in 611, the Jews, disenchanted with Byzantine rule, reinforced Persian regiments with an estimated 20,000 soldiers.

THE JEWS IN ARABIA

It was in the seventh century A.D. that Islam, born in the land called Arabia, began to make its mark on the world. The arrival of the Jews in Arabia and their locations of settlement have importance in the history of Jewish-Arab relations, for it is there where the Jewish-Arab conflict actually began. The locations of Jewish communities in the Arabian Peninsula both before and after Mohammed have influenced Jewish-Arab relationships to this day.

The earliest Jewish settlement of Arabia probably occurred after the fall of Samaria in 720 B.C. The recently discovered Jewish colony of Aswan dates back to that time when Jews fled their ancient northern capital. Several historians have affirmed that the city of Medina, earlier called Yathrib, was first settled by Jewish tribes. They had brought with them advanced agricultural methods and were also skilled artisans. Those skills sustained them well—better than the surrounding cultures. Attracted by the relative prosperity brought by those Jewish tribes, pagan Arabs settled in those areas and, eventually, achieved a majority. But, at the beginning of the seventh century A.D.—the dawn of Islam—Jews still comprised at least 50 percent of the city of Medina.

Jews became the dominant force in the economic life of

Arabia. For example, in the kingdom of Himyar, which was situated on the east coast of the Red Sea, conversion to Judaism was prevalent. Commoners and royalty alike converted to Judaism. The Jewish community in Arabia was swelled by the influx of the Jews who fled persecution by the Persians in the fifth century. It wasn't long before Jews became wealthy landowners there. The economic and cultural supremacy of the Arabian Jews contributed greatly to Arab jealousy and hatred. Their bounty was coveted by Arab tribes in general and, in particular, by the Quaraysh tribe of which Mohammed himself was a member.

MOHAMMED AND THE JEWS

When Mohammed began to proliferate his teachings, he was irritated by the refusal of the Jews to recognize him as a true prophet and to accept his teachings. The basic Jewish tenets would not allow the inclusion of Jesus and Ishmael among the prophets who had already been canonized.

When Mohammed attacked and murdered two Jews and broke precedent by not paying blood money, the stage was set for expulsion, exploitation, expropriation, and forced conversion of the Jewish people. The mass slaughter of Jews at the Jewish oasis of Khaibar and the complete extermination of two Jewish tribes, leaving not even one surviving child, was as heinous as any crusader catastrophe and has no parallel in Jewish history other than the twentieth century Nazi Holocaust.

The prophet Mohammed proclaimed, "Two religions may not dwell together on the Arabian Peninsula." The slaughter of Jews and the expropriation of Jewish property became an extension of Allah's will. As so aptly put in the Koran, "Some you slew and some you took captive. Allah made you masters of the Jews' land, their houses, and their goods."

After the slaughters and the expropriations, those Jews who remained were required to pay a 50 percent tribute for protection. From this evolved the notion of the *dhimmi*—the tolerated minority. (This head tax became an important source of revenue for Islamic caliphs—successors to the prophet Mohammed; a form of this tax is still practiced today in North Yemen.) Many Jews fled Arabia and returned to Palestine. Their return coincided with the conquering of the land of Palestine by the Arabs. The plundering of that land and the Jewish people began in the identical way as in Arabia.

THE ARAB CONQUEST AND ARAB RULE OVER PALESTINE

Although today an Arab nation is one in which Arabic is the official language and an Arab is one whose primary tongue is Arabic, the literal definition of Arab is raider, or nomad, as distinct from one who is sedentary. The Koran uses the term exclusively in this sense. Mohammed and his contemporaries were the Arabs of the desert—Bedouins.

The first wave of the Arab conquest was not deliberately calculated. Bands of pagan Bedouin raiders, forbidden by their new faith, Mohammedanism, to engage in fratricidal combat, had to find new objectives to attack. They never thought in terms of settling in, as that lifestyle was absolutely foreign to their way of life. Nevertheless, Arab bands did manage to carve out pieces of territory which evolved into loosely formed confederacies. They eventually became part of the genuine, but short-lived, Arab Empire. The actual condition of Arabs governing Arabs was indeed a brief phenomenon that lasted much less than 100 years. It occurred only during the Umayyad caliphate (A.D. 661 to 750) in the so-called Damascus period. The Arabs' inability to develop any imperial administration made longevity impossible—their patriarchal system was about all they could manage.

During the first century of the Arab conquest, the caliph and the governors of Syria and Palestine were the sole rulers over their Jewish and Christian subjects. Through a gradual process of expropriation of Christian and Jewish land, they became wealthy landowners themselves. Nevertheless, the Jews and Christians still worked the land, since the Arab nomad (Bedouin) had no use for the rigors of farm labor. The Umayyad caliphate that ruled over Palestine during that period was more concerned with military enforcement than with building an agrarian economy. Islam, at that time, had yet to become widespread.

During the long reign of the subsequent Baghdad caliphate (A.D. 750 to 934), the ministers, administrators, and soldiers were not Arabs. They were Turks, Turkomanians, Iranians, Circassians, and Kurds—all converts to Islam; there were no Arab rulers among them. In other words, the indigenous Arab population was never interested in establishing an empire. Neither were they interested in being rooted to one particular geographic location; it was foreign to their culture. Hence, it was no accident that Palestine in those days was never considered a separate political entity; it was merely an area labeled by Rome. In fact, cultural development in this region may have been an Islamic phenomenon but not an Arab one. It was Islam that allowed the Arab caliphs to co-opt their non-Arab coreligionists, borrow their cultural heritage, and reclaim it as their own. Pure indigenous Arab culture contributed nothing lasting to be remembered by the world.

It was only in the tenth century that the majority of the Middle East converted to Islam. That mass conversion is attributed to the tax exemption given to all adherents of Islam. During that period, the Islamic religion and the Arabic language became commonplace among the multiethnic Moslem community, and the word "Arab" became redefined as a term of social convenience rather than one of ethnic origin.

The conquest of the Holy Land by the Crusaders (A.D. 1099) brought about the decimation of the Moslem and Jewish populations in Jerusalem. The slaughter was so complete that, after the Moslems reconquered the area at the end of the thirteenth century, they had to import foreigners to repopulate the deserted land. Turks, Slavs, Greeks, Georgians, and Circassians were among those transplanted to Palestine during those years. It is clear that at no time was the land either purely or indigenously Arab. Rather, it was a huge multiethnic community of dispossessed, transplanted peoples who spoke the same language—Arabic. There was certainly no Palestinian identity nor any conscious claim by the Arabs over the land at that time.

THE LAND AND ITS PEOPLE

For the 1,250 years between the Arab conquest of the area (A.D. 637) and the beginning of the Jewish return in the 1880s by the Biluim, Palestine was desolate and deserted. The hillsides were barren—devoid of trees and foliage, and the valleys were robbed of their topsoil. In 1687, Nazareth was a small, insignificant village; Nablus consisted of two streets; and Jericho was poor and sparsely populated. As late as 1816, the town of Jaffa was just a small village—certainly not the bustling metropolis it was to become. In 1840, Jerusalem was populated by only 15,000 inhabitants—more than half of whom were Jews. Haifa, at that time, was considered to be one of the great municipalities with a population of 6,000. By the mid-nineteenth century, the total population of Palestine had diminished to only 300,000 people. The status of Palestine at the end of the nineteenth century was appropriately summarized by the noted writer David Landes. He stated, "As a result of Turkish neglect and rule, the land has been given over to land marsh mosquito, clan feuds, and Bedouin marauders."

Periodically, during the nineteenth century when Arabia suffered from "overpopulation" of migrant Arabs, a great number of Bedouin tribes wandered into the region of Palestine, since their lifestyle required vast expanses of exploitable land. When Jewish settlement of Palestine began in the late 1800s, Kurds, Turkomans, Tartars, Turks, Algerians, and Egyptians also moved into the area, attracted by the relative wealth that accompanied Jewish settlement. Today's "Arabs" of Safed are mostly descendants of Kurdish and Moorish settlers from that time.

The vast majority of those immigrants did not, ultimately, strike roots in their new "homeland." Most of the land was owned by several prominent families and was tilled by a sharecropping system. Prominent Moslem families—Al-Huayni, Al-Khalidi, and Al-Nashashibi—acquired huge tracts of land that were worked by peasant immigrants who eventually abandoned the land to escape the yoke of their masters. The land was left without owners and without workers.

The Jews, on the other hand, had begun settlements in the desert, many of which, after much hardship, became viable economic entities. The so-called non-Jewish Palestinians wandered the countryside because they were neither bound to the soil nor attached to the land. It was the opportunity created by Jewish settlements that drew peasant immigrants by the tens of thousands to the area called Palestine.

In 1844, a U.S. expedition under Lynch recorded fewer than 8,000 Turks in Jaffa, which had a population of 13,000. Bustling towns such as Tiberias and Safed had Jewish majorities by 1851. At the same time, Jews counted for half the population of Jerusalem. Smaller Jewish settlements such as Zichron Ya'akov, Hadera, Petach Tikva, and Rishon L'Zion attracted droves of Moslem itinerants who were desperate for work. In 1858, British Consul James Finn reported that the Mohammedans were scarcely one quarter of the entire population. One historian reported that the Moslem population of Palestine in 1882 was 141,000. Of this number, at least 25 percent were newcomers. In 1889, Rishon L'Zion was founded by forty Jewish families. They were followed by more than ten times that many families from Egypt and elsewhere. In 1914, Petach Tikva's population consisted of 2,000 Jewish settlers, 600 resident Arab workers, and 1,100 itinerant Arabs.

Masses of landless, impoverished peasants—endemic to the Middle East—quickly seized the opportunities created by the new Jewish settlements. The wealthy feudal lords, the *effendis,* were selling off their land to the settlers at astronomical prices, while simultaneously inciting violent demonstrations against the Jewish presence and the Jewish settlement. In fact, most Jewish land was appropriated from the *effendis* or from absentee landlords. The Jezreel Valley, for example, was purchased from only two people—a Turkish sultan and a wealthy Syrian banker.

IMMIGRATION DURING THE OTTOMAN EMPIRE (1517 TO 1917)

During the Ottoman Empire (1517 to 1917), the Turks ruled over the entire Middle East, including Palestine. While severely restricting Jewish immigration, the Turks encouraged impoverished Arab itinerants to settle in Palestine. Arab laborers from all over the Middle East found their way to Palestine for the sake of earning higher wages from Jewish settlers who provided employment. The French geographer, Vital Cuinet, described the "enormity" of Arab immigration into Palestine at that time.

Some historians claim Turkish restrictions on Jewish immigration anticipated the Arab awareness that the higher wages offered by Jewish settlers might liberate the peasantry. This put the *effendis* in a bind. The higher wages offered by the infidel

Jew inhibited the traditional exploitative practices of the *effendis* in the region. Yet the situation also encouraged Arab-Moslem immigration to the area.

The problem created by restricted Jewish immigration under Turkish rule escalated when the Biluim (first *aliyah*) from Russia started to flow into Palestine in 1882. By the 1880s, Palestine was an underpopulated land depleted in number because of wanton exploitation of the peasant population by the *effendis* and the total neglect of a land laid to waste. The population of all of Palestine before the period of Jewish settlement in the 1880s was 300,000. There were fewer than 150,000 indigenous Arabs on the land; the balance was comprised of 65,000 nomadic Bedouins, 55,000 Christians, and 35,000 Jews. In 1881, the area of Palestine settled by the Jews west of the Jordan River had a population of only 155,000 of whom 35,000 were Jews. By 1922, there were 84,000 Jews in that area; by 1945, 554,000 Jews. Today, the vast majority of Israel's 3.7 million Jews are settled in this once desolate region.

THE ILLEGAL DIVISION OF PALESTINE

With the demise of the Ottoman Empire in 1918 at the end of World War I, Britain sought to facilitate her own imperialist intentions in the Middle East by requesting a mandate over the area from the League of Nations. The Palestine mandate was originally granted to the British in 1920 at the San Remo Conference. It was approved in 1922 by the League of Nations to establish a Jewish national home that was to cover the entire area of Palestine, which included both the East Bank and West Bank of the Jordan River. The territory was unilaterally and illegally divided by the British for the purpose of compensating the Saudi *Emir* Abdullah for his help in defeating the Turks. His reward became Transjordan—all the mandated territory east of the Jordan River (although a small part, the Golan Heights, was ceded to the French mandate of Syria in 1923). The territory called Transjordan, which covered 38,000 square miles (sq mi) and represented 75 percent of Palestine, was declared closed to Jewish settlement. The territory west of the Jordan, which contained less than 8,000 sq mi and represented only 25 percent of Palestine, was open to Jewish and Arab settlement. Thus, the

British by their mendacity nourished the seeds of Arab-Jewish friction.

IMMIGRATION DURING THE BRITISH MANDATE (1918 TO 1948)

At the beginning of the British mandate, the indigenous Arab population of Palestine was relatively few in number and was immigrant in character. The question remains: where did the myth originate that immigrant Jews displaced the native Arab population of Palestine, and why was that myth misconstrued to be irrefutable fact? The assumption was that the non-Jewish population of Palestine was Arab and was native to the land. But an examination of the 1931 population census of Palestine discloses that twenty-three languages were in use by the Moslem population, while another twenty-eight languages were spoken by the Christian population. In that 1931 census, the non-Jews in Palestine listed twenty-four different lands of origin. What actually happened is that western Palestine, because of the economic climate created by Jewish settlement, became a magnet for migrant Moslems and Christians from faraway lands who were in search of a better life.

Although Arab immigration into western Palestine was to have been limited, British complicity in illegal Arab immigration was incredulous. While Jewish immigration was meticulously recorded, illegal Arab immigration was purposefully concealed by the British authorities. For example, in 1934, 30,000 to 36,000 illegal Arab immigrants from Syria entered Palestine freely without passport or visa; however, the British record showed that only 1,784 non-Jewish immigrants had entered the country legally and that only 3,000 itinerants had remained illegally. Such illegal immigration from Syria, which continued until 1940, had been disclosed by a Syrian leader and substantiated by private and secret British correspondence files. It had been agreed that refugees who appeared to be Syrian, Lebanese, or Palestinian by nationality would be admitted to Palestine without passport or visa. There is no way of evaluating the size of the illegal immigration from Jordan, Saudi Arabia, or any other Arab area, but one can assume that British complicity was prejudicial not only toward the Syrians.

A British official attested, in a confidential correspondence, that the police had no special instructions to pick up Arabs who entered Palestine illegally. The Royal Palestinian Commission heard public testimony that confirmed widespread illegal Arab immigration to Jewish-settled areas and other parts of western Palestine. One official admitted that 50 percent of the Haifa dockworkers originated from Transjordan and that there were also Sudanese from Hejaz and Yemen.

The British were so determined to stop Jewish immigration into Palestine that the British foreign office called its ambassador in Berlin in March 1934 and ordered the British envoy to inform the German government about the means of escape being utilized by Jews and to ask the German authorities to discourage such travel.

The White Paper of 1939—issued by the British government at a time when millions of Jewish refugees would have swum to Palestine to escape the Nazis—was an unalterable betrayal of the pledge to observe the tenets of the internationally mandated Jewish homeland in Palestine. The White Paper's rigid qualifications prohibited most Jews from entering Palestine. The restrictions were so inflexible that even the tiny quota for Jewish settlers—10,000 a year for 5 years with a bonus of 25,000 more refugees—was, tragically, not exhausted at the war's end. Of the Jewish refugees who had reached Palestine, 51,000 were allowed to stay—less than 1 percent. During all the years of the British mandatory control, roughly 400,000 Jews were allowed into the small piece of land that was allocated to the Jewish national home, and all of those were in only the Jewish-settled area of the land called western Palestine.

At the very time that the White Paper was defended and rationalized by the British claim that Palestine had reached the outside limit of her absorptive capacity for Jewish workers, the same British government enacted special legislation that enabled the Palestine administration to import thousands of illegal Arab workers to meet the increased job needs of the government. A survey made later by the Anglo-American community observed that the great majority of Arab laborers from Syria, Lebanon, and Egypt, who were brought by trucks and trains to fill the demand for labor—thereby exceeding the local supply in western Palestine—were presumed to have remained in Palestine illegally.

Those thousands upon thousands of employment opportunities—continually created through the efforts of Palestinian Jews—discredited the British government's unrealistically low estimate of the capacity of the country to absorb new immigrants. Had those jobs been left open to Jews, instead of being usurped by illegal Arab immigrants who were falsely represented as part of the original and existing Palestinian population for thousands of years, many factors would have changed. The Jewish population would have grown by at least 20,000 or more, while the non-Jewish population of western Palestine (Palestinian Arabs) would have decreased by the very minimum of 20,000. The resulting proportional changes in the population might have caused the British to open the gates to the Jews fleeing to their national home in western Palestine, instead of sealing their fates in the extermination camps of Europe.

Malcolm MacDonald, designer of the White Paper that limited Jewish immigration and, therefore, no friend of the Zionists, said in 1938, "The Arabs cannot say that the Jews are driving them out of the country. If not a single Jew had come to Palestine after 1918, I believe that the Arab population of western Palestine today (over 1 million) would still have been around the 600,000 figure." This number referred to the whole of Palestine, not just to the Jewish-settled areas. And that figure never distinguished the Arabs who had been living in western Palestine a long time from those who had just recently arrived. Although it is not clear how many Arabs ever lived in densely Jewish-settled areas before the Jews arrived, it must be understood that Jewish settlements had been relegated to a truncated area consisting of 25 percent of Palestine, while 75 percent had been given to the Arabs.

While Arabs propagated the myth that they were being displaced from their native land, the truth was that they were displacing Jews who had tried to settle in barren areas in the Jewish national homeland. From the outset, an erroneous geographic assumption acquired validity and became ingrained into the conflict. This was that *Jewish-settled areas covered all of Palestine.* Consequently, the assumption extended to the conclusion that Jewish settlers displaced Arab settlers—that Palestinian Arabs were being excluded from Palestine.

However, a question begs to be asked: from which Palestine were the Arabs being excluded? Remember, in 1883, in the 25 percent of Palestine later set aside by the British for Jewish settlement, there were only 120,000 non-Jews of which 55,000 were Christians.

In 1939, Winston Churchill stated explicitly that ". . . Arabs have crowded in greater numbers to Palestine than Jews." The Arabs were a nomadic people who never conceptualized a homeland. Striking roots was an anathema to them. Yet, the wandering Jew never wandered by choice; he was always forced to flee from persecutions, expulsions, pogroms, mass murder, etc.

The return of the Jews to Palestine is unique in the annals of the history of mankind in that they are the only people ever to return to their homeland and re-establish their nation. And they did it three times: (1) Moses and the Exodus, (2) after the destruction of the First Temple, and (3) after 1881 (the first *aliyah*).

Historical Fate of Jews in Arab Lands

There has been a myth that Jews have fared well in Arab lands and that, unlike the Christians, there was no need for the Jews to flee from their Arab cousins. A brief survey of how Jews have fared in Arab lands demonstrates that nothing could have been further from the truth.

YEMEN

In 1948, the Yemenite-Jewish community was at least 2,000 years old; some Yemenite Jews claim their ancestry from the destruction of the First Temple in 586 B.C. The Jews in Yemen lived in ghettos, and, throughout the Middle Ages, were victims of persecution and torture. During the thirteenth century, Maimonides, the venerable Rabbi and physician, had to beseech the Yemenite people not to convert and to keep their Jewish faith. This was documented in the famous Epistle of Yemen. Throughout the nineteenth century, Yemenite Jews were victims of hunger; starvation was so common that no accurate Jewish census could ever be taken. Jews were subjected to Arab attacks on the ghettos and were frequently murdered and robbed.

An age-old Yemenite law demanded that fatherless Jewish children under the age of thirteen be taken from their mothers to be raised as Moslems. This law was reinforced with great vigor until just fifty years ago. The Moslem custom of stoning Jews was still a common tradition at the time of the Jewish mass exodus from Yemen in 1948.

The Jews did not even have the right to leave Yemen, since it was against Shi'ite law for any infidel to go to a land considered enemy territory. The Yemeni Shi'ites considered that every country fell into this category. After the establishment of the State of Israel in 1948, however, 50,000 Yemenite Jews were airlifted to Israel, totally uprooting this ancient community of 2,000 or more years. While it is true that the religious zeal of the Yemenite-Jewish community motivated them to go to Israel, the reason the whole community left (no one stayed behind) was because of their constant deprivation and persecution.

ADEN

Aden, which neighbored Yemen in southern Arabia, had an ancient Jewish community that dated back to A.D. 200. It suffered a plight similar to the Yemenite-Jewish community— all the Moslem laws against infidels were observed, and the Jews lived in a perpetual state of torment.

As late as the twentieth century, Jews in Aden were victimized and humiliated. In 1933, a pogrom made the Jews even more fearful of the erratic volatility of the Aden Arabs. In December of 1947, with the partition of Palestine imminent, eighty-two Jews were murdered; most of the existing Jewish shops were robbed; synagogues were burned to the ground; and over 200 homes were looted, burned, or damaged. Subsequently, for their own security, Jews were cordoned off in a ghetto. In 1958, Jews were brutally victimized again, and the remnant who stayed behind were once more the objects of Arab wrath. After the 1967 Six-Day War, synagogues were burned, and more Jews were murdered. When it was discovered that a mass massacre was being planned, Jews were finally evacuated by the British; Aden became another community where Jews once lived.

IRAQ

The Iraqi Jews took pride in their ancient, scholarly community. For ages, Babylonia (Iraq) was the Olympus of Jewish scholarship. Jews thrived there until the Moslem conquest in A.D. 634. After that, no matter what outside power controlled Iraq, the Jews suffered. During the tenth century, Jews wore a yellow patch, carried the burden of a heavy head tax, and suffered residence restrictions. During the years A.D. 1000 to

1333, the Jews suffered the destruction of their Baghdad synagogues. In 1776, the Jews of Basra (the present Shi'ite capital of Iraq) were slaughtered; in the eighteenth century, anti-Jewish measures imposed by the Turks caused many Jews to flee from Iraq.

During the twentieth century, with Hitler's rise to power and Iraqi independence, Jewish life in Iraq became even more tenuous. In 1941, there was a bloody massacre of Jews, complete with police participation, while British forces benignly ogled the carnage being perpetrated. Nazi propaganda had an enormous effect on the Iraqis and, obviously, fueled their anti-Zionist sentiments. The Iraqi minister of justice declared that Judaism was a threat to mankind. It was estimated that 600 Jews were murdered, hundreds more wounded, and more than 1,000 Jewish homes and businesses destroyed.

After Israel's independence, Iraq's leader, Nuri Said, suggested to the British ambassador that the Jews be transported to the Jordanian-Israeli frontier in trucks to be forced across the border. This was the Iraqi version of the final solution.

Prior to the establishment of the State of Israel in 1948, there were 130,000 Jews in Iraq. In 1950, 123,000 of them fled en masse from Iraq. The few thousand who stayed behind lived in trepidation of being hung in a public square—or slaughtered in their homes, as occurred between 1969 and 1973.

EGYPT

The Jews of Egypt suffered not only at the hands of the ancient pharaohs, which is well documented in the Bible, but also at the hands of modern Egypt's leaders and people. Throughout the nineteenth century, Egypt's ancient Jewish community suffered from accusations of blood libel (drinking the blood). An Egyptian version of the absurd charge that child sacrifice was part of the Talmud was reputed to have documentation and was widespread throughout Egypt in 1890. In 1948, anti-Jewish riots were prevalent. There were eyewitness accounts of as many as 150 Jews being murdered or wounded in a seven-day period.

Nasser, Egypt's modern-day pharaoh, hung Jews as Zionist spies. As late as 1964, he claimed that his sympathies had been with the Nazis in World War II. Even Sadat had been imprisoned by the British during World War II for loyalty to the Nazis. Jews were held in internment camps during the Six-Day War, and as one of the camp commanders candidly admitted, "Egypt has no place for Jews."

MOROCCO

The very ancient Jewish community of Morocco, which dates back to 586 B.C., also suffered from persecutions wrought by the Moslem conquest during the seventh century A.D. In 1032, 6,000 Jews were murdered in Fez, while others were robbed of their women and property. When the Almohad clan attacked Fez in 1146, they tried to persuade the Jews to convert. When that failed, they chose a more persuasive route—they slaughtered 150 Jews; then, the rest converted.

For the several hundred thousand Jews living in Morocco under Moslem rule, sporadic persecutions became part of the Islamic landscape. Since everyone born on Moroccan soil was considered Moslem, Moroccan Jews were deprived of the right to raise their children in the Jewish faith. Jewish marranos were common, but many practiced their Judaism in private, for there was really no place better to go.

Five hundred Moroccan Jews were slaughtered in anti-Jewish riots in 1864. In 1912, another pogrom followed, leaving 60 dead and 10,000 Jews homeless. And in 1948, there was wanton Arab violence against several Jewish communities in northern Morocco, leaving dozens dead. After the establishment of the State of Israel, over 90 percent of the Jews left Morocco; the vast majority went to Israel.

ALGERIA

The Jewish community in Algeria was established 2,500 years ago. Algerian Jews fared no better than their Moroccan brethren. Their fate was harsh. During centuries of Moslem rule the usual *dhimmi* code, persecutions, and humiliations applied. Jews were even accused of sorcery.

In 1830, France occupied Algeria, and Algerian Jews became French citizens. The freedoms they enjoyed outraged the Moslems. Thus, the towns of Oran, Tlemcen, and Algiers became targets for anti-Jewish violence in the late 1800s. One historian states that the town of Tlemcen was an insufferable place of anguish for Jews. He sympathetically wondered how they survived the horrifically oppressive conditions. Jews were forbidden to offer resistance when maltreated by a Moslem no matter what the nature of the violence. Their lives were filled with debasement and outrage. In 1898, anti-Jewish riots erupted all over the major communities in the country.

After Hitler's rise to power, a new wave of anti-Semitism erupted in Algeria. In 1934, for example, a massacre at Constantine left twenty-five dead and many more wounded. By 1948, the 140,000-strong Jewish community rapidly diminished. Most went to France, while a sizable minority left for Israel. This exodus was fortunate for the Algerian Jews because the secular democratic state of Algeria established in 1963 denied citizenship to any non-Moslem.

TUNISIA

Jews have lived in Tunisia continuously for the last 2,300 years. They, too, suffered indignities by and were at the mercy of their Moslem rulers for centuries. While Tunisian Jews fared somewhat better than their Algerian and Moroccan cohorts, they had no freedom, paid the heavy *dhimmi* tax, and were required to wear special identifying clothing. During the fifteenth century, while infidel Christians were given privileged positions, infidel Jews suffered terribly from their Moslem rulers. In 1515, the fanatical founder of the Moroccan Sa'ad Dynasty, while on his way to Mecca, incited Tunisian Moslems against Jews.

Moslem limitations against the Jewish practice of commerce was sporadically enforced throughout the Moslem era. In 1855, when the special *dhimmi* tax on Jews was abolished, a revolt erupted with violent, anti-Jewish rampaging. The violence spread to the city of Tunis where Moslems butchered many Jews in their defenseless ghetto. In 1881, the French protectorate was established, and life improved considerably for many Tunisian Jews.

In 1956, Jews began to flee Tunisia in droves as the process of Arabization took place throughout the country, and it became more difficult for them to practice their occupations. Over one-half of Tunisia's 100,000 Jews went to Israel, while most of the rest emigrated to France and elsewhere. Little remains of a community that had stuck it out for over two millennia.

SYRIA

Here, too, Jews have dwelled continuously for over 2,000 years. And here, too, the Jews' position deteriorated over time. They suffered consistent humiliation and, periodically, were subjected to oppression, extortion, and violence by both local authorities and the Moslem population. Once a haven for Jews fleeing the persecutions of the Spanish Inquisition, Syria became a source of oppression where, once again, the infidel Jew was discriminated against and treated as a second-class citizen.

The famous Damascus blood libel of 1840—a contrived scurrilous anti-Jewish incident—was brought on by Egyptian occupation and was borrowed from their medieval Christian mentors. In 1925, the Jewish quarter of Damascus was attacked. Many Jews were murdered, dozens were wounded, and many businesses were destroyed. In 1936, when there were 35,000 Syrian Jews, an anti-Palestine sentiment raged, and anti-Jewish riots continued throughout the rest of the thirties. Damascus became a center for anti-Jewish activities and a major source of Nazi propaganda in the area.

In 1945, after Syria won her independence, the 13,000 remaining Syrian Jews were prohibited from leaving the country. At that time, the Damascus *mufti* warned at a religious conference that if Jewish immigration into Palestine was not halted, all countries of Islam would wage a holy war against the Jews. In 1947, Syrian mobs burned Torah scrolls and destroyed 150 Jewish homes, 5 Jewish schools, and 50 shops and offices. All Jewish bank accounts were frozen, and in the summer of 1949, the synagogue in Damascus was bombed, leaving over twenty dead and twenty-six wounded. Jews were remanded to a ghetto and were placed under virtual house arrest. Jewish public buildings were given to Palestinian Arabs who were virulently anti-Jewish.

Even today, the few score of Jews in Syria live in terror in a ghetto and do not enjoy the rights of other citizens. They still are prohibited from leaving Syria.

LEBANON

Since at least A.D. 70, there has been a Jewish community in the area defined in recent history as Lebanon. Although the thirty-five Jewish families who lived in Beirut prior to the late eleventh century were slaughtered by the Crusaders, Jews survived in other parts of Lebanon. The Lebanese-Jewish community was reinforced by Jews fleeing the Spanish Inquisition in 1492. During the Ottoman Empire, Jews in Lebanon were required to pay the *dhimmi* to ensure their safety. They were subjected to a severe dress code and harsh legal restrictions.

Anti-Jewish attacks prevailed during the Druse rebellion in the 1840s, culminating with the destruction of the entire Jewish community in the town of Dir el-Qamar. In 1947, a dozen Jews were murdered in Tripoli. In 1950, a Jewish school was bombed and its director killed.

The Lebanese Christian-dominated government established after World War II allowed Jews greater freedom than they had in other Arab lands. Unlike the situation in any other Arab state, the numbers of Jews in Lebanon actually increased in number, until 1958. At that time, there were 9,000 Jews living in Lebanon; today, there are none. In 1958, as a result of greater Moslem participation in the government, the Jewish community no longer enjoyed the freedom it had when the Christians dominated the government, and most Jews fled. In 1975, civil war forced the remaining Jews to flee Lebanon.

LIBYA

The ancient Jewish community of Libya, which dates back to before 300 B.C., has disappeared completely. During the Arab conquest of the seventh century A.D., the Jews were shown no mercy and lived under the same *dhimmi* restrictions as in all the other Arab areas. In the twelfth century, forced conversions terrorized the devout Jewish community in Libya. Jews were restricted to ghettos, and years of distress and famine were their lot during the Middle Ages.

During the 500 years of Ottoman rule, the Jews enjoyed a brief respite from oppression. However, World War II resuscitated their anguish—2,600 Jews were sent to forced labor camps where more than 500 died, and thousands more from

Tripoli were sentenced to forced labor under grievous conditions.

In 1911, Italy occupied Libya, and until the mid-1930s when Libya became Mussolini's Moslem center for Fascist propaganda, the Libyan-Jewish community thrived. In early November 1945, the Jews of Libya, totally unprepared, were subjected to wanton violence and carnage. There was forced conversion, rape, and murder. The attacks, which went on for days, were inspired by earlier anti-Jewish riots in Egypt. One report said that two brothers lost twenty-seven relatives in only one attack.

After the U.N. vote to partition Palestine in November 1947, Libyan mobs murdered more than 130 Jews. Libya's Jewish population at that time was 38,000, but as a result of that pogrom, Libyan Jews began to flee; by 1958, only 8,000 remained. By the end of the 1967 Six-Day War, no Jews remained. When Colonel Qaddafi, the despotic ruler of Libya, came to power in 1970, he officially confiscated all Jewish property that had been abandoned by the Jews who previously had fled the country.

SUMMARY

While the Arab world has been virtually emptied of its Jews, the Jewish state has borne the burden of absorbing over 800,000 *destitute* Jewish refugees from those Arab lands. One wonders where these Jewish refugees would have gone had the establishment of a Jewish state not been achieved. Why aren't these Jews considered refugees? Why is their plight not considered as significant as the plight of the so-called "Palestinians"? Why does the media recognize only the Palestinian-Arab refugees? One reason is obvious: the Jews have successfully been absorbed into a country whose brethren welcomed them with open arms. The Palestinian-Arab refugees, on the other hand, were not welcomed by their Arab-Moslem brethren, except as political pawns in their fight against Israel.

Arab propaganda has reiterated that Jews displaced Arabs in Palestine. Even some Israelis are confused and troubled. Although Israel's older Jewish population can remember the violence perpetrated by the influx of Arab immigrants from neighboring lands, some younger Israelis have become terribly anxious and concerned about Israel's alleged culpability in the displacement of millions of Arabs from their thousand-year homeland

In 1945, there were 570,000 Arabs living in the Jewish-settled territories of Palestine. Shortly after the establishment of the State of Israel in 1948, between 430,000 and 500,000 Arabs were registered with the U.N. Relief and Works Agency (UNRWA) as refugees from Israel. By 1982, UNRWA's count, as reported by the largely Arab-staffed refugee camps, had reached 1,900,000. This figure included descendants—a figure totally inflated by the inclusion of many who were deceased; no deceased Arab is ever removed from the rolls.

Also in 1982, there were 1,500,000 Jewish citizens in Israel who had either themselves fled or were offspring of those who had fled from Arab countries. If the 300,000 Jews who fled Arab lands for countries other than Israel are included, then the number of Jewish refugees matches the reported number of Arab refugees. So, again, the question arises: why does the media focus only on the plight of Palestinian-Arab refugees and not on the fate of Jewish refugees?

The Palestinian-Arab Political Movement

THE GRAND MUFTI OF JERUSALEM

There was no Arab political rebellion in Palestine prior to World War II. The *mufti* of Jerusalem and his political followers were driven by Islamic religious interests, not by Arab nationalism. They began a reign of terror borne primarily of Islamic fanaticism and greed. The *mufti,* Al-Husseini, also held that the Arab nationalists, as well as the Palestinian nationalists, were trying to do something totally unfeasible and contrary to his interests. His own interest was to re-establish his authority and his dominion over the area with the assistance of the local *effendis.* The *mufti* wanted to return to a time when there were rulers and their feudal serfs. It was he who used his clerical power, as the local representative of Allah, to unite all factions against a manufactured common enemy—the Jews. This was a far cry from national aspiration.

The *mufti* not only terrorized the Jews, but he also poured his wrath upon any Arab opposition to his plans. Under the threat of the gun, he extracted large sums of money as "protection" against terror. A number of prominent Arab-Moslem leaders were either murdered or wounded by the *mufti's* henchmen in less than one year, including:

- Sheikh Yamin El-Husseini, head administrator of Al-Aqsa *Mosque*—wounded in March 1938;
- Sheikh Alinur El Khatib of Al-Aqsa *Mosque*—murdered in July 1938;
- Sheikh Nusbi Aboul Rahim, counsel to the Moslem religious court—murdered in Acre in September 1938;

- Sheikh El Manouri—murdered in Hebron in November 1938; and
- Sheikh Daoud Ansari, imam of Al-Aqsa *Mosque*—murdered in December 1938.

Small landowners who were said to have sold land to the Jews as well as suspected informers were mercilessly flogged, tortured, and executed by slow and agonizing means. Some were thrown into pits with snakes and scorpions. Dead bodies, with shoes stuffed into their mouths as a sign of dishonor, were left to rot in the streets. These tactics proved to be successful in that the *mufti's* Arab high committee was all but officially recognized by the British mandatory power as the sole voice of the Palestinian Arabs. The *mufti,* having achieved his legitimacy through terrorist acts, looked to see what else could be achieved through the same type of behavior.

Prior to War World II, Britain pursued a policy based on the Lawrence of Arabia fantasy—the creation of a great British-dominated Arab confederation. As a result, the Arab League—encouraged by Britain and sponsored by Egypt and Iraq—came into existence. The British had made "Palestine" the business of the Arab rulers.

The *mufti* of Jerusalem worked closely with Nazi Germany during World War II. He organized a spy service for the Nazis with sabotage groups working behind British lines. He lent support to the German efforts to form a Moslem SS group in Yugoslavia and was generally considered an ally of Nazi Germany. He anticipated two rewards. First, the total elimination of the Jews would, obviously, nip any Zionist aspirations in the bud. He followed the annihilation of the Jews closely by befriending Adolph Eichmann, mastermind of the "final solution's" implementation. He even made a visit to Auschwitz, the Nazi death camp, to witness the carnage firsthand. Second, upon German victory, the *mufti* was to be rewarded by being the ruler of a vast Arab empire covering the whole of the Middle East.

THE CREATION OF THE PALESTINIAN LIBERATION ORGANIZATION (PLO)

The PLO was created by Egyptian president Gamal Abdel Nasser in 1964 and was founded by the Arab League under his auspices. The concept of a PLO was consistent with the Pan-Arabist nationalistic fervor that ran rampant at that time and with the British scheme that Palestine should be the concern of only the states in the region. The PLO was originally conceived and modeled after the terrorist movement that had been introduced by the Grand *Mufti* of Jerusalem. Nasser's plan was to draw from the only common denominator among all the Arab leaders in the Middle East—an ingrained, Islam-inspired hatred of the Jews. All Arab leaders had lost face because of the Jewish victory in Palestine during the 1948 to 1949 period. It was time to "get even" and forming the PLO was the method of unifying the Arab world under Nasser's leadership against the common enemy—Israel. This would offset the humiliation suffered by Egypt in the loss of two wars to Israel—1948 and 1956.

On June 1, 1964, the PLO proclaimed its resolution and statement of purpose—The Palestinian National Covenant (see Table I). Its specific goal was the liberation of the land occupied by the State of Israel at that time. No mention was made of the "West Bank," which was then occupied by Jordan. The PLO declared its specific intention to obtain sovereignty over only that land occupied by the State of Israel.

TABLE I

The Palestinian National Covenant

The following is the complete and unabridged text of the Palestinian National Covenant, as published officially, in English, by the PLO.

Articles of the Covenant

Article 1: Palestine is the homeland of the Arab Palestinian people; it is an indivisible part of the Arab homeland, and the Palestinian people are an integral part of the Arab nation.

Article 2: Palestine, with the boundaries it had during the British Mandate, is an indivisible territorial unit.

Article 3: The Palestinian people possess the legal right to their homeland and have the right to determine their destiny after achieving the liberation of their country in accordance with their wishes and entirely of their own accord and will.

Article 4: The Palestinian identity is a genuine, essential and inherent characteristic; it is transmitted from parents to children.

The Zionist occupation and the dispersal of the Palestinian Arab people, through the disasters which befell them, do not make them lose their Palestinian identity and their membership of the Palestinian community, nor do they negate them.

Article 5: The Palestinians are those Arab nationals who, until 1947, normally resided in Palestine regardless of whether they were evicted from it or have stayed there. Anyone born, after that date, of a Palestinian father—whether inside Palestine or outside it—is also a Palestinian.

Article 6: The Jews who had normally resided in Palestine until the beginning of the Zionist invasion will be considered Palestinians.

Article 7: That there is a Palestinian community and that it has material, spiritual and historical connections with Palestine are indisputable facts. It is a national duty to bring up individual Palestinians in an Arab revolutionary manner. All means of information and education must be adopted in order to acquaint the Palestinian with his country in the most profound manner, both spiritual and material, that is possible. He must be prepared for the armed struggle and ready to sacrifice his wealth and his life in order to win back his homeland and bring about its liberation.

Article 8: The phase in their history, through which the Palestinian people are now living, is that of national *(watani)* struggle for the liberation of Palestine. Thus the conflicts among the Palestinian national forces are secondary, and should be ended for the sake of the basic conflict that exists between the forces of Zionism and of imperialism on the one hand, and the Palestinian Arab people on the other. On this basis the Palestinian masses, regardless of whether they are residing in the national homeland or in diaspora *(mahajir)* constitute—both their organization and the individuals—one national front working for the retrieval of Palestine and its liberation through armed struggle.

Article 9: Armed struggle is the only way to liberate Palestine. Thus it is the overall strategy, not merely a tactical phase. The Palestinian Arab people assert their absolute determination and firm resolution to continue their armed struggle and to work for an armed popular revolution for the liberation of their country and their return to it. They also assert their right to normal life in Palestine and to exercise their right to self-determination and sovereignty over it.

Article 10: Commando action constitutes the nucleus of the Palestinian popular liberation war. This requires its escalation, comprehensiveness and mobilization of all the Palestinian popular and educational efforts and their organization and involvement in the armed Palestinian revolution. It also requires the achieving of unity for the national *(watani)* struggle among the different groupings of the Palestinian people, and between the Palestinian people and the Arab masses so as to secure the continuation of the revolution, its escalation and victory.

Article 11: The Palestinians will have three mottoes: national *(wataniyya)* unity, national *(qawmiyya)* mobilization and liberation.

Article 12: The Palestinian people believe in Arab unity. In order to contribute their share towards the attainment of that objective, however, they must, at the present stage of their struggle, safeguard their Palestinian identity and develop their consciousness of that identity, and oppose any plan that may dissolve or impair it.

Article 13: Arab unity and the liberation of Palestine are two complementary objectives, the attainment of either of which facilitates the attainment of the other. Thus, Arab unity leads to the liberation of Palestine; the liberation of Palestine leads to Arab unity; and work towards the realization of one objective proceeds side by side with work towards the realization of the other.

Article 14: The destiny of the Arab nation, and indeed Arab existence itself, depends upon the destiny of the Palestinian cause. From this interdependence springs the Arab nation's pursuit of, and striving for, the liberation of Palestine. The people of Palestine play the role of the vanguard in the realization of this sacred national *(qawmi)* goal.

Article 15: The liberation of Palestine, from an Arab viewpoint, is a national *(qawmi)* and it attempts to repel the Zionist and imperialist aggression against the Arab homeland, and aims at the elimination of Zionism in Palestine. Absolute responsibility for this falls upon the Arab nation—peoples and governments—with the Arab people of Palestine in the vanguard.

Accordingly the Arab nation must mobilize all its military, human, and moral and spiritual capabilities to participate actively with the Palestinian people in the liberation of Palestine. It must, particularly in the phase of the armed Palestinian revolution, offer and furnish the Palestinian people with all possible help, and material and human support, and make available to them the means and opportunities that will enable them to continue to carry out their leading role in the armed revolution, until they liberate their homeland.

Article 16: The liberation of Palestine, from a spiritual point of view, will provide the Holy Land with an atmosphere of safety and tranquillity, which in turn will safeguard the country's religious sanctuaries and guarantee freedom of worship and of visit to all, without discrimination of race, colour, language, or religion. Accordingly, the people of Palestine look to all spiritual forces in the world for support.

Article 17: The liberation of Palestine, from a human point of view, will restore to the Palestinian individual his dignity, pride and freedom. Accordingly the Palestinian Arab people look forward to the support of all those who believe in the dignity of man and his freedom in the world.

Article 18: The liberation of Palestine, from an international point of view, is a defensive action necessitated by the demands of self-defence. Accordingly, the Palestinian people, desirous as they are of the friendship of all people, look to freedom-loving, justice-loving and peace-loving states for support in order to restore their legitimate rights in Palestine, to re-establish peace and security in the country, and to enable its people to exercise national sovereignty and freedom.

Article 19: The partition of Palestine in 1947 and the establishment of the State of Israel are entirely illegal, regardless of the passage of time, because they were contrary to the will of the Palestinian people and to their natural right in their homeland, and inconsistent with the principles embodied in the Charter of the United Nations, particularly the right to self-determination.

Article 20: The Balfour Declaration, the Mandate for Palestine and everything that has been based upon them, are deemed null and void. Claims of historical or religious ties of Jews with Palestine are incompatible with the facts of history and the true conception of what constitutes statehood. Judaism, being a religion, is not an independent nationality. Nor do Jews constitute a single nation with an identity of its own; they are citizens of the states to which they belong.

Article 21: The Arab Palestinian people, expressing themselves by the armed Palestinian revolution, reject all solutions which are substitutes for the total liberation of Palestine and reject all proposals aiming at the liquidation of the Palestinian problem, or its internationalization.

Article 22: Zionism is a political movement organically associated with international imperialism and antagonistic to all action for liberation and to progressive movements in the world. It is racist and fanatic in its nature, aggressive, expansionist and colonial in its aims, and fascist in its methods. Israel is the instrument of the Zionist movement, and a geographical base for world imperialism placed strategically in the midst of the Arab homeland to combat the hopes of the Arab nation for liberation, unity and progress. Israel is a constant source of threat *vis-a'-vis* peace in the Middle East and the whole world. Since the liberation of Palestine will destroy the Zionist and imperialist presence and will contribute to the establishment of peace in the

Middle East, the Palestinian people look for the support of all the progressive and peaceful forces and urge them all, irrespective of their affiliations and beliefs, to offer the Palestinian people all aid and support in their just struggle for the liberation of their homeland.

Article 23: The demands of security and peace, as well as the demands of right and justice, require all states to consider Zionism an illegitimate movement, to outlaw its existence, and to ban its operations, in order that friendly relations among people may be preserved, and the loyalty of citizens to their respective homelands safeguarded.

Article 24: The Palestinian people believe in the principles of justice, freedom, sovereignty, self-determination, human dignity, and in the right of all peoples to exercise them.

Article 25: For the realization of the goals of this Charter and its principles, the Palestinian Liberation Organization will perform its role in the liberation of Palestine in accordance with the Constitution of this Organization.

Article 26: The Palestine Liberation Organization, representative of the Palestinian revolutionary forces, is responsible for the Palestinian Arab people's movement in its struggle—to retrieve its homeland, liberate and return to it and exercise the right to self-determination in it—in all military, political and financial fields and also for whatever may be required by the Palestinian case on the inter-Arab and international levels.

Article 27: The Palestinian Liberation Organization shall cooperate with all Arab states, each according to its potentialities; and will adopt a neutral policy among them in the light of the requirements of the war of liberation; and on this basis it shall not interfere in the internal affairs of any Arab state.

Article 28: The Palestinian Arab people assert the genuineness and independence of their national (wataniyya) revolution and reject all forms of intervention, trusteeship and subordination.

Article 29: The Palestinian people possess the fundamental and genuine legal right to liberate and retrieve their homeland. The Palestinian people determine their attitude towards all states and forces on the basis of the stands they adopt vis-a'-vis the Palestinian case and the extent of the support they offer to the Palestinian revolution to fulfil the aims of the Palestinian people.

Article 30: Fighters and carriers of arms in the war of liberation are the nucleus of the popular army which will be the protective force for the gains of the Palestinian Arab people.

Article 31: The Organization shall have a flag, an oath of allegience and an anthem. All this shall be decided upon in accordance with a special regulation.

Article 32: Regulations, which shall be known as the Constitution of the Palestine Liberation Organization, shall be annexed to this Charter. It shall lay down the manner in which the Organization, and its organs and institutions, shall be constituted; the respective competence of each; and the requirements of its obligations under the Charter.

Article 33: This Charter shall not be amended save by (vote of) a majority of two-thirds of the total membership of the National Congress of the Palestine Liberation Organization (taken) at a special session convened for that purpose.

Nasser appointed Ahmed Shuquairy as chairman of the PLO. Nasser's goal was that Shuquairy would replace King Hussein, so Shuquairy, who wanted to control the Jordanian state, claimed that all Jordanians were Palestinians. Actually, the argument was, and still is, whether Jordan should envelop the Palestinians, or the Palestinian entity should envelop Jordan.

At first, Nasser would not allow Shuquairy to mount PLO raids into Israel and, instead, ordered terrorists to attack targets in Amman, East Jerusalem, and other Jordanian cities. In his attempt to become the sole patron of the Palestinian cause, however, Nasser was outmaneuvered by Syria's Assad.

THE CREATION OF *FATAH*

The Syrians, unwilling to permit Egypt to take sole responsibility for the Palestinian cause, created a rival Palestinian organization of their own. They, too, were Pan-Arabists who dreamed of a united Arab empire, but what they envisioned would exist under their flag.

Colonel Ahmad Sweidan, the head of Syrian army intelligence, recruited Palestinian Arabs in Lebanon's refugee camps and trained them as *Fedayeen.* One of Sweidan's agents was approached by eight men who had formed a group called the Movement for the Liberation of Palestine. Their leader was none other than Yasir Arafat who is believed to have been born in 1929 in Cairo. His mother, Mamida, was related to the Grand *Mufti.* Arafat, who graduated from Cairo University as a civil engineer in 1951, had received some military training, along with some young Palestinian Arabs, from the Egyptian army.

It was late in 1964 when Sweidan's agent found the small group of eight in Beirut. Their first assignment was to announce a raid on Israel's National Water Carrier, which was to be damaged by explosives. A communique was written as if the act had already been accomplished and had been a magnificent triumph. The purpose of this announcement was to introduce this group to the Arab world; thus, *Fatah* was born. The name *Fatah* means conquest accomplished by means of *Jihad* (Holy War) and, therefore, is unique to Moslems. The announced raid never took place, yet it still made headlines; and *Fatah,* under the leadership of Yasir Arafat, became a reality.

In an attempt to undermine the Hashemite kingdom's sovereignty, the rulers of Syria, who believed that Jordan rightfully belonged to Syria as part of a "Greater Syria," then began sending raiders into Israel—but always from Jordan. Simultaneously, Nasser attempted to subvert the Jordanian monarchy by sending PLO terrorists from Jordan into Israel, provoking an Israeli retaliation against Jordan.

At first, *Fatah* operated from the area controlled by Jordan west of the Jordan River (the West Bank), but it was forced to move its headquarters to Karameh on the east side of the Jordan River. Shortly after *Fatah* started raiding and shelling across the river on Jewish settlements, the Israelis attacked their headquarters. The Jordanian army inflicted 28 casualties on the Israelis but sustained the loss of 100 of their own. One hundred seventy *Fedayeen* were killed. Despite the very poor performance of the Palestinians, the battle of Karameh was depicted by the Arab media as the heroic resistance of the *Fedayeen.* The battle was hailed as a turning point in the fortunes of the Palestinians. There were public celebrations in the refugee camps. More than 5,000 recruits presented themselves to *Fatah* in the two days following the battle. The bogus victory caused enthusiasm not only in the Arab world but in Europe as well. Young Europeans volunteered. They saw the Palestinian struggle as part of the world revolution. They saw the *Fedayeen* as spearheads of victory against imperialism of which Zionism was an instrument. The *Fedayeen* had been adopted by the international Left.

Then, in May 1967, Nasser closed the Strait of Tiran to Israeli ships and so broke the agreement made after the Sinai Campaign. The ensuing Six-Day War, and its resultant total defeat of the Arab confrontation states, created a sense of despair among all segments of the people who identified themselves as Arab Palestinians. The realization that conventional warfare waged by the Arab nations against Israel had failed and would likely fail again in the future created a shock wave that gave birth to the proliferation—between 1967 and 1969—of terrorist groups that were prepared to wage war through unconventional means.

THE CREATION OF PLO SPLINTER GROUPS

After the Arab defeat in 1967, Arafat and his followers set out to overtake Jordan. Augmented by their rising popularity, they overtook the PLO entirely. By 1968, the PLO included *Fatah,* a small Marxist group established in 1966 by Habash called the Popular Front for the Liberation of Palestine (PFLP), and a large Syrian-organized *Fedayeen* called the Vanguards of the Popular Liberation War with its military arm *Al-Sa'iqa*—an organization that was actually an appendage of the Syrian army. Palestinian officers from the regular Syrian army were transferred to *Al-Sa'iqa,* which was tightly controlled by the Syrian Ba'ath party. Its leader, Zuhayr Muhsin, born in Tulkarm in 1936, was one of the leaders within the PLO who denied the existence of a separate Palestinian people. (See Table II.)

TABLE II

Arab-Palestinian Terrorist Organizations

The Arab Palestinian terrorist organizations created to implement the Palestinian Covenant are identified below. Most of these organizations were established after the 1967 Six-Day War. They have undergone many splits and transformations resulting from ideological and personal differences as well as from the desires of particular Arab states to have their own organization or to control existing ones.

The Palestinian National Liberation Movement—*Fatah*
Organized in 1965 with Yasir Arafat as its leader. It dominates the PLO, and its members hold the most important positions in the PLO. It is nationalistic, pragmatic, without ideological commitments, and tries to maintain good relations with all the Arab states.

Vanguards of the Popular Liberation War—*Al-Sa'iqa*
Established in 1968 by Zuhayr Muhsin and Syria's Ba'ath regime from which it receives and follows instructions. (Muhsin was assassinated in 1979 in France.) It is Pan-Arab and

wants a Palestinian state as part of a united Arab world under Syria's leadership. Within the PLO, *Al-Sa'iqa* is second in size to *Fatah*.

Popular Front for the Liberation of Palestine (PFLP)

Established in late 1966 by its leader, George Habash. It is the largest and most important organization in the rejection front. It is Marxist (new Left) in orientation and closer to anarchist organizations than to Communist parties. It calls for world-wide revolutions and has established close ties to other global terrorist organizations—the Japanese Red Army, the German Bader-Meinhoff group, and the Irish Republican Army. Since 1974, it has dropped terrorist activities outside Israel's borders and has concentrated on terrorism within Israel.

PFLP-Wadi' Haddad Group

The PFLP's 1974 decision to halt terrorist activities outside the Middle East was opposed by Dr. Wadi' Haddad who headed foreign operations. He continued his operations and was responsible for some dramatic terrorist activities that came to a halt in 1978 when, according to reports, he was poisoned to death by Iraqi agents.

Popular Democratic Front for the Liberation of Palestine (PDFLP)

Organized in 1969 by its leader Nayef Hawadmeh after it split from the PFLP. It is Marxist with close ties to the USSR. It followed the political line of Arafat, but since the civil war in Lebanon, it has become much more radical. It originated the theme "secular democratic state" and was the first to establish ties with Israeli Leftist groups. It does not cooperate with moderate Arab states but maneuvers between Arafat and the rejection front. It has objected to terrorist activities abroad and concentrates on the Israel-Lebanon border and inside Israel proper.

PFLP-General Command (GC)

Established in 1968 when it split from PFLP. It is less ideological and was Syrian controlled for a long time. It sided with the Leftists against the Christians at the outbreak of the Lebanon civil war.

Palestine Liberation Front (PLF)

Pro-Iraqi and supported by Iraq with close ties to Libya. It supports terror inside and outside of Israel and is led by Abu Al-Abbas.

Arab Liberation Front (ALF)

Established in April 1969 by Iraq's Ba'ath regime and currently under the leadership of Abd Al-Rahim Ahmad to counter Syrian-controlled *Al-Sa'iqa*. Most of its members are non-Palestinians (Iraqi, Lebanese, Jordanian).

The Front of Palestinian National Struggle
Small organization established by Samir Ghoshe in 1967 in the West Bank. In July 1971, it began, but never completed, a merge with *Fatah*. It joined the rejection front and is supported primarily by Iraq and Libya.

Palestinian National Front (PNF)
Established in the West Bank in 1973 as a political coalition in which the Communist party played a major role. PNF members participated in the April 1976 West Bank municipal elections. PNF leaders—banished by Israel—were given top positions in the PLO Executive Committee.

Fatah Baghdad-based Dissidents
Organized in 1974 by Abu Nidhal as a separate group—not part of the PLO. Nidhal was head of the *Fatah*-Baghdad office. Backed by Iraq, he declared himself independent and acted against Syria and *Fatah*.

PLFP-GC Pro-Syrian Group
Created in April 1977 by Ahmad Dabril. When Leftists and pro-Iraqis in the PLFP-GC, headed by Abu Al-Abas, demanded opposition to Syrian forces in Lebanon and continued alliance with other rejection front organizations, Dabril refused to fight the Syrians and split the Front into two organizations.

Terrorist Cover Organizations

Black September
Named after the September 1976 civil war in Jordan—a cover for *Fatah*.

Black June
Named after the June 1976 entry of Syrian troops into Lebanon. It was activated by Iraq and the Abu Nidhal group and attacked Syrian and Arab targets.

Eagles of the Palestinian Revolution
Appeared on the scene from time to time as a cover for *Al-Sa'iqa*. It attacked the Egyptian embassy in Turkey in July 1979.

Shortly after the Syrian Ba'athists formed *Al-Sa'iqa,* the Iraqi Ba'athists created the Arab Liberation Front (ALF). Some of its members were Palestinians. This group insisted that no state of Palestine should be brought into existence, because it would constitute yet another division within the Arab world.

Some of the terrorist groups were Marxist and had no Palestinian members. One such group was led by a Syrian officer—

Syrian by birth but not Palestinian. Ahmad Jibril formed his group with about twenty other Syrian officers when he split from the PFLP-General Command and created a pro-Syrian splinter group. Through Jibril, Arafat had contacts with the KGB in East Germany and Bulgaria. Another leader of still another splinter group was Nayef Hawadmeh, who was born a Jordanian Christian Bedouin in the town of Solt in Jordan.

In 1968, Wadi Haddad and George Habash, a professed Marxist Leninist and leader of the PFLP, took charge of that group's special operations, which meant acts of terrorism outside the Middle East—chiefly in Europe. Haddad planned and directed a series of hijackings of international flights between July and September 1970. This was the beginning of terror in the skies.

In Jordan, the *Fatah* had gained strength. They had started their own radio station, organized mass demonstrations, and, early in September 1970, even made two attempts on Hussein's life. On September 12, 1970, the King decided to crush the *Fedayeens*. His Bedouin soldiers attacked the *Fatah* camps, bases, and headquarters. According to the PLO organizations, 30,000 people were killed. Most of the survivors either fled to Syria or made their way to the banks of the Jordan River and surrendered to the Israelis. They preferred to face the Israelis rather than Hussein's army.

The *Fatah* leaders, beaten, humiliated, and thirsting for revenge, created a secret organization to overthrow the Jordanian regime. They named it "Black September." Its first act was to murder Wanti-Tol, Jordanian prime minister, in the entrance of the Sheraton Hotel in Cairo. One of the assassins also knelt down and licked the blood that was flowing onto the marble floor.

Since that time, the PLO has been responsible for literally hundreds of raids—primarily focused on innocent women and children—throughout the world. For years, the PLO has brazenly claimed responsibility for such vicious acts of cowardice—always directed against civilian targets, never military. It is only recently that they have decided to be more circumspect with their unspeakable crimes. Now, although these acts are still committed, a forked tongue alludes to the remote possibility for peace.

So-called "moderate Arabs" ask for the establishment of a state in Judea and Samaria in the area of western Palestine re-

ferred to as the "West Bank." But fulfillment of that desire is unlikely to satiate an appetite that has had such grand designs for so
many years. Can anyone deny the turmoil the Lebanese suffered
under the yoke of Palestinian oppression? There was a Palestinian state in Lebanon before the Israeli incursion in 1981.
Would anyone care to investigate the democratic processes introduced in that nation? For that matter, has *any* Arab nation
established a democracy in the Middle East? Is democracy desirable or feasible in an Arab-Moslem world? These are the questions one must ask when considering Arafat's proposition of a
"secular democratic Palestinian state" where Jews, Christians,
and Arab Moslems will live side by side, as equals, with mutual
respect and admiration. Can one believe that any Arab-Moslem
state would ever afford a Jewish minority population equal
status under law? History, Islam, and present attitude and
behavior say *no!*

THE PLO AND LEBANON

Several articles in the Palestinian National Covenant indicate
that the goal of the PLO is to create a secular democratic state in
place of Israel. An understanding of what a PLO state would
really be like can be gleaned from a look at the PLO's activities in
southern Lebanon. The leaders of Egypt, Iraq, and Syria had aspirations to unite the Arab world, each under his own leadership.
Lebanon was one of the countries each wanted to bring under his
own influence, and the PLO was one of the tools each tried to use
for that end.

Early in 1970, after fleeing from Jordan, the PLO entered
Lebanon and immediately embarked upon violent actions that
would destroy the country. Concentrated on the western slopes
of Mount Hermon and supplied militarily from Syria, the PLO
mounted raids and attacked Israeli settlements. Their targets
were exclusively civilian. In May 1970, they attacked an Israeli
school bus. Eight children and four adults were killed.

Within a short period of time, the PLO ruled all the Palestinian camps in Lebanon. They started receiving heavy artillery,
tanks, mortars, antiaircraft artillery, and vast amounts of auto-
matic weapons. After heavy fighting broke out between *Fatah*
and the Lebanese army, an accord was reached between the

Lebanese government and PLO under which the government agreed to abdicate the little control it had retained over Palestinian-occupied portions of its own territory.

What emerged in Lebanon was a state within a state. The PLO established its own military, its own police, and its own civil services, including schools and hospitals. The PLO collected taxes and claimed jurisdiction over every aspect of the lives of the Palestinian refugees.

The PLO's control in Lebanon greatly increased its power in the Arab League, which officially recognized the PLO as the sole representative of the Palestinian people. Furthermore, during the Rabat Conference in October 1974 attended by all the Arab nations and led by Saudi Arabia, a unanimous agreement was reached regarding the disposition of the territory referred to as the West Bank. Hussein and Jordan no longer had territorial rights west of the Jordan River. The sole responsibility for that land was put into the hands of the PLO. The Rabat agreement legitimized the PLO's claim to the West Bank and supported their terrorist activities against Israel. Further, it made acceptable any action undertaken by the PLO to protect Palestinians. Therefore, no Arab state could support the Lebanese government in its conflict with the PLO without defying the Rabat consensus.

The agreements made with the PLO in Lebanon actually legitimized the status of a state within a state and laid the foundation for civil war. It can be said that the PLO aligned itself with the Sunnis and Druse to fight the Maronite Christians. Many massacres and uncountable atrocities were committed during the seventeen months between April 1975 and November 1976—referred to as the first phase of the Lebanese "civil war."

The most heinous offenses committed by the PLO occurred, undoubtedly, in Damour, a town of 25,000 people. Damour was surrounded by a combination of forces—*Al-Sa'iqa,* consisting of 16,000 Palestinians and Syrians; some fifteen other militias; mercenaries from Iran and Pakistan; and a contingent of Libyans. All participated in the massacre. The acts of violence that took place in that city during the attack were unimaginable. The invaders even broke open tombs and flung the bones of the dead into the streets. Five hundred and eight-two people were killed. The ruined town became one of several PLO centers for the promotion of international terrorism. Zuhayr Muhsin, chief of *Al-Sa'iqa* and leader of the combined forces, became known as the "Butcher of Damour." He was assassinated on July 15, 1979 at Cannes in the south of France.

The PLO, together with its allies, made considerable gains throughout southern Lebanon. The Moslems, the Left, and the PLO pressed against the Christians and came very close to total victory until Syria's Assad stepped in in 1976. In pursuit of the dream of "Greater Syria," Assad wanted to dominate Lebanon. However, a new Lebanon under the Lebanese Left—far from accepting Syrian hegemony—would have united all anti-Syrian elements in the Arab world and would have threatened his own position. Therefore, he sent the regular Syrian army to Lebanon to fight the PLO. The Syrians quickly pushed the PLO back to their southern bases. During the process, one of the Palestinian camps was destroyed by the combined forces of Syrians and Christians. In September 1977, after undertaking wearing retaliatory raids in reprisal for the Munich massacre of Israel's Olympic team, Israel briefly occupied a part of southern Lebanon.

The Tripoli-based PLO established a reign of terror in northern Lebanon. The northern Lebanese, and even the Palestinians, began to suffer. There was a loss of public services. For days at a time, there was no water or electric power. Since there was no inspection or licensing of motor vehicles, number plates were invented. PLO power was free of all checks and accountability, secular or religious. PLO rulers were bound by neither written nor custom-established laws. They took charge of the lands, groves, and orchards of Lebanese owners and enjoyed them as they chose. During the ensuing anarchy, every individual group member in possession of his own weapon was a danger to the civilians. They were frequently intoxicated by drugs. Spies and traitors were put to death by torture in public, and the bodies of the executed were often put in polyethylene bags and left in front of the victim's home. Some people whose eyes were gouged out have lived to tell their stories. Even small children were punished by the amputation of fingers and hands.

PLO PROPAGANDA

The PLO controlled the media by terror and intimidation. It was obvious that news sent from Lebanon was incomplete and misleading, but the Western news media correspondents kept this information from their audiences to avoid being victimized. In July 1981, a correspondent from the *London Observer* was murdered, and an ABC television journalist, Sevn Toolan, who had made a film on PLO terrorism, was shot dead in the streets of Beirut. A West German writer, Robert Pfeffer, who had published information on the subject of the training of West German terrorists in PLO camps, was killed. Bernard Debussman, head of the Beirut bureau of Reuters, was shot.

Terror, intimidation, and the law of silence—these were the basic tools used by the PLO to manipulate the international press. Most of the sins committed by Western newsmen under PLO constraint were sins of omission—showing bombed buildings, but not the arms stockpiled in their basements; describing bombed hospitals, but not depicting the PLO fighters whose bases of operation were inside. The list is infinite, but the effect unmistakable—the reverse of international opinion on the moral equation of the Middle East.

THE PLO AND WORLD TERRORISM

The armed struggle of the PLO against Israel took the form of direct shelling of towns and settlements and other terrorist raids. The attacks were made on civilians since the PLO did not willingly seek engagement with the Israeli military. PLO terrorist activities, however, were not confined only to acts against Israel and the Jewish people. The PLO aligned itself with Third World terrorist organizations in their quests for world revolution.

"Black September," Fatah's terrorist organization, blew up oil and gas installations in Holland, Italy, and West Germany; hijacked planes; and shot American and Belgian diplomats in Sudan. In September 1972, they murdered eleven athletes of the Israeli olympic team attending the olympic games in Munich. The plot was encouraged by the Bulgarian Intelligence Service which, for a long time, acted as a subagency for the KGB in promoting acts of international terrorism. Abu Daoud, who was arrested in Amman in February 1973, confirmed his part in the

Munich massacre during a radio broadcast and revealed that it had been planned in Sofia, Bulgaria. The U.N. General Assembly refused to condemn the massacre of the athletes in Munich. Instead, the PLO was rewarded by the United Nations by being invited to participate in its plenary meetings as an observer organization. So Arafat—the leader of the most vicious international terrorist organization—was invited to the rostrum in the hall of the U.N. General Assembly to address the world.

This type of terrorist activity on a worldwide scale was supported by the Soviet Union. She provided the PLO with political backing and arms. The PLO was the chief intermediary and channel of aid between the USSR and most of the world's national liberation movements. Finances came primarily from Saudi Arabia. The PLO functioned as a center for the provision of training and weapons to subversive organizations from most of the non-Communist countries on all continents. To the Communist party of the Soviet Union, those groups were the possible nuclei of future mass movements as well as the disrupters of order in the present. The special position granted by the USSR to the PLO made the seventies a "decade of terrorism." PLO leaders even directed terrorist attacks carried out by foreign groups outside the Middle East, including the attempted assassination of Pope John II in Rome in 1980.

All enemies of Western liberal democracy were friends of the PLO. In only one year (1979), for example, twenty-six Germans, thirty-two Italians, and twenty-two Japanese sought and found training, arms, asylum, financial aid, and contact with the Soviet Union through the PLO.

A constant exchange of information passed between the PLO and the Soviet embassy. An electronic telephone tapping system of the organization called "LISTEN" was established and was housed in a building close to the embassy. It allowed the PLO to tap all internal messages including those passing within East Beirut.

Foreign terrorists entered Lebanon either through Syria or directly by air through Beirut. There was an agreement between the PLO and the Lebanese government—imposed by the PLO—by which foreigners could arrive at Beirut airport and be allowed into Lebanon without having to go through the usual immigration formalities. PLO special baggage containing weapons, explosives, and grenades left Beirut daily on Middle East Airline flights.

The PLO reigned with terror against the Arabs in the West Bank who were contemplating a peaceful solution with Israel as a result of the Camp David Accords. Between Sadat's visit to Jerusalem in 1977 and the summer of 1982, forty-eight political murders of Arabs were committed by PLO agents in the West Bank.

PEACE FOR GALILEE

The intensive shelling of Israeli settlements by the PLO from the hills of southern Lebanon, which resulted in the evacuation of entire Jewish communities near the Lebanese border, created such pressure on the Israeli government that it became necessary to send Israeli forces into southern Lebanon to destroy the PLO bases. Thus began the Peace for Galilee War.

The 1982 Israeli incursion into Lebanon left the PLO isolated—no Arab country came to help them. More shocking to the ideologists of the PLO and to the high command was the failure of the Palestinians in the refugee camps to offer resistance to the enemy. They were armed, trained, and indoctrinated, but the Palestinian masses did not identify themselves with the resistance or the armed struggle. European governments—blind to the terrorist acts of the PLO against their territories—reprimanded Israel in strong terms. The world press played a hideous role in censuring Israel while totally ignoring the central role that the PLO played in international terrorism.

On August 21, 1982, PLO fighters began to leave Beirut. They dispersed to Algeria, Iraq, Jordan, Syria, and Tunisia. Arafat went to Tunisia to set up his new headquarters.

CONCLUSION

Since August 1982, Arafat's PLO has existed only in the columns of Western newspapers, in the briefings of European foreign ministers, and in the long speeches of the United Nations. The PLO Popular Front organizations are under Assad's control as are the rebel factions of *Fatah* and *Al-Sa'iqa.*

For its entire history, the PLO has had a consistent characteristic. From the days of the *mufti* and the White Paper of

1939 to the time of expulsion from Beirut and the Reagan plan, the PLO and its leaders always asked for more than what was politically possible to concede at the time. Since its inception, the organization has served as a savage instrument of inter-Arab politics. It was not designed nor has it been used as a means of liberation. Its actions have placed the Arab population in misery and have allowed them to waste their lives generation after generation. It has been used by the Soviet Union as a tool of international terror to undermine Western democracy and Third World countries all around the world.

The Jewish reaction to Arab terrorism as well as to the brutality of British indifference to the Holocaust during World War II has been used to justify PLO terrorist acts by several elements of society—the British, Israel's detractors, anti-Semites, neo-Facists, some Third World supporters, many Progressives, and parts of the communication media. The very premise of justice and mercy must be affronted by the historical distortions that could give birth to perceptions so twisted that they equate Palestinian Jews with the terrorists of the PLO—that could call the terror of the Arab PLO justice, while dubbing Jewish resistance to such terror injustice. The acceptance of such perverted perceptions may be traceable to any one or a combination of several factors: double standards, refusal to examine facts, racial or religious prejudice, reliance upon misunderstanding and misinformation, and, more prevalently, inadequate information and basic lack of awareness to the truth.

Intifada

"TRANSJORDAN"—THE PALESTINIAN STATE

Seventy-five percent of the land of Palestine as mandated by the United Nations to Britain for the establishment of a Jewish homeland is located east of the Jordan River and is, literally, an independent Palestinian-Arab state—Transjordan (Jordan)— where a Palestinian law of return applies. Jordan's nationality code states, categorically, that all Palestinians are entitled to citizenship by right unless they are Jews.

In 1948, just before formal hostilities were launched against Israel, King Abdullah of Transjordan declared, "Palestine and Transjordan are one, for Palestine is the coastline and Transjordan the hinterland of the same country." His prime minister declared, "We are the army of Palestine." Ahmed Shuquairy declared, "The kingdom of Palestine must become the Palestine republic." And Yasir Arafat has stated that Jordan is Palestine. The Arab advocacy of a secular "democratic" state in Palestine where Jews, Christians, and Moslems can live side by side in peace is ludicrous and profoundly unconvincing.

THE CURRENT UPRISING

In December 1987, the Arab struggle for the liberation of Palestine took on a new direction. For the first time within any territory occupied by Israel, there developed a sustained insurrection (*Intifada*) against the Israeli authorities. It began by organized stone throwing by children and expanded into organized violent acts by young adults, always challenging Israel's authority through the use of civil disobedience.

These riots and acts of civil disobedience in Judea, Samaria, and Gaza have been an attempt to use yet another means of waging war against Israel. Six hundred of the 1,000 Arab terrorists released by Israel several years ago in exchange for two Israeli soldiers held prisoner by Lebanese Shi'ites remained within Israeli territory and have been responsible for most of the organized violence within the territories. The fact that they had not been expelled when initially released is rooted in the nature of Israel's democracy.

Another political dimension has also been added, since the original and primary thrust of this *Intifada* was led by extremist Shi'ite Fundamentalists who have no connection with the PLO. In fact, the PLO's role in the *Intifada* was minimal and now there exist two forces vying actively for control of the Arab population in Judea, Samaria, and Gaza—the PLO and the Shi'ite Fundamentalists.

At first, the Western press, led by journalists like Anthony Lewis, interpreted this revolt as a true organized and unified attempt by the Arabs in Judea, Samaria, and Gaza to seek national independence. In fact, they contrasted these riots to those of 1929 and 1936 at which time the Arabs in Palestine, during their bloody riots, killed not only Jews but also many of their Arab brethren as they struggled to take over the leadership of the riots.

It took only a few months before it became apparent that this current *Intifada* was also a struggle between Arab political forces—mainly, the PLO and Shi'ite Fundamentalists. Daily assassinations and beatings of Arabs by Arabs has become the hallmark of this *Intifada,* thus again dissipating, as in the riots of 1929, 1936, and 1939, any possible lasting political effects toward their goal of Arab (Palestinian) national independence.

THE NATIONS OF THE MIDDLE EAST AND THEIR SOURCES OF CONFLICT: IMPACT ON RELATIONS WITH ISRAEL

Part Two

THE NATIONS OF THE
MIDDLE EAST AND THEIR
SOURCES OF CONFLICT:
IMPACT ON RELATIONS
WITH ISRAEL

The Nations of the Middle East and Their Sources of Conflict: Impact on Relations with Israel

Overview

Twenty-one nations comprise the Arab League, all of which, except for Somalia, share Arabic as their official national language. In all, except for Lebanon, the dominant and official national religion is Islam; and all, except for Egypt, maintain an official state of war with the State of Israel. All, including Egypt, support, to some extent, worldwide economic boycott of Israel; and all, including Egypt, maintain, in varying degrees, a hostile posture against Israel and the Jewish people internally and in world political forums. All profess as a national goal a concept of Arab unity and belong to an organization (the Arab League) designed to promote that unity.

All the Arab nations have the common characteristic of maintaining closed societies—absent are the democratic institutions so characteristic of the Western society of nations, including Israel. Each of the Arab nations is characterized by autocratic authoritarian rule headed by a monarch, dictator, military junta, or president with real power. Except for Egypt, each of the Arab nations is led by a government that does not represent the majority of her people and is, therefore, fundamentally unstable and characteristically repressive.

The Arab world is a region characterized by a history interwoven with the history of Islam. The Arabs maintain a keen sense of the past. They exult in the glories of the seventh and eighth centuries when they carried the word and sword of Islam and built an empire from Persia to the Pyrenees. Their past glories seem to mock their present disappointments. When the Arab empire collapsed, the Arabs spent 400 years under Ottoman (Turkish) rule. Most Arab nations gained independent status only after World War II. To the Arabs, the clash between tradition—as associated with ancient glories—and moderninity focuses on their inability to establish a successful society characteristically Arab as opposed to one drawing from either the Western society of nations or the Socialist society of nations of Eastern Europe.

The most serious common problem facing all Arab nations is the burgeoning population of youth. While published official population figures are invariably altered, actual demographic data exists indicating that the majority of the population of each of the Arab states is under twenty-five years of age. The wealthy Arab states have squandered their wealth on massive military programs, on elaborate infrastructure build-up, and on huge smokestack industries; they now face the problem of providing meaningful employment for their youth. The poor Arab states with their relatively large armies and limited industry maintain high levels of unemployment and cannot employ their youth other than in the military. Although for most of the Arab world this is a potentially explosive situation, for both Algeria and Egypt the problem exists currently. They are struggling desperately to control their restless youth who are turning to Islamic fundamentalism as an expression of their frustration.

All borders in the Middle East between the Arab nations as well as non-Arab nations are in dispute except for Egypt's border with Israel, which has been established by treaty (1979 Camp David Accords). These border disputes, which effect every nation in the Middle East, have been the cause of many wars and armed conflicts—none of which has yet permanently settled a single border (except for that between Egypt and Israel).

While the twenty-one Arab nations that comprise the Arab world have much in common to unite them, they are characterized by unmatched disparity that underlies internal turmoil and hostility between/among them. Some sparsely populated nations—Libya, Saudi Arabia, and Iraq—occupy relatively vast amounts of territory, while others—the Gulf states and Kuwait—are geographically smaller. All of these, however, possess huge deposits of oil and generate (since 1973) exorbitant amounts of money from oil exports. Too much of their oil revenues has been dissipated in military spending, in support of wars, and in the establishment of elaborate development programs they can no longer sustain due to the oil glut since 1982 that has greatly reduced oil income. In contrast, other Arab nations—Egypt, Sudan, Syria, Morocco, Tunisia, and Yemen—for the most part, have larger populations or population densities, are extremely poor, and are grossly underdeveloped. These disparities have not enhanced the cause of Arab nationalism and Arab unity and have heightened the level of insecurity within the region.

The intra-Arab struggle is marked by ethnic and religious animosities; social class hostilities among the poor, wealthy, and military classes; and ideological clashes between Marxists and entrepreneurs. The struggle is fueled by continuing border disputes, the great disparity in wealth between the oil-rich and oil-barren nations, and the conflicts of the transnational movements of Arab nationalism and Islamic fundamentalism.

The most dramatized, over-reported, and little understood conflict that has occupied too much attention in world forums, Western government agencies, and Western communications media is the Arab-Israeli dispute and the Palestinian-Arab problem. Yet, the situation that is most dangerous to existing Arab regimes, potentially the most destabilizing for the region, and probably the most threatening to world security lies within the Arab world itself and between the Arabs and Iran. For the nations of the Middle East, the present delicate order of internal and external things is balanced precariously on a variety of potentially explosive inter- and intra-Arab disputes. The eruption of any one of these disputes could trigger violence and disorderly change and cause the collapse of one or more of the existing Arab regimes, a realignment within the Arab world, and/or a war that would threaten world security. Given the history of the Arabs since their national independence, the probability of the occurrence of such events is quite high.

Paradoxically, the most stabilizing force in the Middle East that might neutralize such a probability is the presence of a strong Israel in conjunction with the existence of the Arab-Israeli conflict.

The dangerous and destabilizing Iraq-Iran War, which temporarily concluded in a stalemate and almost total exhaustion of both parties after eight brutal years, witnessed the indiscriminate use of poison gas against military and civilian personnel, a missile war against large population centers, and U.S. naval involvement in the Persian Gulf against Iran. Ironically, the culmination of that war has created a new and equally dangerous and destabilizing regional situation—the potential of a war over oil production.

From 1973 until 1978, the two largest oil producers in the Organization of Petroleum Exporting Countries (OPEC) were Iraq and Iran. At that time, the non-Communist world's oil consumption was 49.5 million barrels/day (mb/d). Although that oil consumption peaked in 1979 at 52 mb/d, by 1988, it had dropped to the 1978 level of 49.5 mb/d. In 1978, however, OPEC supplied 59 percent of the non-Communist world's oil needs—almost 30 mb/d—while today they supply only 41 percent—a drop of more than 10 mb/d. Since 1981, both Iraq and Iran have produced and shipped only a small portion (less than half) of their peak years' output, thus allowing the other oil-producing countries to absorb their output into a shrinking market.

Today, the problem is that the OPEC nations must divide the oil market into smaller portions. This is the case because Iraq and Iran must increase their oil production in order to pay for the past eight years of war, to rebuild their cities and infrastructures that were destroyed by that war, and to finance preparations for the next war each is planning in order to resolve, finally, their dispute. Both Iraq and Iran need hundreds of billions of dollars and their only potential source is increased oil production. The price of oil will most probably remain depressed for a few years until the pressures created within the OPEC nations bring about an accord by which each producing nation will abide. This is the kind of stuff wars are made of.

This is a region with tremendous ability to export wars and

recessions; however, it is little understood by the outside world. The level of tension, insecurity, and violence within and among the nations of this region is greater than anywhere in the world. The intervention into the region of the great powers—who have shipped in vast arsenals of military weapon systems utilizing the most modern technologies—has fueled an arms race within the region unmatched any place on the globe and unparalleled and unprecedented in history.

Israel's Bordering Nations

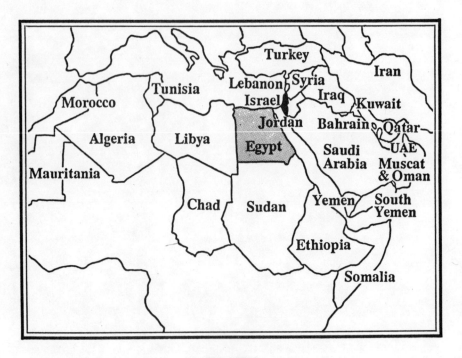

EGYPT

History

Egypt has a recorded history of 5,000 years and is considered one of the birthplaces of civilization. For over 3,000 years, she thrived with a cultural and linguistic continuity matched only by China and the Hebrew nation. Because of her geographic location—where Africa joins the Middle East and the Mediterranean, Egypt has always been a cultural crossroad. She is the only present-day Arab nation that has always had a clear cultural and geographic identity. Egypt maintained her Egyptian identity, despite being conquered by great empires such as the Assyrian, Persian, Greek, and Roman over a period covering 1,200 years (sixth century B.C. to seventh century A.D.). Egypt's strategic geographic position—a gateway to India and China from Europe (not unlike Israel)—made her a natural prize for conquest by the great powers of the time. Throughout the history of Egypt, the Nile River has been the life blood of the Egyptian people and, in ancient times, made Egypt the breadbasket of the Mediterranean civilizations.

In A.D. 642, the Arab conquest of Egypt took place and the Moslem culture replaced the Byzantine influence. The strength of Islam was so intense that, for the first time, the Egyptians submitted to a greater power and adopted Mohammedanism as their religion, and, in 706, Arabic as their language. During the five centuries of Arab rule, Egypt was never a center of Arab power. Rather, she was ruled from either Damascus (by the Umayyad caliphate) or from Baghdad (by the Abassyd caliphate). Although a succession of dynasties and foreign invaders conquered Egypt after the Arab rule—British, Crusaders, Mamelukes, and Ottomans, she maintained Islam as her religion and Arabic as her language.

Egypt was ruled by the Ottoman Empire from 1517 to 1798 when Napoleon invaded and replaced the old Ottoman rule with a Western-type dynasty founded by the Albanian soldier, Mohammed Ali. (He and his descendants ruled over Egypt until 1922 when a monarchal system was established.) The French built the Suez Canal in the 1860s, and, in order to protect this trade route to India, the British invaded Egypt in 1882, took control over the canal, occupied the country, and made Egypt a part of the British Empire. As a result of Egyptian nationalist fervor, the British granted Egypt partial independence in 1922 and full independence in 1936; however, Britain did not relinquish control over the Suez Canal at that time.

As one of six participants in the first Arab-Israeli war, Egypt invaded Israel on May 15, 1948 but suffered a humiliating defeat. As a result, in 1952 a military coup d'etat led by Lt. Colonel Gamal Abdel Nasser and a corps of free officers deposed the ruling monarch, King Farouk—the first of the Arab monarchies to fall. Both General Mohammed Naguib and Anwar Sadat were leaders among the free officers, and General Naguib became the first head of state. Shortly thereafter, Colonel Nasser overthrew Naguib, an Egyptian nationalist, to establish a Pan-Arab-Socialist government with the avowed goal of uniting the entire Arab world under Egyptian leadership.

Shortly after Nasser came to power, he triggered the existing Middle East arms race by entering into a massive arms deal with the Soviet bloc. He militarized the Sinai using those arms and nationalized the Suez Canal. In response to Nasser's moves, Britain, France, and Israel formed a triple-purpose, single-project, short-term alliance. For Britain, the goal was retaining control of the Suez Canal. For France, the aim was curbing the power of Nasser who was arming the Algerian rebels in their secessionist revolution against the French. For Israel, the purpose was to destroy the Egyptian army in the Sinai with arms provided by France before the Egyptians could absorb their Soviet weapon systems and become a permanent threat in the Sinai.

As a result of the 100-hour Sinai Campaign in October 1956, Israel handed Nasser a stunning total military defeat. However, almost simultaneously, the ineptness of the joint British/French Suez expeditionary force allowed Nasser to succeed in thwarting their military action. The ensuing pressure by President Eisenhower on the Israeli and British/French actions forced Israel to relinquish the Sinai and Britain/France to halt all attempts to control the Suez Canal. The ultimate result, therefore, was a perceived political victory of gigantic proportions for Nasser whose prestige among the Arab masses and Third World nations rose to great heights.

Because Britain lost unequivocal access to the Suez Canal, she was forced to decide on a phased withdrawal from her bases east of the Suez. This was to create a military and political vacuum in the Gulf. In 1958, Nasser formed a union with Syria and created the United Arab Republic (UAR), which shortly thereafter became the United Arab States when Yemen joined that union. Within the next four years, Britain gave Yemen her independence and physically withdrew from the territory; Syria, then Yemen, dissolved their union with Egypt; and a civil war broke out in Yemen. Nasser sent an expeditionary force of

40,000 Egyptian troops to Yemen to replace Britain as that area's protector and, of course, effect the outcome of the civil war. After five years of bloody fighting in Yemen, with extensive Egyptian casualties and no positive results, Nasser triggered the 1967 Six-Day War with Israel by withdrawing his expeditionary forces from Yemen, militarily re-entering the Sinai, demanding the removal of all U.N. forces from the Sinai, and closing the Strait of Tiran to all Israeli shipping. These moves were taken, in part, to mask Nasser's failure in Yemen and to rebuild his image.

The ensuing war with Israel in June 1967 was yet another (the third) stunning and humiliating military and political defeat for Egypt and Nasser (and for the entire Arab world). Almost as if he were masochistic, Nasser immediately entered into another arms deal with the Soviets and within a year launched the fourth conflict with Israel—the 1968 to 1970 Canal War. Unable to wrest the Canal from Israel and equally unable to maintain control over his own forces who were abandoning their front-line positions, Nasser enlisted the political intervention of the United States to negotiate with Israel a standstill cease-fire and put an end to his mounting casualties.

Immediately following the August 1970 cease-fire, Nasser, in collusion with the Soviet Union, moved his forces and their newly Soviet-supplied and -manned surface-to-air missiles (SAMs) to the edge of the Canal. This abrogation of the terms of the cease-fire by Egypt triggered the implementation of a condition in the cease-fire agreement between the United States and Israel whereby the United States was obligated to provide Israel with vast quantities of modern weapon systems. It marked the beginning of a new relationship between the United States and Israel that made the United States Israel's sole source of military supplies. In the fall of 1970, after four humiliating defeats by Israel, Nasser died of a heart attack. Shortly thereafter, Anwar Sadat rose to power.

Although he witnessed and actively participated in all four Israeli defeats of Egypt (1948, 1956, 1969, 1970), Sadat negotiated still another massive Soviet arms deal in order to engage Israel in what he proclaimed would be Egypt's redeeming victory. The ensuing war with Israel—the October 1973 Yom Kippur War—ended with a tragic military defeat of huge proportions for Egypt who had to rely on U.S. political intervention to save her army from total annihilation. This marked the beginning of a new approach by Egypt in her conflict with Israel. In short order, Sadat terminated his relationship with the Soviets; established economic, political, and military relations with the United States; and pursued diplomacy to resolve differences with Israel. The process culminated in a peace treaty with Israel, signed in late 1979, and led to Sadat's assassination by the Moslem Brotherhood in late 1981—on the eighth anniversary of the Yom Kippur War. Colonel Hosni Mubarak, Sadat's vice president at that time, became president and, since then, has successfully pursued a three-tiered policy of maintaining, at least minimally, the peace treaty with Israel; returning Egypt into the Arab fold; and keeping alive—at least twelve attempts have been made on his life.

At this point, it is important to review briefly the development of the political ideology of Egypt's ruling class since World War II. From 1936 to 1952, Egypt was a constitutional monarchy ruled by King Farouk, highly influenced by the British and characterized by extreme corruption and a nondescript Moslem ideology. After the Free Officers Revolution of 1952, the monarchy was replaced by Arab socialism, which acquired a Soviet orientation under Nasser. The ideological shift toward the Soviets was a pragmatic move influenced by two events: the 1955 Soviet bloc arms deal and the subsequent financing of the Aswan Dam by the USSR. This Arab socialism, as practiced by Egypt until 1973, was not socialism; and Sadat replaced it with Arab democracy, which was not democracy. In fact, at the time of Sadat's death, Egypt was suffering from "too much democracy."

Several months prior to his public assassination—during a period of social unrest and partial martial law, Sadat was re-elected president, receiving 99.4 percent of the vote. Today, almost a decade since Sadat's assassination by Islamic-Fundamentalist-Egyptian officers, the martial law imposed by his successor, Mubarak, when he assumed power, still has been only partially lifted. Egyptian "democracy," however, is the closest thing to Western democracy that exists in the Arab world. Yet, it is in increasing danger of subversion from the same wave of Arab-Islamic fundamentalism, spearheaded by the Moslem Brotherhood, that killed Sadat. This rise in Islamic fundamentalism has posed the greatest threat to the survival of Egypt's Western orientation.

Present

Egypt covers an area of approximately 1 million square kilometers (sc km) (387,000 sq mi), only 3 percent of which is cultivated and 97 percent of which is desert, waste, or urban. She borders Sudan on the south, Libya on the west, the Mediterranean on the north, Israel on the northwest, and the Red Sea on the east. Her total population of approximately 49 million are 92 percent Moslem (Sunni) and 8 percent Coptic (Christian). Nationally, 90 percent of the population is of eastern Hamitic stock, and the 10 percent balance are Greek, Italian, and Syro-Lebanese. Ninety-nine percent of the population reside on 3.5 percent of the land. Egypt's official language is Arabic, but Nubian is spoken in upper Egypt and among Nubians in lower Egypt. English and French are widely understood among the educated class. The literacy rate, as stated by the government, is 40 percent.

Politically, Egypt—officially called the Arab Republic of Egypt—is ruled by an authoritarian presidential regime, although according to her 1971 constitution, she is to be a "democratic and Socialist republic." Egypt's government can be described as stable in that it represents the majority of the population, however, the Egyptian society is extremely unstable. Ironically, it is in large part the government's desire for greater stability, characterized by its efforts to provide free higher education to its youth, that is creating a precarious nature to its hold over the population and is, thereby, threatening its very stability as representative of the majority will.

All university graduates are promised employment within the government. Since most university students are studying humanities and Arab culture, they are forced to accept employment within the bureaucracy of the government, thereby creating new layers of that bureaucracy with each graduating class. Since the seat of government bureaucracy is in Cairo, and to a lesser extent in Alexandria, the overwhelming majority of these government employees must live in Cairo where the cost of living is exceedingly high, living conditions are extremely poor, and the gap between the opulently wealthy and all others is blatantly obvious. Under such circumstances, the seeds of dissatisfaction are planted and nourished by the frustrations of everyday life—the realization that expectations will never be filled.

These pragmatic concerns of the young intellectuals of the country only tend to re-enforce the ideological issues that were the focus of their university education. They were taught that the universal quests of all Arabs—Arab unification, social justice, cultural rejuvenation, and national independence—have remained unfulfilled in spite of previous experience with the Soviet-Socialist model, as well as the present experience with the Western-Capitalist model. In order to provide hope for the future, masses of university students and recent graduates are seeking a uniquely Arab solution to these problems. They have adopted the only true Arab "legitimacy" that exists for them— Sharia, the Islamic code of law. Their hero is Libya's "strong man," Colonel Qaddafi, whose experience represents a unique model for the universal solution to all Arab problems. His is a synthesis of the social justice and Pan-Arabism of the Ba'ath party with the observance of the Islamic religion, as practiced by Sunni-Islamic Fundamentalists. Egypt is the most fertile of the Arab nations for adopting this model because she has the largest number of youth being educated. It has been reported that as many as 10 million Egyptians have adopted Islamic fundamentalism and that Qaddafi is extremely popular among them. Thus, Egypt's drive for literacy started by Nasser is sowing the seeds for the destruction of the present form of government.

Economically, Egypt is an agrarian society with minimal light industry that depends for its existence on the Nile River, along which the vast majority of the population reside. Since only 2.8 percent of the land is cultivated—of which 70 percent is multiple cropped, the import of billions of dollars of food is required annually. The stated gross national product (GNP) is $32.25 billion, approximately $650 per capita.

Militarily, Egypt spends $4.1 billion annually in support of a standing army of 445,000 men and a paramilitary force equal in number. Additionally, she receives several billion dollars annually in military aid from the United States.

Future

If the present "free officers'" regime—a secular Sunni-Moslem, Western-oriented regime—remains in power through the turn of the century, there will be an orderly replacement of President Hosni Mubarak. This will occur either upon his death or when the national assembly (or some other group representing the desires of the free officers' ruling circle) decides he must be replaced. In this case, the "no war/cold peace" relationship with Israel will remain. The "no war" aspect will hold because there will be no cause for war, since Western orientation enables this regime to receive massive economic and military aid from the United States—Israel's ally. The "cold peace" aspect of this Egyptian-Israeli relationship will be paced by two geopolitical factors: (1) Egypt's need to be an integral part of the so-called "moderate" (Western-oriented) Arab camp and (2) Israel's relationship to the moderate Arab nations.

The continuation of the free officers' regime will see Egypt's relationship with Libya remain strained. Egypt will focus much of her attention on Sudan where she will jealously watch events to assure Sudan's independence in order to keep the Nile River—Egypt's life line—flowing. Egypt will not allow Arab-Moslem Sudan to be threatened either externally by Ethiopia or Libya or, internally, by the secessionist southern animist blacks. Egypt will attempt to re-establish political and economic relations with the Soviet Union in order to pursue a policy of support for the PLO and to challenge Syria's leadership within the Arab world. Additionally, while Egypt will continue to maintain good relations with all the Gulf states, including Saudi Arabia, by not challenging their legitimacy as Nasser did in the sixties, she appears to be developing a three-pronged strategic policy of domination, exploitation, and/or major influence over Sudan, Libya, and the Gulf states.

Internally, under the sustained administration of the free officers' regime, Egypt will continue to attempt to solve burning domestic problems caused by her rapidly expanding population, which could reach 70 million by the year 2000 with almost one-third residing in Cairo. Since an agricultural base is fundamental to nation building, in order to survive, the existing regime must resolve the severe problems that have been created by a population that has increased 1,000 percent since 1800, while arable land growth during the same period has been only 40 percent. Although there have been huge economic benefits for the country as a whole during the post-Camp David period, only a few have shared in those benefits. If more tangible economic results do not trickle down to the growing mass of newly educated youth entering the society, this regime may not endure to the year 2000.

Egypt's survival under the current administration depends on the ability of the regime to establish political stability by creating a broad-based middle class and the appropriate institutions, thereby providing hope for upward mobility for the teeming masses. Egypt is unlike Jordan, Iraq, and Syria where present minority rule governments preclude fundamental societal stability. Egypt's present power structure offers the basic ingredients for a stable society among 90 percent of her population—a common language (Arabic), a common religious belief (Sunni Moslem), a common nationality (Egyptian), and a common cultural heritage (Egyptian).

Time is running out for the current regime in Egypt to resolve the overwhelming domestic problems burdening the society. If the educated youth see no hope for the future, they will lead the masses toward a spiritual/religious solution. The greatest threat to this administration, then, will come from the Islamic Fundamentalists whom the free officers' regime will handle ruthlessly to thwart their efforts and to protect itself.

Should Egypt experience a military coup by Islamic-Fundamentalist officers—as was attempted in the assassination of Sadat, there would be a very serious threat not only to Israel but to the Gulf states and Libya as well. Initially, the immediate threat would be to the existence of Libya as an independent nation.

Surely, a Sunni-Islamic-Fundamentalist regime in Egypt would lose U.S. financial, military, and political support. Libya would be Egypt's first target because she is an oil-wealthy, sparsely populated, bordering nation with a nonhostile, compatible social structure. Since Libya's oil is readily accessible and is shipped from her ports on the Mediterranean to various markets without the danger of shipment through pipelines crossing other countries and/or through the Persian Gulf, her oil wealth would be an immediate source of hard currency for Egypt as a replacement for America's annual $3 billion plus in aid. Additionally, the sparsity of Libya's population, which already includes hundreds of thousands of Egyptian teachers and other civil servants, would invite the flow of many more Egyptians for settlement there.

Such an expanded Islamic-Fundamentalist Egypt would then immediately focus her expansionist intentions toward Sudan, historically—for centuries—an integral part of modern Egypt. Gaining control of northern Sudan would be essential not only in order to protect the flow of the Nile through all of Egypt, but also in order to protect access to arable, fertile land in an area where climatic conditions make it potentially the great breadbasket of the Middle East. Absorption and retention of southern Sudan would be critical to Egypt's economic development because of the vast, yet untapped, oil-bearing deposits recently discovered there. Gaining and maintaining control of this area, however, will be extremely complex for Egypt because the current black animist population, which does not want to be dominated by Arab Moslems, is supported in its ongoing secessionist efforts by neighboring black countries—primarily, Ethiopia—who also covet the great oil potential of southern Sudan.

To such an Egyptian-Islamic-Fundamentalist regime, the existence of a Western-oriented, democratic Jewish state in the region would be ideologically repugnant. In order to gain land access to Israel militarily and to ". . . restore Egyptian national pride," there would have to be a remilitarization—even if slow and scrupulous—of the Sinai. Because the demilitarization of the Sinai is a fundamental element of the Camp David Accords and the key to "peaceful" coexistence from Israel's perspective, Israel would be forced to retake the Sinai as a matter of vital national security the moment Egypt's remilitarization process would begin. Since an Egyptian-Islamic-Fundamentalist regime would be characterized by the transnational nature of Sunni-Islamic fundamentalism manipulated by the force of Egyptian nationalism, it would be a serious threat to the existing monarchies in Saudi Arabia and the surrounding Arab Gulf states, whose populations are predominantly Sunni-Islamic Fundamentalist. Such a synthesis of socialism and Islamic fundamentalism— uniquely Arab in character—would likewise be a threat to the national integrity of the other Arab states and to the status of Saudi Arabia as the dominant Arab political force in the region.

Regardless of who or what the ruling force will be in Egypt, a realignment with the eastern Soviet bloc is most highly improbable because it would require at least two decades for the Egyptian military to be re-equipped and retrained with Soviet weapon systems and tactics. The only thing that can be predicted about the future political forces within Egypt is that the unpredictable will occur.

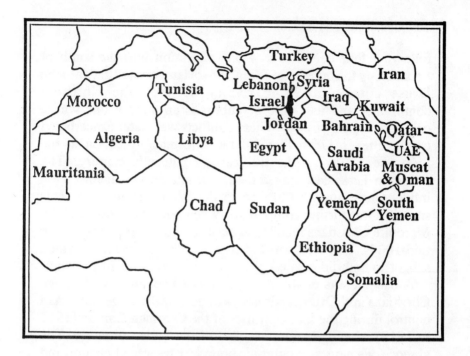

LEBANON

History

Present-day Lebanon's Baaka Valley was part of King David's Biblical kingdom. During the days of King Solomon—approximately 1000 B.C., the Phoenician Empire was established in what is now Lebanon. When the Romans conquered the Middle East during the second century B.C., this entire area became part of the Roman Empire. The Roman legions stationed their troops in the Baaka Valley to protect this "breadbasket" for their empire.

In A.D. 300, Lebanon became part of the Byzantine Empire. In the sixth century, the Monothelite sectaries, who were fleeing from orthodox Byzantine persecutions in northern Syria, colonized the Mount Lebanon area and, apparently, converted it to their brand of Christianity. They appeared in the following century as allies of Justinian II against the ruling caliph and, then, as rebels against his authority, hence their new name, Mardaites. This sect evolved over the centuries into the dominant present-day Maronite-Christian community in Lebanon.

In the seventh century A.D., Islam spread to Lebanon. The

following four centuries saw an infiltration into the south of Lebanon by the heretics of Islam, which later crystallized into the Druse community. The rivalry between the Christian community and its Druse neighbors is an ancient one whose origins are quite obscure. These conflicts were later exacerbated by the French when they offered informal protection to the Lebanese Christians in the early eighteenth century. The Ottoman Turks encouraged the Druse antagonism against these infidel Christians who looked to the West for guidance. This situation was further complicated when both the Druse and the Maronite Christians rebelled against their own leadership in the mid-1800s. This civil war led to European intervention which sought to and did create Lebanon as an independent province.

A bastion was established on Mount Lebanon by Maronite Christians and Druse lords and was never fully under Ottoman control during the four centuries of the Ottoman Empire (1517 to 1918) when Lebanon was part of the Syrian province. The absence of a natural geographic boundary between Lebanon and Syria allowed a free flow of population, therefore, a strong Islamic presence was established in northern Lebanon. In 1920, France held the mandate over Lebanon and Syria. In summary, over the years, each invading force left its mark on the population, which created a large variety of ethnic groups and religions in a very small area.

In 1947, Lebanon achieved statehood. At that time, she consisted of Maronite and Greek Orthodox Christians who together agreed that they represented 60 percent of the indigenous population. The balance was divided among Sunni Moslems, Shi'ite Moslems, and Druse. In 1948, there was a large influx of Arabs from Israel, and in 1970, a large influx of Palestinian-Arab refugees from Jordan via Syria. The government of Lebanon was established according to the agreed-upon religious proportions of the population of the country. The consensus was that the peasant Shi'ite population of the country was not substantial enough to be represented in the government. At that time, Shi'ites inhabited Southern Lebanon, Maronite Christians dwelled in the center, Sunni Moslems lived in the north and Baaka Valley, and the Druse were in the Shouf Mountains. Since feudal lords ruled at the local level, the central government had little control over the sectarian elements.

Lebanon's main sources of income came from truck farming, banking, commerce, and transit shipping of goods and oil to the Arab countries through her ports. Because Beirut became the banking capital of the Arab world and the Lebanese ports were handling such large volumes of transit goods, there was no incentive to establish industries other than commerce and simple agriculture.

When France assumed the mandate over the Ottoman-Syrian province in 1920, she created a Lebanese entity envisioned to be Christian-Arab ruled and a Syrian entity to be Moslem-Arab ruled. When Lebanon attained independence from the United Nations in 1947, she was, likewise, perceived to be a Christian-Arab nation. The first challenge to Lebanon's Christian national identity came from Nasser's Pan-Arabism in 1958. The United States intervened and President Eisenhower sent the U.S. Marines. At that time, Lebanon was preserved in her original intended form—a Christian-Arab nation.

The original proportions for religious representation in the government were established in 1932 and never changed until 1984. Since 1932, the real demographic make-up of Lebanon's population has been either unknown or one of the world's best-guarded secrets. Each sect established its own armed militia; procured weapons on the world market including tanks, armor, and heavy artillery; and trained its own mini-armies.

The real political struggle for power in Lebanon began in 1975, when the Lebanese-Sunni Moslems demanded a greater share of power upon their uniting with the refugee Palestinian-Sunni Moslems. They demanded a redistribution of representation based on a new population census. At that time, the ruling Lebanese positions of power were divided with a Christian as president, a Sunni Moslem as prime minister, and a Druse as chief of staff. Despite their being the largest single population in Lebanon, there was still no Shi'ite representation in a position of power. This was a result of their depressed economic condition and their lack of sophistication in political organizations. During the first eight years of civil strife, which began in 1975, hundreds of thousands died—75,000 died in 1975 alone—and over 500,000 Lebanese left the country. In 1976, Syrian peace-keeping forces entered Lebanon, fought the Sunni and the PLO, and literally saved the Christians from being massacred. Israel entered in both 1978 and 1982 to maintain the Christian-Arab character of Lebanon by neutralizing the Palestinians and destroying the PLO.

The original aims of the Begin government at the start of the 1982 Peace for Galilee War in Lebanon were numerous and politically far-reaching:

- termination of hostilities and terrorism against towns and settlements in northern Israel through destruction of PLO military build-up and infrastructure in Southern Lebanon and Beirut;
- destruction of the PLO as an effective political force for change in the Middle East, thus foiling the Reagan administration's trend (started under President Carter) toward the recognition of the PLO as a relevant political partner in future peace negotiations;
- termination of Syrian domination of Lebanon by militarily humiliating the Syrian forces, thereby discouraging what was believed to be a Syrian preparation for a major war against Israel—a mini-preventive war;
- creation in Lebanon of the first non-Moslem-Arab state in the Arab world and the achievement of a formal peace treaty with a second Arab nation; and
- discouragement of organized rebellion by Arab inhabitants of Judea, Samaria, and Gaza (there was extreme unrest at the time) as well as by Israeli Arabs.

Although these aims were somewhat overly ambitious, given Israel's political status among the world community of nations and the converging interests of the major powers in the area, the immediate results of the 1982 Peace for Galilee War in Lebanon were impressive and include:

- peace, calm, and security for Israel's northern towns and settlements—except for an isolated terrorist incursion from time to time;
- military destruction and political neutralization of the PLO;
- military humiliation of Syria by—
  - the destruction of her most advanced, complex SAM systems (located in the Baaka Valley) and one-half of her interceptor forces (without the loss of a single Israeli plane in either operation), and

- the explosion of the myth of the invincibility of the Soviet
  T-72 tank;
- forced withdrawal of Syria from most of Lebanon;
- re-establishment of Israel as the dominant military power in
  the region; and
- neutralization of Arab unrest in Judea, Samaria, and Gaza,
  yielding calm and tranquility within those territories.

Of the original aims of the Begin government's 1982 Peace for
Galilee War in Lebanon, what Israel did not achieve included:

- establishment of a unified Lebanon as the first non-Moslem-
  Arab state in the Arab world (decisive forces within were too
  numerous and too powerful);
- formalization of a peace treaty with a second Arab nation;
- conclusion of a swift enough military victory by Israel—one
  week instead of three weeks—so as to
  - limit the number of casualties sustained by the Israeli
    Defense Forces (IDF);
  - minimize the economic dislocation caused by the total
    manpower mobilization required; and, most importantly;
  - preclude the establishment by the Free World nations—
    led by the United States—of a counterpolicy to thwart the
    achievement by Israel of her far-reaching political goals.

The intervention of the U.S.-led multinational peace force in
Lebanon brought about fundamental political changes in the
area. For the United States—whose purposes in this initiative
were to neutralize politically Israel's military achievements, to
implement her own policies, and to demonstrate her ability to
determine events in the Middle East—this endeavor was a
foreign policy fiasco! Although she succeeded in denying Israel
the fruits of military victory and enforcing the withdrawal of
Israeli troops from Lebanon, she was unable to project her
influence into the area and, in the effort, exposed several totally
unanticipated weaknesses—the very existence of which
demonstrated impaired crisis assessment. The United States
failed in both the appraisal of her tactical military preparedness
and the recognition that the absence of a U.S. national purpose
would not sustain even minimal losses (Vietnam War
syndrome). A third major U.S. failure was in the evaluation of
her political reliance on agreements with Arab nations in that:

- Saudi Arabia failed to provide the political support promised after pressuring the United States to change significantly her Middle East policy by intervening politically and militarily in Lebanon;
- Egypt, Jordan, and Saudi Arabia—as moderate Arab countries—disappointed the United States by their lack of political influence on events in Lebanon;
- Jordan rejected Reagan's 1982 Peace Plan for the West Bank and Gaza after privately implying acceptance; and
- Syria deceived the United States by breaking her agreement for a withdrawal from Lebanon simultaneously with Israel.

Unexpectedly, the most valuable outcome of U.S. intervention in Lebanon was the long-term strategic military alliance between Israel and the United States. This alliance was forged as a direct result of the realization by the United States that Israel's military power was significant and not transient; the exposure of the interests of the United States and the Arab nations in the area is divergent, not convergent, in the overall dynamics of the war. This alliance—a twist of events development—is likely to be the most valuable product of the 1982 Peace for Galilee War in Lebanon for both Israel and the United States.

A simultaneous escalation of the Iraq-Iran War not only forced the United States to refocus her political attention from the Lebanon-Arab-Israeli confrontation and the Palestinian issue to the security of the Persian Gulf, but it also provided the United States with an opportunity to redirect world attention away from one of her greatest foreign policy blunders in the Middle East.

Summarization of the overall results of the 1982 Lebanon Peace for Galilee War indicates that the political behavior of the Arab leaders exposed U.S. military weakness and political impotence in the area—virtually rendering U.S. political influence in the Middle East ineffective. The ensuing realignment of forces in Lebanon spawned the emergence of the politically dormant Shi'ites as a real political force.

Present

Lebanon, bordered by the Mediterranean Sea on the west, presently occupies approximately 10,360 sq km (4,015 sq mi) of which 1 percent is meadows and pastures, 7 percent is forested, 29 percent is agricultural, and 63 percent is desert, waste, or

urban. Except for a narrow southern border with Israel, her
territorial boundaries are with Syria on the south and on the east.

Lebanon's population is "guesstimated" at 2,675,000—93
percent Arab (83 percent Lebanese, 10 percent Palestinian), 6
percent Armenian, and 1 percent other (including Syrian and
Kurd). Estimates of the religious composition of the population
indicate that 57 percent are Moslem (32 percent Shi'ite, 20
percent Sunni, and 5 percent Druse); 42 percent Christian (24.5
percent Maronite Christian, 6.5 percent Greek Orthodox, 4
percent Greek Catholic, 4 percent Armenian Orthodox, and 3
percent Armenian and Roman Catholic, Syrian Orthodox, and
Protestant); and 1 percent other. Because the political system is
based on the population proportions of the individual religious
communities, and there has been no official census since 1932,
the precise ratios are in dispute. Population figures of the various
sects are grossly inflated to make each group appear stronger and
protect its safety. Although the political system is officially based
on a 6:5 ratio of Christians to Moslems/Druse, most recent
estimates suggest the present ratio is actually 6:4 or 6:5
Moslems/Druse to Christians.

Arabic is the official language of Lebanon, although French
and English are widely used, and Armenian is spoken in Beirut.
The literacy rate is reported to be 75 percent.

Lebanon, officially known as the Republic of Lebanon, is a
"republic" with an elected president and legislature. However,
since 1985—because of the ongoing civil war—governmental
functions have, in effect, been taken over by various militia and/
or foreign "peace-keeping" forces. For the most part, the Druse
control the Shouf Mountains; the Christians control East Beirut
and the central coastal area; the Shi'ites control most of the south
(Amal), part of the Baaka Valley (Hesbullah), and part of West
Beirut (Amal); and the Sunni control part of West Beirut
(Morabund). Syrian forces now control part of the Baaka Valley
and the north where they center their activity in Tripoli, formerly
under the domination of the Sunni-Moslem Brotherhood and the
PLO.

Currently, Israel's forces, in conjunction with the Southern
Lebanese Army and U.N. forces, are attempting to maintain
peace between the various rival factions in the south, while
Syrian forces are responsible for peace-keeping in the rest of the

country. Sporadic terrorist activity and outbursts of factional rivalry continue to occur, however, throughout the Lebanese territory. Today, Lebanon is a microcosm of the inter-Arab Middle East struggle in that there are influences present of just about every national and religious entity and subentity in the Arab world attempting to control events.

Because Syria's Alawi minority government is aligned with Syrian Christians (and Druse), she must continue to demonstrate her support of the Christians in Lebanon by containing the power of the Shi'ites. Additionally, she must maintain control over Shi'ite power to prevent the fervor of Islamic fundamentalism from spilling over into Syria. The Druse have expanded their territorial control and assumed more power in Lebanon than their demographic proportions dictate; therefore, Syria must continue in her effort to reduce Druse power to correspond to their actual population ratio. Since Syria's minority government rules over a Sunni majority population, she cannot permit the Sunni to become the dominant force in Lebanon, especially since those Sunni in the north (Tripoli) are controlled by the Moslem Brotherhood—Sunni Fundamentalists who are dedicated to the destruction of the present Syrian regime.

The basis, then, of the present political unrest in Lebanon is clear. There are many factions (each with its own militia) vying for power, none of which is strong enough to obtain absolute control. All of these factions, with the exception of one, have allies in the Arab world external to Lebanon. The Maronite Christians, however, rely solely on their external support from Israel. Israel's political position in Lebanon is much stronger than it appears. She has real influence with the Christians, Druse, and part of the Shi'ites (those opposed to Khomeini—Amal).

Economically, Lebanon is also in a state of utter chaos. The cataclysmic, multifactioned civil war that has raged since 1975 has completely devastated Lebanon's commercial, industrial, and agricultural infrastructure. Although Beirut was for decades the banking capital of the Arab world, the effect of the war has resulted in a shift from Beirut to Amman as the Arab nations' financial center. Likewise, Lebanon's status as the tourist center of the Arab world—at one time the second highest foreign currency earner—has disappeared. At the present time, Lebanon's dominant foreign currency earner and her chief agricultural crop and export is illicit drugs—opium poppies, cannabis, hashish— for the international drug trade. Lebanon's GNP is estimated at $5.5 billion—$1,956 per capita.

Militarily, Lebanon cannot be compared to or even discussed in the same way as other nations since the country is deeply divided among warring militias. The size of armaments and the amount of expenditures of the individual militias are not public information. All arms purchases are through private arms merchants on the open market—not through governments.

Future

To predict the future of Lebanon as a unified independent nation, one would need to rely on tarot cards, a crystal ball, or a psychic. The best that can be foreseen is a weak, superficial central authority (whose only purpose is to communicate with other nations) and a number of autonomous cantons (with no official international recognition). Close ties between Israel and the Christians and secular Shi'ites (Amal) in southern Lebanon, near Israel's border, will be required for the security of northern Israel.

Regardless of events in Lebanon, there will always be a Syrian influence there with the goal to annex Lebanon to fulfill "greater Syria." If Syria remains under Alawi control, she will continue to have only a limited influence in Lebanon—the Alawi don't have friends. If the Sunni rise to power in Syria, then she will have a strong influence over the Sunni in Lebanon, but both the Amal- and Hesbullah-Shi'ite factions would oppose a Sunni-dominated government in Lebanon.

In the future, Israel will continue to maintain her policies in southern Lebanon—her friendly ties with the Christians (to help them maintain their position and to keep Lebanon from becoming an enemy Arab-Moslem state) and cordial relations with the Druse.

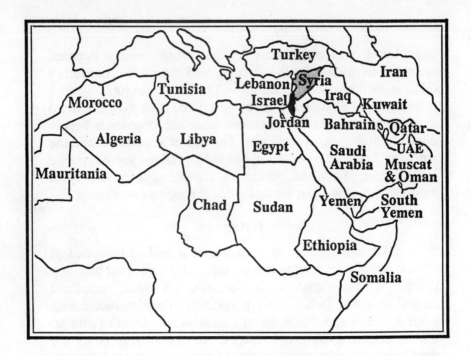

SYRIA

History

The Moslem presence in Syria can be traced back to the year A.D. 636. In 660, the Umayyad Dynasty conquered Damascus and from there the Arab caliphate ruled over what was called the "Greater Syrian Empire" until 750. That area included present-day Israel, Jordan, Lebanon, and Syria. The Umayyad Dynasty fell when the Damascus region was conquered by the Abassyd caliphate, which moved to Baghdad, leaving present-day Syria largely unattended and ignored. Subsequently, Syria was bombarded and occupied by quarreling caliphate factions, the Christian Crusaders, and the Egyptians.

Between 1516 and 1918, this region became a fixture of the Ottoman Empire. After the dismantling of the Ottoman Empire following World War I, the French received a mandate over Syria from the League of Nations. Syria remained a French protectorate until 1946 when she received her independence. Since then, Syria has been wracked by a succession of coup d'etats prompted, in part, by her diversity.

In 1958, Syria and Egypt merged to form the United Arab

Republic (UAR) under Nasser. Syria became the northern region of the UAR and was ruled as a province by Egypt. Egyptian dominance of Syria was resented, and Syria broke from the UAR in 1961.

The Syrian Ba'athists—an Alawi secular Moslem-Socialist party—took power in 1963 through a violent military coup led by Alawi Ba'athist officers. Then, in 1970, in yet another coup, Hafez al-Assad, the air force commander, took power when a Syrian-led and -supported Palestinian invasion of Jordan failed. Even though Assad was (and is) an Alawi—a group representing only 11.5 percent of the population—he came to power because of a unique societal phenomenon. The peasant class Alawis, as a result of their economic circumstances, comprised the majority of the French-trained army officer corps, while the wealthy Sunni majority remained totally aloof from military affairs. After Syrian independence, it became clear that he who controlled the army (Assad) would eventually control the country.

Assad has remained in power through the brutal extermination of his opponents and has withstood a number of attempts to overthrow his regime by the Fundamentalist Sunni-Moslem Brotherhood. In so doing, he has also ruthlessly slaughtered tens of thousands of Sunni-Moslem civilians—most recently an estimated 25,000 in the city of Hama—as well as scores of Alawis.

The noble Ba'athist ideal that allows sectarianism to be curbed and, perhaps, eventually eliminated has not been realized in over two decades of secularly inspired but sectarian minority-dominated Syrian-Ba'athist rule. Ironically, since her independence, modern-day Syria has become more distant than ever from this ostensible Ba'athist ideal of a secular society in which all Arabs, irrespective of religion, can equally participate.

Present

Today, Syria covers an area of 185,000 sq km (71,500 sq mi) at the eastern end of the Mediterranean Sea. She is bordered by Turkey on the north, Iraq on the east, Jordan on the southeast, Israel on the southwest, and Lebanon on the west. Nearly half of her land is arable, 30 percent is grazing pasture, 21 percent is desert, and 2 percent is forested. As a result of the June 1967 Six-Day War, Syria lost to Israel 1,300 sq km (800 sq mi)—an area known as the Golan Heights that represents less than 1 percent of Syrian territory.

Syria's population is estimated at 11 million and is comprised of the following religious groups: 74 percent Sunni Moslems; 16 percent Alawi; and the balance Christian, Druse, and others. In terms of nationalities, approximately 90 percent are Arab and 10 percent Armenians, Kurds, and Turks. While Arabic is the official language, Aramaic, Armenian, Circassian, and Kurdish are minority languages. English and French are understood widely. The literacy rate, as reported by the government, is 50 percent.

Politically, Syria, officially known as the Syrian Arab Republic, is a republic dominated by a military government under the authoritarian leadership of President Hafez al-Assad. Today, Syria continues to be controlled by the Ba'ath party which purports to be a secular, Socialist, progressive Arab party, when, in fact, it is controlled by a small group of Alawi officers who, in turn, are controlled by the Assad family of five brothers. The Alawi Ba'athists are aligned with the Christians, Druse, and other small minorities; together, they represent under 30 percent of the total Syrian population. The Moslem Brotherhood, which represents a minority of the Sunni, wants to establish an Islamic-Sunni-Fundamentalist state, while the Sunni majority want a secular Sunni state. The present Assad regime describes itself as a Pan-Arab secular Socialist state.

The legitimacy of Assad's rule is under constant challenge because the Sunni, who comprise almost 70 percent of the Syrian population, have only minority representation in the ruling Ba'ath party and, therefore, have no power over government institutions, government policy, or the military. The declared aims of the Ba'ath party are Socialist aims illuminated by humanitarian principles. The Ba'athist struggle was supposed to be a class struggle of the rich against the poor, but, in reality, it has deteriorated to that of a religious and ethnic struggle within the Syrian society pitting, not rich against poor, but Alawi, Christian, and Druse against Sunni Moslems.

Today, Syria is controlled by a "minority within a minority" representing an ideology that has failed to achieve its main objective. Its retention of power has been based on terrorism, violent intimidations, periodic mass slaughters, selective assassinations, and political incarcerations. It is a ruthless military dictatorship that has alienated and harmed a sufficient portion of the society to have created an immense pool of enemies. Its survival is constantly threatened because its existence is constantly challenged.

Economically, Syria—like Jordan—is basically agrarian with very limited light industry, no technological infrastructure, and no scientific community to speak of. Her GNP is estimated at just over $17 billion—$1,660 per capita.

Militarily, Syria maintains a standing armed force of 500,000 and spends approximately $3.5 billion annually for defense. This represents about 18 percent of her GNP.

Future

In projecting the future of Syria as a nation at the turn of the century, the analysis depends on whether the Alawi-dominated alignment of Alawis, Christians, and Druse will continue to rule, or whether Sunnis—either secular or Islamic Fundamentalist led by the Moslem Brotherhood—will come to power.

Continued Alawi-Ba'athist domination of Syria will make her relationship with Iraq even more strained and hostile. The basis for the animosity is that in Syria the Ba'ath party is Alawi controlled over a Sunni majority, while in Iraq the Ba'ath—also a secular Socialist progressive party—is Sunni controlled over a Shi'ite majority. Both Alawis and Shi'ites are despised by the Sunni.

Syrian construction of a dam on the Euphrates River, a water source she shares with Iraq, will further exacerbate the relationship between the two nations. Their relationship is still further complicated by the Iran-Iraq War in which Syria, unlike the vast majority of her Arab brethren, has allied herself with Shi'ite Iran. Since Iraq is burdened by the war with Iran, a military confrontation with Syria does not seem to be on the horizon, but enmity between the two countries will continue to intensify and is not likely to subside unless there is an end to that war.

Additionally, Syria's intervention in the Lebanon civil war— particularly her occupation of West Beirut and her support of Lebanese Shi'ites—emphasizes the precarious nature of the continued Alawi-dominated Syria. Her support of Shi'ite

Fundamentalists in Iran and Lebanon is implausible policy for a secular regime under the constant threat of rebellion from the Sunni-Fundamentalist-Moslem Brotherhood at home.

Because of such internal instability, an Alawi-Ba'ath-led Syria must focus on Israel as a common enemy of all Syrians. She will, therefore, continue to maintain a political, economic, and military struggle against Israel—a Western, democratic, capitalist state.

An Alawi-Ba'ath-led Syria may sooner or later attempt to destroy the constitutional monarchy of Jordan and establish a Ba'athist government there controlled by Socialist Christians and Socialist-Sunni Moslems. Syria would accomplish this by coordinating the rebellious activities of the Syrian-controlled PLO and Palestinians in Jordan. This is why Assad has continually supported George Habash and his Christian-Arab-Communist terrorist organization.

The strong-arm politics of an Alawi-dominated regime will continue as Syria attempts to maintain the facade of a Pan-Arabic secular Socialist state, while remaining in control of her volatile situation. The ultimate aim of such a government, however, is the revolutionary establishment of a Ba'athist-Arab world of secular Socialist societies. Since the original Nasser-led Pan-Arab concept with Cairo as the capital was never realized, Syria will continue to see herself as the center of the Arab world with Damascus as the capital. For the Syrian Ba'athists, Syrian national imperialism overrides Ba'athist Pan-Arabism. The Syrian Ba'athist see their role as the implementers of a Syrian-controlled Arab world—secular and Socialist. This becomes obvious when one realizes that the Syrian constitution—written two decades prior to Ba'athist ascension to power—does not recognize Lebanon, Jordan, or Israel as independent states and has as its goal the establishment of a modern Umayyad Empire referred to as "Greater Syria."

What further underscores the instability of Syria's minority-led Ba'athist regime is the tribal nature of her society. Entire cities and sectors are controlled by various hostile ethnic and religious groups—similar to what exists in Lebanon. It is most likely, therefore, that a bloody civil war, such as occurred in Lebanon, will destroy the national character that exists today within the present boundaries of Syria.

If there will be a Sunni majority in a Ba'athist-led Syria, there will be a massive slaughter of the ruling Alawis, Christians, and Druse in an attempt to decimate those societies and render them politically ineffectual. If successful, then, Syria would support mainstream PLO to overthrow the Jordanian monarchy and join with an Arafat Sunni-Ba'athist PLO state in a union dominated by Syria. If that union occurs, it will support the destruction of the Christian and Druse communities in Lebanon and establish there a Lebanese secular Ba'athist state to be joined with Syria. There would be a temporary rapprochement with the Iraqi-Ba'athist-led government; however, the *national* interests of each will eventually collide over the issue of which center will dominate the Arab world—Damascus or Baghdad. Relations with Israel will be the same whether Syria is a Sunni-Ba'athist or Alawi-Ba'athist nation—one of constant conflict.

If there were to be a Sunni takeover in Syria, it is most likely to be an Islamic-Fundamentalist movement spearheaded and controlled by the Moslem Brotherhood. Such a takeover would occur through violent revolution and would witness the bloody and ruthless slaughter of masses of Alawis, Christians, Druse, and Sunni secularists. This Sunni-Islamic-Fundamentalist government would form an alliance with the Jordanian monarchy and would support actively the Moslem Brotherhood in Egypt in its effort to depose the ruling military junta there. Such a government would be in conflict with a Ba'athist-Iraqi regime, while also seeking battle with Israel.

The final possible alternative is that Syria will go the way of Lebanon and break into semiautonomous regions in constant battle. Regardless of which scenario emerges, as we enter the twenty-first century, there can be no peace between Syria and Israel.

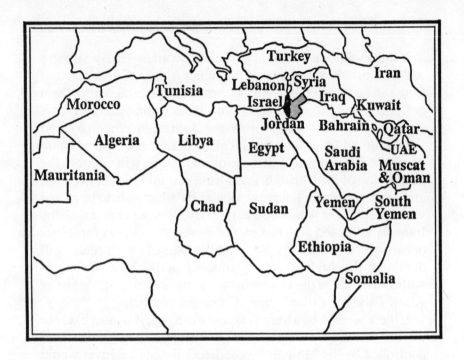

JORDAN

History

All of the land east of the Jordan River presently occupied by the nation of Jordan was a part of what the Romans called Palestine in A.D. 300. At that time, the Romans renamed the entire Jewish state (both sides of the Jordan River) Palestina after a people who no longer existed (the Philistines). They did this in order to punish the Jews because of the Bar-Kochba uprising and to eradicate all traces of Jewish connection to that land. The Roman emperor, Hadrian, took the land identified in the Bible as the tribal land of the Hebrew people who had inhabited that land continuously from 1200 B.C. Between A.D. 300 (Hadrian's renaming of the land to Palestine) and 1918 (the fall of the Ottoman Empire), there was *one* land called Palestine, and it covered the entire area east of the Jordan River—now occupied by the nation of Jordan—and the entire area west of the Jordan River—now occupied by the nation of Israel. During that 1,600 years, the land of Palestine was never a nation; it never had a government nor was it ever identified with any people other than the continuous Jewish population.

For the 500 years prior to 1918, all of Palestine—both sides of the Jordan River—as well as all other lands occupied by Arabs, were ruled by the Turks (the Ottoman Empire). Before 1918 and until 1948, when the spirit of nationalism peaked throughout the world, the only people who claimed Palestinian national identity were the Jews. The remaining population of Palestine—either Arabs, Bedouins, Christians, Moslems, or other transients— never identified themselves as Palestinians. The non-Jewish population in all of Palestine never created commerce, never established institutions, and never built cities or any other type of permanent settlements. Rather, they exploited the land. They tilled and cultivated the land improperly, shepherded their animals inappropriately, chopped down trees indiscriminately, killed the indigenous animals for food, and created malaria-infested swamps.

In 1922, three years after the League of Nations Mandate for Palestine, Britain usurped the authority vested in her by the League of Nations to create a Jewish national homeland in Palestine by dividing the land of Palestine into two pieces. She created an area east of the Jordan River (75 percent of the land) which she called Transjordan. At that time, although the area was only sparsely inhabited by Nomads—Bedouins, Jewish settlement in Transjordan was forbidden *(Judenfrei)*. Only the area west of the Jordan River (25 percent of the land) was open for Jewish (and Arab) settlement.

The legitimacy of this act was forged by a thirty-minute meeting of two British generals in a hotel in Jerusalem. Britain, in an effort to eliminate the internal war in Arabia between the Saud family and the Hashemite family, compensated the Hashemite *emir,* Abdullah, by giving him that part of Palestine east of the Jordan River—Transjordan. In order to protect this area from Jewish settlement and future claims to it as part of Palestine, it was written into law that no Jew could settle, live, own property, or make commerce within Transjordan—the area now occupied by Jordan. Even at the present time, such *Judenfrei* is part of Jordan's written law and is meticulously enforced. From a Biblical and, for that matter, modern historical point of view, that area east of the Jordan River now called Jordan is no less Palestine than the area west of the Jordan River now called Israel.

In 1928, after the Arab League was formed, Britain recognized Transjordan as an "independent" nation, despite the fact that she maintained fiscal and military control as well as the formal mandate, which she only relinquished in 1948. Transjordan was proclaimed a kingdom in 1946, and the British knighted the Hashemite *emir,* Abdullah, who had been expelled from Arabia (Saudi), king of Transjordan. At that time, Transjordan had a population of 400,000 Bedouins.

In 1948, after Transjordan invaded the then new State of Israel, she conquered land west of the Jordan River, which later became known as the "West Bank." King Abdullah then officially annexed that territory and changed the name of his country from Transjordan to Jordan. Later, Jordan lost that territory west of the Jordan River as a result of the Six-Day War in June 1967 during which she invaded Israel—including Jerusalem—on the third day.

During the 1948 to 1967 period of Jordanian occupation of the West Bank, neither King Abdullah nor his grandson and successor, King Hussein, ever recognized Palestinian-Arab rights. Theirs was an autonomous regime that invested no money for commercial, industrial, or educational development. No colleges or universities were established. In fact, a distinct Palestinian-Arab identity was prohibited. During that time, the population of Jordan, including the West Bank, consisted of 85 percent who identified as Palestinians and 15 percent who identified as Bedouins whose loyalty was to King Hussein's monarchy. There was no movement for a Palestinian state among that population until Israel recaptured the West Bank during the 1967 War. Between 1948 and 1967, no Jews were permitted in the area of the West Bank (Judea and Samaria), despite the fact that Jews had been living in settlements in the Etzion block, Hebron, Nablus, and east Jerusalem prior to the invasion of Israel by Jordan on May 15, 1948. For those nineteen years, Jordan made that entire area *Judenfrei* and blatantly desecrated Jewish holy places.

Present

Jordan presently occupies approximately 85,000 sq km east of the Jordan River. (The territory west of the river, which she conquered in 1948 and lost in 1967, covers 6,000 sq km—less than 7 percent of the territory she occupied between 1948 and 1967.) Jordan borders Israel on the west, Syria on the north, Iraq on the northeast, and Saudi Arabia on the east and south. Approximately 1 percent of the land is forest, meadow, or pasture; 9 percent is agricultural; and 90 percent is wasteland (mostly desert), urban, or other.

Today, the population of Jordan approximates 2.85 million. Religiously, 95 percent of the population is Sunni Moslem and 5 percent is Christian. Nationally, the Jordanian government claims that 60 percent of the present population identify as Palestinians—a figure that is most probably understated by as much as 15 percent. Ethnically, it is estimated that 98 percent of the population is Arab, 1 percent Circassian, and 1 percent Armenian. The official language of Jordan is Arabic, although English is understood widely by the middle and upper classes. The literacy rate is claimed to be 70 percent.

Politically, Jordan, officially known as the Hashemite Kingdom of Jordan, is a secular Sunni constitutional monarchy. The country, ruled by a Bedouin minority consisting of twenty-two tribes, does not provide the four basic freedoms found in Western-style democracies—assembly, speech, worship, and the press. The ruling Bedouin minority has no common cultural heritage with the majority who now identify as Palestinian Arabs. Among the Bedouin, there is no real feeling of national identity—their allegiance to the tribe is much stronger than to the state.

One reason for this apathy toward national identity is that there is no history of national struggle for independence. Their country was a gift given by the British. The territory was never actually settled by Arabs. No Jordanian city has any Arab or Moslem historic significance. (There are, however, many Jewish historical cities and places in Jordan.) There is no ancient history of the land other than its Biblical heritage and the history of tribes that disappeared hundreds of years ago. Jordan is an area inhabited by two "peoples" with no historical, cultural, or religious roots in that territory. Even more incredulous is that Jordan is ruled by a foreign sheik, whose family originates from Saudi Arabia, dubbed king by the English.

This artificial state, created by two British generals meeting in a hotel room and sanctioned by a British-Jewish high commissioner of Palestine without previous consultation with the League of Nations, is presently coveted by two very strong political forces. Both the PLO, whose charter calls for Jordan becoming Palestine, and Syria, which sees Jordan as an integral part of Greater Syria, are Jordan's enemies. The State of Israel is not Jordan's enemy; Jordan is the enemy of the State of Israel.

Economically, Jordan is basically agrarian with limited light industry; there is no technological infrastructure and no scientific community to speak of. Amman, the Jordanian capital, has replaced Beirut as the center of Arab banking since the outbreak of the Lebanese civil war. Jordan's GNP is reported to be approximately $4,010,000,000—$1,520 per capita.

Militarily, Jordan expends approximately $600 million, or 25 percent of her national budget, to support her armed forces—85,000 men-under-arms and their Bedouin officer corps. This represents 12 to 15 percent of her GNP.

Although Jordanian political activity, economic development, and military establishment engage Palestinian talents and energies at the moment, the monarchy has never yielded and cannot yield to the "Palestinian" national aspirations that have developed only since June 1967. This applies to those "Jordanians" whose origins were from either the East or West Bank of the Jordan River.

Future

Within the next twenty years, Jordan will most probably be ruled by her majority Palestinian population and will be Palestinian, if the Syrians do not, within that period, conquer her by either subversion or invasion. To complicate Jordan's future, Iraq would like to build an oil pipeline to Aqaba to bypass any future Iranian blockade and the potential danger of the closing of the Persian Gulf. Iraq is preparing for a long period of animosity and struggle, and Jordan provides the only outlet to the sea. Syria, who is in conflict with Iraq, will not want such a pipeline to function. Iraq and Syria could go to war over Jordan.

The only thing that can be predicted about the future political arrangement within Jordan and for her political relationship with her neighbors is that something unpredictable will occur. This is due to the fundamental built-in instability within the country and within the region.

By the turn of the century, the existence of the nation now called Jordan and her relationship with Israel will depend upon four possible scenarios:

- If the minority Hashemite kingdom survives, the probability of war with Israel would be extremely negligible because of the overwhelming impact of Israel's demonstrated power. The monarch would do everything politically possible to prevent the establishment of a Palestinian state in the West Bank—Judea and Samaria. There would be no formalized peace treaty or agreement with Israel because of the tenuousness of the majority-ruled monarchy.

- Should Jordan's Palestinian majority gain control of the government, a revolutionary antimonarchial government would be established. There would be an attempt to make a deal with Israel for a political treaty with all the Arabs within the territory Israel controls, including areas within her pre-1967 borders. Such a Jordanian state would build an army equipped and trained by the Soviet Union. Her first military venture, by necessity, would be a continuation of the antimonarchial trend and would focus on Saudi Arabia—the largest existing monarchy in the Middle East. The fall of the Saudi monarchy—the protectorate of the Sunni sheikdoms in the Gulf—would unleash Palestinian revolutionary forces in Kuwait where 30 percent of the population are Palestinians who do not share in the benefits that accrue to Kuwaiti citizens.

The remaining two possible scenarios project a Syrian takeover of Jordan:

- If an Alawi-governed Ba'athist Syria were to gain control over the territory, then what currently is Jordan would become a secular-oriented Socialist-Moslem state. Such an extension of the present Syria—another phase in establishing the Greater Syria—would be a threat to Iraq, Saudi Arabia, and Israel. The new state's first military objective would be Iraq for the purpose of changing the Sunni regime there to one similar to her own. The next military/political objective would be Saudi Arabia to achieve a similar result. The final step in establishing Greater Syria would be the attempt to conquer Israel and destroy the Jewish presence.

- If a Sunni regime were to gain control in Syria, it would, most likely, be a Sunni-Islamic-Fundamentalist regime that would form an alliance with the Sunni monarchy in Jordan. The Islamic religious fervor that would develop as a result of such an alliance would spread throughout the area and would be in greatest conflict with Iraq's secular Socialist regime, despite the fact that it, too, is Sunni. Such an alliance between Syria and Jordan would, likewise, pose a great threat to Israel if, as a result, they were to establish a joint military command.

Iraq

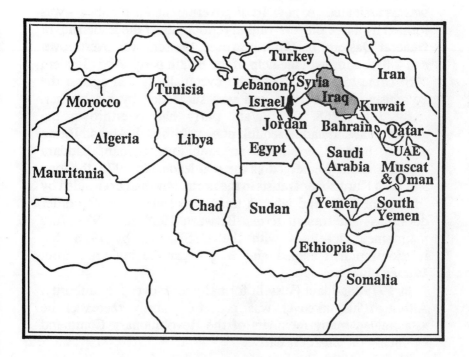

History

Ancient Iraq formed part of Babylonia and became known as Mesopotamia. Persians occupied the territory until A.D. 635 when it was conquered by Arab Moslems and became part of the Umayyad Dynasty and the center for Shi'ite Moslems. In 750, the territory was conquered by Abassyds, non-Arab Moslems, who controlled the area from Morocco to northern India. Mongols invaded and occupied the area in 1400. Then, in 1534, Suleiman the Magnificent conquered the entire Middle East, with the exception of Persia, and established the Ottoman Empire, which lasted until 1918. After World War II, by League of Nations mandate, the British were given control of Iraq—along with other territories in the Middle East wrested from the Turks.

In 1932, Iraq became an independent nation with the establishment of the constitutional monarchy of King Faisal whose Hashemite family also ruled Jordan. Early in 1958, the two Hashemite kings—Faisal of Iraq and Hussein of Jordan—formed a union, but during a revolt later that year, King Faisal was assassinated. A new Iraqi government—a republic—was formed by a free officers' military group under the leadership of General Qassem. In 1963, however, Qassem was overthrown and killed, and, with the help of the Ba'ath party, Abd al-Salem 'Arif came to power. Arif, who eventually turned against the Ba'athists, died in 1966 and was succeeded by his brother.

By July 1968, the Ba'ath party had overthrown the government and had seized full power. Although Ahmad Hasan al-Bakr became president, an ambitious civilian, Saddam Hussein, quickly emerged as the real leader. In 1975, the long war with Kurdish separatists in the north, who had been aided by Iran, came to an end when a treaty was signed settling border questions—on Iranian terms. Between 1968 and 1978, Iraq maintained close ties with the USSR, but by 1978 that relationship had cooled and Iraq began buying arms from Western Europe.

In 1979, Saddam Hussein formally took over full authority. Although his takeover was peaceful, shortly thereafter he assassinated many members of the Revolutionary Command Council—the Ba'athist party.

Then, in 1980, Saddam Hussein and the Ba'ath party saw a unique opportunity to achieve seven strategic goals, simultaneously, by invading Iran to fulfill Iraqi-Ba'ath ideology.

- The first goal was to insure the survival of the Iraqi minority Sunni regime. Iran's ayatollah was inciting the Shi'ite majority in southern Iraq to revolt against Saddam Hussein's Sunni government.
- The second goal was to conquer Khuzistan, the major oil-bearing sector, which was inhabited by Iranian-Sunni Arabs. This area called Khuzistan by Iran is known as Arabastan by

Iraq. Saddam Hussein wanted a reunification of Iran's Sunni Arabs with Iraq's Sunni Arabs and control over the oil wealth of Khuzistan.

* The third goal was to weaken and neutralize the ayatollah's Iranian-Shi'ite regime. This would provide Hussein with the ability to attain total control over the Gulf states and move west.
* The fourth goal was to establish Iraq as the dominant power, not only in the Gulf region, but in the entire Arab world as well.
* The fifth goal was to neutralize and challenge the Syrians and establish Baghdad as the capital of the Arab world.
* The sixth goal was to use Iraq's economic, military, and political power to intimidate the Western world so that they would force Israel into an unfavorable settlement on the Palestinian issue.
* The seventh goal was to subvert the sheikdoms of the Gulf states and establish secular, Socialist, progressive states according to the Ba'ath ideology.

Saddam Hussein and his Ba'athist brothers became mesmerized by the projected benefits to be accrued through a successful invasion of Iran.

The ayatollah's response to Iraq's invasion of Iran was shocking to Hussein and his followers. The ayatollah understood well that Iraq was not a nation that could wage a sustained war—she had no agricultural or industrial base and no common culture to engender the required maturation among her populace. She was, rather, a highly illiterate, underpopulated, desert country whose only asset was an annual income of $35 billion from oil exports. Therefore, the ayatollah did the unthinkable—he immediately attacked and destroyed the Iraqi oil infrastructure, which shut down the world's second largest oil exporter for two years. After that, Iraq could only resume exporting a small percentage of her prewar output.

Present

Iraq covers an area of 445,480 sq km (167,881 sq mi) of which 68 percent is desert, waste, or urban; 18 percent is cultivated; 10 percent is meadows and pastures; and 4 percent is forested. Her borders are with Iran on the northeast, Kuwait on the southeast, Saudi Arabia on the south, Jordan on the southwest, Syria on the west, and Turkey on the north.

The total population of Iraq is estimated at 16.5 million—one-third that of Iran. Ethnically, 75 percent are Arabs; 15 to 20 percent are Kurds; and 5 to 10 percent are others, including Turkmen, Persians, and Assyrians. Religiously, 95 percent are Moslem (55 percent Shi'ite and 40 percent Sunni) and 5 percent are other—mostly Christian. Although Arabic is the official language, Kurdish is spoken by the Kurds and Farsi, and Armenian and Assyrian (Aramaic) are spoken by other minorities. Iraq's literacy rate is reported to be approximately 50 percent.

The only legitimate political expression in Iraq is the Ba'ath party, just as in Syria. A small group of officers led by Saddam Hussein, a Sunni Moslem, controls the Ba'ath party, which, supposedly, is comprised of a Shi'ite majority and some Kurds. The animosity between Iraq's and Syria's Ba'ath parties stems from the old rivalry concerning the location of the center of the Arab world—whether it would be established in Damascus or Baghdad. It is the same rivalry that existed between the Umayyad and Abassyd caliphates centuries ago.

Just prior to the Iraqi invasion of Iran in September 1980, Iraq was the world's second largest oil exporter with earnings of $35 billion per year of oil income. The oil boom dominated Iraq's economy while all other sectors—industry and agriculture—were ignored. She developed no industrial base worth mentioning. At that time, 75 percent of the population were engaged in agriculture, which produced 8 percent of Iraq's GNP. Many farmers abandoned their lands and migrated to the cities. Oil exports account for 98 percent of Iraq's foreign currency earnings. However, when her single-commodity oil economy was destroyed by the Iran-Iraq War, it left her an extremely poor country with a GNP, excluding oil, of less than $3 billion.

Today, Iraq has become a beggar nation having fought an "endless" war with money provided by the very Gulf states she previously had intended to undermine. Presently, these Gulf states are being subverted by the ayatollah. For Saddam Hussein and Iraq, as well as for the Sunni-Arab world, the war with Iran has been a disaster of the highest order. Iraq's prewar $35 billion per year oil income, reduced drastically because of the war and lower oil prices, still remains under $10 billion per year.

Iraq drained her $35 billion reserve and for years had to borrow as much as a billion dollars a month from the Gulf states in order to finance the war. Presently, her external debt because of the war is well in excess of $60 billion. During the first five years of the war, she lost many billions of dollars in equipment and sacrificed 275,000 men in battle (killed, wounded, or taken prisoner of war). Iraq also suffered very heavy casualties during the past three years with estimates of her total manpower loss as high as 600,000—200,000 dead and the balance wounded or captured. With a population of 7 million males, 2 million of which are fit for duty, such casualties mean that Iraq has lost as much as 25 percent of her military potential, with every household being affected.

Future

Iraq has no industrial or agricultural base, no technologically trained manpower, and an enormous illiteracy rate. Her oil production, however, has been restored from a low of 700,000 barrels/day to about 2 mb/d by doubling the capacity of the Turkish pipeline, by building a new pipeline to Saudi Arabia, and by transshipping her oil through Kuwaiti and Saudi ports.

The war with Iran will never be completely settled because it is an ideological struggle between two opposing religious philosophies (secular Islam and Shia fundamentalism) and two opposing political philosophies (Arab-Marxist socialism and non-Arab-Moslem theocracy). The animosity created by Iraq's use of missiles against Iranian civilian targets and chemical warfare (including poison gas) against the Iranian military has fomented a hate that time cannot heal, unless one side becomes a victor. The Iraqi-Ba'ath regime's survival is being challenged by Iran's ayatollah. Saddam Hussein has survived a coup from within the Ba'ath leadership because the ayatollah has made it clear that he wants not only Saddam's head, but the heads of all of his Ba'ath ruling brothers.

Any projection of the future of Iraq as a nation at the turn of the century will depend upon whether she continues to be controlled by the Sunnis or whether, like Lebanon, she will divide into three distinct autonomous regions. If there is division, there are certain implications. The south, which possesses vast oil wealth, is almost totally populated by Shi'ites who comprise 60 percent of Iraq's population. The north, which is also rich in oil, is inhabited by Kurds who represent 15 percent of the population. The center, which is barren of oil wealth, is inhabited by the 25 percent Sunni who presently rule Iraq according to the Ba'athist ideology—one united secular Socialist Arab-Moslem nation encompassing the entire Middle East. Division would result in Iraq's Shi'ites joining with Iran's Shi'ites—a dangerous situation for the rest of the Middle East. If there is no division of Iraq, she will either continue to be ruled by her Sunni minority or the Shi'ite majority will rise to power.

The survival of the minority Sunni Ba'ath until the turn of the century is doubtful at best. If there remains a Shi'ite-Fundamentalist government in Iran and the war resumes, it is highly unlikely that a sovereign Iraq will be able to survive the continued loss of manpower. From the perspective of 1989, it is extremely difficult to project Iraq's survival as a nation-state led by a Sunni minority. However, if the Shi'ites gain control of Iraq, then the entire Middle East will go through a series of military and political convulsions, which can only be deleterious to the West and not necessarily of any value to the Eastern bloc. The Gulf states, including Saudi Arabia, will not survive such a Shi'ite neighbor. One thing that can be predicted is that the unpredictable will once again take place.

Until the Ba'ath political party took power in Iraq, the monarchy was not committed and dedicated to the destruction of Israel; however, the Ba'athists, in accordance with their ideology, are vociferously dedicated to the destruction of the Jewish state. Their goal is a united secular Socialist Arab-Moslem world encompassing the entire Middle East. To them, Israel is perceived as a knife placed in the heart of the Arab world.

The African Arab Nations

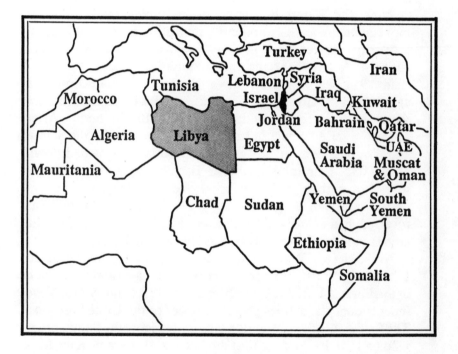

LIBYA

History

Present-day Libya evolved historically as three separate entities—in three different locations: Tripolitania (around the city of Tripoli) in the west, Cyrenaica (around ancient Cyrene and modern Benghazi) in the east, and the Fezzan in the Saharan interior.

The nomadic population of ancient times was linked

ethnically to North Africa (Berber in culture and language) and to Egypt. The area was successively occupied by Phoenicians, Greeks, Romans, and Byzantines before the Arab conquest in the seventh century. Under Arab occupation, Libya became Moslem and the Berber population adopted the Arabic language. While Tripoli tended to maintain cultural and political ties to northwest Africa, Cyrenaica leaned toward Egypt in culture and dialect.

During the sixteenth century, Libya was conquered by the Ottoman Turks who occupied the coastal areas but exercised little authority over the tribes of the interior. By the nineteenth century, the Sanusi Brotherhood—a tribally based religious movement preaching holiness, revivalist Islam, and tribal solidarity—had emerged in Cyrenaica instilling a sense of quasi-national identity that transcended individual, tribes.

In 1911, Italy invaded Libya, the last Ottoman-controlled area in North Africa, and was confronted with resistance from local Turkish forces and the Sanusi Brotherhood. After Mussolini seized power in Italy in 1923, uprisings by the Sanusi and Tripolitanians in Libya kept the Italian troops tied down until 1932. During World War II, Libya was the arena for several major battles. The British drove the Italians out of Libya only to be driven back, in turn, by the Germans until the tide was reversed again (in Egypt) by the British. These represented the largest tank battles ever fought in the Libyan desert.

At the close of World War II, the British and French occupied Libya—the British in Tripolitania and Cyrenaica and the French in the Fezzan. In 1951, Libya became the first country to achieve independent status through the auspices of the United Nations. The first to rule the new nation was the leader of the Sanusi order who had led the revolt against the Italians. He became King Idris I and ruled over the loose federation of three provinces. The king's authority was limited by local autonomy, and the population remained predominantly tribal.

When oil was discovered in Libya in 1959, she was still a poor, backward, largely tribal country. When commercial quantities of oil were found in the early 1960s, almost over night this sparsely populated nation, which was almost entirely illiterate, was faced with a newfound wealth too overwhelming for such a society. Corruption was rampant.

A group of young army officers led by a twenty-seven-year-old Bedouin colonel overthrew the monarchy and seized power in September 1969. They proclaimed a republic under the leadership of young Colonel Mu'ammar Qaddafi, an admirer of Egypt's Nasser. Colonel Qaddafi immediately thrust Libya into the violent intrigue of inter-Arab politics aligning Libya with Nasser in the euphoric and elusive quest for Arab unity. Nasser's view of Arab nationalism was based on secular socialism with Islam as the guiding force but not the law of the land. After the death of Colonel Nasser in 1970—only one year after Qaddafi's rise to power—Qaddafi began to establish his own unique brand of Arab nationalism. He combined puritanical Islamic legal regulations (similar to those of Saudi Arabia) with social and political radicalism—Islamic fundamentalism and socialism—in a way not previously experienced in the Arab world. He was anti-West and anti-East with a desire to establish a new "third international system," combining Islamic fundamentalism with social revolution. Extensive development projects and social programs at home as well as favored causes abroad were supported by Libya's fabulous oil riches.

Qaddafi's goals and ideas were expressed in a collection that became known as the "Green Book." The government was officially abolished with the establishment of the *"Jamahiriya"*—a state based on the masses. Cabinet powers were transferred to officers of the congress; embassies became "People's Officers." Qaddafi, with no formal constitutional power, was addressed as "Brother Colonel" or "Revolutionary Leader."

In 1977, Egypt attacked Libyan air bases in response to border tensions. During 1980, Qaddafi attempted to form a union with Syria, but it failed to materialize. Later that year he sent Libyan forces into Chad in an attempt to form a union between the two countries.

During the 1980s, Qaddafi was active in supporting radical national revolutionary forces throughout the Middle East and Africa as well as radical terrorist groups operating against Western targets. In 1981, during a confrontation between the U.S. Navy and Libya in the Gulf of Sidra, two Libyan SU-22 fighters were shot down. At that time, also, Libya formed a tripartite alliance with the Marxist Soviet-aligned nations of South Yemen and Ethiopia. There were a number of attempts to overthrow Qaddafi during the 1980s.

In 1984, Qaddafi attempted to form a union with Morocco, a traditional Arab monarchy led by King Hassan II. The alliance between the radical Libyan *Jamahiriya* and the traditional Moroccan kingdom ended two years later—in 1986—as a result of a visit to Morocco by Israeli Prime Minister Shimon Peres.

There was another confrontation between Qaddafi and the United States in 1986 when the Reagan administration branded Libya "the major supporter of international terrorism." U.S. naval aircraft destroyed a SA-5 base and attacked Libyan naval vessels in the Gulf. A few months later, U.S. F-111 planes operating from Britain bombed Tripoli and Benghazi, destroying Qaddafi's personal quarters.

In her war with Chad, the modern Libyan army suffered a humiliating defeat at the hands of the primitive Chad army. This marked the end of over a decade of Libyan adventurism in Chad.

Present

Libya occupies approximately 1,765,000 sq km (681,500 sq mi) on the Mediterranean coast of North Africa, 93 percent of which is desert, waste, or urban; 6 percent of which is agricultural; and 1 percent of which is forested. Her land borders are shared with Egypt on the east, Sudan on the southeast, Chad and Nigeria on the south, and Algeria on the west.

Of her total 4 million population, 97 percent are Arab and Berber; the other 3 percent represent over a dozen nationalities, including Egyptians, Tunisians, Italians, Pakistanis, Turks, Indians, and Greeks. Prior to the August 1985 expulsion of foreign workers, however, 87.3 percent were Libyans, 8.3 percent were Egyptians, 2.4 percent were Tunisians, and 2 percent were from other countries. Religiously, 97 percent are Sunni Moslems; the balance are European Christians. Arabic (the official language) and Berber dialects are spoken; Italian and English are widely understood in the major cities. The literacy rate is purported to be 50 to 60 percent.

Libya, legally known as the Socialist People's Libyan Arab *Jamahiriya,* is a *Jamahiriya* or "mass-based state" under the authoritarian rule of Colonel Mu'ammar Qaddafi. There are no political parties or elections, and no formal governmental structure exists.

Economically, Libya relies solely on petroleum exports. Her GNP of approximately $27 billion yields a per capita income of approximately $7,130.

Libya is the only Arab country to have built a significant agricultural infrastructure. She is close to agricultural independence, presently producing 35 percent of her agricultural needs. Currently, within Egypt, Jordan, Morocco, and Saudi Arabia, there are mass movements toward the adoption of a Qaddafi-style regime. His ideology and successful experiment, with a pure solution to establishing a working society with an Arab sense of social justice, is glamorous and successful enough to provide a prototype to those unfulfilled societies whose present system leaves too many frustrated.

Militarily, Libya spends $1.2 billion per year on defense, while maintaining 76,000 men in her armed forces. Qaddafi has been seeking to create an "armed populace" which would formally replace the present military, but resistance from the military has prevented full implementation of this plan. There is presently a proliferation of internal security and intelligence organizations. An "Islamic legion"—a foreign legion consisting of personnel from a number of Arab and African countries who have been trained in Libya—is now serving with Libyan forces in Chad. Libya has acquired vast quantities of military equipment, primarily from the Soviet bloc and France, which is prepositioned as an Arab arsenal for use in any future wars in the Middle East.

Libya's Sunni-Islamic-Fundamentalist society is legislated by Islamic *Sharia* law. Qaddafi has been able to impose upon this deeply fanatical religious society a Nasser brand of socialism and social justice. He has nationalized all basic enterprises and confiscated the land; he has succeeded in establishing a Ba'ath-type socialism and system of social justice. While it may appear on the surface to be an anomaly and a contradiction, it must be remembered that Soviet Marxism is full of contradictions—yet, it has survived. The real danger of Qaddafi is not his grand plan for an Islamic world nor his support of terrorism, but his successful experiment of superimposing socialism upon this

Islamic-Fundamentalist society. In fact, the time has passed when Qaddafi himself represents the danger; now the danger comes from his example, which is likely to outlive him.

Future

Libya possesses vast oil wealth that is not endangered by the vulnerability of the Persian Gulf. Since hers is the closest oil to Europe with no choke points to block its flow during any adverse political conditions that may prevail in the area, Libya's wealth is insured for a long time to come. Because of her huge territory, small population, and what appears to be noncorrupt government—a unique set of geopolitical/economic conditions, Libya should emerge as the society in which there is the best distribution of oil wealth anywhere within the Arab world.

Qaddafi's unheralded success *within* Libya—not his public pronouncements on foreign policy and highly publicized acts of terrorism—makes him a deadly enemy to the rest of the Arab world. By both the Arabs and the West, Qaddafi is probably the most misunderstood and underestimated leader in the Arab world. This alone makes him extremely dangerous. The world community stresses his semiliterate education as a reason for dismissing him as a potential threat; yet, it must be remembered that Mohammed died an illiterate and, within twenty years, the huge Byzantine Empire that had ruled for hundreds of years crumbled due to his ideology.

Egypt presents the only external threat to Libya. The potential of an Egyptian attempt to conquer Libya, which would be stimulated by a movement within Egypt to establish a Qaddafi-style regime, cannot be dismissed.

Libya covets Chad because of her vast empty territory with immense natural resources, especially uranium. A takeover would provide Qaddafi with bargaining chips for the acquisition of a nuclear weapon. Qaddafi's primary interest is in the northern half of Chad, which is sparsely populated by black nomads. Additionally, Qaddafi is trying to subvert black African countries that lie south of Libya. His goal is to establish Islamic-Fundamentalist religious societies with socialism as the economic base. Israel will always be a prime target of any leader of Libya as long as she remains an Islamic-Fundamentalist society.

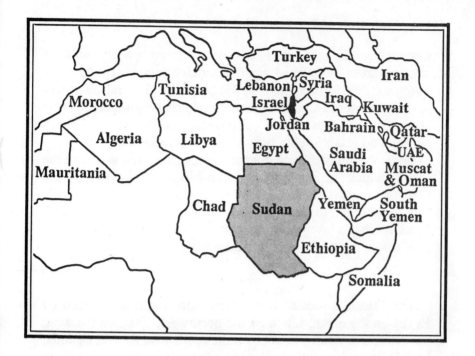

SUDAN

History

Ancient Egypt often conquered northern Sudan (known then as Nubia), and, occasionally, Nubian pharaohs ruled over Egypt proper. Nubia, which converted early to Coptic Christianity, avoided Moslem conquest by paying tribute to Moslem Egypt, and only in the late Middle Ages adopted Islam.

In 1821, Egypt conquered, unified, and occupied Sudan, which she ruled until 1881. At that time, under the leadership of a self-proclaimed *Mahdi*—expected messiah, Sudan defeated Egypt and gained her independence. Then, in 1898, a combined Egyptian-British force, led by General Horatio Kitchener, marched on Khartoum (the capital city) and reconquered Sudan, which remained under Egyptian-English rule until 1954.

In 1956, despite Egyptian objections, Sudan became an independent nation with a democratic parliamentary government. In 1958, however, there was a military coup led by General Ibrahim Abboud. General Abboud ruled the country until 1964 when a civilian movement—an alliance of professional unions, student groups, and religious orders—overthrew the military regime and re-established a parliamentary democracy. Again in 1969, a military coup, this time led by Major General Gaafar al-Nimeiry, restored a military dictatorship that maintained power until 1985. At that time, a coup d'etat overthrew the Nimeiry regime and established a provisional government.

Since its independence, Sudan has fought a civil war with the south, which is inhabited by non-Moslem blacks who are Christians and animists. Nimeiry abrogated the autonomous self-rule that he had granted to the south and attempted to impose Moslem Sharia law on the black inhabitants. During this bloody revolution, over 500,000 Sudanese were killed.

Present

The Sudan is located in northern Africa and is bounded by Egypt on the north; Libya on the northwest; Chad on the west; the Central African Republic on the southwest; Kenya, Uganda, and Zaire on the south; Ethiopia on the east; and the Red Sea on the northeast. Sudan's 2.5 million sq km (nearly 1 million sq mi) makes her two and one-half times the size of Egypt and the largest nation in Africa. Although 37 percent of her land is arable—an area the size of all of Egypt—only 3 percent is cultivated by utilizing the most primitive agricultural techniques. Fifteen percent of Sudan is suitable for grazing; a little more than 15 percent is forested; and 33 percent is either desert, waste, or urban.

Sudan, which literally means "land of the black peoples," is inhabited exclusively by blacks in the southern region—an area tied geographically and ethnically to east Africa while religiously animist and Christian. Northern Sudan, ethnically Arab, is religiously Islamic (Sunni Moslem) and tied historically to Egypt.

Sudan's current population totals approximately 25.5 million of which 50 percent are Arab, 11 percent Dinka, 8 percent Nubian, 6 percent Beja, and 2 percent foreigners. (The lack of an official census—caused by poor infrastructure and a low literacy rate—contributes to discrepancies in population breakdown.) Religiously, 73 percent are Sunni Moslem, 23 percent are animist, and 4 percent are Christian. Although Arabic is the "official" language, Nubian, Ta Bedawie, and various dialects of Nilotic, Nilo-Hamitic, and Sudanie languages are common. English is spoken by the small educated class. A program of Arabization is in progress. The northern Sunni-Moslem Arabs have no common language, religion, history, culture, or relations with the black animist and Christian inhabitants in the south. The overall literacy rate is estimated at 20 percent.

Politically, Sudan, officially known as the Democratic Republic of Sudan, has a parliamentary form of government that is technically called a constituent council. In reality, the country is ruled by the Arabs who occupy the northern half of the nation and who have continued to impose Islamic *Sharia* law on all inhabitants, including the non-Moslem southern Blacks.

Economically, Sudan is neither an industrial nor an agrarian society since she has no industrial, agricultural, technical, or cultural infrastructure. With an estimated $7.3 billion GNP—an annual per capita income of $310, Sudan is one of the world's poorest nations.

Militarily, Sudan expends approximately $250 million annually to support her armed forces. She maintains 61,000 men under arms of whom 6,000 have mutinied to join the Sudan Peoples Liberation Army (SPLA) and are fighting for increased equality and power sharing (autonomy) as well as the removal of Islamic *Sharia* law. Libyan and Ethiopian support of the SPLA threaten to undermine Sudan's hold on the south.

Although she is one of the world's most backward countries, nature has provided Sudan the basis for a strategically vital relationship with Egypt in that the Nile River—Egypt's life line—originates in Sudan. Additionally, recently discovered vast oil reserves in the south make Sudan an important prize not only for Egypt but for Ethiopia (who had been promised southern Sudan by Britain) as well.

Future

The Arabs of Sudan who occupy the north and control the government will not be able to maintain power over the Blacks of the south by their own means. External forces such as Ethiopia, plus violent animosity in the south, will make it impossible for the Arabs to stop secession without strong intervention by Egypt.

The future independence of Sudan in her present form is highly unlikely since there exists within the country not only an active secessionist movement in the south but also a very strong politically active Islamic-Fundamentalist movement in the north. Because Sudan controls the flow of the Nile River, possesses vast, yet untapped, oil reserves, and has huge tracts of arable land available for cultivation, Egypt will move either proactively to form a union and integrate Sudan or reactively to intercede in any attempt by an outside force (Ethiopia) to take over Sudan.

The Gulf States

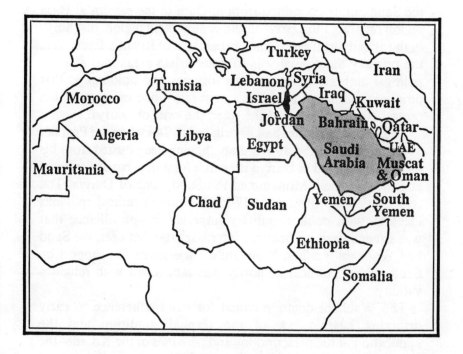

SAUDI ARABIA

History

Historically, the area that is now Saudi Arabia was a buffer zone between the great empires of antiquity. The great Yemen civilizations of the past spilled over into this home of several ancient cultures.

Early in the seventh century, Mecca—a city in the Hejaz (western) region of Arabia—became the birthplace of Islam. In

A.D. 622, the Prophet Mohammed—founder of Islam—emigrated from Mecca to Medina and established not only a religious community but a political entity as well. By the time of his death in 632, most of the Arabian Peninsula was Moslem. In the midst of a civil war in the late 650s, the Prophet's son-in-law and successor moved his capital from Medina to Kufa in Iraq, thus removing from Arabia the political center of the Islamic caliphate. The religious center of Islam, however, remained in Mecca and Medina.

During the fifteenth century, the earliest traceable ancestors of the Saud family emigrated from al-Qatif in the eastern al-Hasa region of Arabia to Dariya in the central Nejd region, just north of the already well-established urban area of Riyadh. Even then, the primary Saudi goal was to unite urban areas into a single political authority. The family's fortunes and holdings at that time were sufficient to call it an emirate—one of many in the central Nejd region—and the ruler, the *emir* of Dariya.

The first Saudi realm had its origins in 1744 when the Prophet Mohammed ibn Abd al-Wahhabi, having been ousted from his own town, landed in Dariya in search for a new base of support and met the sheik Mohammed ibn Saud, *emir* of Dariya. The two formed an alliance in 1745 that united radical religious ideology with political-military imperialism—an alliance that was strengthened by frequent intermarriages between the Saud and Wahhabi families. Wahhabiism was given full support by Saud, whose political authority was sanctioned with religious validity.

The Wahhabi doctrine called for strict adherence to early orthodox Islamic law of the Hanbali tradition and the application of the prescriptions and penalties of the Koran—the sole basis of knowledge. It required austere living and condemned saint worship and indulgence in luxuries such as smoking, music, and the wearing of silk. Islamic law—the *Sharia*—was to be "interpreted" by *ulama*—learned religious men.

The most fundamental principle of the Wahhabi doctrine is absolute monotheism—the oneness of Allah. Basic concepts include:

- the supremacy of *umma*—the Wahhabi fold—over all other social/tribal bonds, therefore equalizing all *ichwan*—

brothers of Wahhabiism—and sharing with all equal rights and responsibilities;
- the liability of all nonbelievers to *jihad*—holy war—and the laws governing Islamic warfare; and
- the departure from all that does not allow for total immersion in the Wahhabi doctrine—*hijra,* including emigration from lands where *ichwan* are not free to claim their religion and the abandonment of a previous lifestyle (tribal laws and bonds) in favor of the lifestyle required of a Wahhabi adherent.

In its quest for power, the Wahhabi-Saudi movement relied heavily on the natural outgrowth of these principles. They weakened tribal loyalties while strengthening the central authority; they encouraged strict adherence to a degree of radicalism; and they encouraged militant conquest with its inherent rewards.

Armed with the military power of the Saud family and the radical ideology of Wahhabiism, the movement spread rapidly throughout the central and northern Nejd region and, shortly thereafter, to the western Hejaz on the Red Sea, then eastern al-Hasa on the Persian Gulf, and the Asir in the south. In the east, the Saudi-Wahhabi forces captured Qatif and destroyed the places of worship of the sectarian Shi'ites; subjugated Bahrain and what are now the United Arab Emirates (UAE); and required the payment of tribute from what is now part of Oman. In the south, the Wahhabis reached as far as the ports of Yemen, although the Zaydi-Shi'ite sect of the Yemen highlands remained in tact. In the north, the Wahhabis advanced into Syria and Iraq. In Syria, they raided Damascus, and further north, in Iraq, they destroyed one of the holiest places of Shi'ism—the tomb of Hussein, the martyred grandson of the Prophet Mohammed. In the west, the Saudi-Wahhabi forces captured, lost, and recaptured the holy cities of Mecca and Medina. By 1806, most of the Arabian Peninsula had been converted to Wahhabiism and was under Saudi rule.

The Saud family was confronted by the Ottoman Empire over the occupation of the Hejaz—particularly, the holy cities of Mecca and Medina and the pilgrimage routes. Mohammed Ali, the ruler of Egypt, was requested by the Turks to conquer the Hejaz and expel the Wahhabi fanatics. Egyptian forces launched an expedition in 1811, recaptured the Hejaz (including Mecca and Medina) in 1814, and, in 1818, completely defeated the Saud family at their capital in Dariya, which they totally destroyed and rendered uninhabitable. Having recaptured the holy cities and believing he had crushed the Saud family and destroyed Wahhabi power, Mohammed Ali withdrew his forces from the poor and restless Nejd area in 1819.

Within five years, however, a grandson of the founder of the first Saudi realm—Turki—re-established a Saudi-Wahhabi power base in Riyadh (1824) and began consolidating Saudi rule in the Nejd. By 1830, he had conquered al-Hasa, and by 1833, the entire Persian Gulf coast recognized Wahhabi rule.

Since Turki kept a lid on Wahhabi fanaticism and avoided clashes with outside powers—Ottoman and Egyptian in the Hejaz and British in the Persian Gulf and on the coast, external problems were minimal. His major challenges came from internal sources—first, lawlessness among the tribes; second, discontent among the religious leaders; and third, rivalry within the Saud family. In fact, Turki was assassinated in 1834 by a cousin, Mishari, who was under house arrest. Forty days later, however, Turki's son, Faisal, returned from battle in Bahrain, defeated and executed Mishari, and became the Saudi ruler.

During his first reign (1834 to 1838), Faisal was faced with continuing family dissension; repudiation of Saudi suzerainty by Qatar and Bahrain; and tremendous pressure from the Egyptian ruler, Mohammed Ali, who had severed his relations with the Ottoman sultan and had captured what is today Lebanon, Palestine, and Syria. Ali wanted to incorporate the Arabian Peninsula into his empire. In 1836, Egyptian forces, joined by Khalid—a rival Saudi cousin of Faisal—marched on the Nejd, intimidated Faisal's forces, and entered the capital of Riyadh in 1837. For a short time, the Egyptians recognized the rules of both Faisal and Khalid over a partitioned Nejd, but by 1838, they marched against Faisal and sent him for detention to Cairo.

Egyptian forces went on to conquer all of Arabia except for Asir. At that time, control was firm because of the energetic leadership of their superior forces and because they worked with Khalid and became Wahhabi allies. Following the stunning victory of Mohammed Ali and his Egyptian forces over the Ottoman sultan in 1839, European powers intervened. Mohammed Ali was confined to the hereditary leadership of Egypt, and by 1841, the bulk of Egyptian forces were withdrawn from the Nejd. After their withdrawal, Khalid, challenged by rival Saudi cousins, attempted to maintain his fortunes and his control of the Nejd from Riyadh, but he was unsuccessful. By 1843, Faisal, having escaped from his Egyptian jail, had made his way back to the Nejd, had raised forces, and had marched on Riyadh.

Faisal's second reign (1843 to 1865) was considered the golden age of the second Saudi realm. Although territorial holdings were smaller and dynamism was significantly less than during the first realm, there was far greater acceptance both externally and internally. Faisal was careful not to challenge Ottoman rule in the Hejaz region and paid a small tribute for Ottoman recognition that he was ruler of all Arabs. He avoided clashes with the British (until very close to the end of his life) in his assertions of authority in Bahrain, the Gulf sheikdoms (now the UAE), northern Oman, and Qatar.

Under Faisal, Wahhabiism ceased to be the driving force for endless holy wars externally and became less of an issue internally. Although Wahhabiism was strictly enforced in certain areas such as Riyadh and the central Nejd, in other places it was practiced more loosely. All of Faisal's territories, however, found it acceptable.

Administratively, Faisal was likewise flexible. He selectively allowed locally emergent leadership to govern in some circumstances (including the Rishadi in the northwestern Nejd) and appointed governors supported by garrisons in others. Although he had to campaign constantly to keep recalcitrant tribes subdued, Faisal possessed the energy, the will, and the wisdom to maintain Saudi-Wahhabi control under such conditions.

After Faisal's death in 1865, his sons/successors—none of whom emulated his father—engaged in such internal strife that they brought about the end of the second Saudi-Wahhabi realm. Their control of the Nejd diminished as they fought each other, and the rival al-Rishad family took advantage. Rishadi forces took control of the Nejd and its capital, Riyadh, and, after putting down several Saudi uprisings over a twenty-year period, finally forced the remaining Saud family into exile in Kuwait in 1891. By the turn of the century, then, the Rishadi family controlled the central/northern Nejd region; the Ottomans controlled the western Hejaz region and the eastern al-Hasa area; and the British had varying degrees of control over Aden and the southern Arabian statelets as well as Bahrain, Kuwait, the Gulf sheikdoms (UAE), and Oman in the Persian Gulf area.

In 1902, operating from the Saud family exile base in Kuwait, twenty-year-old 'Abd Al 'Aziz al-Saud (Ibn Saud) initiated his empire-building career and comeback of the Saud family by defeating the rival House of Rishad and recapturing Riyadh— the traditional family capital in the central Nejd region—in a surprise attack. He continued to expand his dominion in the central and northern part of the peninsula; then, in 1913, he ousted the Turks from Hufuf—the inland capital of the eastern al-Hasa region—and expanded his domain to the Persian Gulf. After agreeing to formalize his status as a Turkish vassal in 1914, Ibn Saud was appointed governor general with power over the Nejd and al-Hasa regions.

The western part of the peninsula, the Hejaz, was under Turkish-Ottoman rule in 1916 when an Arab revolt, led by the Hashemite sharif of Mecca, succeeded—with British help—in freeing the area from Ottoman rule and establishing Hussein as king of Hejaz. After a series of clashes between Hussein and Ibn Saud escalated in 1919, the Saudi ruler turned his attention westward and, as a result of a 1924 military campaign, conquered the Hejaz region. By 1925, the Hashemites were deposed, and in 1926, Ibn Saud was proclaimed king of Hejaz and sultan of Nejd and its dependencies. He appointed his son, Crown Prince Saud, as governor of Nejd, and his son, Faisal, as governor of Hejaz. He established a consultative council of sheiks and other notables in Hejaz.

Prior to his settlement with Hussein in the Hejaz region, Ibn Saud had taken advantage of an opportunity to move into the adjoining, relatively rich Asir highlands. He had been asked by the local chieftains for help against the Idrissi who had taken over after the Turks evacuated the area. Ibn Saud defeated the Idrissi forces, laid claim to the Asir highlands by asserting that the province had previously belonged to his ancestors, and absorbed the area into his realm. In 1927, in exchange for recognition of his control over his entire domain, Ibn Saud agreed to acknowledge both the British protectorate status of the gulf sheikdoms as well as the legitimacy of Hussein's sons as rulers of Iraq and Transjordan.

Between 1929 and 1930, Ibn Saud put down a rebellion of tribal leaders and *ichwan*—the militant "brethren" of Wahhabiism—who insisted that conquests continue beyond the existing northern borders. In 1932, after achieving some stability, Ibn Saud declared the union of the two major parts of his domain as the kingdom of Saudi Arabia; then, after he put down a revolt by Idrissi forces over the Asir region in 1933, he formally annexed Asir to his kingdom—a move disputed by Yemen. In 1934, Ibn Saud declared war on Yemen, quickly conquered large portions of the country, then later signed a peace treaty agreeing to evacuate the areas he had conquered.

During this period (1932 to 1934), Ibn Saud, in dire need for funds because of the sharp decline in the number of people making pilgrimages to the holy cities—the kingdom's main source of revenue, granted the first oil exploration right to one, then another, U.S. company which, together, formed the Arabian American Oil Company (ARAMCO). Although commercial production of oil began in 1938, revenue didn't contribute significantly to Saudi Arabia's wealth until after World War II.

During most of World War II, Saudi Arabia remained neutral, although Ibn Saud leaned toward the Allies. Just before the end of the war, Saudi Arabia joined the Allies without officially declaring war against the Axis powers—while maintaining neutrality of the holy places. She was able, therefore, to join the United Nations as a charter member. Also in 1945, Saudi Arabia became one of the founders of the Arab League.

Although relations between Saudi Arabia and the United States continued to strengthen after the war, differences between them regarding Israel remained prominent. Ibn Saud stressed his anti-Zionist stand with Roosevelt, opposed Truman's plan to permit the immigration of 100,000 Jewish Holocaust survivors to Palestine, and resented both U.S. support for the partition of Palestine and U.S. aid to Israel. He did not, however, carry out threats of retaliation against U.S. interests at the time because it was not in his best interests to do so.

Increasing oil revenues enabled Ibn Saud to begin several development projects, including a railroad, a network of roads, and an internal air communication system. He curbed Wahhabi fanaticism, to some degree, when he abolished the ban on smoking and allowed the ban on music to die with the advent of radio broadcasts. The king's private coffers and the national treasury were one in the same and loose financial accounting prevailed during most of Ibn Saud's reign; however, at the end of 1951, the first national budget was published and, shortly thereafter (1952), the first bank opened.

Although his kingdom was not really united and remained a collection of disparate tribal groups, Ibn Saud was king and the absolute ruler of Saudi Arabia. His success, to a large extent, was based on the fact that he was recovering a kingdom his ancestors had created, ruled, lost, recreated, and lost again. Additionally, he married over 100 women who were the daughters of various tribal leaders and, thereby, created a huge royal family (numbering today over 3,000 princes and 7,000 members). Ibn Saud gave huge land grants and gifts to many tribal leaders to encourage their continued support, but he also severely punished those who acted against him, those who raided other tribes for plunder, and those who failed to maintain order. He selectively established and maintained relationships with Arab neighbors and the powers of his time, as he required, and used militant Wahhabiism when and in ways that met his and Saudi Arabian needs.

When Ibn Saud died at the end of 1953, his son, Saud ibn 'Abd al-'Aziz, became King Saud and prime minister. King Saud increased the pace of change instituted by his father and lived even more lavishly. Oil income soared to over $300 million; emerging social strata—college graduates, army officers, civil servants, technicians, and workers—demanded part of the sociopolitical pie; the number of foreign technicians and experts increased; and minimal funds were expended for a bare-bones infrastructure—mainly to benefit the royal family and U.S. construction companies and exporters.

During King Saud's reign, the entire royal family lived extravagantly and became a source of waste and corruption. King Saud built himself a $140 million marble palace, and several hundred princes and their relatives likewise built magnificent palaces. The royal household spent 17 percent of state revenues. Luxury spread to a new privileged class among the tribes and to a new class of entrepreneurs.

Although oil revenues had reached $341 million by 1955, there was a financial crisis by 1956—a public debt of $95 million; and by 1957, the national debt was $500 million. Other sources of internal pressure faced by King Saud came from within the royal family as various princes vied for power and from among the Wahhabi religious leaders who reacted strenuously against the dissolute way of life and the spread of Arab nationalist ideology. The significant Egyptian presence—especially as teachers and military aides—had aroused interest in Nasser's Arab nationalism.

Foreign affairs was still another area of grave concern to King Saud whose reign witnessed critical threats to the survival of the kingdom. The basis of the difficulty he faced was the contradiction between maintaining Western ties—particularly to the United States and Britain—while cooperating with Egypt to check the Hashemites. Within the Arab League, Saudi rulers had always taken an anti-Hashemite stand and had cooperated with Egyptian and Syrian leaders to oppose any extension of influence of the rulers of Jordan and Iraq. King Saud opposed the Western-sponsored Baghdad Pact and worked against Iraqi influence in Syria. With Nasser, he attempted to alienate Jordan from the West. As Nasser became more radical and revolutionary in his quest for Arab nationalism and emerged as the dominant influence in the Arab world, Saudi-Egyptian relations deteriorated. Saud tried to effect a reconciliation with the Hashemites and, simultaneously, supported U.S. efforts to have Saudi Arabia fill the Middle East leadership vacuum— before the Soviets could do so through Egypt and pro-Soviet Nasser.

By March 1958, because of his poor foreign affairs policies, the financial crisis, and the continuing quarrel with his brother Faisal, Saud was forced to transfer all power to Faisal who immediately implemented several changes. He placated Nasser, introduced reforms, modified the government by bringing four ministries (including the treasury) under his personal supervision, and cut royal household expenditures from 17 percent to 5 percent. By 1960, there was a national surplus of $185 million.

Saud regained power from Faisal in December 1960 and continued the stringent fiscal guidelines. Because Saud's failing health required that he go to the United States for medical treatment, in November 1961, Faisal resumed leadership. In March 1962, Saud regained his position of authority, but, by that summer, he had to return to the United States for further treatment. The struggle between the two brothers continued; however, Faisal succeeded in removing Saud's supporters from key positions and refused to restore power to Saud. In November 1964, the Council of *Ulama* deposed Saud, made Faisal king, and Faisal's half-brother, Khalid, crown prince.

Faisal sought to avoid the family power struggle he had previously experienced and to protect his realm and the dynasty. He reunited the prime ministership and the crown and kept both for himself. He also saw to it that the person designated as crown prince was incapable of presenting a challenge to him. Faisal created the position of second deputy prime minister and offered it to Fahd, his energetic minister of interior. He balanced Fahd's increased power by delegating more to other key princes, expanding and diversifying the royal family power circle.

Domestically, Faisal used his absolute leadership to weaken centers of power that had arisen under Saud—royal princes, clergy, foreign expatriates. Vastly increasing oil revenues allowed him to upgrade the infrastructure and undertake several major development projects. A huge oil-based petrochemical industry was begun. To assure the status of the religious establishment—discontent about all the modern development—Faisal maintained *Sharia* as the law of the land, including its code of punishments, and the religious police were permitted to continue enforcement of obligatory prayer and other religious duties.

From both the inter-Arab and international perspectives, Faisal ruled Saudi Arabia during a period of great complexity. Throughout most of Faisal's reign, Saudi Arabia was reactive, rather than proactive, to several regional and international events that impacted her strategic environment and status. These included the continuation of revolutionary activities in the Yemens and Nasserist movement activities by Egypt during the mid-1960s; the Arab-Israeli (Six-Day) War and the British withdrawal from southern Arabia in 1967; the British announcement of their intent to withdraw from the Persian Gulf in 1968; violent changes in regimes in Iraq, Sudan, Libya, and

Syria between 1968 and 1970; the War of Attrition from 1969 to 1970; Nasser's death in 1970; Iran's assertion of territorial claims in the Persian Gulf; Iraq's treaty with the USSR in 1972; Iraq's border dispute with Kuwait in 1973; and the Arab-Israeli (Yom Kippur) war in October 1973. Faisal continued to exercise constraint in the use of Saudi Arabia's escalating oil revenues to respond to the problems created by these and other internal, regional, and international events.

In his inter-Arab relations, Faisal attempted to thwart Egyptian attempts to penetrate the Arabian Peninsula. During the civil war in Yemen, he supported the Yemeni Royalists against the Republicans who were aided by Egyptian expeditionary forces. And in Aden and south Arabia, he supported an underground anti-Nasserist movement. Relations with Egypt continued to deteriorate, and Egypt was accused of activating a subversive underground movement in Saudi Arabia that committed acts of sabotage against Saudi cities and her oil pipeline.

Efforts to find a solution to the Yemen conflict and to mend ties with Egypt were increased in the mid-1960s. Relations between Saudi Arabia and Egypt improved considerably when Nasser toned down his interventionist activities and withdrew Egyptian forces from Yemen. Saudi Arabia (as well as other Arab states) disregarded inter-Arab disputes to support Egypt when she became involved in the Six-Day War in 1967.

During the late 1960s and early 1970s, Faisal attempted to stabilize the Arabian Peninsula by improving Saudi relations with bordering nations. Territorial and border disputes were "resolved" with Jordan, Kuwait, Iraq, Yemen, Oman, the UAE, and Qatar. Faisal even attempted to resolve some differences with Iran, and, in 1975, the shah visited Saudi Arabia.

Within the international arena, Faisal continued to cultivate close ties with the United States, and Saudi Arabia was considered by the United States as a moderate ally. With the advent of the Arab-Israeli (Yom Kippur) war in October 1973 and the subsequent oil embargo, Saudi-U.S. relations were shaken. Although Saudi Arabia's earlier attempt (1967) at imposing an oil boycott against the United States and the West had failed, in 1973 the Saudis were successful in leading the other oil producers in an oil embargo that changed the power structure in the region and propelled Saudi Arabia into leadership of the Arab world.

In spite of the oil embargo, the United States continued to view Saudi Arabia as reasonable and moderate among the oil-producing nations. Although the publicly proclaimed Saudi policy regarding Israel was certainly not moderate, the United States endeavored to involve her in the Middle East peace process.

In June 1974 and January 1975, new economic and military agreements between Saudi Arabia and the United States were finalized. They included the large-scale supply of advanced U.S. military equipment to Saudi Arabia. In his effort to enhance the Saudi regular armed forces with advanced military technology, Faisal also contracted with Britain and France for weapon systems.

When Faisal was assassinated by his nephew in March 1975, his half-brother, Khalid, became king and prime minister; Fahd became crown prince and first deputy prime minister; and Abdullah became second deputy prime minister and commander of the national guard. During the first few years of Khalid's reign, there was agreement to continue Faisal's policies. Fahd played the prominent role—for the most part in foreign affairs and defense—while the more conservative Khalid busied himself attending to relations with the tribes that supported the regime.

While under Faisal's single leadership reign, he had ruled with complete authority—moderated only by his need to maintain the consent of his supporters upon his death, leadership became collective—with Khalid as final arbiter, but Fahd as the more pronounced wielder of responsibility. A 1979 rift among the leadership nearly caused the demise of the kingdom and demonstrated that the royal family didn't necessarily close ranks in the face of adversity. Although subsequent circumstances healed the split, since that time, the kingdom has demonstrated all the earmarks of collective leadership—delay in decision making, inconsistency in policy, lack of clarity of responsibility, ruthlessness as viewed by outsiders, and poor internal discipline.

In addition, during Khalid's reign, many of Ibn Saud's younger sons and grandsons came of age, proliferating the royal family. While senior princes were active in the central and provincial governments, junior princes were in the upper ranks of the civil service, the armed forces, quasi-governmental agencies, and large private businesses. The size and diversity of the royal family diluted its sense of cohesiveness and unity; diminished, in the eyes of others, the aura of royalty, reducing it to a privileged class; increased the opportunity for abuse; enhanced the complexity of power/successor struggles; and strained further the disenfranchisement of the growing middle class.

Between the beginning and the end of Khalid's reign, oil revenues peaked, then dropped. Oil income rose from its 1975 level of $25.7 billion to $36.5 billion in 1977, $48.4 billion in 1979, and an astronomical $102.1 billion in 1981. A recession in oil production and subsequent fall in oil prices resulted in a drop in oil revenues in 1982 to $70.5 billion.

Khalid's reign witnessed the implementation of Saudi Arabia's second five-year development plan (1975 to 1980)— designed during Faisal's time—and part of the third. The first five-year plan (1970 to 1975)—budgeted at $9.2 billion— resulted in an annual growth rate of 13.4 percent (14.8 percent in the oil sector and 11.7 percent in the non-oil sector). The second five-year plan—budgeted at $142 billion but costing an additional $40 billion—showed an annual growth rate of only 8 percent (4.8 percent in the oil sector and 15 percent in the non-oil sector).

The aims of the second plan were to strengthen defense, build a physical infrastructure, improve social services, and develop the non-oil production sectors in an effort to reduce dependency on oil. Much more than anticipated was spent on defense; expected revenues were used for infrastructure and social services; and considerably less than budgeted was spent on non-oil sector development.

The third five-year plan budgeted $237 billion for civilian projects and $100 billion for defense, security, and foreign aid. It projected an annual growth rate of 19 percent. Its aims were less emphasis on infrastructure and more emphasis on diversification of the economy. After the first year (1980 to 1981), however, the combined contribution of non-oil-related industry and agriculture to the GNP was only 2.6 percent—less than 4 percent of the oil sector's contribution. The two major constraints to

Saudi Arabia's overall development—her geography and her population—loomed as barriers.

Between 1975 and 1981, Saudi Arabia vastly increased her imports. Therefore, if she opted to use her oil weapon, she was vulnerable to retaliation by suppliers of essential goods and subject to disruption of the flow of her oil through one of the three choke points (Suez, Bab el Mandeb, Strait of Hormuz).

During Khalid's reign, huge petrochemical plants were constructed in Jubail and Yanbo. In an effort to ease the geographic constraint of Saudi Arabia's vast disconnected territory, a massive transportation and communication network was developed. Although this infrastructure development was a great improvement over what occurred during Faisal's reign, it was still considered by many to be inadequate. For example, Israel—one-hundredth the size of Saudi Arabia—had proportionally about forty times as many miles of paved roads.

Manpower requirements for the development plan were met by massive numbers of imported foreign laborers. At the end of the first five-year plan—the beginning of Khalid's reign—there were 314,000 foreign workers. By 1980, the end of the second five-year plan, there were 2,100,000 (plus 400,000 dependents)—1,000,000 from North Yemen; 200,000 each from Egypt and Jordan (Palestinians); 50,000 to 100,000 each from the Sudan, South Yemen, Lebanon (Palestinians), Pakistan, India, South Korea, and the Philippines; and 100,000 from Western countries (the United States, Britain, France, Italy, and West Germany). Although foreigners comprised half of the total Saudi Arabian population in 1980, they represented twice the number of Saudis in the work force. The Saudi national labor force amounted to 1 million, or about 22 percent of the population (compared to 42 percent for Egypt and 50 percent for Israel).

The use of foreign labor on such a vast scale enabled Saudi Arabia to implement her ambitious development plans and to maintain a larger and more sophisticated military establishment. On the other hand, however, it increased her security problems, exposed Saudi society to political and social values and notions counter to those rooted in Saudi tradition, and raised questions about equal rights based on Islamic and Arab principles.

The rapid acceleration of development during Khalid's reign set the entire Saudi society in motion and unleashed forces the conservative regime could neither comprehend nor control. The growth rate was dizzying and created a chasm between urban and rural-tribal ways of life. There were further splits within the urban sector that separated the masses of foreign workers, the emerging new classes, and the traditional urban groupings. The strain and tensions characteristic of such changes erupted in November 1979 when a group of insurgent Islamic Fundamentalists—comprised of students of religion, members of the national guard, tribe members, and foreigners—seized the Grand *Mosque* in Mecca and sent shock waves throughout the Saudi security establishment.

The new classes to have emerged from the Saudi modernization effort include an industrial proletariat—concentrated in the oil industry and historically activist; a mercantile bourgeoisie—comprised of Hejaz trading families and newcomers who, in collusion with members of the royal family, have amassed wealth by both fair and foul means; and an educated middle class made up of teachers of modern subjects, mid- and upper-level civil servants, military officers, and self-employed professionals. This new middle class is perhaps the most threatening of the new social strata because, while it lacks the cohesiveness to be revolutionary itself, it undermines the regime by its alienation and encourages insurrection by others. Its members increased fourfold between 1970 and 1980—from 22,000 (2.5 percent of the labor force) to 86,200 (7.2 percent of the labor force).

For the first few years of Khalid's reign, Fahd was able to pursue, and even improve upon, Faisal's foreign policy and defense strategy. Khalid inherited a Riyadh-Cairo-Damascus alignment that protected the Saudis from attack by Arab radicals, strengthened their security in the Gulf, facilitated their handling of the Yemen situation, and allowed them to cultivate their U.S. connections. Even after Egypt signed the U.S.-mediated Sinai II agreement with Israel in September 1975, Syria intervened in the Lebanese war in 1975 and 1976, and Sadat visited Jerusalem in his quest for peace in November 1977, the Saudis were able to maintain their connections with both Egypt and Syria. In addition, the March 1975 signing of the Algiers agreement settling differences between Iraq and Iran encouraged the formation of a Riyadh-Tehran-Baghdad triangle that permitted Saudi Arabia to play Iraq and Iran against each other to neutralize the dangers from each direction while she pursued her own interests—influence among the smaller Gulf states.

Early success with their other inter-Arab relations encouraged the Saudis to pursue their preferred resolution to the Aden-San'a (South Yemen-North Yemen) affair. Efforts were made to recognize and cooperate more with the Peoples Democratic Republic of Yemen (PDRY), give the Yemen Arab Republic (YAR) more leeway, provide both with financial assistance, and balance the two against each other. This Saudi approach was at first supported by the heads of government in both Aden and San'a, and slow but steady progress was made. However, residual hostilities toward the Saudis and between the two Yemens surfaced and erupted during the end of 1977 and throughout 1978. Three heads of state were assassinated, and border clashes and mutually subversive activities occurred frequently. The Saudis backed the YAR.

Also during the first few years of Khalid's reign, the Saudis managed to maintain their post-1973 relationship of interdependence with the United States. At the end of 1977 and throughout 1978, however, as problems escalated in various Saudi-related arenas, the U.S.-Saudi relationship showed signs of inconsistency, doubt, and disappointment.

By the end of 1978, events occurring in the Arab-Israeli arena, the Gulf, and southern Arabia began developing into an intermeshed set of external circumstances that erupted early in 1979, triggering a debate among Saudi leaders that resulted in the major change in the regime's power structure. 1979, then, was a year emblazoned in Saudi Arabia's history because of three major external events—the Iranian revolution and the fall of the shah (January and February); the PDRY incursion into YAR (February) and the outbreak of war between the Yemens; and the signing of the U.S.-sponsored Egyptian-Israeli peace treaty (March)—and the Saudi responses to them by way of significant changes in regional and international policies.

In January and March of 1979, in an effort to appease Iranian revolutionaries, Saudi Arabia reduced her oil production and precipitated a worldwide oil crisis that sent oil prices skyrocketing. Other external events in late 1979—the taking of

U.S. hostages by Iran, the seizure of the Grand *Mosque* in Mecca by fundamentalist insurgents, and the Soviet invasion of Afghanistan—created additional problems and forced the Saudis to make choices they would rather have avoided. To compensate for the tarnished image of security and the challenge to her Islamic credentials that resulted from the Mecca incident, Saudi Arabia led an Islamic opposition to the Soviet invasion—a move that somewhat isolated pro-Soviet Syria and, momentarily, brought the United States a bit closer. When Sadam Hussein countered with the threat of a Pan-Arab charter and the Soviets promised less interference in the Yemen situation, the Saudis withdrew.

The 1980 Iraqi invasion of Iran and the subsequent short-lived gains of one, then the other, posed serious threats to the Saudis who, in their fear of an Iranian victory, turned to the United States, then Syria for help. As the war settled into a stalemate, Saudi Arabia openly assumed a position of neutrality and the role of a mediator. She organized the Gulf Cooperation Council (GCC) and, as its leading power, encouraged it to maintain neutrality. Behind the scenes, however, the Khalid regime supported Iraq financially and assisted in the shipment of Iraqi oil. When the Saudis attempted to use the GCC to enlist Egyptian military aid for Iraq on the promise of support for Egypt's reinstatement into the Arab world, and Mubarak refused, again they turned to Syria to persuade Iran not to attack Iraq proper. Syria agreed, at least verbally, to keep the Saudis away from the United States, but she continued to support Iran. Although the "special" relationship between Saudi Arabia and the United States continued unofficially, Saudi Arabia rejected the U.S. proposal for an open strategic alliance because it conflicted with her own security plan for the Gulf, her arrangement with the Soviets regarding the Yemens, and her Iraqi and Syrian connections.

In the Arab-Israeli arena, the March 1979 signing of the Egyptian-Israeli peace treaty spawned debate and various alignments among the Saudi leaders. Although Khalid personally may have preferred to side with the United States, the collective decision was to oppose the peace treaty. Saudi Arabia joined the hard-line confrontation states against Egypt and, along with Jordan, turned it into an all-Arab mainline. After making their choice to join the Arab bloc against the U.S.-sponsored peace treaty, the Saudi leaders attempted to mend their U.S. connection while simultaneously cooperating with the Arab coalition opposing Egypt.

The void in leadership of the Arab world left by the ouster of Egypt provided an arena for the struggle for dominance of the region among Iraq, Syria, and Saudi Arabia. Iraq's subsequent engagement in her war with Iran reduced the contest to two—pro-Soviet Syria and pro-Western Saudi Arabia.

Events that occurred in the region during the remainder of Khalid's reign (1979 to 1982) exposed the contradictions in Saudi orientation as the collective leadership compromised, improvised, and continued to push and pull the kingdom first one way, then another. Two consistencies that appeared, however, were (1) that there was no intention to realign strategically with Egypt during Sadat's lifetime and (2) that Syrian opposition almost always caused the Saudis to yield. Syrian counteractions to Saudi activity occurred many times.

In the southern Arabia area, the unity agreement that terminated the 1979 war between the YAR and PDRY presented problems for Saudi Arabia. She couldn't manipulate YAR's political forces to subvert the agreement, as she had done in 1972. Saudi Arabia, YAR, and PDRY managed to tolerate the strains in their relations throughout Khalid's reign.

During the last few years of Khalid's reign—1979 to 1982—Saudi Arabia vacillated in her East (USSR)-West (United States) orientation. Early in 1979, U.S.-Saudi relations reached a post-1973 low when the U.S. request for Saudi Arabia's commitment to her Middle East political strategy, which centered on the Egyptian-Israeli peace treaty, was denied and the Saudi leaders—after a split decision—joined the anti-Camp David Arab coalition. The chasm was deepened by Saudi Arabia's decision to cut oil production—to appease Iran—and the subsequent oil crisis. Shortly thereafter, however, the royal family factions compromised in an effort to preserve the Saudi-U.S. strategic connection in order to protect areas of mutual interest—keeping navigation in the Gulf open and Soviet influence out, to safeguard the purchase of advanced U.S. arms, and to secure the availability of assistance in times of emergency. Abdullah and his followers continued to believe that Saudi oil was a sufficient bargaining chip for U.S. cooperation; however,

Fahd and his followers believed that additional efforts to secure U.S. cooperation were required on some occasions.

At least five times between the 1979 crisis and Khalid's death in 1982, Saudi Arabia's attempts to strengthen her U.S. ties were reversed—usually as a result, at least in part, of Syrian opposition. In 1980, the United States, as part of her plan for defense of the Persian Gulf and the Middle East, asked Saudi Arabia to store U.S. materials and host U.S. base facilities. The Saudis, concerned about the reactions of the Arab coalition, were not prepared to agree formally.

After Iran succeeded in a major offensive against Iraq, Iraq and Saudi Arabia's GCC partners appealed to Egypt to intervene militarily. When Egypt refused, the Saudis were left without a coherent policy to face the deteriorating situation. At the time of Khalid's death in June 1982, Saudi Arabia was just hoping for the best as she continued to sit out the Iraq-Iran War crisis and ponder what would develop in the new war in Lebanon.

When Khalid died, Fahd became king and prime minister. Prince Abdullah (Commander of the National Guard) became crown prince and first deputy prime minister, and Fahd's full brother Prince Sultan (Minister of Defense and Aviation) became second deputy prime minister (and likely the successor after Abdullah).

On the domestic scene, Fahd's major problems have evolved from and have revolved around the oil recession—the decline in oil production, export, and prices; the decrease in revenues; the expenditure of reserves; the slashing of budgets; the cutbacks in development projects; and the vicissitudes of oil policies (Saudi and OPEC) to confront the problems. Oil discoveries in the North Sea and Mexico created additional problems. The OPEC nations found themselves strapped by huge expenditures they had incurred, and some began underselling the OPEC price. OPEC agreement became difficult to achieve. As the largest source of OPEC's (and the world's) oil reserves, Saudi Arabia could actually control OPEC (and world) oil prices. Under Oil Minister Yamani's direction, Saudi Arabia increased oil production in an effort to force OPEC agreement, but the plan backfired and in the mid-1980s, oil prices plummeted to below $10 per barrel—unheard of since prices began to increase in 1973.

Oil income dropped to $70.5 billion in 1982, and by 1983, it had dropped to less than half of its 1981 peak—$40 to $43 billion; by 1985, it was $28 billion; and by 1986, it was even less. There was deficit spending, and imports continued to outstrip exports. Operating expenses could be met only by drawing on reserves which declined to $70 billion by 1985. The situation was so bad that there was no announced 1986 budget. (There was one, though, in 1987.) Severe cutbacks were required in several of the ongoing development projects and social services, as well as in the extravagant lifestyle of many. By 1985, there was a monthly exodus of tens of thousands of foreign workers.

Late in 1986, Fahd dismissed Yamani—oil minister since 1962—who had been unpopular with Fahd for several years and whose authority as one not a member of the royal family had become problematic. Following Yamani's ouster, the Saudis became committed to raising the price of oil toward $20 a barrel.

Although Fahd had effectively been in control of foreign policy during Khalid's reign, since his ascendancy to king, he has been somewhat more vigorous in his foreign affairs. His Fahd Plan—rejected at the first Arab summit in 1981, much to the embarrassment of Fahd and anger of the Saudis—was endorsed at the beginning of the second summit in September 1982. Under Fahd, Saudi Arabia has continued to strengthen ties (still short of formal relations, however) with Egypt, cooperate with Jordan, and improve connections with other GCC states.

The greatest source of regional concern for Fahd, of course, has been the Iraq-Iran War, now in a shaky (and probably temporary) cease-fire. The Saudi air force's 1984 engagement of Iranian F-4 Phantoms and the downing of one Iranian plane gave rise to fears of the war's escalation, but the incident—which renewed the confidence of the Saudi armed forces—was not repeated. The Saudis remain threatened by Iran's Islamic-Fundamentalist movement and by Iraq's desire to become the major regional power. Fahd maintains a careful watch over the radical Marxist government in South Yemen, particularly in light of the January 1986 coup.

In order to back his ambitious foreign policy and to protect the essential, but vulnerable, Saudi oil establishment, Fahd has continued, and even expanded, the military build-up started during earlier regimes. All Saudi military and security services are undergoing modernization. In spite of close Saudi-U.S.

relations, Saudi Arabia's diversification of arms' sales from other than the United States—particularly France and Britain—continues.

Present

Saudi Arabia occupies approximately 2.24 million sq km (864,800 sq mi)—80 percent of the Arabian Peninsula—of which 98 percent is desert, waste, or urban; 1 percent is forested; and less than 1 percent is agricultural. Her borders, many of which are disputed, are with the UAE and Qatar on the northeast; Kuwait and Iraq on the north; Jordan on the northwest; the Yemen Arab Republic (North Yemen) on the south, and the People's Democratic Republic of Yemen (South Yemen) and Oman on the southeast and east. On her eastern coast, she has the Persian Gulf separating her from Iran and the Gulf of Bahrain separating her from Bahrain. On her western coast, she is separated from Egypt, Ethiopia, and Sudan by the Gulf of Aqaba and the Red Sea.

Saudi Arabia's three largest deserts account for over two-fifths of her total land mass. The Rub al-Khali, often called the empty quarter, covers about 250,000 sq mi across the south; it is the world's largest continuous sand area. The an-Nafud—22,000 sq mi—lies across most of the north. And a great area of sand, the ad-Dahna—almost 900 miles long and in some places only 30 miles wide—lies between the central Nejd region and the Persian Gulf in the east and joins the Rub al-Khali with the an-Nafud. The vast majority of the remainder of Saudi Arabia's land is wilderness covered by gravel and lava beds. There are neither rivers nor perennial streams, only some wells and a few springs, the larger of which form oases for settlements and some agriculture. Only a small part of her very limited arable land—that located in the Asir region in the southwest—is watered by rain. Agriculture in the Nejd region is dependent on irrigation.

The published population figures of every Arab state are only estimates provided by their governments. Because an official census is not taken and for security reasons, actual population figures are either not available or are grossly exaggerated. Although these population estimates for most Arab countries—for any year—vary from source to source, the disparity in figures related to the population of Saudi Arabia is so extreme that the highest "best estimates" are more than double those of the lowest. And in every reference there is commentary about the difficulty in obtaining even near accurate population information about Saudi Arabia. Total population estimates for Saudi Arabia vary from 5 to 6 million to over 12 million and include foreign resident estimates ranging from 1 to 2.5 million (15 to 21 percent).

Ethnically, 90 percent of Saudi Arabian citizens are Arab and 10 percent are Afro-Asian. Religiously, 100 percent are Moslems, the overwhelming majority of which are Wahhabi Sunni. There are a small number of Yemenite Zaydi in Asir and a few hundred thousand Shi'ites in the al-Hasa region. Interestingly, for decades the Saudis have been estimating their Shi'ite-Arab population at approximately 300,000 souls— implying no population growth—while the balance of the population has been estimated to have one of the world's highest birthrates—one that would double the Saudi population every twenty-three years. In all other nations throughout the Middle East, it has been acknowledged that the Shi'ite portion of the population either exceeds or equals the growth rate of the general population.

The only Christians in Saudi Arabia are noncitizens—those who are counted among the foreign residents. Those foreigners employed in the military are Pakistanis. Those employed in the oil industry are mostly Asians and Indians, and their numbers are declining due to the drop in oil production and revenues. Foreigners employed in administrative and teaching positions are mostly Egyptians and Jordanians (Palestinians). Their numbers, too, are decreasing because the Saudis they have trained are taking their place, thus reducing foreign influence and its inherent conflicting mores.

Arabic is the official language of Saudi Arabia, but English is taught in some schools. The literacy rate is reported to be approximately 50 percent.

The four major regions, or provinces, of Saudi Arabia, rooted in her tribal history, still play a significant role in her present-day geopolitical and socioeconomic make-up. Population settlement patterns follow those natural geopolitical regions and are separated by vast, sparsely inhabited spaces both within and between each other. Approximately one-half of the total population resides in the western mountainous belt along the Red Sea comprised of the Hejaz region in the north and the Asir region in the south. This area includes the religious capitals of Mecca and Medina as well as the major port cities of Jidda—considered the commercial capital—and Yanbo. A second cluster of population centers follows an archipelago of oases in the central Nejd region. This area includes the official royal and administrative capital city of Riyadh. The third population belt is in the eastern al-Hasa region on the Persian Gulf coast. This area includes the Shi'ite population center and the main petrol-producing fields and facilities as well as Dhahran—the site of a major airport and military base—and the new port city of Jubail.

According to most reports, approximately 50 percent of Saudi Arabia's population is urban while 20 percent remain nomadic or seminomadic. Since less than 1 percent of the land is suitable for agriculture and most industrial areas are in or near urban centers, it's difficult to understand where the other 30 percent of the total population reside and what they do.

Saudi Arabia possesses the most modern and best-equipped hospital in the world and officially claims to provide medical care, social services, and other educational and welfare benefits to her inhabitants. Despite these official claims, she has one of the highest infant mortality rates in the world—approximately twenty-five times that of Israel's, which is one of the world's lowest. Diseases that are rare and hardly exist in the Western world, especially Israel, are rampant in Saudi Arabia—trachoma, tuberculosis, malaria, syphilis, gonorrhea, dysentery, cholera, spinal meningitis, yellow fever, typhoid, and other lung infections. These diseases are but one measure of the basic sanitary and health conditions that prevail in the overall society. The more than twenty-year difference in life expectancy between Israelis and Saudis is another reflection of how health and social benefits fail to reach ordinary Saudi inhabitants—those other than the royal family or the elite bureaucracy that serves the kingdom.

Saudi Arabia is a society closed by a "curtain of sand" that surrounds and seals her from the outside world and is tighter and exceedingly more difficult to penetrate than either the "Iron Curtain" of the Soviet Union or the "Bamboo Curtain" of the Peoples Republic (Mainland) of China. Foreigners may enter

Saudi Arabia *only* by invitation and official consent of the Saudi government and only after extensive screening to keep out undesirables—Jews and journalists are among the many groups that fit that category. Foreign workers residing in Saudi Arabia who are employed by foreign firms have been effectively silenced. Their failure to speak out publicly on conditions within Saudi Arabia is traced to the punishment of permanent banishment from that country, plus the loss of their jobs back in their country of origin. Rare exceptions reveal a society in which Islamic law *(Sharia)* is ruthlessly administered and where the concept of human rights and individual freedoms of speech, assembly, press, and suffrage are totally nonexistent.

Political

The Kingdom of Saudi Arabia, as she is legally known, is an absolute monarchy. The king is chosen by and responsible to the royal council, which is comprised of various princes of the royal family, and is assisted by a council of ministers appointed by and responsible to him. The Saud family and the majority of the tribal population adhere to the Wahhabi branch of Sunni-Islamic fundamentalism; therefore, *Sharia* law is strictly observed and is enforced as the law of the land. Saudi Arabia is a feudal autocratic society in which elections, political parties, suffrage, and political and religious dissent are prohibited. In fact, dissent is dealt with ruthlessly by the Saud family who don't allow any of the freedoms that exist and are taken for granted in the United States and other Western-style democracies—freedom of speech, religion, assembly, and press.

Each successive ruling member of the Saud family who has come to power has reasserted the Saudi political/religious position that the Saudis are the leaders of Islam and that, as such, have led in the organization of all Moslem nations in the world—Arab and non-Arab—in an effort to create a worldwide Moslem political force.

Saudi Arabia's stated political goals include the control of Jerusalem and the elimination of the Jewish State of Israel in the land of Palestine. In support of these stated political goals, the Saud family has financed the armies of the Arab Confrontation States—"radical" as well as "moderate"—in their continuing struggle against Israel and has liberally financed the terrorist activities of the PLO and its splinter organizations. She opposed Sadat's peace initiative with Israel and has opposed the Camp David Accords and the resultant peace treaty with Israel. There are absolutely *no* conditions under which Saudi Arabia—as long as she is a Wahhabi-Islamic-Fundamentalist state—can ever recognize or live in peace with an independent Jewish state in any piece of the land of what was known as Palestine. In this respect, she does not differ in attitude toward Israel from the Shi'ite-Islamic state of Iran under the Ayatollah Khomeini and/or from Qaddafi's Libyan Sunni-Fundamentalist state—all are dedicated to Israel's destruction.

Saudi Arabia's political goals are only an extension of her Wahhabi-Islamic-Fundamentalist religious convictions. She has pursued virulent anti-Jewish policies during her entire national existence. In the mid-seventies, Saudi Arabia led the anti-Israel political fight within the United Nations and sponsored the resolution that equated Zionism with racism and denounced Israel as a racist state. The Free World stood by silently, failing to speak out against injustice—intimidated by the power of oil and money.

Today, Saudi Arabia, especially because of her military vulnerability and lack of real military power, continues to resort to political and economic means to fight the State of Israel. No Jew can enter Saudi Arabia, work for any foreign company in Saudi Arabia, or be assigned to the diplomatic corps of any nation within Saudi Arabia. This places friendly Western nations (such as the United States) in the extremely embarrassing political position of screening all military and diplomatic personnel for Jews and legally permitting all U.S. companies, such as Bechtel and ARAMCO, to screen their employees in order that no Jewish employee will ever enter or be stationed in Saudi Arabia. Although Saudi Arabia is currently not a military threat to Israel, her long-term military build-up and her proximity to Israel's southern borders makes her a potential deadly adversary. Saudi Arabia will then add another element of power in her struggle against Israel.

The U.S.-Jewish and -Christian communities' support for the State of Israel is motivated by ideological (shared Western values) and religious beliefs. Whether there is agreement or disagreement with the Israeli political program is immaterial, since they are utilizing perfectly legitimate ways to promote policies they believe to be in the best interest of the United States. Their efforts in support of Israel reflect the democratic political process in the United States.

The emergence of the pro-Saudi petrol dollar lobby creates a very serious problem, since it is a vested lobby with commercial interests tied to foreign governments purporting to represent U.S. national interests. Even though there is a law requiring all agents of foreign powers to register publicly as foreign agents and submit regular disclosure reports, very few members of this vast corporate lobby are registered as foreign agents—despite the fact that their corporate interests are intricately linked to those of Saudi Arabia. This results in the subversion of the integrity of the U.S. decision-making process by the lobby, which is controlled, directed, and influenced by Saudi Arabia as she secretly attempts to manipulate U.S. policy. The primary motivators of the United States in the petrol dollar lobby are the maintenance of business in the Arab world and financial gain.

In recognition of the lack of popular support for the Arab cause within the U.S. public, successive presidential administrations since 1948 have agreed to initiate pro-Arab (anti-Israel) policies. U.S. policies have often followed the dictates of Arab nations. The executive branch's sponsorship has thus shielded the Arab nations from accusations that they have intervened in U.S. politics. In effect, the executive branch has created a dual approach to foreign policy. It passed onto Congress the area of U.S.-Israeli relations but maintained the responsibility of protecting the interests of Saudi Arabia as well as the other Arab states.

The result of this division of responsibility in foreign policy is the perception that the Jewish lobby for Israel is extremely powerful because of the highly profiled public process it must undertake in its efforts to influence Congress. The Arab nations can sit back while the executive branch does their work for them.

Another example of both the dual political policy of the United States toward Israel and her Arab neighbors and the powerful influence of the Arab nations on shaping U.S. foreign policy can be observed in the communications media. There is an almost universal demand by the media for factual news from Israel, regardless of whether or not it is favorable toward Israel.

In fact, news that reflects negatively on Israel is often amplified and repeated ad nauseam. On the other hand, factual news from the Arab nations is almost impossible to obtain, and, when it is available and reflects negatively on the moderate Arabs, it is suppressed. In the case of Saudi Arabia, no hard news is ever available through what the Saudis consider legal sources. Should there be leaks, every attempt is made within the United States to suppress it.

For example, the documentary television film "Death of a Princess," which depicted the execution of a nineteen-year-old Arabian princess who illegally married an Arabian commoner—not a member of the Saud royal family, created a diplomatic storm that reverberated throughout the Western world. She was shot, and he was beheaded in a car in the port city of Jidda. The royal Saud family perceived the film to be an attack on them and an attack on the Islamic world. By using its influence with friendly congressmen, entrepreneurs doing business or hoping to do business with Saudi Arabia, U.S. State Department officials, and members of the Carter administration, tremendous pressure was applied on the Public Broadcasting System's affiliated stations—many of whom canceled the program. A form of censorship was being imposed by public and private institutions as a method of mollifying Saudi Arabia who has so aptly been portrayed as a friend and ally of the United States.

Economic

The economy of Saudi Arabia has been structured upon a single commodity source of income since the conclusion of the second world war when oil far outstripped the only other source of revenue—the yearly Moslem pilgrimages to Mecca and Medina. Prior to the second world war, income from the pilgrimages represented the major portion of state revenue. In the 1920s, 50,000 pilgrims made the yearly trek to Mecca and Medina. By the 1930s, the number of pilgrims reached 200,000; but by 1938, oil produced in commercial quantities provided a level of income that outstripped that from the pilgrims. (Today, many millions of pilgrims visit Mecca and Medina each year; however, that source of revenue represents only a small portion compared to that provided by oil.)

During the reign of Ibn Saud, especially after World War II,

Saudi oil revenues increased substantially—from $10 million in 1946 to $53 million in 1948, $57 million in 1950, and $212 million in 1952. However, oil income was flittered away and spent extravagantly on the royal family—waste and imprudent spending squandered the money. Little was invested in development. Under the rule of King Saud, the outrageous royal family spending habits continued, and, even though oil revenues reached $341 million in 1955, a $95 million national dept was incurred in 1956 and soared to $500 million by 1957. During a year when oil revenue reached $300 million, King Saud spent $140 million on a marble palace and about 350 princes and their relatives, who also built huge palaces, lived lavishly at royal expense. The royal family spent 17 percent of state revenues while satiating their appetite for the "good life." Expenditures for development remained negligible.

In November 1964, Faisal became king and began to control expenditures, funneling money into the development of the country. In 1964, oil income was $.5 billion; in 1969, $1 billion; in 1972, $3 billion; and by 1975, $25 billion.

After the humiliating defeat of Egypt, Jordan, and Syria by Israel in the June 1967 War, Saudi Arabia began using surplus money to provide financial assistance—to the tune of $85 million—to shore up the war-torn economies of Egypt and Jordan which had been shattered by their defeat in that war. That was the beginning of a Saudi platform of diplomacy which attempted to influence her Arab neighbors' policies through the use of financial grants.

The Yom Kippur War of October 1973 was fought on two fronts:

- the battlefield—the invasions by Egypt and Syria which, after twenty-one days of intense fighting, ended, again, in their devastating military defeat and
- the economic field—the oil embargo by all the Arab exporting states, led by Saudi Arabia, which resulted in a worldwide panic in a world thirsty for oil and not prepared for such a political move by the Arabs (primarily, Saudis).

The oil consumers were much more dependent on oil imports in 1973 than they had been in 1967—the previous time Saudi Arabia attempted an embargo (aptly termed the "oil weapon") as a means of supporting the Arab Confrontation States in their war against Israel. In 1967, the Saudi embargo failed, but the Western oil importing nations did not learn the proper lessons from that experience. They didn't build up reserves, seek alternative energy sources, exploit indigenous sources, or practice energy conservation—all of which the oil-guzzling nations were forced to do after the 1973 oil embargo.

Saudi Arabia's two political motives for initiating the embargoes during the June 1967 War and the 1973 Yom Kippur War were to provide political support for Arab "cousins" on the battlefield and to increase the price of oil, which she had felt was grossly underpriced. The shah of Iran was not interested in joining an embargo, but he shared Saudi Arabia's interest in raising the price of oil in order to finance his grand dreams of re-establishing the great Persian empire. The price of oil rose rapidly and dramatically as the entire Free World capitulated to this new form of warfare.

Saudi Arabia soon learned that because of her tremendous petroleum reserves—the world's largest (purported to be 25 percent of the world's reserves)—and because she had the largest production capacity of all the oil exporting nations, she could become the "swing producer" of the OPEC nations. Saudi Arabia had the capability, by regulating her production of petroleum, to force the price of oil down when there was a surplus of oil on the world market and force the price of oil up when there was a market shortage. Three times she utilized that capability (1974, 1979, and 1983) to influence the price of oil. In 1974 and 1979, this technique caused the price of oil to jump dramatically, while in 1983, by pumping millions of barrels of oil per day in excess of what the market could absorb, she caused a dramatic drop in the price.

Saudi Arabia used her post-Yom Kippur War swollen oil revenues to finance her Middle East diplomacy policy by continuing to provide financial grants to pay for Syrian, Egyptian, and Jordanian weapons purchases; to underwrite PLO activities; and to construct a $1.5 mb/d capacity pipeline from the Persian Gulf to the Red Sea. In addition, she spent huge sums on defense, financed massive national projects such as oil refineries and a petrochemical industry, and squandered fortunes (approximately $10 billion) on the construction of the world's largest and most grandiose airport in Riyadh.

By 1981, Saudi Arabia had accumulated reserves of approximately $155 billion. Every year since 1983, however, she has incurred a considerable budget deficit of between $15 and $20 billion and, thus, has diminished her reserves. Total Saudi oil income since 1974 approximates three-fourths of a trillion dollars or about half of all the oil income accrued to all the Arab oil-exporting countries. Now and in the near future, Saudi Arabia's oil income will stay at approximately current levels, so her government spending levels will create serious deficits that she will find difficult to reduce. Her current GNP is reported to be over $102 billion—$8,500 per capita.

The dangers created by the never-ending Iraq-Iran War, not withstanding the present cease-fire, challenge Saudi security interests and prevent her from seriously trimming her defense budget which is not much lower than her income from oil exports. However, a reduction in Saudi oil income—from $22 billion in 1986 to $17 billion (projected) in 1988—has resulted in a reluctant but comparable decrease in defense spending—from $19.3 billion in 1986 to $16.2 billion in 1987.

Saudi Arabia is entering a period when her diminished oil income and bloated defense and social services budgets will force her to spend her dwindling financial reserves. It is a period when economic forces rather than familiar political ones will pose a threat to her and her neighbors. Saudi Arabia is probably the only Arab oil-exporting country with sufficient monetary and oil reserves and sufficient excess production capacity to weather an economic crisis. Since her Arab oil-producing neighbors can't, there could be serious political repercussions for Saudi Arabia. Already she has had to cut back on some social services. If oil revenues continue to fall in the future, Saudi ability to influence the policies of her neighbors through the use of financial grants and her questionable ability to exert a stabilizing influence in the region will be greatly compromised.

Military

It is extremely important that the current military situation in Saudi Arabia be understood. To achieve this, a brief historical review of the defense of the Gulf region as it relates to Western interests is essential.

After the fall of the Ottoman Empire in 1918, Great Britain controlled and defended the entire Gulf region east of Suez. She was the caretaker over Western interests in that region. With the loss of the Suez Canal to Egypt's Colonel Nasser in 1956, Great Britain could no longer maintain her position east of Suez and in the Gulf and was forced to pull out, leaving a military as well as political vacuum.

The shah of Iran (with U.S. encouragement) embarked upon a program of military build-up in order to assume the responsibility for the defense of the entire Persian Gulf. The United States supported the shah by selling Iran massive amounts of the most modern weapon systems, many of which had not been sold or provided to any other nation in the world.

Why such U.S. support for the shah and Iran? In some ways, it was a U.S. response to Soviet involvement in the Gulf. The radical Arab state of Iraq, with assistance from the Soviet Union, had embarked upon a military build-up using Soviet weapon systems, training, and tactics. The selection of Iran as a surrogate for protection of Western interests in the Gulf region had a logic at that time. Iran was the most strategically positioned state in that she bordered the Soviet Union, encompassed a large land mass, had a sizable population of 45 million, and maintained a stable government in that it represented Persian Moslems, the vast majority of the population.

On paper, the shah had built the most awesome military force in the entire Middle East equipped with the most advanced tactical weapon systems assembled anywhere outside the United States. Then, in 1979, the shah fell to the Ayatollah Khomeini who established an Islamic-Fundamentalist state, and the Iranian military establishment immediately became a force in the Gulf potentially hostile to Western interests. In retrospect, the analysis that spawned the U.S. support of Iran policy erred in that it didn't take into account the impact and destabilizing effect the rapid modernization of Iran would have on the culture, population, and political forces within the country.

To the dismay of the West—particularly the United States, who had assumed the role of maintaining the political status quo in the Persian Gulf—the collapse of the shah created yet another political-military vacuum in that region. During the post-Vietnam political environment in the United States, a direct U.S.

military presence in the Gulf was politically unthinkable, yet, again, in retrospect, it would have been the only effective solution. This was proven by the need for a U.S. presence in the Gulf that began during the summer of 1987, when the United States embarked upon a program of direct naval involvement in the Gulf through her naval escort of reflagged Kuwaiti tankers, an activity that helped to influence the ensuing Iraq-Iran cease-fire.

However, in the post-1973 Yom Kippur War era, the United States embarked upon a program, accelerated in 1979 with the demise of the shah, of building up the military infrastructure and establishment of Saudi Arabia and making her the recipient of the most technologically advanced weapon systems. In so doing, the United States assisted Saudi Arabia in one of the world's most lavish military build-ups since the reign of the shah. This appears to be yet another attempt at seeking a surrogate military force which would represent and defend Western interests in the Gulf as a substitute for a significant U.S. military presence. However, since Saudi Arabia is not Iran, that policy made little sense, even applying the same criteria as those used during the shah's reign in Iran. The decision was very risky because of Saudi Arabia's huge land mass, the locations of her oil-producing fields, the nature of her population concentrations, the sparsity and low density of her population, the presence of large numbers of transient foreign workers, the absence of a scientific or technical infrastructure, the lack of an industrial base, and the nonexistence of a native educated class.

Events of the past decade do not support the wisdom of U.S. reliance on Saudi Arabia for maintaining the political or military balance in the area. One wonders whether an important consideration at that time—perhaps even the determinant one— was the economic impact of massive advanced weapon systems sales to Saudi Arabia on U.S. military industries which were being adversely affected by the continual erosion of the defense budget during the Ford and Carter administrations. During the past decade, Saudi Arabia has spent in excess of $200 billion on defense, making her fourth only to the United States, China, and the USSR; yet, she is as defenseless as ever.

It becomes obvious why Saudi Arabia is still defenseless when an analysis is made of how oil income was spent over the last decade. In 1981—the peak selling year—Saudi Arabia spent

$25 billion on defense, representing the highest per capita defense spending in the world—twice as high as Israel and three times that of the United States. In that year, Saudi Arabia spent, in actual terms, twice the combined spending of Egypt, Iraq, Israel, Jordan, and Syria. At that time, these five Middle East countries, combined, could field 60 divisions, 10,000 tanks, and 2,000 combat aircraft, while with equivalent spending, Saudi Arabia could field only 5 divisions, 500 tanks, and 200 combat aircraft (about the size of Jordan's military at that time).

The reasons for this lack of cost effectiveness include the duplication of defense installations due to the massive size of the country; the lack of any initial infrastructure and the grandiose manner in which attempts were made to build one; the inability to train expeditiously unqualified personnel to fill highly skilled jobs; the lack of a qualified manpower pool from which to build a modern military establishment; incompetence at the planning and implementation levels; and a combination of false starts, waste, spoilage, and corruption. The ratio of hardware spending to that for training and construction over ten years was 1:4.

In 1952, Saudi Arabia's defense budget was $60 million—30 percent of government revenues. By 1981, her defense spending reached $25 billion—a growth of 415 times—while her government revenues had grown by 383 times. In 1987, Saudi Arabia spent $16.23 billion dollars—32 percent of her total government revenues—on defense, fielding an armed force of 83,000 full-time military personnel. Of that number, 15,000 are Bedouin who comprise the national guard—a small elite force organized to protect the Saud family, their palaces, and their key institutions; it is not an army.

A potential internal threat to the Saud regime emanates from the emerging middle class who staff positions that operate the country but who have no authority. They are being trained to operate the highly sophisticated military weapon systems being acquired by Saudi Arabia, and, since they are trained in England, France, and the United States, are a potential source of unrest due to their exposure to Western culture. Their attempt to circumvent strict *Sharia* law as imposed by this Wahhabi (Sunni Fundamentalist) society—prohibition of alcohol, tobacco, drugs, sexual freedom, secular films, literature, etc.—will cause strain on the society and potential danger to the Saud regime.

Another internal threat comes from the 300 to 400,000

Shi'ites who reside in eastern Saudi Arabia and work in the oil fields. Twice they have posed a serious challenge to the regime when they attempted to capture the great *mosque* in Mecca during the holy period of Ramadan: once in 1979 and another time in 1987. Paradoxically, Saudi Arabia's petroleum infrastructure (including her 5 major oil fields with their 1,500 oil wells, her refineries, and her pumping stations) is located in an area 250 miles long by 50 miles wide along the Persian Gulf—the population center of the Shi'ites (the natural enemies of the Wahhabi-Saud family). Since Shi'ites constitute a majority of the workers operating the entire petroleum industry, especially the oil fields, Saudi Arabia is extremely vulnerable to sabotage by hostile workers, a small hostile commando, or guerrilla forces—a kind of hostility extremely difficult to defend against.

The external threats to Saudi Arabia are from Iran, Iraq, Syria, and Marxist Yemen. In addition, there are the threats on the personal lives of the Saudi princes who are being blackmailed and extorted by the PLO. In order to defend herself—by herself—from surrounding external threats, Saudi Arabia must expand her military as the massive growth in infrastructure nears completion. More funds can then be allocated for military hardware such as combat ships, combat planes, armored fighting vehicles, and missiles.

Saudi Arabia spans a vast territory with a 1,500 mile coastline bounded on either side by two seas, access to which can be readily blocked by three narrow straits. Passage can be blocked along the Red Sea at the twenty-mile wide Bab al Mandeb Strait—adjacent to South Yemen—between the Red Sea and the Gulf of Aden, while the Suez Canal acts as a choke point between the Red Sea and the Mediterranean. On the Persian Gulf, the link to the Arabian Sea is the thirty-mile wide Strait of Hormuz, bordered on one side by Iran and on the other side by Oman. This makes Saudi Arabia extremely vulnerable to both hostilities between neighbors and aggression from a regional enemy.

This is especially true given the nature of Saudi Arabia's other serious security problems—her neighbors. She is bordered on all sides by a dozen countries—some of which are very strong (Egypt, Iran, Iraq), while others are very weak (Bahrain, Kuwait, North Yemen, Oman, Qatar, South Yemen, and the UAE);

some of which are extremely wealthy (Bahrain, Kuwait, Oman, Qatar, and the UAE), while others are very poor (Jordan, Egypt, North Yemen, and South Yemen); and some of which are pro-Western (Egypt, Israel, Jordan) while others are radical and pro-Soviet (Ethiopia, Iraq, and South Yemen), or radical and not influenced by either East or West (Iran). Of all of Saudi Arabia's neighbors, only Iran has a stable government—a government that represents the majority of the population.

Additionally, there is the potentially destabilizing situation that none of Saudi Arabia's boundaries with her neighbors and none of the boundaries between her neighbors are mutually accepted or recognized. In that part of the world—where sizable amounts of wealth may be locked beneath the surface of the land—relatively small amounts of territory could yield enormous wealth, spawning the greed that is the catalyst for war and other aggressive behavior between nations.

Saudi Arabia, then, is vulnerable to both internal subversion and sabotage and outside aggression. Her location; the vastness of her territory; the nature and sparsity of her population; and the concentration of the majority of her population in a few locations—in the central area (Riyadh), along the Red Sea (especially Mecca and Medina), in the ports of Jidda and Yanbo, and along the Persian Gulf—make her impossible to defend. In addition is the threat of dwindling oil revenues—the main source of income from which the huge military budget is funded. (During the last four years, the military budget has had to be cut, and in order to fund it, the Saudi treasury had to draw on its foreign currency reserves accumulated during the late seventies and early eighties when oil revenues were at their peak.) These dilemmas, as well as the inherent instability of a society controlled by a few thousand people whose loyalty must always be a source of concern, make Saudi Arabia's obsession with security and her budget emphasis on military build-up very real. Her ability to establish sufficient military power to provide real security is more than questionable; it is most doubtful.

Future

When analyzing the future of Saudi Arabia and attempting to assess the dangers the existing power structure (Saud family) faces in the next ten to twenty years, it is first necessary to evaluate the internal forces which could bring about change in the environment. A large middle class who are not members of the Saud family is being created from the general population. They have been trained and influenced in commerce by the West but are forced to observe *Sharia* law while having no direct power or influence on any decision-making process in the government. They have established a group who will represent an ever-present danger to the family-run and controlled government. As this group administers but does not rule, they represent a force for change within a ruling structure not equipped to provide changes. Within the next ten to twenty years, a whole new generation of emerging middle class engaged in bureaucracy—banking, military service, and commerce—will join their fathers in the ranks of this disenfranchised body.

An alliance between the burgeoning middle class and the military is the most probable scenario for the termination of Saud family rule. While the PLO has represented a personal danger to individual Saudi princes, it has not been a threat to the state. Assassination of princes will only result in an orderly replacement by other members of the family.

Any internal political change rejecting the Saud family can only result in a political system based on Sunni-Islamic fundamentalism. No political infrastructure or experience exists within Saudi Arabia for the creation from within of an Islamic secular state. Therefore, the greatest ideological threat to the present regime is Qaddafi's brand of Islamic socialism and social justice. A country sparsely inhabited by 20 percent nomads and an emerging disenfranchised wealthy middle class already steeped in Islamic fundamentalism is hope for an Arab brand of social order. It is inconceivable that a Soviet-style communism, Western culture's secular humanism, or Ba'athist secular socialism—all of which reject *Sharia* law—could be established in Saudi Arabia.

A Qaddafi-type regime in Saudi Arabia would be anti-Soviet, anti-West, and actively anti-Israel. It would buy arms from the East structured around Soviet military doctrine utilizing simpler weapon systems, as they discover that what they purchased from the West were massive armaments but not an army. This regime, however, would still do the bulk of its commerce with the West.

Such a hypothetical regime—if it were to come into existence—would most certainly expand its borders to include Bahrain, Qatar, Oman, and the UAE but not Kuwait—Iraq's domain—and not the Yemens. Such a Sunni-Islamic-Fundamentalist, non-Marxist-Socialist state would find a Shi'ite-dominated Iran a real active enemy. The Shi'ites within Saudi Arabia, then, could become a serious political fifth column.

The external threats to Saudi Arabia by the turn of the century will depend upon what kinds of governments are in power in her neighboring states.

- Yemen—The threat from Yemen will be one of intimidation and challenge to Saudi Arabia's indefendable borders. While an invasion by a Marxist Yemen could conquer the land of Saudi Arabia, the PDRY could not rule the fiercely religious Wahhabis. The threat from Yemen, then, is one of challenging Saudi regional policies but not Saudi survival.
- Syria—If Syria were successful in undermining Jordan and establishing a Ba'athist-style regime in place of the Hashemite kingdom, she could become a threat and a serious nuisance to Saudi Arabia and the Gulf states—but only to intimidate or to block their regional influence. Invasion by Syrian forces could not result in the establishment of a political system that would be in alliance with Ba'athist Syria.
- Jordan—If the PLO were successful in toppling the Hashemite kingdom and establishing a Qaddafi-type Sunni-Islamic-Fundamentalist Socialist state with a militarily proficient army, it could conquer and establish similar regimes in Saudi Arabia as well as the other Gulf states. Ultimately, however, the power base of such a combined Sunni-Islamic-Fundamentalist state would reside in Riyadh, as opposed to Amman, because of the disparity of wealth and population.
- Iraq—If Iraq becomes a Shi'ite-Fundamentalist- dominated state with a relationship with a Shi'ite-Fundamentalist-controlled Iran, then the Saudi regime would automatically be in mortal danger, as would the rest of the Gulf states. Internally, the 300,000 Shi'ites living within and working in the eastern Saudi oil infrastructure would become a dangerous fifth column. A Shi'ite Iraqi-Iranian army would

be the external threat to Saudi Arabia. The entire area, including Kuwait, could not survive.

- Iran—If the present Shi'ite-Islamic-Fundamentalist leadership survives, the direct danger from Iran will be subversive activity of the Shi'ites in Saudi Arabia.

No matter which type of government will exist in Saudi Arabia—whether Saudi-Islamic Fundamentalist, Qaddafi-style Islamic-Fundamentalist Socialist, or Ba'athist controlled by either Iraq or Iran—the Arabian Gulf's relationship with Israel will be one of hostility. There will be no recognition of a Jewish state in Palestine. Saudi Arabia's ability in the future to utilize her emerging military power in conjunction with one or more of the other Arab states in a war against Israel presents a grave danger for Israel.

Because of a number of noncoincidence of interests in the region between the United States and Saudi Arabia—the Camp David Accords sponsored by President Carter, the undermining of the shah during Carter's presidency, the escalation of Israel to strategic ally during the Reagan administration, and the U.S. Congress' reluctance to continue to sell Saudi Arabia massive quantities of advanced weapon systems—Saudi Arabia has embarked upon a program of diversification of weapons purchases. She is buying the advanced Tornado fighter from Europe and equipping her navy with combat ships from France. The Saudi diversification plan encompasses the purchase of a new modern tank from Europe and long-range ballistic missiles from the People's Republic of China (PROC) for expansion of her armed forces.

The relief from dependence on the United States as a source of weapon systems that Saudi Arabia seeks will be more than offset by the complexity of maintaining and operating equipment supplied by a number of different nations. While she may become less dependent on the United States, she will most certainly become even more dependent on foreign military advisors and their growing military elite, whose political loyalties will be questionable. Saudi Arabia has thus embarked upon building a military establishment in which the key personnel are Saudi, the support personnel are mercenaries, and the technical advisors are American, French, German, British, and Chinese.

The commander in chief of this military goulash will always be a member of the royal family—a deserving prince. It is difficult to conceive of such a contrived military force either achieving a military objective that requires the professional use of a military organization or surviving without revolt or massive unrest—certainly not within the next twenty years.

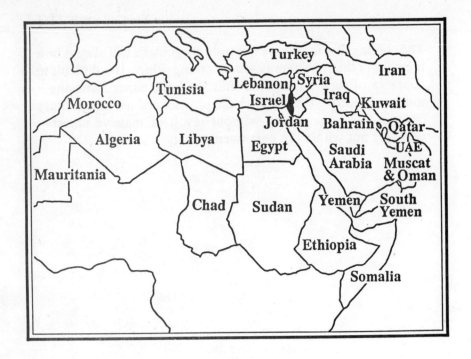

BAHRAIN

History

Bahrain, as with much of the Gulf coast, was a backwater known only for pearl fishing until the twentieth century. At various times, she was ruled by local tribes from Qatar, by Portugal, and by Persia (Iran). In 1783, the Khalifa clan drove the Iranians out of Bahrain and established a regime that, basically, has ruled the state ever since. In 1820, the British established a treaty relationship with the Khalifa clan.

In 1932, when oil was discovered in Bahrain, she became one of the first oil centers on the Arab side of the Gulf. She experienced an oil boom long before her neighbors—prior to World War II—and was the first Gulf state to bring in large-scale expatriate labor to work the oil fields. A huge foreign community of Egyptians, Indians, Pakistanis, and Palestinians swelled Bahrain's work force and produced the same potential for societal tension and instability as was later created in the other oil-producing states throughout the Gulf region.

Bahrain, also, was the first of the Gulf states to be faced with the problem of depleting oil reserves. In order to maintain her living standard, she diversified her economy by building the region's largest aluminum factory, a dry-dock second only to that of Dubai, and an offshore banking facility—the pillar of her diversification program, which is making Bahrain "the Singapore of the Persian Gulf."

The Sunni minority-ruling Khalifa family was threatened in December 1981 when an Iranian-backed plot for a Shi'ite coup was discovered. The government house was to have been seized by local Shi'ites who then were to call in Iranian troops. The Shi'ite plotters had been trained in Iran. As a result of that threat, Bahrain signed a mutual security agreement with Saudi Arabia.

The Iraq-Iran War alerted Bahrain to her vulnerability. Bahraini defense forces have been expanded and modernized, and Bahrain has joined the GCC with Oman, Qatar, Saudi Arabia, and UAE—all of whom have pledged $1 billion to Bahrain for modernization of her military forces.

Early in 1986, there was a dispute between Bahrain and Qatar over the coral reef of Fasht al-Dibal—east of Bahrain—where a Dutch company under contract with Bahrain was using landfill to raise the reef. In April, Qatari forces landed on the island, took the European and Filipino workers as prisoners, and made the area an "exclusion zone" patrolled by Qatari aircraft and naval vessels. The dispute was settled through the mediation efforts of the Saudis and the GCC.

Present

The state of Bahrain is comprised of a number of islands in the Persian Gulf. These include the two larger islands of Bahrain and Muharraq—site of Manama, the capital—which occupy approximately 622 sq km (240 sq mi), plus thirty-two smaller islands. Only 5 percent of Bahrain's land is cultivated; the remainder is either desert, waste, or urban. Across the Gulf from Iran, Bahrain lies about fifteen miles off the coast of Saudi Arabia and is just about equally distant from Qatar—Saudi Arabia to her west and south, Qatar to her east and south.

Bahrain's population of approximately 480,000 is 65 percent Bahraini Arab; 25 percent Iranian, Indian, and Pakistani; 5 percent other Arab; 3 percent European; and 1 percent other.

Religiously, the population is 85 percent Moslem (60 percent Shi'ite and 25 percent Sunni), 7.3 percent Christian, and 7.7 percent other. The most destabilizing factor within the Bahraini society is that the ruling house, the Khalifas, is Sunni while the vast majority of the indigenous population is Shi'ite. These tensions have been exacerbated by the rise to power in Iran of the Ayatollah Khomeini and his Shi'ite-Islamic-Fundamentalist government. Although the official language of Bahrain is Arabic, English, Farsi, and Urdu are also spoken. The official literacy rate is given as 40 percent.

Politically, Bahrain, officially known as the State of Bahrain, is an independent emirate—an autocracy ruled by the same royal family since 1782. There are no elections, and all political parties are prohibited. (A 1973 political experiment resulted in the election of a parliament that was dissolved one and one-half years later.)

Economically, Bahrain relies on oil exporting, offshore banking, petroleum processing and refining, aluminum smelting, and ship repair. Her GNP is approximately $4.1 billion and her per capita income, $9,290.

Militarily, the state of Bahrain spends $300 million a year on defense, while maintaining 2,800 men in the armed forces. She shares a $1 billion defense fund with Oman—provided by the GCC—for modernization of her armed forces. While Bahrain's small military force provides internal security and her navy, very limited regional patrolling, Saudi Arabia provides for the basic defense of Bahrain.

Bahrain and Saudi Arabia are now connected by a causeway and the mutual accessibility has created concern for both ruling families. There is Saudi pressure on Bahrain to curb her traditionally free and open lifestyle, and there is Saudi fear that Bahrain's Shi'ite population might affect Saudi society negatively.

Future

The threats to the future independent status of minority-ruled Bahrain—a mini state surrounded by giant adversaries—come from both internal and external sources. Internally, the greatest threat to the ruling family—Sunni Moslems—comes from the 70 percent of the population who are Shi'ite Moslems. Iran has sent agents to Bahrain to organize unrest among the Shi'ites with an aim toward takeover. The internal political situation does not bode well for the future.

Externally, Iran's long-term claim to Bahrain could erupt at any time if Iran were to neutralize Iraq and bring down the ruling Iraqi military government. Saudi Arabia's present protectorate status over Bahrain could easily deteriorate to that of absorbing Bahrain as part of Saudi Arabia and imposing conservative *Sharia* law on that freewheeling society—the soft underbelly of the Sunni-dominated region and the prostitution center for religiously esthetic Gulf states. Saudi Arabia has always had ambitions to absorb the entire Gulf area into a greater Saudi Arabia. Bahrain is the most vulnerable of all; thus, her future independent status lies very much in doubt.

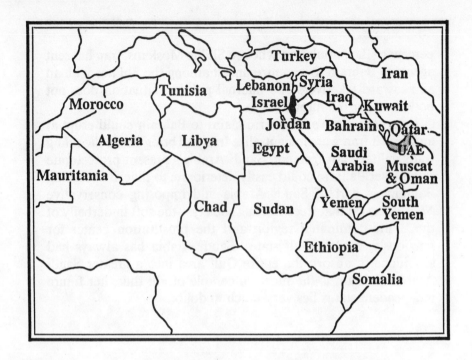

THE UNITED ARAB EMIRATES (UAE)

History

Until the nineteenth century, the area of the Gulf sheikdoms—historically called the "pirate coast" and currently comprised of Abu Dhabi, Ajman, Dubai, Fujira, Ras al-Khaima, Sharjah, and Umm al Qaiwain—was known for its pearl fishing, smuggling, and intertribal warfare. With British mediation, an 1820 treaty that brought about peace among the sheikdoms developed into an 1853 truce and the acquisition of the name Trucial States. These agreements culminated in the 1892 treaty—mediated and signed by Great Britain as in other Gulf principalities—that gave Great Britain protectorate status but left internal affairs to the local sheiks. Rivalries among the sheikdoms, often violent, continued.

In 1955, Britain intervened militarily when Saudi Arabian troops occupied a portion of Abu Dhabi—the Burhaimi Oasis—in a classical regional border dispute. Later, Iran attempted to occupy three islands in the Strait of Hormuz—Greater Tunb and Lesser Tunb, which had been controlled by Ras al-Khaima, and Abu Musa, which was held by Sharjah. Although Iran negotiated a division of authority and oil revenues, these three islands later became an issue that helped to "justify" Iraq's invasion of Iran in September 1980.

Discussions about the formation of a federal union to include the seven trucial states as well as Bahrain and Qatar were begun by the British after they announced their intention to leave the Gulf area by 1971. Bahrain, Qatar, and, at first, Ras al-Khaima declined to join the Federation of Arab Emirates, later renamed the UAE (and joined, shortly thereafter, by Ras al-Khaima).

Abu Dhabi, the largest oil exporter of the emirates, had already become a major Gulf oil producer by the time of independence in 1971. Oil was also discovered in Dubai and, later, in Sharjah and Ras al-Khaima. The oil boom of the 1970s brought with it the influx of a gigantic foreign labor force and a huge expansion in the federal budget, including expenditures for defense, social services, and infrastructure development. This created a serious problem when the oil glut of the 1980s forced the emirates to enter into deficit spending. Construction and new infrastructure development were severely curtailed and the expatriate population cut back.

Present

The UAE is strategically located along the southern Persian Gulf, which provides her northern coastline of nearly 1,000 miles. She occupies approximately 84,000 sq km (32,500 sq mi) and is bounded by Oman on the east and Saudi Arabia on the south and west. Iran lies on the other side of the Gulf. Over 97 percent of the land is desert, waste, or urban; about 2.5 percent is pastured; and less than .5 percent is arable—the Burhaimi and Liwa oases.

Of the UAE's total population of 1,850,000, only 19 percent are native inhabitants of the emirates; 23 percent are foreign Arabs; 50 percent are South Asian (mostly Indian and Pakistani); and 8 percent are other expatriates. Religiously, the population is 96 percent Moslem (80 percent Sunni, 20 percent Shi'ite), and 4 percent are Christian, Hindu, and other. Although the official language is Arabic, English is the language of commerce. The literacy rate is officially estimated at 56.3 percent.

Abu Dhabi, the largest of the emirates in territory and population, is the capital of the federation. The internal boundaries of the sheikdoms remain a maze as a result of centuries of tribal rivalries.

Politically, the UAE is a federation of seven member states which are sheikdoms. A provisional constitution, signed December 1971, delegated specific powers to the UAE central government and other powers to the seven sheikdoms. There are no elections and no political parties. The legal system is influenced and guided by Islamic law, while the executive power lies with a supreme council composed of representatives of the seven emirates. The council elects a president and vice president who are assisted by a council of ministers that is headed by a prime minister. Both the prime minister and the council of ministers are selected and controlled by the supreme council. Rivalry among the emirates is so great that it has led to much infrastructure redundancy, for example, two modern international airports only a short distance from each other.

There is a continuing internal political rivalry between Abu Dhabi—the largest oil producer—and Dubai—the only emirate with any pre-oil income other than from pearling or fishing. Abu Dhabi wants a strong, centralized union of the emirates which she, as the largest and wealthiest, would presumably dominate. Dubai, the most cosmopolitan of the sheikdoms, proposes a looser federation in order to preserve her cosmopolitan identity. Abu Dhabi has been able to attain the political support of the smaller non-oil-producing sheikdoms.

Internally, the UAE suffers from the same sociopolitical problems as her other Gulf state neighbors. A massive labor force of foreigners to help in the oil fields and man the bureaucracy, which in Abu Dhabi alone represents half of the population, is sowing the seeds of discontentment. Political pressures for greater democratization emanate from Western-educated, younger groups. Although the federation has a common foreign policy, the individual emirates often speak with several voices.

Economically, the UAE is a society focused primarily on oil production, with minor exports of dried fish, dates, and pearls. Her GNP is estimated at $26.4 billion—$17,000 per capita.

Militarily, the UAE spends approximately $2 billion per year on defense—nearly 45 percent of her total budget—making her the largest defense spender per capita in the world. She maintains 43,000 men in the armed forces, most of whom are foreign—

traditionally, 60 percent have been Omani. Another 11 percent are accounted for by the 5,000 Moroccan troops that have been incorporated into the UAE army recently. Although the armed forces are, theoretically, integrated, Dubai actually maintains her own military force of 6,000 men. Until integration is complete, consequently, there are two military forces—the federal forces and Dubai's forces.

The relatively large oil reserves of the UAE, her location along the Gulf, her proximity to Iran, her relatively large Shi'ite population, her high percentage of foreign workers, and her low population density make her extremely vulnerable to aggression from without as well as from within. She is almost totally indefendable, given the size of her population and population density. During the tanker war of 1986 to 1987 in the Gulf, a number of bombing raids struck her facilities, presumably, by error, although it hasn't been substantiated whether by Iranian or Iraqi planes.

Future

As with most Gulf states, the future of the UAE is threatened by both internal and external sources. Although the most immediate internal threat is the foment of troubles—particularly in Dubai—from the Iranian revolution, there are several other problematic situations. The political struggle between those who favor a strong, centralized power and those who prefer a looser federation will persist. The vast differences between the Bedouin traditions of most of the emirates and the freewheeling, sea-going, smuggling traditions of Dubai are a potential source of instability. The massive percentage of foreign workers and the cries for further democratization of younger educated groups also represent serious threats to internal stability. Another potential source of trouble is the great number of Shi'ites that inhabit the UAE who are basic adversaries of the Sunni sheikdoms.

Externally, any political change in Saudi Arabia could spell the end to the independence of the UAE—an area Saudi Arabia has always coveted. A decisive victory by either Iran or Iraq in their ongoing struggle, likewise, would mean an eventual end to the existing political independence of the emirates. The future of the UAE is bleak.

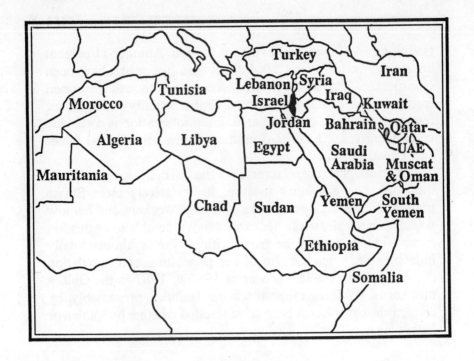

QATAR

History

Qatar, like her Gulf neighbors, was an undeveloped sheikdom relying on fishing and pearling before oil was discovered. She was ruled by Persia (Iran) and then, in 1776, came under the control of Bahrain's Khalifa Dynasty. In 1868, in exchange for tribute, Britain negotiated a Bahraini withdrawal from Qatar and installed the al-Thani clan as Qatar's rulers. (Although the peninsula was occupied by Ottoman Turks in 1872, they never really controlled the area.) Qatar became a British protectorate in 1916; then, upon Britain's withdrawal from the Gulf in 1971, Qatar became a fully independent state. Conflicts and rivalries within the ruling family have continuously marred internal politics.

Although oil was discovered in 1940, World War II delayed production until the late 1940s. Because of the rapid expansion of the oil industry, there was a huge influx of foreign laborers (who now comprise over half the population). In addition, rapidly acquired prosperity by the native Qataris resulted in their social isolation from these foreigners. Oil revenues were used to expand the economy, to build a communications infrastructure (ports, roads), and to establish a network of social/educational services and institutions, including a university.

Present

Qatar, a small peninsula jutting north into the Persian Gulf from the Arabian Peninsula, occupies 11,500 sq km (4,200 sq mi), nearly all of which is desert, waste, or urban. Her land borders are shared by Saudi Arabia on the southwest and the UAE on the south. Well over half of her 410,000 population reside in Doha, her capital and only major city; another 30 percent reside in Musay'id. Approximately 80 percent of her residents are foreign expatriates. Of her total population, 45 percent are Arab (20 percent Qatari, 25 percent other Arab); 10 to 20 percent are Iranian; and 40 to 50 percent are Indian, Pakistani, and other. Religiously, 95 percent are Moslem—mostly followers of the Sunni-Wahhabi sect—but expatriates include Christians, Hindus, and others. Arabic is the official language; the literacy rate is reported to be 40 percent.

Politically, The State of Qatar is a traditional monarchy under the reign of the Sunni-Moslem al-Thani clan. Although a constitutional provision calls for an election (through limited suffrage) of part of the thirty-member advisory council, there has yet to be an election; all members are still appointed by and responsible to the *emir*.

Qatar's majority nonnative population precludes as puritanical an implementation of Islamic law as neighboring Saudi Arabia, but there are close ties between the two countries. There are continuing (but often quieted) disputes with Bahrain based on territorial claims and the long-standing rivalry between the two ruling dynasties. Qatar also has latent desert boundary disputes with Saudi Arabia and the UAE. The greatest external threat to Qatar, however, comes from Iran and the possibility of attack by her militant Shi'ite-Islamic Fundamentalists.

Perhaps an even greater threat to Qatar than those from outside attack is the internal threat of Iranian (or Libyan) subversion, as the number of Iranian Shi'ites residing in Qatar continues to increase. Additionally, internal stability is threatened by resentment of the privileges of the native Qatari minority by the majority expatriate population, and, to a lesser degree, by the quieted but long-standing conflict among members of the ruling al-Thani family.

Economically, Qatar depends upon her oil production, refining, and export. Her economic concerns over future oil reserves have recently been allayed because of the discovery of huge natural gas fields—among the world's largest. She provides economic aid to Arab and Islamic countries; she receives none. Her GNP is approximately $5.1 billion—$15,723 per capita.

Militarily, Qatar's armed forces are primarily concerned with internal security and the protection of the monarchy from internal threats. She has 6,000 men under arms with an annual military expenditure of $166 million—only a little over 2 percent of her GNP. She depends on military assistance from Saudi Arabia and the other GCC countries should she face the probability of external attack.

Future

Since the Qatari and Saudi societies are both Wahhabi (Sunni-Islamic Fundamentalist) and their territories share a common border, Qatar's destiny as an independent state is tightly linked to that of the Saudi monarchy—a collapse of the Saudi monarchy in the future would spell the demise of the Qatari monarchy as well. Even with the continued existence of the Saudi monarchy, Qatar is dependent upon its good will. Any collapse of government within the Gulf states would have a great impact on the independent status of Qatar.

It is highly unlikely that Qatar (or any of the other Gulf states) would be able to maintain her present political status given the emergence of a clear-cut victor in the Iraq-Iran conflict. An Iranian victory in that war would surely result in the presence in Qatar of Iranian Shi'ite-Islamic-Fundamentalist agents for the purpose of instigating a revolution—a not-too-difficult task to accomplish, given there are already in Qatar many resentful, dis-enfranchised Iranian-Shi'ite expatriates. Should Iraq emerge the victor in the war, the Iraqi-Ba'athist party would, likewise, instigate a revolution in Qatar (and in the other Gulf states as well) in order to further its Pan-Arab cause. Qatar's security as an independent state depends on the continuation of the Iraq-Iran War either as a stalemate, as it was for so long, or as it is at a temporary cease-fire—a respite from war—during which each country would use the time to rebuild her forces in preparation for the war's resumption.

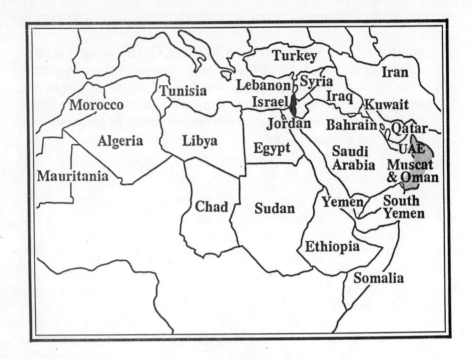

OMAN

History

Because of Oman's location on the southeastern corner of the Arabian Peninsula, she has always had closer ties with South Asia and East Africa—accessible by sea—than she has with her neighbor, Saudi Arabia, from which she is separated by a vast impassable desert. As a result of her imperialistic endeavors, for centuries Oman maintained colonies in Persia and India, and until as recently as the 1960s, a branch of the Omani Dynasty ruled over Zanzibar in East Africa.

During the lifetime of the Prophet Mohammed, Oman converted to Islam but soon rejected both Sunni and Shi'ite principles in favor of those of the Khariji sect—the Ibadi branch, in particular. Historically, there has been a conflict between the undeveloped interior—still tribal and energetically Ibadi—and the more cosmopolitan coastal area, especially the capital, Muscat.

In 1741, the Turks were expelled from Oman, and, in 1749, the currently ruling Al Bu Sa'id Dynasty was established. Throughout most of this dynasty's reign, an *imamate*—

established by strict Ibadi tribes and ruled by *imams* representative of the Ibadi sect—has been maintained. In the 1920 Treaty of Sib, Al Bu Sa'id Sultan of Muscat—supported by the British—was recognized as ruler over the interior. In 1950, Ghalib, a new *imam* from the interior, rebelled, with Saudi Arabian support. However, by 1959, the British had ousted the Saudis and terminated Ghalib's rebellion. Although British military activity was more substantial in Oman than in most other nearby areas, Oman was not a protectorate in the same way as other Gulf states.

Oman was kept isolated by the Sultan Sa'id bin Taimur, who maintained slavery, hoarded revenues from the country's newfound oil, and forbade the construction of roads and schools. Until his overthrow in 1970 by his son, Qabus, who was supported by the British, Oman was one of the most backward countries in the world. Immediately upon becoming sultan, Qabus abolished slavery and began to use oil revenues to implement a modernization program.

By that time (1970), however, guerrilla activities in Dhofar province were threatening the Omani sultanate. Followers of the deposed *Imam* Ghalib and rebellious slaves had formed the Popular Front for the Liberation of the Arabian Gulf (PFLAG), which soon after became the Popular Front for the Liberation of Oman (PFLO), and adopted the principles of Marxism. (When South Yemen gained her independence in 1967, she became an ally to and supplier for the PFLO.) Qabus solicited help from Iran in suppressing the rebel forces in Dhofar. The sultan's armed forces were staffed by British officers, and British, Jordanian, and Iranian troops lent support. Having driven the PFLO out of most of Dhofar province, Qabus declared the war over in 1975.

Since 1981, Oman has been joined with other traditional Gulf states in the GCC where defense cooperation activities and the construction of new pipelines across Oman—avoiding the dangers of the Strait of Hormuz—are being planned. As a result of resurgent uprisings on Oman's South Yemen border early in 1982, a "normalization" accord between the two countries, mediated by the UAE and Kuwait, was reached in June of the same year. U.S. maneuvers in the area in December 1982 and in 1983 and 1985 were protested by South Yemen.

Oman has historically demonstrated her courage to stand

"alone" among, and perhaps even alienate, other Arab nations. Her closer ties with East Africa and South Asia than with Arabia and her adoption of Khariji Islam are early examples. Her status as an oil-producing Arab nation that is not a member of OPEC, her alliance with Iran, her support of Sadat in his Egyptian-Israeli peace effort, and her ties with the United States are later examples of her "independence."

Present

Oman covers approximately 300,000 sq km (120,000 sq mi) on the southeastern corner of the Arabian Peninsula. She borders South Yemen on her southwest, Saudi Arabia on her west, and the UAE on her northwest. Her enclave on the northern most point of the Musandam Peninsula controls the Strait of Hormuz on the Persian Gulf; her capital, Muscat, faces east toward the Gulf of Oman and the Arabian Sea; her western province, Dhofar, faces south into the Indian Ocean. The vast majority of her land (95.1 percent) is desert, waste, or urban, while only fractional parts are either pastures and meadows (4.7 percent) or agricultural (0.2 percent).

Ethnically, her population, estimated between 1.27 and 1.5 million, is approximately 80 percent Omani Arab but includes as many as 15 percent Indians, and smaller numbers of Pakistanis (mostly Baluchis), Iranians, Bengalis, and others. Religiously, Oman is the only Kharijite-Islamic country; over 86 percent of her population are Moslem, nearly all of whom are Ibadi, with some Sunni and fewer Shi'ite. Approximately 13 percent of the population is Hindu. The official language is Arabic, but English is commonly used in government and business. Baluchi, Urdu, and Indian dialects are also spoken. Oman's reported literacy rate varies from 20 to 30 percent.

Politically, Oman—officially the Sultanate of Oman—is an absolute monarchy, currently led by Sultan Qabus bin Sa'id. His "cabinet" is more a royal court than a government body and his key ministers, more technocrats than politicians. The smooth functioning of his government is dependent upon expatriate support. Qabus' throne, in spite of minor sporadic threats, appears secure, although there is no apparent successor.

Oman maintains enormous strategic importance. Considering

her borders at the entrance to the Strait of Hormuz and with Saudi Arabia, the UAE, and Marxist-controlled South Yemen, the fall of Oman could spell disaster to the political integrity of the whole region. The Iraq-Iran War was—and is likely to be again—fought at her doorstep, and recent Iranian and Iraqi policies make her patrols of the Strait of Hormuz increasingly significant. Oman's strategic importance was magnified by the U.S. military escort of reflagged Kuwaiti tankers in the Gulf.

Economically, Oman is faced with the challenges of modernization. Although hurt somewhat by the international decline in oil prices, recent oil discoveries in the south have increased production and revenues. Her GNP approximates $8.3 billion—$6,730 per capita.

Militarily, Oman is in the midst of a gigantic build-up so that she can meet increasing challenges in her efforts to protect the Strait of Hormuz. Her military expenditures in support of an armed force of 21,500 men exceed $2 billion annually—over 37.5 percent of government spending. She receives Western assistance as well as help from her richer cohorts in the GCC.

Oman's continuing ten-year base-facility agreement with the United States, although hesitatingly reassessed in 1985 at its halfway point, demonstrates, publicly, her cooperation with the United States. She is one of only a few Gulf states to do so.

Future

Although Oman has developed significantly since 1970, she does not have the means between now and the turn of the century to establish the agricultural or industrial infrastructure sufficient to serve her economic stability. Remnants of the Dhofar War, tribal rivalries, and border disputes represent additional potential internal threats to the security of this absolute monarchy for which there is no apparent successor.

Oman is so important strategically to the West that it is highly unlikely any U.S. government—other than an extremely isolationist one—would allow her to be conquered by a local invading army. However, should an external force such as Iran or Iraq—if either decisively wins the war when it resumes—move to take over the entire Gulf region, U.S. intervention on Oman's behalf is unlikely.

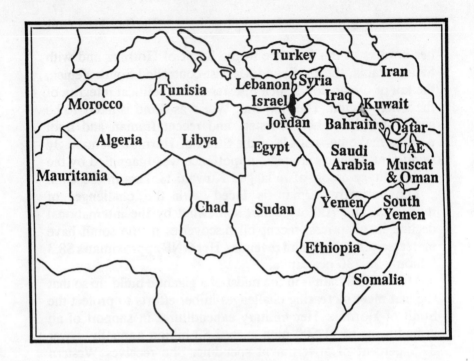

KUWAIT

History

The country known today as Kuwait, like other territories in the region, was inhabited for centuries by transient nomadic tribes. She became part of the Abbasyd Empire of Baghdad in A.D. 650 and from then until the eighteenth century was influenced by Baghdad. Known throughout much of her history for pearl fishing, Kuwait—previously called Qurain—was a popular stop for British and Portuguese traders.

The first tribe to settle in Kuwait—in 1710—was from Nejd, the eastern province of Arabia, but other tribes soon followed. In 1756, a leader among the tribes was selected, primarily to deal with pressure from the Ottoman Empire. The man selected was the first sheik of the al-Sabah Dynasty, to this day still Kuwait's ruling family.

During the nineteenth century, Kuwait was caught between the Ottoman Empire rule in Iraq and the Wahhabi movement representing the rising power of the house of Saud in Arabia. In 1899, Kuwaiti Sheik Mubarak the Great requested protection from the British in order to stay Ottoman rule. A protectorate status for Kuwait—similar to those of other Gulf sheikdoms—was negotiated, and a British military garrison was established there.

By 1910, the population of Kuwait, which had grown considerably, was still only 35,000. Having granted the first oil concessions in 1937, by the post-World War II period, Kuwait was rapidly becoming one of the world's richest nations. Although there had been a continuing direct positive British influence in maintaining the role of the al-Sabah sheik dating from 1756, in 1961, Kuwait became the first British protectorate in the Gulf to receive independent nationhood.

Within a week after her declaration of independence, Kuwait faced the challenge by Iraq's ruler, Kassem, that she was an integral part of Iraq—a claim rooted in the breakup of the Ottoman Empire in the wake of World War I. (During Ottoman rule, Kuwait had been a district under the indirect administration of the governor of Basra—capital of Southern Iraq.) The British, then Arab League forces, occupied Kuwait to thwart a planned Iraqi invasion.

As world demand for Arab oil mushroomed and Kuwait became a major export country, the need for immigrant laborers to operate the oil fields grew tremendously. From the mid-sixties until 1981, there was a huge influx of foreign workers—Palestinian-Jordanians, Egyptians, Syrians, Iraqis, South Asians, and East Asians.

The advent of the Iraq-Iran War, and the subsequent material and financial aid provided Iraq by the Kuwaiti government, placed Kuwait in mortal danger from Iranian-backed Shi'ite terrorists. They placed deadly car bombs in Kuwait to terrorize the community and destroy installations, and began a rash of assassinations of Iraqi diplomats.

Present

Kuwait, which encircles a protected harbor at the north end of the Persian Gulf, covers approximately 17,800 sq km (6,800 sq mi), including her islands. Nearly all her territory is either desert, waste, or urban; only 1 percent is cultivated. She borders Saudi Arabia on the south, Iraq on the north and west, and the Persian Gulf on the east. Because Kuwait City, the capital, is the only major city and is a major port, Kuwait is usually referred to as a "city-state."

While her total population estimates vary from 1,300,000 to 1,870,000, composition figures are relatively consistent: approximately 40 percent are native Kuwaiti and 60 percent are foreigners—expatriates from countries such as Iraq, Syria, Egypt, and Jordan. Of her total population, 78 percent are Arab (39 percent Kuwaiti and 39 percent non-Kuwaiti); 9 percent are South Asian (Indian, Pakistani, and Sri Lankan); 4 percent are Iranian; and 9 percent are other (including East Asians). Religiously, 85 percent are Moslem (70 percent Sunni and 30 percent Shi'ite), and 15 percent are Christian, Hindu, Parsee, and other. Arabic is the official language; English is the most commonly found foreign language; and Parsee and South Asian languages are spoken by the expatriates. Estimates of the literacy rate range from 55 to 70 percent and appear to be rising. This is most likely as a result of the creation of a new middle class. Educated administrators and teachers have been imported from Egypt and Jordan (Palestinian) to administer the social service bureaucracy and operate the school system.

The State of Kuwait, as she is legally known, is a constitutional monarchy headed by an *emir*. Since descendants of the original al-Sabah sheik have ruled continuously since 1756, today, Kuwait is the state with the longest ruling monarchy in the entire Arab world. By constitutional provision, there is a national constituent assembly elected by and comprised of male Kuwaiti citizens who represent the total electorate of 57,000—3.5 percent of the population. Although most of the members of the assembly support the *emir* and his government, at the present time (and on other occasions in the past), the assembly has been dissolved to reduce the threat of dissent.

By design of the sheik, there has been no economic investment in developing either an agricultural or industrial base other than in the petrochemical field. The sheik has no interest in development in any industrial area other than petrochemical for two major reasons: Kuwaiti citizens are too spoiled to work in industry, and the import of more foreign laborers would jeopardize further the stability of the regime. The need either to import or to desalinate 75 percent of her water makes agricultural pursuits impractical for Kuwait.

Kuwait's enormous oil wealth has enabled her to provide her *citizens* one of the world's highest standards of living, to create a sophisticated commercial center, to build an ultramodern transportation and communications infrastructure, and to invest vast financial reserves in foreign markets. Her GNP is approximately $25 billion—nearly $14,500 per capita.

Militarily, Kuwait supports 12,500 men under arms; her annual military expenditure is $1.6 billion—approximately 7 to 7.5 percent of her GNP. Her modernly equipped forces comprise part of the GCC. Kuwait is violently anti-Israel and has consistently provided financial support to the various terrorist factions of the PLO as well as to the confrontation states (Syria and Jordan) in their struggle against Israel.

Of all the nations in the Gulf, Kuwait has been placed in the greatest danger by the Iraq-Iran War. Almost from the inception of the confrontation, Kuwait provided Iraq with very substantial financial and material support in the form of grants and loans as well as the use of Kuwaiti port and airfield facilities. That support was viewed by Iran's ayatollah as a war-like act and provoked an Iranian military response. Iran's war with Iraq was fought close to Kuwait's border with Iraq. Kuwait was directly challenged militarily by the tanker war that took place in the Persian Gulf in which Iranian missiles and armed gunboats attacked tankers carrying Kuwaiti oil. The U.S. escort of reflagged Kuwaiti-owned tankers was a desperate attempt by Kuwait to limit Iran's challenge to the flow of Kuwaiti oil. Kuwait's financial as well as material support of Iraq in the Iraq-Iran conflict postponed, at least until the war's real (and final) termination, any territorial designs on Kuwait by Iraq.

Internally, Iranian terrorists have been organizing the Kuwaiti-Shi'ite population (30 percent of all Moslem nationals) to rise up against the monarchy and replace it with a Shi'ite-Islamic-Fundamentalist nation. Another internal threat to Kuwait's monarchy comes from the growing *majority* of disenfranchised foreign Arab residents whose income and available social services are only a fraction of those of the Kuwaiti nationals and who bitterly resent the prerogatives of the local minority.

Future

Threats to the survival of the independent status of Kuwait as a nation and/or to the Kuwaiti monarchy will emanate from a number of sources.

Internally, the threats will continue to come from the growing Arab majority of disenfranchised foreign residents and from the potential rise to power of the Shi'ites who would establish an Islamic-Fundamentalist state. In either case, since all administrative services and government activity are centered in Kuwait City, a takeover could be effectuated by a relatively small number.

Externally, threats will come from Saudi Arabia, Iran, and Iraq. Should a revolutionary Islamic government arise in Saudi Arabia, Kuwait would be overtaken and probably divided between Saudi Arabia and Iraq—as Poland was divided between Russia and Germany in 1940. Should there be an Iranian military conquest of all or just the south of Iraq, Kuwait would be overtaken and would become a Shi'ite-Islamic-Fundamentalist nation.

Since 60 percent of Iraq's population is Shi'ite, a revolution could take place, and Iraq could become Shi'ite governed. Should this occur, then, too, Kuwait would be overthrown and become a Shi'ite-Fundamentalist nation. Iraq has never recognized Kuwait as an independent entity; in fact, on all Iraqi maps, Kuwait is shown as part of Iraq. There have been many border clashes, and only pressure from the Arab League—in addition to the long-lasting Iraq-Iran War—temporarily contained Iraq from occupying and annexing Kuwait. Should Iraq emerge the real victor in her conflict with Iran, she would renew her Kuwaiti territorial claim. Militarily, Kuwait is no match for Iraq, so the monarchy would fall and the Iraqi-Pan-Arabist/Socialist-Ba'ath party would reign.

The only hope for the preservation of the Kuwaiti monarchy is the continuation of the Iraq-Iran War as is—in a temporary cease-fire during which the two countries can rebuild their forces in preparation for the war's resumption—or in a stalemate, as previously existed for so long. Otherwise, there is no future for Kuwait as an independent state.

The Yemens

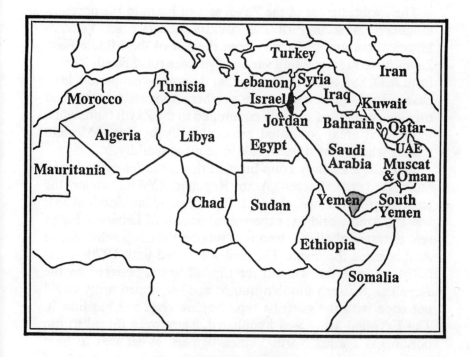

NORTH YEMEN
YEMEN ARAB REPUBLIC (YAR)

History

Yemen, often referred to as North Yemen to distinguish her from her neighbor, South Yemen, has a history that can be traced back to 1000 B.C. Classically famous for her spices, which she traded throughout the ancient world, North Yemen was the area noted in the Old Testament as the "Kingdom of Sheba" (from which the Queen of Sheba originated). The early kingdoms, whose inhabitants were speakers of a semitic language, were succeeded by the Himyarites. There were close ties with Ethiopia, which had been colonized from Yemen. From early on, Christians and Jews resided in Yemen, and there were rulers of both faiths.

By the sixth century, Yemen had become a battleground between Persia and Ethiopia, and by the seventh century, Islam had arrived. Yemen became a Moslem nation while retaining (until 1948) a sizable Jewish population.

The establishment of the Zaydi sect of Islam in the northern mountainous section of the country underscored Yemen's historical cultural difference from the rest of the Middle East. Zaydi *imams* representing various dynasties ruled North Yemen from A.D. 898 to 1962. During that thousand-year period, little changed in the country—the northern mountains remained tribal in nature and strongly committed to the Zaydi faith, while the coastal area, populated predominantly by Sunni-Moslem traders who resented *imam* rule, was more worldly.

In 1962, a military coup brought down the *Imam* Badr and established the Yemen Arab Republic (YAR) under the leadership of Abdullah al-Sallal. This triggered the bloodiest civil war the Arab world has experienced outside of Lebanon. Egypt sent upwards of 40,000 troops to support the coup, while Saudi Arabia aided the *imam*. The civil war lasted until 1970—after Sallal was overthrown and the capital, San'a, besieged by the Royalists. Nasser's modern-trained and -equipped army could not cope with the guerrilla-type warfare conducted against it. The Egyptian army was humiliated. They were forced to use poison gas against North Yemen fighters. What was to be a quick, easy victory for Egypt turned out to be years of embarrassment and a high cost in men and material. By 1971, after almost ten years of bitter fighting, there was relative peace. The new government was a compromise—a republican government with a pro-Saudi and tribal orientation.

Border wars between the YAR and the PDRY flared during 1972 and 1973 and, in 1974, Ibrahim al-Hamdi seized power. Hamdi, who became very popular, moved away from Saudi Arabia, retained close ties with the West (the United States and Europe), and encouraged ties with the USSR. He also tried to improve relations with South Yemen. The Saudis were dissatisfied with Hamdi, and he was assassinated in 1977. His successor, Ahmad al-Ghashmi, was more pro-Saudi, but he, too, was assassinated in June 1978. Ghashmi was succeeded by North Yemen's current president, Ali-Abdullah Saleh. Again, in 1979, border disputes between North and South Yemen erupted. Saleh requested and was granted aid from the United States, but when Saudi Arabia interfered, he accepted aid from the USSR.

Although Saleh made gallant efforts to maintain a careful balance between pressures from Saudi Arabia and South Yemen as well as between the Saudi-supported tribes of the north and the PDRY-supported tribes of the south, between 1981 and 1987, border disputes and internal disruptions continued.

Present

North Yemen contains the only fertile land in Arabia naturally watered by a regular monsoon. Because of undemarcated and disputed borders, her area estimates vary from 120,000 sq km (46,160 sq mi) according to British sources to 200,000 sq km (77,200 sq mi) as reported by the YAR government. The Swiss Technical Cooperation Service, however, indicates her area is 135,200 sq km (52,210 sq mi). Twenty percent of the land is agricultural; 1 percent is forested; and 79 percent is desert, waste, or urban. Located on the southwestern corner of the Arabian Peninsula, North Yemen borders Saudi Arabia from northwest to northeast, South Yemen on the southeast, and the Red Sea on the west. Much of her land borders, however, remain undefined and, therefore, a cause for political tension.

North Yemen's population of approximately 8.3 million represents nearly half the population of the entire Arabian Peninsula. Ninety percent are Arab and 10 percent Afro-Arab. Religiously, the population is almost 100 percent Moslem—40 percent Sunni and 60 percent Zaydi (Shi'ite). The language spoken is exclusively Arabic. The official literacy rate of 15 percent is most probably exaggerated.

Politically, North Yemen, officially known as the Yemen Arab Republic (YAR), is a republic controlled by the military. There are no elections and no legal political parties; it is a virtual military dictatorship run by President Saleh, who appoints a cabinet headed by a prime minister for "assistance."

North Yemen is of key importance on the international scene. She is the major center of population and cultivated land on the Arabian Peninsula. Strategically located just above the Strait of Bab el Mandeb—at the choke point between the Red Sea and the Indian Ocean—she borders pro-Western Saudi Arabia on one side and pro-Soviet South Yemen on the other and lies across the Strait from pro-Western Somalia, pro-Soviet Ethiopia, and French-supported Djibouti. Hers is a politically precarious position.

Economically, North Yemen is a rudimentary agrarian society which concentrates her agricultural efforts on growing a narcotic called *qat,* mostly for domestic use—it is chewed daily by most male adult Yemenis—but also as an export commodity. As a result, domestic agricultural potential has been blighted, and other export crops have suffered. Wealth and economic progress anticipated when oil was discovered in late 1984 have yet to be realized. North Yemen's $4.15 billion GNP—$600 per capita—makes her one of the poorest nations in the world, in a class with Sudan and Bangladesh. Much of North Yemen's male population has found employment in Saudi Arabia, and their cash remittances have made that the single largest item of foreign currency in the YAR balance of payments.

Militarily, North Yemen spends approximately $600 million a year on defense, while maintaining 36,500 men in the armed forces. Her military structure, however, remains inadequate to defend against attack, particularly by the PDRY, because tribal allegiances still dominate the society. Saleh has maintained a balance in arms purchases from the East and the West, and North Yemeni air bases are among the few in the world to have had both U.S. and Soviet advisers present, simultaneously, on the same base.

Future

Disputes between the YAR's northern and southern tribes will remain a threat to internal security. Certainly, the Zaydi clans in the north will continue to resist change, and the tribes of the south will continue to resist the influence of the Zaydi sect. Border disputes with both Saudi Arabia and South Yemen (PDRY) will continue to be an acute cause for concern and may become a more serious problem given the recent discovery of oil in commercial quantities.

The major military threat to North Yemen continues to be South Yemen. Even though North Yemen has two and one-half times the population of South Yemen, the Marxist nation is extremely militant and highly organized. While both Yemens conceptually agree on a unified Yemen, it appears highly unlikely that the coastal plain people of Marxist-run South Yemen could come to terms with the tribal Islamic-Fundamentalist mountain people of Saudi-backed North Yemen.

Yemeni concern about Saudi control of northern tribes will remain a source of contention as will Saudi concern about North Yemen's desire for the return of the Dizan and Najran provinces (yielded to Saudi Arabia in 1932). Since the Saudis fear a takeover of the YAR by the PDRY, they will continue to arm the YAR during periods of threat.

Her location just above the Bab el Mandeb Strait, straddled on either side by Eastern- and Western-oriented nations, places North Yemen in an extremely unenviable position. The future independent status of this nation is questionable. Between internal strife and external forces, it is doubtful that this government or an independent status can survive through the balance of this century.

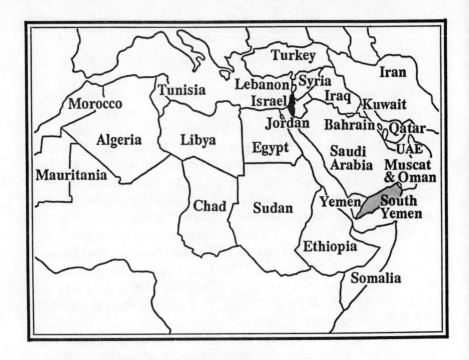

SOUTH YEMEN
PEOPLES DEMOCRATIC REPUBLIC OF YEMEN
(PDRY)

History

Between 1200 B.C. and A.D. 525, South Yemen was part of the Minaean, Sabaean, and Himyarite kingdoms. The Ethiopians and then the Persians ruled the area until the seventh century when Islam overran the entire region. The coastal regions were subsequently dominated by the Egyptian and Ottoman Empires.

British control of the region in the nineteenth century marked the beginning of South Yemen's "modern" history. Several treaties with tribal sheiks were concluded, and the city of Aden was developed into an important port for British trade and naval routes. From the vantage point of Aden, the British could control and protect the Bab el Mandeb Strait and, indirectly, the Suez Canal. By the time Britain withdrew from Aden and South Yemen in 1967, she left behind a thriving harbor and major military installations.

By the mid-1970s, South Yemen was fast becoming a Soviet

"friend," moving along the path of "scientific socialism." With Soviet military and economic assistance, South Yemen became an unfriendly neighbor to both North Yemen and Oman. In 1977, she waged war with Oman and, in 1979, launched an invasion of North Yemen. In each case, South Yemen failed to achieve victory because of outside interference—Iran saved Oman, and Iraqi, Jordanian, and Syrian intervention saved North Yemen.

In January 1986, a civil war broke out in Aden between the two major factions—those urging better relations with the Arab world against those favoring full dedication to the world Marxist revolution. While the civil war didn't last long, it was extremely bloody. Both sides used maximum firepower and caused the deaths of 10,000 people—a devastating toll on South Yemen. The fighting demonstrated that tribal allegiances had not been wiped out in the "tribe-free, classless" South Yemen.

This civil war decapitated the entire leadership of the country. The key figures either died or fled into Ethiopia. Although a new pro-Soviet leadership emerged, the fighting had virtually destroyed the old politburo and soured relations with Ethiopia.

Present

South Yemen is located in the southern part of the Arabian Peninsula and is bordered on the north by Saudi Arabia, on the northwest by North Yemen (YAR), on the south by the Gulf of Aden and the Arabian Sea (the northwestern part of the Indian Ocean), and on the east by the sultanate of Oman. Many of the boundaries of South Yemen's approximate 330,000 sq km (127,400 sq mi) are undefined, a cause for constant tension and concern over border disputes. Only 1 percent of the land is arable and less than half of that is cultivated. The vast majority of the land is desert and other waste; only the coastal area is urban.

South Yemen's population of approximately 2.3 million is 92 percent Arab and the balance Indian, Somali, and European. Religiously, the vast majority are Sunni Moslem with some Christian and Hindu. The primary language is Arabic, although some English is spoken, primarily, in Aden. The official literacy rate of South Yemen is 25 percent and is purported to be the world's fastest growing. This is most probably due to the influence over the society of the Marxist regime utilizing compulsory education (indoctrination) to influence and consolidate its hold over the population.

Politically, South Yemen, officially known as the People's Democratic Republic of Yemen (PDRY), is a republic with power centered in the ruling Yemeni-Socialist party—a Marxist-Leninist vanguard party and the sole political party permitted. The constitution provides for suffrage for all citizens over eighteen years of age; however, the last election for the legislature was in 1978. Although others have been announced since then, none have taken place. The country is run by the chairman of the presidium who, as in all other Communist countries, is appointed by the "Party." Haydar Abu Bakr al'-Attas, the present chairman, heads a faction of technocrats and managers. South Yemen is a part of the Soviet bloc of nations.·

Economically, South Yemen is a rudimentary agrarian society with a major petroleum refining industry (that operates when crude is available) located at Aden, her major port. Cotton is the major agricultural export. South Yemen's approximate $1.13 billion GNP—$490 per capita—makes her one of the poorest nations in the world. Although South Yemen covers an area more than twice the size of North Yemen, her population is less than 30 percent that of North Yemen, yielding her a population density roughly on par with that of her northern neighbor, Saudi Arabia.

Militarily, South Yemen spends approximately $200 million per year on defense—well over 17 percent of her GNP. She maintains 27,500 men in the armed forces. As the only Marxist-Leninist nation in the Arab world, South Yemen is of enormous strategic importance. She, along with Ethiopia (the other Marxist-Leninist state in the area), controls the Strait of Bab el Mandeb. While South Yemen herself does not have the military strength to keep the Bab el Mandeb closed, substantial deployment of Soviet forces in South Yemen—presently 10,000 technical advisers and 44,000 troops—during a major war would create a serious problem for a nation trying to neutralize that power to keep the Bab el Mandeb open.

The Soviets have replaced the British at Aden and control the area around South Yemen. They maintain five air bases in the area with a command headquarters in Aden. Additionally, a Soviet fleet headquarters command is based there. During the past decade, Soviet, Cuban, and east European military activities have increased. The Soviet Union is continually expanding her military presence in South Yemen—building bases and upgrading facilities—which now includes new air defense missile batteries.

During the January 1986 civil war, when South Yemen's armed forces were severely damaged and a high percentage of its command and leadership were either killed or exiled, a large portion of the navy defected to Ethiopia. Many of the ships were not returned for months. The process of rebuilding the military is presently taking place.

Future

This Marxist Soviet-backed Arab nation will pose a serious threat to her neighbors now that the Soviet military maintains such a large military presence. Border disputes with Saudi Arabia, North Yemen, and Oman will continue to play a part in South Yemen's geopolitical behavior. The discovery of a major oil-bearing area in North Yemen and its forthcoming oil production would make it a valuable prize for South Yemen as a source of oil for her port and petroleum-refining facilities at Aden. The union of South Yemen with North Yemen, under South Yemen's control, remains the number one policy goal of this Marxist-Leninist state. A united Yemen under Marxist-Leninist leadership would pose a serious threat to Oman, a real nuisance to Saudi Arabia, and another worry for Western interests in the region.

The Maghreb Nations

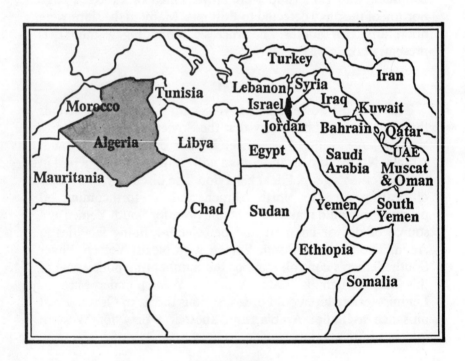

ALGERIA

History

North Africa was inhabited in ancient times by Berbers. The area became part of the Byzantine Empire; then, by the end of the seventh century A.D., Arab armies took over northwestern Africa or Barbary—so named because of its predominantly Berber population—from the Byzantines. Algeria was a vaguely defined region situated between Morocco and Tunisia, both of which were historically prominent civilizations. Although the Moslem conquest did not lead to the settlement of the country by Arabs, the Berber inhabitants of the Algerian territory converted to Islam—sometimes to orthodox but often to heterodox varieties. In classical Arab terms, northwest Africa was referred to as the Maghreb, and Algeria was called the "Middle Maghreb" to distinguish her from the "Farther Maghreb"—Morocco—and the "Nearer Maghreb"—Tunisia.

Between the eighth and fifteenth centuries, several different kingdoms rose and fell in Algeria, often pitting Eastern and Western influences of the times against each other. The Christian reconquest of Spain in 1492 unleashed an influx of Spanish Moslems into Algeria. Islamic-Spanish forces occupied several coastal positions, including a harbor protected by islands referred to in Arabic as "the islands," which in corrupted Arabic became Algiers. The local sultan accepted a Spanish protectorate, and the payment of tribute was levied by Spain in many cities. The Moslem population appealed to the Turkish pirates for help.

The Ottoman Turks expelled the Spanish from Algeria in the sixteenth century, and Algeria became a vassal state of the Ottoman Empire. The Barbary pirates controlled the coastal area and made Algiers a flourishing city during the seventeenth century. They became less active during the eighteenth century and the early years of the nineteenth, when Algeria declined in importance.

In 1830, the French took over Algeria and remained there for 132 years. The French occupation was strictly a colonial one. France, determined to make Algeria French, encouraged her citizens to settle there and also encouraged Greek, Italian, and Maltese settlement in the area. Arabic was not taught in the schools, and the Moslems were denied political rights. By the 1900s, Algeria had been incorporated into metropolitan France, and the local population was denied political rights unless they literally cut themselves off from Islam.

Throughout the period of French occupation, resistance to French domination existed whenever there was a leader to organize it. In 1954, under leadership based in Cairo, a bloody revolution for Algerian national independence began and was waged for eight years. During that period, one French government after another fell because of that revolution. All the

Arab countries supported the Algerian revolution, including Morocco and Tunisia—once they received their independent status. In 1962, Charles De Gaulle negotiated Algeria's independence.

The new independent nation of Algeria became a radical state which, eventually, devoted most of her energies and oil revenues from the Sahara inward to building the nation rather than outward for adventurism. She has taken an aggressive stance in her historic dispute with Morocco. Algeria has actively opposed Morocco's annexation of the western Sahara not only by supporting materially the Polisario front but also by allowing the Polisario to operate from bases in western Algeria.

Algeria has undergone a continuous process of Arabization— a process which has been opposed by an Algerian elite who are barely literate in Arabic and use French as their basic language. The attempt to teach only Arabic in the Algerian school system has not only been opposed by the French-speaking urban Arab elite but also by the Berber-speaking people in the mountain regions.

Algeria became a member of the front for steadfastness and confrontation joining Libya, the PDRY, the PLO, and Syria. However, Algeria has supported Tunisia in her growing tensions with Libya to the point of sending troops to the Tunisian border.

Present

Algeria's approximately 2,400,000 sq km (920,000 sq mi) makes her by far the largest of all the Maghreb states—in fact, one of the ten largest countries in the world. However, like her neighbor, Libya, she is 80 percent desert, waste, or urban with only 3 percent of the land cultivated and 17 percent pasture, meadows, or wooded. Algeria is located along the Mediterranean coast of North Africa. She borders Libya and Tunisia on the east, Niger to the southeast, Mali and Mauritania to the southwest, and Morocco and the Spanish Sahara to the west.

Algeria's present population of approximately 23 million is 99 percent Arab Berber and less than 1 percent European. Religiously, 99 percent are Sunni Moslem and 1 percent are Christian. The state religion is Sunni Moslem. Arabic is the official state language and is spoken by approximately 80 percent of the Algerians; however, nearly 20 percent speak Berber, and French is the major foreign language. The official literacy rate is 52 percent.

Politically, Algeria, officially known as the Democratic and Popular Republic of Algeria, is an independent Socialist republic. She is a highly centralized Islamic single-party state.

Algeria is an OPEC nation. Economically, her main source of income is from petroleum and natural gas which account for 98 percent of her export income. Algeria's GNP is $55.2 billion—$2,530 per capita.

Militarily, Algeria spends approximately $1 billion annually on defense, while maintaining 169,000 men under arms. This represents a reduction from the $1.5 billion previously budgeted for defense and reflects a drop in oil income. The Soviet Union has been the major arms supplier to Algeria—between 1980 and 1985 she supplied Algeria with $3.5 billion worth of weapon systems. The basic role of the Algerian armed forces is to maintain the security of the regime and the governance of the nation. They must be prepared to deal with the unresolved border dispute with Morocco and the challenge from Morocco created by Algeria's provision of bases for the Polisario in eastern Algeria.

Future

Algeria is presently one of the radical Arab states that opposes peace with Israel under any terms and supports those forces bent on the destruction of the Jewish state. There is no serious external threat to the present Algerian government; however, Islamic Fundamentalists inspired by Khomeini have been operating effectively within Algeria; therefore, she would not be immune to the effects of a wave of Islamic fundamentalism in the area.

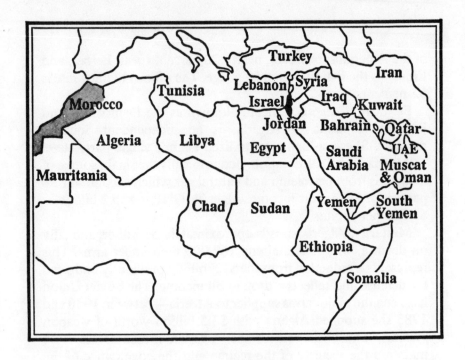

MOROCCO

History

Because of her location—on the Strait of Gibraltar—Morocco, since ancient times, has been an important strategic prize. She was home to ancient Carthaginian colonies and an integral part of the Roman Empire.

During the seventh and eighth centuries A.D., Morocco was conquered by Arab forces and converted to Islam. Arabic replaced Berber as the spoken language. Morocco began her long history of independence in 788 and by the sixteenth century had become a sultanate of great significance. The great Moroccan empires of the sixteenth and seventeenth centuries extended deep into the Sahara. Although she was able to confront Spanish expansion and maintain her diplomatic ties with other European countries for an extended period of time, by the early twentieth century, Morocco was threatened by European colonial expansion. In 1912, she was partitioned by the European powers into Tangier—an international city, French Morocco, and the Spanish territories.

French Morocco gained independence in 1956, and most of

the Spanish territories were incorporated soon thereafter. The Spanish Sahara—maintained by Madrid until 1975—and the towns of Ceuta and Melilla opposite Gibraltar remain a thorny issue in Morocco's various international affairs. The battle for the former Spanish Sahara has continued for more than ten years and has led to strained relationships for Morocco with Algeria, Mauritania, and even the United States.

Morocco's King Hassan called an emergency Arab summit for August 1985 to address the Hussein-Arafat-Arab-Israeli peace initiative. He had not consulted with all the other Arab states; and Algeria, Lebanon, South Yemen, and Syria refused to attend. Although inconclusive, the summit did not openly oppose the peace initiatives. As a result of Shimon Peres' 1986 visit to Morocco and talks with King Hassan, there were denunciations by Libya and Syria, and Libya broke off the "union" with Morocco under the Oujda Accords.

Present

Morocco, located on the northwest corner of North Africa on the southern shore of the Strait of Gibraltar, is bordered by Algeria on the east and western Sahara on the south. The remainder of her borders are coastline—the Atlantic Ocean on the west and the Mediterranean Sea on the north.

Morocco's land area is approximately 450,000 sq km (175,000 sq mi) not including the contested area of western Sahara. Approximately 18 percent of the land is forested; 32 percent is meadows, pastures, or under permanent cultivation; and the remaining 50 percent is desert, waste, or urban. Morocco's current population of approximately 23 million is 99.1 percent Arab-Berber; the balance are non-Moroccan. Religiously, 98.7 percent are Moslem, and the rest are Christian. While the official language is Arabic, French is used in diplomatic, government, and business circles; Spanish is still spoken in northern Morocco, the area that was formerly Spanish Morocco; and several Berber dialects are spoken. The official literacy rate, as stated by the government, is 28 percent.

Politically, Morocco is legally known as the Kingdom of Morocco and is a hereditary constitutional monarchy with a multiparty system. However, the king, now Hasan II, serves as head of state and maintains the real power. Elections are held for the National Assembly which the king has the power to dissolve. The two pro-monarchy parties form the current government.

Economically, Morocco is a poor country and, basically, an agrarian society with some mining of minerals and phosphates. Her GNP of $13.4 billion, $610 per capita, ranks her among the poorer nations of the world.

Militarily, Morocco is forced to spend $3.3 billion annually in defense—almost half of her general budget and over one-fourth of her GNP. She has a serious border dispute with Algeria that could, at any time, deteriorate into armed conflict given the appropriate political climate. More consuming, however, is Morocco's long-lasting—over ten years—war with the Polisario over control of the western Sahara. Algeria has given financial, military, and political support to the Polisario in its struggle against Morocco over possession of the western Sahara.

The north African Maghreb states have split into two groupings with opposing views on the disposition of the western Sahara territory which Morocco annexed. Algeria, Mauritania, and Tunisia signed a treaty of fraternity in 1983 in search of creating a "Greater Maghreb." Their political position was in support of the Polisario claims over the western Sahara in total opposition to Morocco's annexation and claims to that territory. To help neutralize this political move by Algeria, Morocco sought Libyan support for her claim to the western Sahara, and they formed a loose alliance. The war with the Polisario has been contained by Morocco and limited to sporadic fighting through the construction of a defensive wall around the "useful" part of the Sahara under contention. Morocco has refrained from "hot pursuit" of the Polisario into Algerian territory, which the Polisario uses as a haven.

Morocco's monarchy has dropped her claims of establishing the "Great Moroccan Empire" as existed in the sixteenth and seventeenth centuries, thus dropping her claim over all of Mauritania. Morocco continues her policy of defense ties with the United States and France while still maintaining cordial relations with the Soviet Union.

Future

For two major geopolitical reasons, Algeria will continue to be Morocco's natural enemy. Morocco, which controls access to the Mediterranean via the Strait of Gibraltar, has a very long coastline along the Atlantic Ocean. Algeria's only access to the Atlantic Ocean is through the very Strait of Gibraltar that Morocco controls. Additionally, Morocco, one-fifth the size of Algeria in area and one-third in population, insists on her claim to the western Sahara, which she annexed in 1974. It is doubtful whether any Algerian government will ever honor Morocco's claim to that territory.

Islamic fundamentalism is on the rise in Algeria. If that nation should ever be governed by Islamic Fundamentalists, then, the independent integrity of the Moroccan monarchy would be challenged directly and Morocco would likely become an Islamic-Fundamentalist nation.

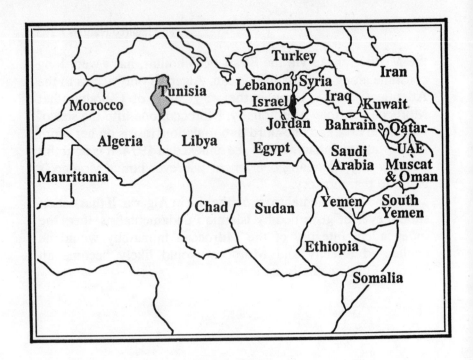

TUNISIA

History

Jutting into the Mediterranean as she does, Tunisia has always been of strategic importance in the region. Her history dates back to the twelfth century B.C. when Levantine colonies may have been there. By the sixth century B.C., the powerful Phoenician colony at Carthage had risen to power. In turn followed the Romans, the Vandals, the Byzantines, and—by the end of the seventh century A.D.—the Arabs.

During the Middle Ages, Tunisia was the major political center of several powerful dynasties; then, in 1574, she became part of the Ottoman Empire. An autonomous, hereditary dynasty ruled in Tunis by the eighteenth century. In 1881, France—as a logical follow-up to colonization of Algeria—occupied Tunisia.

By the 1930s, the Destour (Constitution) movement for independence, under the leadership of Habib Bourguiba had emerged. After World War II, during which Tunisia was a major battlefield, Bourguiba's Neo-Destour party moved toward independence, finally granted in 1956. During the Algerian revolution (1954 to 1962), Tunisia became a major support base for Algeria, thereby alienating France.

Within the Arab arena, Tunisia has been very active diplomatically. She sent a regiment to take part in the Arab-Israeli war of 1967; however, it arrived too late to participate in that war. Then, in 1968, Bourguiba went so far as to call for a compromise with Israel. In 1973, Tunisia sent a regiment that did participate in the October Arab-Israeli war. Tunis replaced Cairo as the headquarters of the Arab League after Camp David and also replaced Beirut as the main headquarters of the PLO after the Lebanon evacuation.

A 1974 unity agreement with Libya was immediately repudiated, and incidents of Libyan infiltration and confrontation were of major concern until 1986 when U.S. clashes with Libya muted Libyan threats to Tunisia. Since their 1983 treaty, Algeria and Tunisia have been moving closer together, in part to counterbalance the 1984 alliance between Morocco and Libya. Israel's attack of PLO headquarters in Tunis in 1985 temporarily postponed U.S. arms talks.

Present

Tunisia, one of the three Maghreb nations in the northwestern part of North Africa, covers an area of approximately 164,000 sq km (60,000 sq mi). She is bordered by the Mediterranean on the north and east, by Libya on the southeast, and by Algeria on the west. Approximately 6 percent of her land is forested; 23 percent is grass and range; 28 percent is agricultural; and 43 percent is desert, waste, or urban.

Tunisia's population is estimated at just over 7.6 million of whom 98 percent are Arab, 1 percent are European, and less than 1 percent are Tunisian Jews—the remnants of a once thriving Jewish community. Religiously, over 95 percent are Moslem, 4 percent are Christian, and less than 1 percent are Jewish. While Arabic is the official language, French is also utilized in commerce. The official literacy rate is stated to be 62 percent.

Politically, Tunisia—officially known as The Republic of Tunisia—is dominated by President Habib Bourguiba who became president in 1956 and who, since 1974, has had a lifetime job. Although Bourguiba is assisted by a cabinet headed by a prime minister, all are selected by and responsible to him. His dominance renders even the elected National Assembly insubordinate and ineffective. Bourguiba heads the Destour-Socialist party which advocates socialism Tunisian style—based on economic planning and a nonaligned foreign policy. There are ties with the West and support for a negotiated settlement in the Arab-Israeli conflict. There are elections for the National Assembly in which one party, the Front National, led by Bourguiba, holds all the seats.

Economically, Tunisia relies heavily on agriculture and her petroleum-related industries. Her GNP is $8.73 billion with $1,220 per capita.

Militarily, Tunisia expends approximately $250 million annually on defense, while maintaining 28,800 men in the armed forces. Her major arms purchases—quietly funded by Saudi Arabia—have been from the United States and France, although in 1985 and 1986, during periods of confrontation with Libya, Algeria sided with Tunisia by sending her surface-to-air missiles.

Future

Although labor unrest is a continuing problem, Tunisia's major uncertainty domestically is the succession to Bourguiba who is nearly ninety years old. Serious internal rivalries over succession are likely to remain problematic. There is a high probability that with the death of this man, who has maintained power as a leader of the Tunisian people for over fifty years and as the president of the country for the last thirty-two years, will come a takeover by the military and security forces.

Of the nations that neighbor Tunisia, Libya will remain a threat militarily and politically. Tunisia, with her relatively weak defense forces, is no more likely in the future to be involved militarily beyond her borders than she has been in the past.

Iran

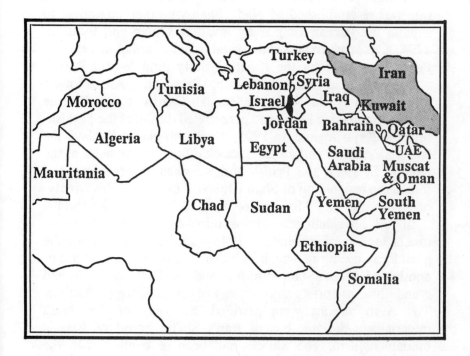

History

In 550 B.C., King Cyrus established the Achaemenid Dynasty on the territory that covers present Iran. At that time, the Zoroastrian religion was born. The regime was theocratic and based on an elite priesthood. The state, called Persia, survived as an independent entity until A.D. 642 at which time it was conquered by Arab forces. The local Persian population welcomed the conquering Arabs because they recognized Islam as a more egalitarian religion than the hierarchical structure of the Zoroastrian religion. Persia was dominated by the Arab caliphate for 900 years until the sixteenth century, despite invasion for brief periods by the Mongols and Tatars in the thirteenth and fourteenth centuries.

During the sixteenth century, the first Persian Dynasty was established by Safavid; Shi'ite Islam became (and still remains) the official religion of Persia (Iran). During the early eighteenth century, the Safavid Dynasty fell to invading Afghans who ruled for a short period. During the mid-eighteenth century, Persian rule was re-established by Nadir Shah who then attempted to expand the Persian Empire by invading Oman and India. In 1794, Kajar rose to power and established a capital in Teheran. Persia was ruled by the Kajar Dynasty until World War I.

During World War I, the British, Turks, and Russians fought and ravaged Persia. After the Russian Czarist regime fell, the British remained in Persia and perpetrated the fall of the Turkish-oriented Kajar regime. In 1925, the British placed Pahlavi, the late shah's father and an ex-Cossack officer, at the helm of the regime. In 1941, the British and Russians invaded Iran and forced the resignation of Shah Pahlavi. They placed his twenty-one year old son, Mohammed Reza Pahlavi, on the throne.

In 1977, the shah, after almost thirty-eight years in power—except for a brief interlude in 1946—attempted to recreate the great Persian Empire, which included domination in one form or another of Afghanistan, Pakistan, and the Gulf states. He had grand illusions and a grand strategy of conquest for his lifetime. The Arab nations were petrified, not only of the shah's imperialistic designs, but of Iran's Shi'ite brand of Islamic fundamentalism. The Shi'ites had been in conflict with the Sunnis throughout their history. In 1979, the Ayatollah Khomeini came to power and created the world's only existing theocratic state.

The experts on Iran totally ignored the tremendous potential power and cohesive force of the Islamic-Shi'ite Fundamentalists. The inability to assess the value and importance of the structured organizational nature of the Shi'ites in Iran, which runs totally counter to their loosely organized Sunni-Fundamentalist counterparts throughout the Arab world, certainly contributed to the poor assessment of the Iranian revolution by the world body of "experts." Only the Catholic church has an organizational structure and a hierarchy not totally unlike the Iranian-Shi'ite structure; none of the other world religions possesses this attribute. It is a quality that assisted the Ayatollah Khomeini in succeeding so swiftly and completely in totally taking over that nation's institutions and establishing a pure Islamic-Shi'ite theocracy in their wake. Historically, Iran had been dominated for 900 years (A.D. 642 to 1500) by Arab states. During that period, the Shi'ite-Persian hierarchy served as the only opposition or alternative to Arab-Islamic domination. Remember, it was in the sixteenth century when Persia became an independent Shi'ite-Islamic state under the Safavid-Shi'ite monarchy. Thus, the Shi'ites had already functioned as both the rulers and the opposition with their political structure totally in tact.

Prior to the 1979 Shi'ite revolution, two theories dominated the thinking of the experts on Iran. The mainstream theory projected that Iran would develop into a democratic, liberal, humanistic society—a true model for the Third World. One may believe that this optimistic forecast developed from a desperate need to find an alternative to the failing Third World societies, which had been created by the Western nations after World War II. They were supposed to have become democratic societies modeled after Western Europe and the United States; however, the lack of an educated middle class, history of democracy, and Western institutions, as well as an overemphasis on defense, prevented the plan from succeeding. Iran, then, became the model nation because much of her wealth was utilized to create a large middle class that included the military.

The second theory was one purported by the non-Soviet Marxists from the Western world. They believed that the growing wealth of the middle class, which was concentrated in the main cities, especially Teheran, would be in violent conflict with the growing number of peasants who streamed into the cities. These peasants lived in abject poverty amidst the sea of newfound middle-class wealth and opulence. This created a perverse condition in which a booming commerce based on luxury cars; exclusive condominiums; plush and expensive restaurants, cabarets, and villas; diamonds; and the world's most expensive furs thrived in the midst of teaming poverty.

In addition, there were highly paid, foreign, skilled workers and experts hired to help absorb the multibillion dollar import of both turnkey industries and the world's most exotic and advanced-technology weapon systems. Not only were those imported weapon systems totally unabsorbable by the local military establishment, but the commissions on their purchases created a new wealthy class of opulent spenders. This underscored the contrast created by the influx of great numbers of peasants to the cities from the impoverished, backward, rural areas. These peasants created tin hut areas and literally lived an existence of starvation and squalor. To the (non-Soviet) Western-Marxist theoretician who sees everything in secular class struggle terms, Iran was overripe for a revolution by the following newly created classes: the peasant class; the lower middle class who served the opulently wealthy; and the expanded working class. What these Marxist theoreticians didn't understand was that these three classes were dominated by their religious Islamic-Shi'ite fundamentalism.

In retrospect, to be generous to the experts, the modern world has never before experienced a true theocratic revolution with a government run by the "almighty." Ancient Egypt was run by the Pharaohs 4,000 years ago, and ancient Israel was run by the prophets 2,800 years ago. The Moslem caliphates in the seventh and eighth centuries are the only models of true theocratic regimes that the embarrassed "experts" could have used as precedent-setting models for the Iranian, or any societal, revolution. Their total disregard for the power of Islamic-Shi'ite fundamentalism and their total ignorance of the role of the 350,000 *imans*, or *mullahs*, involved in the Shi'ite hierarchy and network throughout the entire nation seems incredulous. The shah had refused to tolerate the existence of a political opposition party or a chief of staff to coordinate the military; thus, he unwittingly allowed the Shi'ite hierarchy to be the only organized force in Iran. The experts also failed to evaluate the meaning of this situation.

The question is why the shah didn't allow a political opposition and, more significantly, why he chose to maintain total personal control and coordination of the military rather than operate through a chief of staff. The most workable theory appears to be historically based. The shah's grandfather, an ex-

Cossack officer, seized power in Iran by a military coup in 1921. The shah feared a similar fate; thus, he kept the Iranian military from establishing a centralized military command.

The shah was attempting to control a dynamic, growing society of immense contrasts, which was beset with enormous social problems. His rule was undermined by the then newly elected president of the United States, Jimmy Carter. Carter attempted to define the world in simplistic human terms such as good and bad, righteous and evil, virtuous and sinful. In so doing, he attempted to force the shah, who from the perspective of U.S. national interests was our best friend in the East-West struggle, to provide for his society more equitably. Jimmy Carter wanted this important friendly nation to introduce to her society and provide for her citizens more goodness, more righteousness, and more virtue. He became the champion of human rights for the Iranian population, and, by his quest, he weakened the shah's ability to rule. Inadvertently, through his "Good Samaritan" naive approach to a nation totally alien to him, he helped to bring to power the champion of the people—the Ayatollah Khomeini—who also saw the world in terms similar to Carter.

The ayatollah, the epitome of theocracy, provided a classical totalitarian approach to governing the society. He views the world and the society in the following terms:

- The world is divided into good and evil, virtue and sin, right and wrong.
- Individual freedom is not a relevant value, and the correct life of collectivity is the main goal.
- Human society is perfectible, and the structure for perfection must be implemented immediately.
- There exists a body of truths in which the mandate for human behavior is provided and which must be applied.
- Whoever does not participate in this effort and share these values is not only wrong but evil and, therefore, must be treated as an enemy.

Present

The size of Iran is three times that of France. She has a population in excess of 50 million, evenly divided between cities and rural communities. Approximately 50 percent of the population are Farsi (Persian), and the other half are divided into minorities; the largest minority is Azerbaijanese—Shi'ite Moslems who are of Turkish, not Persian, descent. The balance of the minorities consists of Kurds, Baluchi, Asserians, Armenians, and several million Arabs. Although the area inhabited by the Arabs is called Khuzistan by Iran, Iraq refers to this area as Arabastan. The Khuzistan Arabs are all Sunni Moslems who live in the major oil-bearing area in Iran. Conquest of that territory was one of the goals of Saddam Hussein when his Iraqi forces invaded Iran in September 1980.

Only 10 to 12 percent of Iran is irrigable land; the rest is a vast desert. She cannot, therefore, establish an agricultural industry that will provide food self-sufficiency. In 1977, Iran imported $2.7 billion worth of food to feed a rapidly increasing—3 percent per year—population. Today, food distribution is made through *mosques* and controlled by the *mullahs;* thus, making the population dependent on the ayatollah for its continued sustenance. The agricultural sector cannot expand by developing more acreage. Expansion can only be achieved through the application of highly sophisticated, modern farming techniques, which runs counter to the present trends within Iran. Therefore, the move of rural inhabitants to the cities continues, and the nation not only becomes more dependent on imported food but also must be satisfied with a more limited diet in types and quantity.

In 1978, Iran, then one of the world's great oil producers, had a GNP of $55 billion, $21 billion of which was from oil. Since the 1978 revolution and the subsequent invasion in 1980 by Iraq, the Iranian economy has stalled, and her oil income has dropped drastically. After the revolution, the ayatollah's revolutionary council canceled $80 billion in foreign contracts. The great move toward the industrialization of Iran, which had been started by the shah and which, at its peak in 1979 employed 2.5 million people, collapsed. By 1985, only a fraction of that number were still employed because of the purge of the scientific, engineering, and technical sector of the society—most of whom had left the country during the turmoil after the revolution.

In 1979, manufactured goods made up one-third of the non-oil output of Iran—about $3 billion; today, it is only a small portion of this amount. The ayatollah destroyed the possibility for future economic growth in all sectors by driving away the managerial and technical class the shah so arduously developed within the society. He purged, executed, or jailed the military leadership and then established the Islamic revolutionary guards—a disorganized and poorly trained, but highly motivated and loyal, army—in addition to the regular armed forces. He did this to diminish the potential for a military coup d'etat.

Presently, the possibility of an internal revolution to bring down this Islamic-Fundamentalist regime is very unlikely. Unlike the shah's, this regime is brutal and will crush, by any means necessary, any identifiable sign of opposition. The shah's rule was mild compared to that of the ayatollah. Today, there is no organized ideological force that could be rallied into opposition like the one that opposed the shah. The ayatollah— the best reminder of Hitler to emerge since World War II—is literally mad with illusions of grandeur and aspirations of world conquest by invasion and massive subversion. However, there does still exist today, within the Shi'ite clergy, a group who believes that the approach to achieve an Islamic-Shi'ite world is through building, within Iran, an ideological Islamic society that will spread throughout the world by example of its success. This is in contrast to the present regime that is dedicated to spreading its ideology by world subversion. To support the subversive strategy of his regime, the ayatollah has allocated $1.5 billion per year to world terrorism.

Because the ayatollah destroyed the means for future economic growth, he has very little choice but to maintain the nation on a militant footing and continually seek battle with the enemy. It was fortuitous for the ayatollah that Saddam Hussein was idiotic enough to invade Iran, attempting to conquer some territory and then negotiate a favorable settlement. Iran has a population growth of 1.5 million people per year, and, with the present system, which doesn't encourage technical education and doesn't provide an atmosphere for industrial development, there is no way to expand the economy to absorb the growth in the work force. The increasing population of unemployable youth must be sacrificed in battle in the name of Allah. If Saddam Hussein hadn't initiated the war, eventually, the ayatollah would have had to seek battle with some enemy, although he would not have chosen a direct invasion of Iraq. It is more likely he would have chosen the route of massive subversion of his neighbors. The invasion of Iran by Iraq, therefore, was a blessing in disguise for the ayatollah. It helped to solidify his revolution, unite the nation against a common enemy, and keep the Iranian army engaged in war instead of meddling in internal affairs. This war is one from which all parts of the world have benefited—except for the Arabs, who were either fighting the war (Iraq) or supporting it financially (the Gulf states).

The Ayatollah Khomeini has established a governmental dictatorship not much different in its savagery, tyranny, oppression, and global aspirations than that of Fascist Hitler's Germany and Bolshevik Stalin's Russia. Tyranny from the right as exemplified by Hitler's nazism, tyranny from the left as exemplified by Stalin's communism, and cleric tyranny as exemplified by Khomeini's Islamic fundamentalism utilized the same means to achieve the same goal—transnational world domination. All three were both nationalistic and imperialistic in their grand design, although only Hitler openly admitted that his goal was German domination and German nationalism. Stalin and Khomeini, while both imperialists, never openly admitted that the real purpose of their conquests was the glorification of their nations.

Presently, Khomeini has several goals. Although he espouses generic Islamic internationalism, he really is promoting Shi'ism—at the expense of Sunniism. He openly supported the slaughter of 20,000 Islamic-Sunni Fundamentalists in Syria by Alawi soldiers led by Rifat Assad. The Alawi, although not Fundamentalist, are a branch of Shia.

Khomeini views both the United States and the Soviet Union as powers in competition for world domination and, therefore, expresses hostility toward both superpowers. Paradoxically, in regard to long-term strategic goals for Iran, the ayatollah's grand design does not differ significantly from that of the shah's. The only difference is that the shah lacked an ideological motivation and was using modern technology to achieve his ends, while Khomeini has the ideological motivation but, because of his theological doctrinaire approach, can't harness the means. The shah wanted Iran to become the Prussia of the Middle East. The ayatollah wants to usher in his version of the "Kingdom of G-d."

The ayatollah views Jewish political control of Jerusalem and the Moslem holy places as heretical and, therefore, is violently opposed to Zionism and the State of Israel. If the State of Israel were to yield the entire city of Jerusalem to the Moslems, the ayatollah's zealous opposition to the State still would not diminish—only Jerusalem as a symbol would be removed. His attitude toward Christianity and Christian nations is no less charitable. He believes that there is no place in the world where Christians or Jews can live side by side as equals to Shi'ite Moslems. To the ayatollah, the concept of ecumenicalism is nonexistent, even among Moslems. Sunni Moslems view Shi'ites as a heretic sect because Shi'ism recognizes two prophets subsequent to Mohammed, while the Koran claims that the Prophet Mohammed, the messenger of G-d, was to be the world's last prophet. The ayatollah will not tolerate the Sunni rejection of his theology.

Khomeini wants to unite the entire Islamic world under the Shi'ite banner, including countries such as the Arab nations, Indonesia, Malaysia, Nigeria, Pakistan, and Turkey—a collective population that exceeds one-half billion. If the ayatollah can succeed in such an endeavor, then he could become the leader of the Third World and use this as a base for his grand design of world conquest for Islam. Thus, he would achieve his goal to establish "G-d's world" on earth.

Ayatollah Khomeini's present theocratic regime views every single nation in the world, except Libya and Syria, as its enemy. There can be no politically negotiated settlement on any major issue with this ideological government.

Iran is the most glaring example of a country that has refused to succumb to the experts' theories of social development. Counter to the conventional wisdom of prediction based on existing trends, forces that were considered relatively dormant caused a revolution that caught the world and its experts totally by surprise. The Iranian revolution of 1979 and its aftermath shocked the entire world community of politicians, businessmen, military men, area specialists, and academicians. It was totally unpredicted and has put into serious question, once again, the wisdom of the experts. In 1959, no one predicted the results of Fidel Castro's Cuban revolution. From 1929 to 1933, no one predicted the results of Adolph Hitler's German revolution, even though he rose to power by democratic means. And, in 1917, no one understood the results of Lenin's Soviet revolution. The lesson of Iran recounts the unpredictability of cataclysmic political upheavals and reminds us of the volatile nature of this explosive region.

A bare majority of the population of present-day Iran is comprised of Persian-Shi'ite Moslems. This majority shares in common a cultural heritage, a language, a history of struggle against foreign domination, and a long history of designs of national grandeur. These Persians sustained a 1,000 year Arab rule. The re-establishment of the great Persian Empire of several thousand years ago is a dream ingrained in the culture of the people. Therefore, the words of both the shah and the ayatollah, similar but sung to a different melody, are music to the ears of the Iranian people—not very much unlike the words of Hitler to the German people who yearned for great conquest. Since nearly 50 percent of Iran's population consists of national or religious minorities, there is a serious problem for the future. In order to maintain repressive autocratic domination, these minorities must be controlled and, at the same time, shielded from external influence. Despite the near decimation of Iran's industrial, physical, and human resources by the ayatollah, at present, she does have a surviving educational and industrial rudimentary infrastructure, which could be rebuilt for possible future alternatives.

Future

In the following analyses, the basic assumption can be made that Iraq will not be able to conquer Iran.

For the near future, the first possible scenario is the death of the Ayatollah Khomeini—he is near ninety years old—and the continuation of his policies by his successor. In that event, Iran will continue her policy of massive subversion of Islamic regimes and continue warfare with Iraq. If Iraq is conquered by Iran, or if the present military regime of Iraq collapses and a Shi'ite government replaces it, then Iran will possess tremendous power due to the formation of a combined Iraqi-Iranian-Shi'ite army controlled by Iran. Through a combination of invasion and subversion, Iran would conquer the Gulf states with Saudi Arabia as the ultimate target. The minority regimes of Kuwait and Bahrain would collapse immediately due to the uprising of their Shi'ite majority. Since the United States doesn't have the means to block such a combined army of Shi'ites, there would be no way to protect the Gulf states or defend them without Soviet participation. This would most likely include the threat of invasion or the actual occupation of the Iranian province of Azerbaijan. This Soviet intervention would create a real threat to Iran.

The largest single religious group in Iraq are the Shi'ites; they represent 55 percent of the population. If Iran were to succeed in conquering militarily either southern Iraq—an area exclusively inhabited by Shi'ite Arabs—or Baghdad—the capital of Iraq—and installing a Shi'ite government, or if she successfully supported a revolution from within, then both the United States and the Soviet Union would have a mutual interest in trying to contain any further expansion of an Iranian-Iraqi Shi'ite axis.

The Soviet Union would become extremely vulnerable to the influence of Islamic fundamentalism on her almost 90 million Moslems who inhabit a large territory bordering Iran. Any Fundamentalist resurgence would be a literal nightmare for the Soviets. For obvious reasons, the United States would also find such an eventuality less than desirable. Additionally, the balance of the Arab world, including the secular Shi'ite state of Syria and Qaddafi's Libya, would feel threatened. The very existence of Jordan would be challenged immediately. Only Israel could act on behalf of Jordan by helping her to maintain her independent statehood. This projected scenario of an aggressive theocratic Iranian-Shi'ite regime that would succeed in dominating Iraq is one that is extremely dangerous for Israel.

The second scenario is one in which the Iranian struggle against Iraq would continue on and off until the turn of the century, and the successor to the present ayatollah would pursue the same domestic and foreign policy tactics and strategy. In this scenario, the future ayatollah would continue massive investment in the subversion of every Islamic regime in order to achieve his ends by promoting revolution. Iraq is the only possible outlet for a policy of conquest by invasion.

In this scenario, every Arab nation would be engaged in protecting herself from internal revolution. Each would economically share the burdens of Iraq because the "on and off" war would keep Iraq's economy in shambles without massive continuous aid from the Gulf states. Saddam Hussein's decision to build a pipeline through Aqaba in order to export Iraqi oil indicates that he believes that the war will resume and continue for many years. The basis for this belief is that there can't be a negotiated settlement in the Western sense because this is the first ideological war in this area in hundreds of years. A prolonged war between Iraq and Iran would, eventually, dominate Arab politics, placing Israel and the Palestinian problem as a secondary issue.

This scenario poses some serious questions to which there appear to be no predictable answers. How is the Iranian government going to feed and employ its youthful, prolific population which grows by 1.5 million per year? If future demand for Middle East oil continues to decrease, and the world either taps other more reliable oil resources or switches to other energy sources, how will the currently rich Arab Gulf states be able to continue to finance the war? One thing is certain—only the unpredictable will occur.

The third scenario would also be based on the death of the present ayatollah. In this case, however, a new regime would emerge that would pattern itself after the successful Libyan experiment established by Qaddafi, which combined *state* Islamic fundamentalism with a Socialist economic structure. It is not possible to present a scenario in which a secular government could be formed from the forces that presently exist in Iran. The most change that could occur is a modified theocracy as in Libya. The primary short- and long-term goals of such a government would be, once again, to introduce technology into the country, expand the agriculture, and industrialize. Such activities would re-employ the people. The domination of Islamic neighbors would become a long-term goal.

It is doubtful, however, that such a Socialist-Islamic republic would be any less dangerous to its neighbors than the regimes projected in the two previous scenarios. In fact, in the long run, this is the most dangerous scenario because such a government could become a great economic/military power and a model for others to emulate. Its active subversive methods would have a greater chance of success in motivating the revolutionary movements in the neighboring states. This scenario, which is extremely dangerous for the Arab-Moslem world, is the most desirable for the West and Israel and would pose a serious problem for the Soviet Union. It is possible that such a Socialist-Islamic republic could, for an interim lengthy period, have good economic and political relations with Israel. This would be very similar to the conditions that existed between Iran and Israel during the reign of the shah.

Events in Iran could very well eclipse the present media focus on the Palestinian question and the Arab-Israeli conflict. The fate of Iran must be of primary concern because it is the most strategically important country in the Middle East to both Israel and the West. An Iran independent of Soviet influence acts as a block to the long-standing Soviet desire for expansion into the Middle East and Asia.

Part Three

NON-AMERICAN GLOBAL POWER CENTERS AND THE MIDDLE EAST: THEIR INTERESTS, INVOLVEMENT, INFLUENCE, AND IMPACT

Non-American Global Power Centers and the Middle East: Their Interests, Involvement, Influence, and Impact

Overview

Meddling, involvement, and outright intervention in the affairs of the peoples of the Middle East by powerful nations has been a hallmark for almost 4,000 years, nearly the entire history of the region. So it is today as the global power centers perceive their national interests requiring that they attempt to control events in the area in order to gain access to the region's assets.

The primary focus of the global power centers has been, and continues to be, accruing the benefits of access. By providing the nations of the Middle East with the means to wage wars (thereby destabilizing the region), and then constantly intervening in these wars, the global powers have created an aura of stability. A volatile and dangerous Middle East, however, makes the rest of the world a more dangerous place to live.

It is apparent that the two greatest global powers—the United States and the Soviet Union—have come to a number of common conclusions independently. First, nuclear war is unthinkable; thus each is pursuing a policy leading toward the destruction of all nuclear weapons. It is likely they will, eventually, attempt to place a global ban on these weapons by treaty. It is also apparent they are determined to avoid a ground war that would necessitate their armies fighting each other. From their recent military experiences—the Soviet Union in Afghanistan and the United States in Vietnam, it also appears obvious they will both attempt to influence events throughout the world through surrogates (not their armies), since both learned the same bitter lesson about the limitations of their military power.

But each will continue to attempt to gain influence and control events in various regions through the use of military weapon sales or grants to client states who may do battle using those resources from the great powers. In each case, however, they will attempt to limit the war or contain it so that it does not disturb world peace. Until now, the global powers have successfully played this game in the Middle East. The last major war—Iraq versus Iran—wound down, through the exhaustion of both sides, to an uneasy truce that may hold for a few years until—each side looks for, and finds, the right opportunity to begin again. Until now, the wars in the Middle East—fed and fueled by the great power centers—have been contained. And for the first time since World War II, it appears that the United States and the Soviet Union are interested in the avoidance of war by their client states. Perhaps they both wish to eliminate the interferences of such wars with their own relations.

The great global power centers have shipped into the region such vast amounts of weapons that, in a very real sense, they have lost their ability to influence their client states about entering into war. Therefore, the superpowers will be pushing their client states into political accommodation to avoid the risk of war and its spread.

Whether or not the global powers can continue to dump vast amounts of weapons into the region, attempt to improve their political and economic hold, and still avoid wars is yet to be proven. Until now, their record has not been good. Former President Jimmy Carter once said, "Weapons don't make war; people do." But people cannot make war without weapons, and the Middle East has plenty of them. If the cease-fire between Iraq and Iran holds, then it is highly likely that world attention will be on political accommodation in the region and will focus on the real problems among the Arabs, especially the Palestinian Arabs.

Western Europe

BRITAIN

History

During the seventeenth, eighteenth, and nineteenth centuries, Britain was one of the great imperialist powers of the world. She continually sought to extend her influence and power to the various continents where there were raw materials and the possibility of trade. After Egypt gained independence from Turkish rule in the early 1900s, Britain took control over Egypt. At that time, Disraeli bought the Suez Canal for Britain from the French, with funds provided by the Rothchilds. Although Britain controlled the Suez Canal, the gateway to three continents— Europe, Asia, and Africa, she wanted to enhance her hold on the entire Middle East, which she viewed as being of vital, strategic importance.

Prior to World War I, the British supported the Zionist movement against Turkish rule over Palestine, and the British consul in Jerusalem became the protector of the Jews. One of the aims of the British during World War I was to destroy the Ottoman Empire's wrenching control of the Middle East. Therefore, with the demise of the Ottoman Empire at the war's end in 1918, the disposition of Turkey's possessions in the Middle East was of great concern to Britain. To help insure her control over most of those possessions, Britain pursued a mandate from the League of Nations to legalize her imperialist designs.

By decree of the League of Nations, the British attained legal control over all the Middle East territories, except for Lebanon, North Africa, and Syria. Morocco, Algeria, Tunisia, Lebanon, and Syria were placed under French control, while Libya was assigned to the Italians. To the victors, went the spoils. The U.S. Congress had never ratified membership in the League of Nations, despite the valiant effort of then President Woodrow Wilson, and established only an indirect presence in Saudi Arabia through the good offices of Britain.

Once she received the mandate over Palestine from the League of Nations, Britain was no longer interested in Zionist national aspirations in Palestine. In fact, since Jewish national aspirations were shown to be in conflict with British imperialist aims, British policy was shaped to thwart all Zionist efforts. Britain maintained a dual policy in Palestine through the encouragement of an increasing Arab presence and the limitation of Jewish immigration in that territory. Since her goal in the Middle East was to control the entire area (and, thereby, replace the Ottoman Empire with the British Empire), imperialist Britain did not want an advanced and enlightened society (such as Zionism would implant) to set an example for the Arabs to emulate.

Not only did British interest in fulfilling the spirit of the mandate—the establishment of a Jewish national home in Palestine—wane, but Britain actually undermined the mandate's intention. Although the Palestine referred to in the mandate as the area to be established as a Jewish homeland included both sides of the Jordan River, 75 percent of the land became inaccessible for Jewish settlement when Britain established the territory east of the Jordan as Transjordan—to be ruled by the Hashemite king and thereby designated *Judenrein.* Thus, Britain avoided the potential of a Jewish state being of any significant size. Only the 25 percent balance of Palestine—the portion west of the Jordan—was designated for settlement by Jews and Arabs.

Under the guise of monitoring absorptive capacity, Britain controlled immigration into western Palestine. Although all immigration—Jewish and Arab—was to be limited, in reality, Britain restricted Jews from entering while encouraging Arabs to settle there. That action was intended to preclude the Jews from achieving a majority population and, therefore, hamper the establishment of an independent Jewish state. Throughout the mandate period, Zionism faced not only the political watering down of the mandate rooted in British imperialistic designs but also deep-seated antipathy from anti-Semitic British officials. In their efforts to appease the Arabs and avoid Arab acts of terror, the British violently discriminated against the Jews in what presumably was to be their country. A definition of illegal immigration evolved through the Palestine mandatory adminis-tration's design and imposition of a series of regulations and restrictions. All were directed against the immigration of Jews into the Jewish national home. At the same time, there was no Arab quota within the system. Illegal immigration meant only Jewish immigration.

During the 1920s, the British government withheld immi-gration certificates from qualified Jewish immigrants. Within the same period, they issued unlimited blank passes to the northern borders to accommodate Syrian Arabs wishing to leave the turmoil in Syria. When Arab violence manifested itself in either anti-Jewish riots (as occurred in Hebron) or in individual acts of terror, British law enforcement was either inept or ineffectual. Although the possession of arms was illegal for Arabs and Jews, enforcement was prejudicial toward the Jews.

Prior to Britain's entry into the war in 1939, British officials actually collaborated with the Nazis to stop Jews from entering Palestine. Even though a million Jews had already been crushed under the heels of nazism in Austria, Germany, and Czechoslovakia, the British government was informing the Nazis about the boatloads of Jewish refugees headed toward the Jewish national home. Not only were Jews fleeing Nazi Europe denied entry to Palestine, but the Nazis were being warned by the British about Jewish escape routes.

With the outbreak of World War II, the Jews unanimously agreed to put aside their differences with the British policy and demonstrate their loyalty to the cause. The British didn't need to placate them. As past experience had taught the British, the Jews' cooperation with the Allies could be taken for granted. The British had been assured by Joseph Kennedy in April 1939 that they need not overestimate the problems that might be presented by the influence of the Jewish community in the United States.

That fact was central to many British officials concerned with placating the Arabs. One British official, the minister in Egypt, remarked, "The Jews are anybody's game these days."

Even after Britain entered the war, she blocked the sea routes that Jews, who had escaped from Europe, used on their way to Palestine. The collaboration between the British and Nazis on the Jewish question found a very fertile ground in the Arab world.

The greatest contemporary hero in the Arab world was Hitler. The symbiotic relationship between muftism and nazism was well documented. In the files of the German high command in Flensburg, Germany, evidence was found that only through funds made available by Germany to the Grand *Mufti* of Jerusalem was it possible to carry out the revolt in Palestine. The Grand *Mufti,* who operated from Berlin after 1941, was a staunch friend of Hitler and a coordinator with Germany in the final solution to the Jewish problem. He was personally responsible for the slaughter of hundreds of thousands of Jews. For example, when the *mufti* learned that the Hungarian government was planning to allow 900 Jewish children to escape from the Nazis to Palestine, he immediately demanded the reverse of the plan. Instead of going to Palestine, the Jewish children were sent to the extermination camps in Poland.

Well-documented evidence shows that whenever the possible rescue of Jews became known, those rescues that were not prevented by the *mufti* or other Arab axis supporters were effectively protested against and, eventually, foiled by the British government. It can be said in simple terms—the British were prepared to accept the probable death of thousands of Jews in every territory because of the difficulties of relocating any considerable number of Jews should they be rescued.

The British had made their choice in 1939 by issuing the White Paper restrictions. In the context of Hitler's war against the Jews, it became a death warrant. Even in 1942, England's war cabinet declared that the British would continue to take all practicable steps to discourage illegal Jewish immigration into Palestine.

So the British virtually sealed the fate of countless Jews in mortal danger of extinction by engaging the right of the British Empire to enforce strict laws against Jewish immigration. Simultaneously, the government declared an excess of jobs in western Palestine amounting to near emergency proportions. The government not only encouraged but officially enacted the illegal immigration of thousands of Arabs from neighboring and more distant lands to take jobs in the Jewish national home that might have saved the lives of Jewish concentration camp victims. This action seen in the proper context matches the barbarism that the Allies were battling to deflect. That deed by Britain constituted an active participation in the social genocide of the Jews in Eastern Europe.

It is horrifying to realize that the British—a civilized people— were willing to see Jews in Europe put to death by the Nazis either for fear of Arab comment or reprise or because of the anti-Semitic feeling of the ruling government officials. Britain's rationalization for her political appeasement of the Arabs, virtually halting Jewish immigration to the Jewish national home at the time of greatest peril in Europe, was perhaps the most cynical and grave chapter in the tragic record of the Holocaust.

Between World War I and World War II, Britain established quasi-independent states in the Middle East in Egypt, Iraq, Kuwait, Saudi Arabia, and Transjordan. She controlled their armed forces by putting British officers in charge. She maintained political influence by helping to organize and run the administrative institutions of the kingdoms she established, while economically exploiting the territories. During the second world war, Britain accumulated a huge debt to the United States. As a consequence of that war debt, Britain lost control over Saudi Arabia to the United States.

The British abandoned their Palestinian mandate on May 14, 1948. The next day, May 15, 1948, the State of Israel was established—an event that triggered the British collapse in the Middle East. They were thrown out of Transjordan by King Abdullah. They were pushed out of Iraq after the assassination of King Faisal by Kassem who then established a Ba'athist-Socialist government. They were thrown out of Egypt by Nasser after he nationalized the Suez Canal. And they were pushed out of Kuwait. As a consequence of losing control of the Suez Canal, the British were forced to abandon their presence east of the Suez (in the Gulf states), finally leaving Aden and the Yemens by 1970. Although Egypt attempted to gain control east of the Suez by entering Yemen in the mid-sixties, ultimately, the military vacuum created by the British pullout was filled by Iran and the Soviet Union who were more than eager to fill it.

A closer look at British-Israeli relations immediately prior to and after the establishment of the State of Israel in 1948 is revealing. The British supported the Arabs during Israel's War of Independence politically, economically, and militarily (through weapon sales). They actively supported Transjordan's invasion of Israel by encouraging the British officer corps to lead the Jordanian army. Britain wanted Israel to collapse after her independence and believed she would. Britain defined her interests in the Middle East as having strong ties with Jordan and maintaining influence over Egypt and Iraq. She had absolutely no interest in the Jewish state.

Nasser's nationalization of the Suez Canal and the anti-British sentiment among Egypt's Arab neighbors forced Britain to re-evaluate her attitude toward Israel. Unofficially, Britain cooperated with Israel during the 1956 Sinai Campaign, although in that same Sinai area six years earlier—during the War of Independence—Israel's General Weizmann had shot down five British planes that were trying to assist Egypt.

Since 1956, Britain's relationship with Israel has been *cool, perfidious,* or *proper,* depending upon the issue. After the 1956 Sinai Campaign, trade between Britain and Israel expanded through official trade agreements; however, Britain opposed Israel's entry as an economic member of the European Common Market. On the political level, Britain has taken an adversarial posture toward Israel in public forums, as a matter of official British policy. Militarily, Britain has maintained an official arms embargo on weapon sales to Israel since 1973, while aggressively soliciting weapon sales to Arab nations.

Superficially, one would believe that Britain—the only Western European country, except for Norway, that is not dependent on imported oil for energy consumption—would have softened her public animosity toward Israel. However, despite her position—not only as a nation self-sufficient in oil, but also as a major non-OPEC exporter—she maintained an aggressively anti-Israel policy prior to the Yom Kippur War.

Today, the overriding interests of Britain in the Middle East are based on a combination of commercial ties with the Gulf states—Kuwait, Oman, and the UAE—and an emotional nostalgia within the British ruling circles rooted in the vestiges of a well-developed "Lawrence of Arabia" syndrome. The fact that London has become the tourist and commercial center for the Arabs from the Gulf states only tends to cement the ties between the Arabs and the British. It is a combination of factors with which it is very difficult to compete.

Future

There is no future for close relations between Israel and Britain, unless they become of vital interest to the British. As long as the British don't violate basic Arab interests, and as long as London remains the financial, recreational, vice, and buying center of the Arab world, Israel will have to settle for a very poor secondary position of interest.

In the past, the British developed a propensity for not investing in their own nation's industry; they exported their capital. This led to a lower standard of living, higher unemployment, and the loss of pace with technological developments. Britain's industry didn't benefit from the advances of technology until Margaret Thatcher's conservative government came to power. She not only stopped the erosion but reversed the trend. No longer is Britain destined to be the "poor man" of Europe. There is every reason to believe that by the twenty-first century technology in Britain will be on a par with that of Germany and France.

FRANCE

History

France has a several hundred year history of involvement in North Africa—Algeria, Morocco, and Tunisia. In the mid-1800s, France supported the Sudanese revolt against Egypt during which control of the Sudan was wrested from Egypt by the *Mahdi*. In the late 1800s, the French financed and built the Suez Canal, which they later sold to the British.

After World War I, under the Sykes-Picot Agreement, France was given Lebanon. This included the piece of Palestine that was bounded by the Litani River, which became part of Lebanon, and the piece of Palestine called the Golan Heights, which became part of Syria. Both of these parcels came under French mandate.

After the establishment of the State of Israel, the French were most helpful in providing physical support for the fledgling nation. In spite of fundamental French anti-Semitism, their purposes for this support were to undermine British interests in the Middle East, to retaliate for what they felt was a double-deal by the British and the League of Nations in the Sykes-Picot Agreement, and to maintain their influence in Lebanon and Syria.

The "French connection" began in 1955 with a fundamental political attempt to thwart Egypt's Nasser, who was supplying political, financial, and military aid to the Algerian rebels during the French-Algerian War. Between 1955 and 1962, the Franco-Israeli relationship provided Israel with her only partner or ally. Military, economic, cultural, and political ties were forged. The whole Israeli military modernization program began in 1955 entirely around French weapon systems. Nuclear know-how was transferred. The major weapon platforms of the Israeli air force, navy, and army came from France.

In 1962, DeGaulle gave Algeria total independence and withdrew the French army as well as 400,000 French citizens from the area. Then, he shifted French political orientation from an Israeli focus to a focus on improving relations with the Arab nations. The real break in French relations with Israel occurred on the eve of the 1967 war. DeGaulle informed Abba Eban that if Israel were to start a war against Nasser, instead of pursuing a political solution, he would place a total embargo on Israeli military shipments. Upon the conclusion of the Six-Day War, DeGaulle attempted, rather successfully, to have France replace the United States—with whom most of the Arab nations broke diplomatic relations—as the West's foil against Soviet dominance in the Middle East.

Relations between France and Israel remained strained until the rise to power of the Socialist government of Mitterand. At present, while these relations are more friendly and cordial on a ceremonial and cultural level, they remain strained on a political level. France maintains a real Arab orientation because of massive weapon sales to a number of Arab countries—Egypt, Iraq, Kuwait, Saudi Arabia, Syria, and the North African nations, including Libya. Interestingly, the French have become a second source of weapon systems for the Arab nations—second only to the two primary suppliers, the Soviet Union and the United States.

Future

France's relationship with Israel will remain strained in the future. France sees herself as the alternative to the Soviet Union for the supply of arms. Because she has the most well-developed weapons industry in Western Europe, she must sell to any market that will buy. France's primary markets are extremist Arab states to which the United States has traditionally refused to sell. Since she's in competition with the Soviet Union for these markets, she feels she must maintain a pro-Arab position, which, of course, she interprets to include a bias against Israel. There is no reason to expect that France's position will change as she enters the twenty-first century as one of Western Europe's four leading powers.

GERMANY

History

German interest in the Middle East dates back to the days of the Crusaders (A.D. 1100 to 1200). The Order of the Templars, a German religious order, led the Crusades. The origins of German interest in the area, obviously, had much to do with reclaiming the Holy Land from what they considered to be heretic invaders.

Centuries later, the Germans used their favorable alliance with the non-Christian (Moslem) Ottoman Turks to exert influence over the region. Through the political support of the Ottoman Turks, Germans settled in colonies throughout the Middle East and established markets for their goods. The Germans were united under Bismarck, and in 1871, they fought the French, gaining Alsace-Lorraine and a huge indemnity from France. This resulted in Germany's establishing trade and colonies in the Middle East by building the Berlin-to-Baghdad railroad, the Istanbul-Damascus-Jeddah railroad, and the Istanbul-Jaffa-Suez-Cairo railroad. All of this was done with the blessings of their Ottoman ally.

After World War I and the Allied powers' defeat of Germany

and Turkey, the British and French divided the spoils of the war. The Germans re-entered the Middle East through political and economic support for Arab nationalist movements aimed at undermining British colonial control in the area. The Zionist movement (the Jewish national movement) was viewed by the Germans as pro-British. After the rise to power of nazism in the early 1930s, Germany viewed support of the Arabs as a means of implementing her anti-English and anti-Jewish policies. In Baghdad and Cairo, Nazi-organized revolts were contained by the British, while the German colony in Palestine became a hornets' nest of Nazi spies and Nazi subversion in the Middle East.

As a result of the bombing of the Reichstag in 1933 and the subsequent anti-Jewish backlash, there was a massive emigration of intellectual German Jews to Israel *(aliyah)*. Although prior settlement in Israel had reflected the Socialist-Zionist emphasis on agriculture, these German Jews established basic urban industries that did not adhere to Socialist-Zionist principles.

After the defeat of Hitler's Germany in World War II and the end of the Holocaust that had resulted in the death of 6 million Jews, a German program of financial reparation paid large sums of money to the State of Israel and to individuals in Israel as well. It was the first large influx of government aid to Israel. The initial post-State infrastructure was built with German reparation money and German know-how.

In the early 1960s, Germany was used by the United States as a third party for supplying military armaments to Israel. U.S. helicopters, Patton tanks, and artillery were sold to Israel by Germany under U.S. direction. This activity initiated German-Israeli intelligence cooperation. As a result of this relationship, Germany saw the possibilities of exchanging operational intelligence data.

Since the end of World War II, the West German government has lived under the implied threat that the Soviet Union would launch against Germany an invasion similar to "Operation Barbarosa"—Germany's June 1941 surprise invasion of the Soviet Union. Germany, like Israel, has no interest in preparing for the ability to launch a first-strike invasion of her adversaries; however, she, also like Israel, must be prepared to stall—for at least three days—an invasion by her enemies, who would start with superior numerical forces. In Germany's case, the time is needed for a combination of German reserves and NATO forces to be brought in to assist; in Israel's case, the time is required for the reserves to be mobilized.

There has developed, then, a great coincidence of interests between Germany and Israel based on the similarity of tactical and strategic military threats—facing both—from the Soviets or Soviet-equipped and -trained forces. Since the tactics facing them are identical, the size of the imbalance is somewhat alike, and the military threat facing both nations' populations and armies is extremely similar, the solutions must be alike. Therefore, joint cooperation to seek a solution is mutually beneficial to both.

Future

The trend in Germany today is away from development and deployment of nuclear tactical weapons toward nonnuclear kill (NNK) weapons. Therefore, Germany is planning her future defense by neutralizing her tactical nuclear weapons and building mass-destruct NNK weapons. This requires development, production, and deployment of a whole host of new nonnuclear tactical weapon systems for the purpose of mass destruction of tanks and soldiers. Because she can't depend upon NATO for defense support in the early stages of a war, Germany must defend herself (by herself). She must be able to stall a force far superior in numbers of tanks, equipment, and men.

For the next two decades, Germany will face the identical military dilemma as Israel. Since the United States is not developing tactical weapon systems to meet their unique challenges, it will be in the best national interest of both Germany and Israel to cooperate in the technical and scientific areas and to develop similar solutions. Such cooperation could result in joint projects in which each nation would provide her own expertise and resources to develop, manufacture, and deploy appropriate weapon systems. Germany's need will be more important than simply protecting her political and economic interest in the Arab world; her need will be a matter of survival.

Given that this set of conditions will prevail for the next few decades, Germany will become the most important nation in

Europe for Israel and the second most important friend of the United States. In fact, West Germany should enter the twenty-first century as Western Europe's leading power. And this is the historical paradox—Germany will be Israel's second most important ally in the Western world politically, economically, and militarily, but not *culturally*.

TURKEY

History

During the fifteenth century, Turks came to the Middle East from Turkmenistan, the southern part of Russia, and conquered what was left of the Byzantine Empire; thus, the Ottoman Empire was established. These eastern Turks were Moslems who established rule over the territory that covers present-day Turkey; all of the Arab countries in the Middle East; North Africa; and the Balkan countries, including Albania, Bulgaria, Greece, and Yugoslavia.

Although the reign of the Ottoman Empire lasted 500 years, it went through various stages of reduction. First, it was forced to give up Europe, then North Africa, then Egypt. As a result of World War I, during which Germany and the Ottoman Empire were allied, the Ottoman Empire lost all of Arabia and the Middle East, including all of the Gulf states, Iraq, Lebanon, Palestine, and Syria. As the Empire diminished, it abandoned territories that had been entirely decimated—places where no administrative services or centers for governing were provided. A series of wars developed as the forces within the abandoned territories jockeyed for power. This left a basic Arab animosity toward the Turks because of the 500 years of abuse they had suffered at the hands of their Turkish masters.

In 1923, the nation-state of present-day Turkey was created under Ataturk. During the 1920s, the Turks slaughtered 1 million Christian Armenians, who represented an educated class within the society. Today, Turkey is one of the few nations in the entire region, including southern Europe, in which the government represents the majority of its people—90 percent are Turkish-speaking Sunni Moslems. Of the total 50 million population, 45 million are Turks, 3.5 million are Kurds, and there are over 1 million others. Presently, there is a strong

Islamic-Fundamentalist movement within Turkey.

Although Turkey entered NATO in 1952, she has not been accepted as a full member of the European Common Market because she is not fully democratic. Presently, Turkey is ruled by a parliamentary republic, and her president comes from the general staff.

Turkey is bordered by Bulgaria, Greece, Iran, Iraq, the Soviet Union, and Syria. Presently, she has border disputes with Syria in the north, with Greece over Cyprus, and with the Soviet Union over the Bosporus and Dardanelles Straits. She has a dispute with Bulgaria over a Turkish minority in Bulgaria and a Bulgarian minority in Turkey. The dispute between Turkey and Greece goes back 600 years to the time the Ottoman Empire destroyed the Byzantine Empire, which had emanated from Greece. The Byzantines, remember, spoke Greek. This ongoing dispute has come to fruition in Cyprus.

Today, Turkey maintains the largest land army in Western Europe, which is required because of the length of her border with the Soviet Union with whom she has fought numerous wars. The USSR, Turkey's main enemy, has established a military relationship with Syria, which has a major dispute with Turkey; therefore, Turkey is flanked by two major enemies on both sides—the Soviet Union and Syria.

Presently, Turkey maintains commercial ties at many levels with Israel, but their political ties have weakened over the past decade due to the emergence of Pan-Islam forces led by oil-rich Saudi Arabia.

Future

Turkey will continue to be threatened by the Soviet Union on one border and the massive Soviet-equipped Syrian army on another. She has no fundamental political interests in the Arab world but is dependent upon Arab oil. With the waning political and economic power of Arab OPEC countries, however, Turkey will be less sensitive to Arab interests in the Arab-Israeli dispute.

Although Turkey maintains the largest standing army in Western Europe, that army is the poorest equipped and must be modernized. Since the threats to Turkey will not change, because of vital national interests, she will strengthen political, economic, and, by sheer necessity, military ties with Israel.

Union of Soviet Socialist Republics (USSR)

Any understanding of the turmoil that has existed, does exist, or will exist in the Middle East requires an appreciation of the Russian (pre-Soviet) historical involvement and aspirations in that region of the world as well as her attitude toward and treatment of her Jewish inhabitants. Only then can one begin to appreciate the nature of the post-revolutionary and present Soviet involvement in the Middle East, attitude toward Israel, and treatment of Jewish inhabitants (citizens) of the USSR.

IMPERIALISM

There have been several significant events in the history of Russian imperialism that impact the Middle East and the Jewish people.

- A.D. 800—Prince Valdimir brought Byzantine culture into Russia and created a local Christian church, which has influenced Russia through modern times.
- 1682—Peter the Great reached out to the West and built St. Petersburg (now Leningrad).
- 1762 to 1796—Catherine II conquered great areas and created imperial Russia. In expanding eastward, she captured vast quantities of land including Uzbekistan, Kazakhstan, and Siberia; in expanding westward, she acquired the territories of Latvia, Estonia, Lithuania, and a large portion of Poland. At that time, the Russian Empire assimilated much of her Moslem population.
- 1855 to 1881—Alexander II made the wide-reaching

reforms that set the stage for the Russian Revolution. His equivocal nature regarding these reforms and his ambivalent responses to the reforms he had initiated, created unrest, which helped fuel the revolutionary fervor of the time. This era marked the end of serfdom and, ostensibly, the feudal state.

- 1875—Russia acquired vast territory from China (Vladivostok and southern Siberia) by coercion. By 1880, Russia controlled all of Siberia, including the only seaport on the continent to the Pacific (Vladivostok).
- 1905—Nicholas II ruled over Russia when she was defeated by Japan. The Russo-Japanese War created an atmosphere for revolution. The attempted revolts failed, but the method of suppression fostered the evolution and growth of communism in Russia.
- 1917—Nicholas II's reign ended. He was the last ruling czar, and, by peaceful means, czarist Russia was transformed into a democratic state under Kerensky. The czar then became a figurehead.
- 1917, February to November—the Bolshevik Revolution took place. The czar and his family were murdered by Svedluff—a Jewish Communist. Kerensky escaped to the United States, and Lenin came to power. The Communist revolution liberated the nations within Russia, and they voluntarily united to form the Union of Soviet Socialist Republics (USSR).
- 1919 to 1920—Lenin attempted to expand the borders of the newly created USSR to include much of Poland. The attempt failed because of the Polish army's victories on the battlefield.
- 1939—Stalin invaded Finland. That military attempt to expand the borders of the USSR failed because of the fighting capability of the small but effective Finnish army.
- 1939 to 1940—Stalin absorbed the eastern half of Poland (as a result of a treaty with Hitler), Latvia, Lithuania, and Estonia.
- 1945 to 1948—Stalin, after World War II, subjugated Bulgaria, Czechoslovakia, East Germany, Hungary, Outer Mongolia, the balance of Poland, Rumania, and half of the Sakhalin and Kuril Islands.

- 1945—Stalin attempted militarily to take over northern Iran but was forced to leave due to U.S. intervention. Stalin, also, attempted to take over half of Austria as well, but he was successfully thwarted again by U.S. action.
- 1956—Khrushchev and Bulganin suppressed revolts in both Poland and Hungary through the use of brutal military force by the Polish army in Poland and the Soviet army in Hungary.
- 1979—Brezhnev triggered a war by sending Soviet forces into the Peoples Republic of Afghanistan to bolster the Communist puppet regime that was being threatened by revolution.

The Russian adoption of the Byzantine culture, which was based on secret and violent change in government—cruel and ruthless reign over its population—set the seeds for the modern-day Communist USSR. Today, the Soviet Union is only an extension of the pattern that was established in A.D. 800 and that has carried over through the centuries. The imperial expansion of Russia that was begun by Catherine II during the late eighteenth century continues throughout modern Soviet history. Even today, although she is withdrawing militarily, the USSR is still attempting to establish a puppet Communist state in Afghanistan.

After World War I, the Turkish imperialist empire in the Middle East was dissolved, and the territories were mandated by the League of Nations to the British and the French. These mandates expired after World War II, allowing for the establishment of over 100 new nation-states from the territories relinquished by the West. Simultaneously, after World War II, the Western society of nations—primarily, Belgium, Britain, France, Germany, Holland, Italy, Portugal, Spain, and the United States—gave up possessions and territories that they had controlled in Africa, Asia, and South America. The USSR, however, reversed the process in Eastern Europe and absorbed national groups and territories by what was then very clever means—she placed Communist leaders in positions of power and destroyed forces of national opposition. But the USSR never gained the love, admiration, or respect of the people inhabiting those lands; she only created tens of millions of enemies within her area of control.

The USSR is the modern-day "imperialist." Since World War II, in order to maintain her imperialist posture, the USSR has been forced to utilize Soviet troops in Czechoslovakia, East Germany, and Hungary to put down rebellions against the puppet governments. The Soviet internal security police (KGB) intervened twice in Poland to put down popular uprisings against puppet Communist governments. In 1981, in order to consolidate the Soviet Union's hold on her southern states of Kazakhstan, Tadzhikistan, Turkmenistan, and Uzbekistan, which are almost totally populated by Moslems, the Soviet leaders felt compelled to send their military into Afghanistan. This was done to foil the establishment of a hostile Shi'ite-Moslem government, which could influence the Moslems of the Soviet Union bordering Afghanistan.

What most Americans fail to realize is that while today the population of the USSR is approximately one-third Moslem, by the early part of the next century the Moslem population there will reach 50 percent. There are approximately 20 million Byelorussians, *80 million Moslems,* 60 million Russians, 40 million Ukrainians, and 40 million varied minorities, including 3 million Jews. These figures do not include the satellite populations of the Eastern bloc countries of Albania, Bulgaria, Czechoslovakia, East Germany, Hungary, Poland, and Rumania.

In 1935, in order to put down an uprising within the Moslem population, Stalin slaughtered millions of Moslems in Kazakhstan. The memory of this uprising was still fresh in the minds of the septuagenarians ruling the Politburo when the Soviet Union invaded Afghanistan. They also realized that many of the Afghans were blood relatives of the Kazakhs and Uzbeks. The Shi'ite uprising in Iran several years prior to the Soviet invasion of Afghanistan didn't help to allay the worst fears of the aging Soviet leadership. Obviously, this leadership never believed that it would require a bloody war that has lasted over eight years (and only now appears to be in the process of winding down) to impose a Communist puppet regime in Kabul, the capital of Afghanistan. The quick suppression, by force, of the Czech, East German, Hungarian, and Polish uprisings, which were successfully measured in days, turned out not to be a proper model for the solution of the Afghanistan problem.

Not only was the Soviet military unable to neutralize the uprising against the Soviet-Communist puppet government established in Kabul, but its invasion of Afghanistan triggered fear in the capitals of the Western world. This forced the Carter regime, in its last year, to reverse its domestic arms policy and move toward rearmament, which the Reagan administration has since expanded. The Soviet invasion of Afghanistan was responsible not only for U.S. rearmament but also for the placement of U.S.-supplied, medium-range nuclear weapons in Western Europe. This invasion also created additional friction and aroused fears within the ruling circles of the Peoples Republic of China who, when looking at a globe, saw themselves being encircled by the Soviets. They realized that Afghanistan is separated from them by only a small strip of land.

The invasion of Afghanistan put an end to the twenty-five year military build-up of the Soviet Union, which had gone unmatched by the Western democracies. The West had not perceived the USSR to be an aggressive military threat to Western Europe. However, the invasion dealt a serious blow to the burgeoning peace movements within Western societies. These peace movements had been becoming a serious political force for Western unilateral disarmament because it was perceived that Soviet armament expenditures were based not on aggression, but on fundamental insecurity triggered by past wars caused by the West.

The Soviet military's use of poison gas and deadly antipersonnel weapons against civilian targets in Afghanistan totally neutralized the peace movement and catapulted the Soviet Union into the role of an aggressive nation capable of using military aggression any place in the world. This perception was supported by the Soviet use of surrogates, such as the Cubans, to foster military intervention in black Africa. The Soviet military struggle in Angola and Ethiopia, which continues, is supported by black Cuban soldiers financed by the Soviets. In the latter half of the twentieth century, the Soviet Union stands alone as the only imperial power in the world that utilizes nineteenth century imperial techniques to control and conquer territories by establishing puppet regimes with a bogus ideology which she controls.

INTERNAL POLITICAL STRUCTURE

Since A.D. 800, Russia has neither experienced democracy nor had a democratic form of government (except for a brief eight-month trial period by Kerensky). Never has there been an established entrepreneurship middle class that evolved from either the agricultural or the business sector. Although twice such a middle-class structure—evolving once from each sector—was formulated, both times it was brutally exterminated in order to avoid the germination of a middle-class political power.

In 1918, Lenin established millions of small peasant farm holders (private entrepreneurs) by breaking up the holdings of the wealthy Russian land barons; then, in 1921, he created the New Economic Policy (NEP), abandoning basic Communist principles by establishing small privately held businesses. In 1924, Stalin eliminated Lenin's NEP for fear of its capitalist tendencies and began the extermination of millions of men who had maintained small entrepreneurial enterprises established under Lenin.

From 1927 to 1933, Stalin forced collectivization of the millions of small peasant farm holders who had started their farms as a result of the land distribution policy of Lenin in 1918. Stalin redistributed the land of the peasant farmers and created the Kolkhozy (collective voluntary farms) and the Sovkhozy (government-owned and -run farms with salaried workers). This act of eliminating the enterprise of small privately owned farms created hunger and starvation throughout the USSR. Then, in 1933, Stalin again stamped out the possibility of a strong entrepreneurship middle class by exterminating millions of successful peasant farmers created by Lenin's land reform program. The only middle class allowed to be formed was the ruling bureaucratic middle class who controlled the wealth of the nation and distributed the spoils of political power. During Stalin's reign, he alone accounted for the slaughter of 30 to 50 million people who were under Soviet rule, while the Germans accounted for the slaughter of an additional 20 million Soviets. One estimate claims that a total of 90 million people have been murdered in the USSR since the time of the Revolution until today.

There is a real wealthy class in the Soviet Union that has been created, not by the creation of agriculture, banking, commerce, or industry, but by the possession of bureaucratic power. This is in contrast to Western democratic states in which creation of wealth lies in the hands of those who produce goods and services, while government bureaucratic officials and leadership receive only wages. This Soviet system of wealth creation by government leaders is a parasitic system because it does not reward initiative for the creation of agriculture, banking, commerce, industry, and services; it rewards only those who can retain positions of political power. There is no reward for excellence at or in any sector of the society. That is why the country has been operated politically by septuagenarians. The means for survival is not excellence but ruthlessness, cunningness, and/or nepotism (family influence).

The existing Soviet power structure is a power triad, delicately balanced in order to provide no single force total control. The KGB, the military, and the Communist party's apparatus actually run all aspects of life within the Soviet Union. Since the demise of Khrushchev, the Politburo has been controlled by the Communist party, which has maintained a member of the KGB and one seat for the military. Since the Russian Revolution after World War I, the basic Soviet economy has been a centrally run military economy—one that is always preparing for the next military confrontation. Only once in the eighty years since the Revolution has there been an attempt to expand the civilian economy. So, three parallel organizations run a country whose industrial production is dedicated to the military and whose agricultural sector, which employs almost half the people, can't produce enough to feed the other half.

Khrushchev demobilized 1.2 million men, scrapped ships under construction, and abandoned weapon system projects. This brought about the demise of Khrushchev because, inadvertently, he caused an imbalance in the power triad. The military reacted to preserve its power by allying itself with the KGB in order to bring Brezhnev into power. Since then, the Soviet Union has carried on a massive arms build-up policy despite a decade of detente. During this period, there has been continued obsolescence of Western military weapon systems. Despite the Strategic Arms Limitation Talks (SALT agreements), the Soviet Union has continued a massive growth in her tactical conventional military build-up.

Since the Soviet economy is based on the production of military weapon systems, the majority of the industrial manpower and capital resources are dedicated to producing those systems. Given that approximately 40 to 45 percent of Soviet manpower is engaged in agricultural pursuits (in contrast to the 2.5 percent of U.S. manpower now in agriculture), the Soviet economy can't shift manpower to the manufacture and distribution of consumer goods. Because of its total inefficiency in agriculture and its dedication to military production, the entire economic structure is in a rigid straitjacket. The system can't be changed because of the power triad and the lack of incentives in the production section of the society. Presently, however, Gorbachev is attempting to institute changes to reform the society. It appears that under Gorbachev there is an attempt to modernize Soviet industries, to reduce the impact of the bureaucracy on the economic system, and to tackle the growing technological gap between the Western world—primarily the United States—and the Soviet Union. Since it has been a totally nonproductive society, completely centralized and controlled, only time will tell to what extent Gorbachev will be successful.

Despite the fact that Gorbachev has spearheaded a nuclear disarmament agreement and despite his realization that nuclear war is unthinkable (there is no doubt that both the Reagan administration and Gorbachev's people believed that all tactical and strategic nuclear weapons must be banned as poison gas was after World War I), there is no indication that Gorbachev wants to or can slow down the build-up of conventional forces as Khrushchev did. Certainly, there is no indication that *Glasnost* and *Perostroika* can be viewed as a shift in Soviet imperialism. Gorbachev is still the ruler of imperialist mother Russia. His goals haven't changed, only the means of achievement.

While Marx proposed an egalitarian society, his most famous adherents have established the antithesis to egalitarianism. The new upper class who possess unlimited wealth have gained this wealth based purely on bureaucratic political power. The higher one's position in government, the more power, money, and privileges one possesses. The Soviet Union's bureaucratic governmental system that operates the country in parallel at every level requires a control that consists of a member of the Communist party and the KGB to assist the technocrat in each position. Since the penalty for failure is so great and each official is being watched so carefully, the decision-making process is automatically removed from an individual to that of a committee, which creates a cumbersome system to initiate even small changes. The need to diffuse responsibility and cover up mistakes is essential for survival. Since there is too little regard for success and too much punishment for failure, a totally corrupt managerial class has been created.

The Soviet masses are totally isolated from the world outside the Soviet Union and are constantly reminded of the success attributed to the Marxist-Leninist doctrine. Despite the knowledge of the ruling elite that that doctrine is a complete and total failure, they desperately try to isolate the society from any knowledge of what is actually taking place in the rest of the world. Soviet policy, therefore, is dedicated to establishing similar models throughout the world to prove to their people that Marxism is a success in other places. According to Brezhnev doctrine, in order to stifle the perception of failure, the Soviets can't retreat from any place where they have established a local Communist regime. This is the reason that the United States cannot provide financial aid to Vietnam; she can only hope for a collapse or internal revolution, which would make Vietnam the first Communist regime to fall.

Cuba, Nicaragua, and Vietnam are the three Communist regimes the Soviet military does not have direct (contiguous land) access to. The Soviet regime must continuously prove to her masses the failure of the West and the great economic success of her revolutionary Marxist society. The military, the beneficiary of this political arm of worldwide expansion, has been given the task to support and help implement this Marxist-Lenin policy. That is why the Soviets have embarked upon extension of their strategic reach by building a huge navy and a massive long-range airlift capability. This military expansion will help implement the long-term Soviet strategic goals of world domination through the establishment of Marxist-Leninist regimes and will help support the Soviet short-term tactical aims of seeking political allies from anti-Western, non-Marxist radical states in the Middle East such as Algeria, Iraq, Libya, and Syria.

The formation of a fourth or fifth power center within the Soviet Union cannot be permitted because the most stable force is a triad. For example, in Poland, when the Solidarity labor union (a fourth power center) and the Catholic church (a fifth power center) both rose to challenge the triad (Polish Secret Police, the Polish military, and the Polish Communist party), they were stifled. In order to put down the power of the Solidarity union and the Catholic church, the Polish military rose to share power with the Polish Secret Police leaving the Polish Communist party totally neutralized.

The advanced industrial nations of the West are in the midst of a high technological explosion. In order to cope with the requirements of full utilization of this technological revolution, a process of decentralization of research and development (R & D), manufacturing, information, and mass media education is taking place. In contrast, within the rigid structure of the Soviet Union, all planning is centralized and all power is concentrated in the hands of a few. The secretiveness and oppressiveness of the Soviet society does not allow the conditions necessary to enable the Soviet Union to enter into this new technological revolution.

Today, the Soviet Union is a ruthless autocratic regime parading under the banner of the Marxist-Lenin ideology. When one understands the society-government relationship, however, it is not difficult to compare the similarities that exist between the Islamic-Fundamentalist nation of Iran and the modern revolutionary Soviet Union.

Iran is a fanatical, ruthless theocratic state run by the ayatollah with a structure staffed by a clergy known as the *mullahs* whose religion is Islamic-Shi'ite fundamentalism. They are actually operating the country by a religious dogma that disregards reality and the well-being of the citizens. Iran offers her citizens only hope for an afterlife in heaven, while she provides a hell on earth based on sacrifice for the good of the theocratic state.

The Soviet Union, also, has her high priest, the secretary of the Party, who provides dogma on the ideology of the state, which also disregards reality and the well-being of Soviet citizens. The Soviet Union promises, and has promised for the last seventy years, a better life for the future. In the meantime, people who have been denied an official religion, or a G-d to whom they can pray, are told that atheism is the official spiritual philosophy of the state. Instead of having *mullahs* to protect the purity of the dogma, the Soviets provide secretaries of local Communist parties. Just as the ideology of Islamic-Shi'ite fundamentalism seeks to spread its dogma to other societies all over the world, the Soviet-Marxist officials are attempting to achieve the same goal. In one case, it is in the name of Allah, and in the other case, it is in the name of Marxist-Leninism—both of which are *transnational imperialist* movements.

There are only two differences between these two autocratic theocracies. One uses technology to attempt to achieve its ends, while the other uses faith in Allah; one provides for hope and salvation after death, while the other provides for hope on earth, which it hasn't been able to deliver. The Soviet people have replaced prayer and hope with vodka; thereby, literally, creating a nation of drunkards. The Soviet people, who have been stripped of hope because they have been denied access to a belief in G-d, have no access to material goods, with the exception of the lucky few who maintain the power. Both the Iranian and the Soviet societies have extremely dangerous transnational movements dedicated to establishing other societies in their own image by force.

The Soviet Union is the only nation in modern world history that periodically purges and destroys masses of her own people in order to intimidate and maintain control of her society. Under Lenin, the Soviet regime established terror as a policy and slaughtered millions of anti-Communist Russians and Socialists who opposed the regime. Then, Stalin came to power, and, in 1925, his regime slaughtered the community of small businessmen that had been created by the NEP of Lenin. In 1927, Stalin decided to eliminate the class of small individual farmers created by Lenin through the process of collectivism. By 1933, he had slaughtered millions of farmers. In 1936, there was a purge to destroy his own bureaucracy and political deviates. In the process, he slaughtered the old-time Communists. Between 1937 and 1938 came the purge of the army with the slaughter of 32,000 officers, including the entire general staff.

World War II brought a respite to the self-destruction of the Soviet people; however, immediately after the end of World War II, Stalin sent all of the repatriated prisoners of war to fill the *gulags* (concentration camps). During 1943 and 1944, after the

German retreat from Soviet-occupied territory, Stalin ordered the complete resettling of national entities, accusing them of collaborating with the Germans. For example, the people who inhabited the cold, high altitude of Caucasus were resettled in Kazakhstan—a dry, hot, sandy, low altitude area—where they contracted tuberculosis by the masses. The Tartars from Crimea were resettled in Siberia where they couldn't survive the harsh climatic conditions. The resettlement was a technique for eliminating the population who couldn't survive their new environments. This was Stalin's method of exterminating those national groups.

1953 witnessed the infamous Jewish doctors' plot—a scheme devised by Stalin to discredit Russian-Jewish doctors and, therefore, all Russian Jews. He created an incident to justify the resettlement of the entire Soviet-Jewish population to Siberia, and only his death during the winter of that year stopped his plan from being implemented. Since the Stalin era, there has been no purge of large groups of people, although the system, tradition, experience, and methods to reinstitute the destruction of sectors of Soviet society still exist. Now, however, there is a greater awareness by the Soviet-ruling elite that such techniques could be used against them by the KGB, the military, or their supreme ruler.

In the last decade, the Cambodian-Marxist regime of Pot Pol, which came to power as a reaction to the U.S. intervention in the early 1970s, brutally eradicated—by the most cruel and inhuman methods—millions of its own Cambodian people. The Marxist leaders totally depopulated the cities and exterminated almost one-third of the Cambodian population. This Marxist ideology created two countries in which the societies (Soviet and Cambodian) slaughtered masses within their own majority population.

THE SOVIET UNION AND THE MIDDLE EAST

For the Soviet Union, the Middle East represents a network of interests. If she can succeed in controlling the area, it would provide her with limitless possibilities for success in other parts of the world. A brief description of Soviet interests in the Middle East follows:

- The Soviets want to protect and maintain their Russian-Orthodox church holdings in the Middle East, especially in Jerusalem, which were established by the czar who was also the leader of the national church prior to the 1917 Russian Revolution.
- Access to the Middle East would provide the Soviets with the means to subvert religious institutions throughout the world through their influence and control of the major holy places of Islam and Christianity.
- Establishing revolutionary regimes in the Arab world would bypass Turkey and provide the Soviets with allies undermining NATO's southern flank.
- The Middle East is the crossroads of Africa, which controls the main waterways from Europe to the Indian Ocean and the Pacific Ocean.
- Control of the region's vast oil resources would provide not only a reliable, cheap oil supply for the Eastern bloc nations and the Soviet Union but also a means of blackmailing the West, primarily Europe.

For defensive purposes, the Soviet Union has massed two-thirds of her military might facing Western Europe and one-third along the Chinese borders. However, for the purposes of expansion, there is no area in the world more vital to the Soviet Union than the Middle East. It is more vital to the Soviet Union than Europe or Asia. All Soviet activities in the Middle East are directed toward future expansion, primarily as a jumping point to the continents of Africa, Asia, and India. No *imperialist-Soviet* regime will ever abandon its desire to control and influence the Middle East.

SOVIET-ISRAELI RELATIONS

History

Prior to the establishment of the State of Israel in May 1948, Zionism in the Soviet Union was detested and attacked viciously. Known or suspected Zionists were jailed. Except for a brief period during Lenin's regime, Zionism was perceived as a crime against the state.

At the time of the establishment of the State of Israel, the

Soviet Union provided political support, offered quick recognition, and established diplomatic relations in the United Nations. At that time, the Soviet Union had two basic reasons for supporting the creation of an independent Jewish state and helping to insure her survival from Arab invasion. First, the Soviets wanted to drive British influence out of the Middle East. Additionally, the Soviets believed that the Jewish state, with her strong Socialist and Marxist core (the Mapam party was extremely Marxist oriented), might become part of the Soviet sphere of influence or, at a minimum, not align with the West.

In 1948, Israel purchased weapons from Czechoslovakia with Soviet approval. In fact, it was the first weapons sale made by any Soviet bloc nation to any nation outside of the Soviet bloc. The Czechoslovakian military transaction provided fighter planes and pilot training; rifles, guns, and ammunition; and training for a complete infantry brigade. It is safe to say that this transaction had an affect on the outcome of the War of Independence and the final armistice borders. While the Arab nations had access to weapons from the West—primarily Britain, Israel's only official source of weapons and training was from the East.

By 1949, Israel was no longer able to purchase arms from Czechoslovakia or any other Eastern bloc nation. And by 1955, relations with the Soviets and the Eastern bloc nations deteriorated to the point where Nasser was able to make massive weapons purchases under extremely favorable conditions. The Soviet Union had concluded that Israel was not going to become a Socialist nation and, simultaneously, found an opportunity to enter the Middle East through Nasser's Egypt. That was the first arms deal to any Middle East country that supplied Soviet weaponry.

During the 1956 Sinai Campaign, Prime Minister Bulganin of the Soviet Union initiated a threat against Israel: to use ballistic missiles if she didn't evacuate the Sinai. Bulganin also broke diplomatic relations with Israel, and they were not re-established until several years later.

After the 1956 Sinai Campaign, the Soviets began a systematic process of massive arms shipments to Algeria, Egypt, Iraq, and Syria. They adopted a totally hostile attitude toward Israel within the United Nations on every issue. They attempted, along with the Arabs, to paint Israel and Zionism as the evil force facing the entire world. Prior to the 1967 War, at a meeting of all Soviet ambassadors on the subject of the Middle East, a decision was made to switch their entire political support to the Arab nations.

During May and June of 1967, Soviet political activity in the region created the atmosphere for the 1967 Six-Day War. The Soviets convinced Nasser that Israel was massing her army along the Syrian border in preparation for an invasion of Syria. When the ideological head of the Mapam party, Chazan, went to see the Soviet ambassador to invite him to inspect the border area and see for himself that the Israeli army was not massed there, he received the reply, "Pravda printed the information and not only must it be true, but the Arabs are going to drive the Jews into the sea." Chazan replied, "We shall show you that the pillars of the Kremlin will tremble." Chazan had been pro-Soviet until that time.

After the 1967 Six-Day War, the Soviet Union broke diplomatic relations with Israel and organized the Third World and the entire Soviet bloc against Israel. The Soviets began vicious propaganda campaigns, which have continued to this very day, while abrogating all commercial ties and existing trade agreements with Israel.

In 1969, Soviet military personnel manned missiles at the Suez Canal. Soviet pilots flew missions over the Canal in defense of Egypt against Israel. Soviet military personnel, including pilots, were killed in combat at the Canal. In fact, in one brief dogfight, four Soviet fighter planes—manned by Soviet pilots—were shot down by Israeli fighters.

In 1973, prior to and during the Yom Kippur War, the Soviets shipped massive amounts of arms to both Egypt and Syria. After the war, the shipments continued to Syria but not to Egypt. It was during this war that the Soviets brought in ballistic missiles with nuclear warheads, which they removed after the war. During the cease-fire, First Secretary Brezhnev threatened to send Soviet military personnel to help defend Egypt, thus triggering the worldwide nuclear alert initiated by Henry Kissinger.

Since the Yom Kippur War, Israel has become the second greatest enemy of the Soviet Union—second only to the United

States. The Soviets began training and supplying the PLO and all its factions to terrorize Israel. They condoned, supported, and organized terror against the State of Israel, while supporting or leading every anti-Israel resolution in the United Nations. During the military confrontation with Syrian military forces in the 1982 Peace for Galilee War, the destruction of their most modern weapon systems dealt the Soviets the fifth major military defeat of their weapon systems and tactics by Israel: 1956, 1967, 1969, 1973, and 1982.

Relations Between Pre-revolutionary Russia and Her Jews

For several hundred years, pre-revolutionary czarist Russia actively pursued anti-Semitism as a government policy. Pogroms were government organized and instigated in order to divert the attention of the masses from their miserable lot in life: hunger and extremely poor living conditions. The Ukrainians, for example, had a long tradition of pogroms, and it was the great Kishinev pogrom in the early 1900s that created a mass exodus of Jews from Russia.

The Jews lived under conditions of abject poverty and persecution by the government and the Russian people. They were forced to live in designated rural ghettos (never in cities) and were treated as second- or third-class citizens. Because the czarist regime was very corrupt, Jews with any money who were able to find their way into the cities could bribe officials and receive a secular education generally denied the Jewish community.

The enlightenment period that swept through Europe, including Russia, found fertile ground among the Jewish youth who shed their religious observance to seek another G-d—a G-d of change. Thus Jews became activists in the revolutionary movement that arose during the Russian enlightenment period. Several political activist movements in which Jews were extremely involved emerged from pre-revolutionary Russia. The Jewish movements were Zionism (a Jewish-Socialist movement) and Bundism (an internationalist-Socialist movement that was anti-Zionist but promoted Jewish culture). The Russian national movements were social democracy and communism. Jews were extremely involved in the organization and direction of the Communist movement and its splinters and, therefore, had great influence over these movements.

Relations Between the Soviet Union and Her Jews

After the Russian Revolution, the first Communist Politburo contained close to a majority of Jews led by Leon Trotsky, the minister of defense. Until Stalin came to power, the post-revolutionary Soviet Union had a great influence over the Communist party and the operations of the government, including the secret service and the military. Slowly, Stalin removed positions of influence from the Party apparatus, secret police, and military; however, it wasn't until the mid-thirties that he undertook a massive purge of Jews from the Soviet power structure.

In 1948, after the creation of the State of Israel, there was a display of mass support for Israel within the Soviet-Jewish community. Stalin, who was paranoid about power, turned totally against the Soviet-Jewish community. He slaughtered Jewish intellectuals, such as the Mikals from the Jewish stage, and closed Jewish theatres, newspapers, and Yiddish schools. Then, he created the name *cosmopolit* to describe a Jew—a worldly person, one not loyal to the state. He considered this a crime against the state, and only Jews were accused of being *cosmopolit.*

This frenetic demonstration of anti-Semitic policies within the Soviet Union was carried over to the Soviet satellites—particularly, Poland and Czechoslovakia. The famous Slansky Trial, which indicted and convicted Slansky, a Czech Jew and a leader of the Mapam party of Israel who was visiting Czechoslovakia, was based on the accusation that he was spying. He spent many years in jail despite his innocence. During the period after World War II until Stalin's death in 1953, every Soviet bloc nation publicly promoted the Jewish trial.

In 1953, when Stalin staged the famous doctors' plot, he made preparations to expel all the Jews from the cities of the Soviet Union and planned to relocate them in the barrens of Siberia to be, in one way or another, exterminated. Stalin's timely death in the winter of 1953, therefore, saved the lives of millions of Jews. Before he died, however, some Jewish doctors died from the treatment they had been subjected to in preparation for the trial. Stalin created a vicious anti-Semitic atmosphere—not dissimilar to that of Hitler's Nazi Germany—and spread it throughout the Soviet Union and the Soviet bloc countries. It must not be forgotten that Hitler's extermination of the vast majority of Jews had taken place in Eastern Europe; therefore, Stalin had fertile ground in which to implement his vicious anti-Semitic actions.

After Stalin's death, the corrosion of the Jewish position within the Soviet society continued to take place as a matter of policy. The Soviets made it more difficult for Jews to enter universities to study the sciences, closed the foreign service totally to Jews, and limited Jewish employment opportunities. This policy continues unabated today.

During the period of detente initiated by Brezhnev, the Soviets reversed Stalin's policy of not permitting Jews to emigrate from the Soviet Union. However, this reversal of Stalin's policy stopped when detente stopped—just after the Soviet invasion of Afghanistan.

The important difference between the treatment of Jews in the Soviet Union and that of other minorities is that Jews are not officially recognized; therefore, being Jewish does not afford one the national, religious, or cultural privileges enjoyed by other minorities. The Jews have become a nonentity. This is true even under Gorbachev despite his policy of liberalization.

At this time, the conclusion that must be drawn is that the Soviet attitude toward Israel as a nation and the Soviet Jews as a people is the same entity. Despite seventy years of Communist persecution, the Soviet Jews—without access to any form of Jewish education, without religious practices, and without the ability to relate in any way to the State of Israel—have managed to keep their Jewish national identity blossoming.

The Present

Several elements contribute to the existing (and projected) relationship between the Soviet Union and Israel.
- Communism and Zionism become competitive because they are both transnational movements. As a matter of faith, communism opposes all transnational movements. Zionism is a significant enemy because it influences Soviet Jewry.

- Israel is the only successful example in the Middle East of Western democracy. Her social values and institutions, especially freedom of speech and the press, are totally rejected by the Soviet brand of communism in spite of the Marxist belief in such freedoms. All of the other twenty-three nations in the region are transitional military regimes, autocracies, monarchies, or theocracies, but all are totalitarian in nature and ripe for revolution.
- Israel is a vital, successful example of utilization of modern agricultural methods. She is self-sufficient in food with only 4 1/2 percent of her population engaged in agriculture. She also exports several billion dollars in agricultural products. Her agricultural methods could be adopted by agrarian, backward Third World nations. In contrast, the Soviet Union who cannot feed half of her population, despite the agricultural effort of the other half, is not engaged in agricultural aid.
- The Israeli-Arab conflicts have shown that Soviet weapons are inferior to Western weapon systems. This situation:
  — lessens the perception of Soviet power in Western Europe and the Far East;
  — diminishes Soviet ability to market their weapon systems for export; and
  — diminishes Soviet ability to influence Third World countries, since weapon sales or agricultural assistance are traditional means of entering less-developed countries.
- The Jewish lobby for Israel in the United States has influenced U.S.-U.S.S.R. relations, and there is every reason to believe it will continue to do so.
- Israel has become a technomilitary intermediary for the West—primarily for the United States—with Third World countries; thus, she is a serious competitor for the Soviet Union.
- Israel appears to be becoming a source for technical innovations in the area of tactical military weapon systems for Communist China. This works against Soviet interests.

The Future

The Soviet inability to enter into the technological industrial revolution and keep pace with the explosion of technology that the West is experiencing, by all indications, will continue through the end of the twentieth century. The basis for progress in this electronic age is the free transmission of information at all levels. The Soviet system cannot allow such freedom to exist in its society for the simple reason that it contradicts all the basic principles upon which Soviet society is based. Gorbachev stands against the formidable forces of a middle-class bureaucracy, a central committee apparatus, a nonexistent rooted peasantry, and a society based on the principles of information control. It sounds like much too much for one man to undertake. For these reasons, the gaps between Soviet and Western technological development, standard of living, quality of life, and military sophistication will continue to widen.

Even with Gorbachev's attempt to loosen the economic grip that the totalitarian regime has on Russia by allowing small business enterprise, nothing will be able to change the continuing economic deterioration without a *revolution* within the system (which Gorbachev seems to be attempting). Gorbachev watched neighboring China in horror as she became not only self-sufficient but also an exporter of food only four years after the introduction of similar kinds of economic reforms. This was only possible in China because the Chinese cultural revolution did not completely destroy the agricultural infrastructure. Stalin, however, completely and mercilessly annihilated a complete class of Russian peasants. Now, Gorbachev needs, magically, to create a new class of peasants. This ambitious desire will never come to fruition in the near future because of the profound distrust of the government shared by all. It is the perpetuation of the system that will cause the Soviets to continue to stay far behind in both agriculture and technology and will, ultimately, make their weapon systems obsolete as well. The great disappointment in the lack of any economic improvement within the Soviet Union, to date, has given rise to a popular anti-semitic movement among the people, creating a new anti-semitic organization—*Pamiat.*

The results of the growing technological gap between the Soviet nations and the West will be far reaching. There will be a comparative deterioration in the Soviet standard of living, which will create a growing discontentment and hatred of the government by the people. The Soviets will be unable to spread their influence to nations outside of the Soviet bloc through aid because those nations will seek Western technological aid that is more advanced in agriculture, industry, and weapon systems. Even today, the Soviet Union cannot offer agricultural know-how, except for major infrastructural national projects. Only military aid is still sought from the Soviets, and it's only a matter of time before no country will accept Soviet modern weapon systems and relevant tactics.

In the Middle East, the primary focus of the disputes between nations within that region will shift from the Arab-Israeli question and the centrality of the Palestinians to the threat from Sunni- and Shi'ite-Islamic fundamentalism—a threat to the national integrity of all the nations within the region. Given the size of the Soviet-Moslem population, what is most significant is that they can't feel immune to such a force. Today, the Soviets are supplying the Iraqis with weapon systems to insure their ability to defend themselves against Iran, the spearhead of Shi'ite-Islamic fundamentalism.

Until now, the major thrust of Soviet penetration in the Middle East has been based on an involvement in the Arab-Israeli dispute. However, if the Moslem religious struggle takes center stage, then the Soviets will have to find another method through which to penetrate the Middle East. They will not be able to establish a Communist-type regime within the Middle East nor will they be able to have any influence through agriculture, industry, or weapon systems. Therefore, the only method of entering into the Middle East will be by subversion of the region governments.

Since the existing Arab regimes in the Middle East are totalitarian, the only method of subverting their governments is through the PLO. With the PLO weakened, it is highly improbable that it can be used to intimidate existing regimes anymore. Thus, the only nation left with which the Soviets could try using techniques of undermining and destabilizing the existing government would be Israel, since she has a democratic society with a large hostile minority. It is, therefore, plausible to believe that the Soviet Union, before the end of the century, will be forced to attempt to re-establish diplomatic relations with Israel. Also, there appears to be a convergence of interests between Israel and the Soviet Union because both of them desire to thwart the spread of Islamic fundamentalism.

The other prevailing reason for the Soviets to re-establish diplomatic relations with Israel is that Israel is quickly becoming the major stronghold in the Middle East. A diplomatic relationship with Israel is imperative for the Soviets, given Israel's military power and dominance over the region. However, from Israel's perspective, there are no urgent interests in allowing a Soviet diplomatic presence, except for one— Israel's desire to resume Soviet-Jewish emigration directly to Israel from the Soviet Union. This is the *only* carrot the Soviets can extend to entice Israel to any diplomatic relationship.

A point must be made that there is a serious probability that the present political structure of the Soviet Union will change by a collapse of the imperial Soviet system, if Gorbachev does not succeed in his attempt to modernize the economy.

People's Republic of China

The geopolitical world of the 1980s will force nations to seek new and perceptibly strange alliances as the twenty-first century approaches. As never before, countries face dangers generated by an uncontrolled global arms race and a worldwide economic crisis that has developed from commodity pricing based on political factors and not on market conditions. The never-ending quest for national security creates a search for survival.

Presently, from Israel's perspective, the world contains four power centers: the Eastern bloc of nations led by the Soviet Union; the Western European nations led by Germany, France, and England; the United States; and mainland China. The absence of natural resources and a credible military infra-structure—two criteria required for a nation to become a world power—diminish Japan's role as a fifth power center, despite her population in excess of 100 million and her gigantic industrialized economy—two other criteria that enable a nation to become a world power.

If the Soviet Union, Western Europe, and the United States continue to tighten the political noose around Israel—each doing so for different reasons—Israel will need to establish additional alliances to counterbalance and neutralize political strangulation by both her "friends" (the United States and Western Europe) and her "enemies" (the Soviet Union and the Arab nations). Presently, from an Israeli point of view, only mainland China can partially fulfill her needs. By the turn of the century, as China modernizes and grows more powerful—thus gaining more influence in world political forums—all political, economic, and military relationships that have developed will become more significant vis-à-vis the other global powers.

Before there can be a clear understanding of the benefits that can accrue to both Israel and mainland China as a result of their relationships, it is essential to review, briefly, Israel's current and projected ties with the other world powers.

THE WESTERN NATIONS, THE EASTERN BLOC, AND ISRAEL

As early as 1944, U.S. President Franklin D. Roosevelt commented, "The trouble with this country is that you can't win an election without the oil bloc and you can't even govern with it." If Roosevelt's statement was true in 1944, how much more appropriate would that statement be if made in 1989 by President Bush? Roosevelt's observation was made when oil was an inexpensive, abundantly available commodity priced by the law of the marketplace—supply and demand. But oil is now an expensive, perceptively scarce resource priced by political factors and not the economics of the marketplace.

The control of too much of this valuable commodity, and therefore of a significant portion of the world's monetary reserves, has been in the hands of a relatively few medieval-style Arabian sheiks, princes, and sultans. This hold has enabled this small group to wield immense influence over the major oil companies, multinational corporations, the international banking community, the communications media, and Western foreign policy formulators. The judgment of Western politicians is obscured by the narrowly prejudiced need for power of these Arab elite—at the expense of compromising issues of fundamental economic and political concern to Western security.

Ever since October 1973, when the oil-controlling Arab elite determined to neutralize the stunning military defeat of their Arab brethren in the Yom Kippur War by using oil as a weapon to their economic and political advantage, a cloud of paranoia has reigned over the nations of the entire Free World—the fear of being cut off from the available oil supply and/or an escalation of oil prices that would strangle their economies. Western leaders, since the 1973 Yom Kippur War, have failed to recognize or to react publicly to the threat to their national interests created by the bitter inter- and intra-Arab rivalries.

Additionally, Western policymakers refuse to understand the real strength of the non-Arab forces within the so-called Arab domain. Many policy failures, of both omission and commission, have permitted a series of events to continue without an appropriate response, which now places the Middle East on the brink of disaster and anarchy. These events include the Lebanese civil war, the Iraq-Iran War, and unbridled and unpunished Arab terrorism (except for the Reagan administration countermeasures after 1986).

In addition to ignoring the destabilizing effect that the sudden oil wealth has created in what are, essentially, feudal societies, Western policymakers also:

- have been blind to the rise of Islamic fundamentalism and incapable of projecting its effect on the area's fragile regimes (e.g., the fall of the shah, the rise of Shi'ite political power in Lebanon, the threat to the internal security of Bahrain and Saudi Arabia from Shi'ite Fundamentalists and of Egypt from Sunni Fundamentalists);
- have declined to focus on the essential stabilizing nature of Israel's growing military power and failed to appreciate the need for an U.S. military presence in the region to offset the unreliable character of local surrogates (only partially rectified by the interjection of the U.S. fleet in the Gulf in the fall of 1987); and
- have neglected to assess properly the risks of indiscriminate massive sales of weapon systems to nations of the Middle East or the effects of the peace and stability these sales could have on the region.

Despite this shortsightedness, the United States and Western Europe have chosen to cater to the elite of the Arab world, to wit, the mission of the U.S. fleet in the Persian Gulf. A perceived mutuality of interests has prevailed between the West and these Arab elite. The West has pursued policies that have satisfied the interests of the Arabs while undermining their own economic well-being (except for a number of large, multinational corporations and defense contractors who have benefited economically).

To placate and pacify the Arab oil bloc, U.S. decision makers have found it necessary to view Middle East insecurity and instability primarily within the narrowly defined context of the Arab-Israeli dispute. They have focused on the "just rights" of the Palestinians as the core issue to the complete exclusion of all other disputes within that region. In addition, the United States has continued to support as reasonable expectation a policy of "selling pieces" of Israel to the Arabs in return for a "piece of peace." As Israel continues to resist agreement to such a formula for peace, a public image of Israel as an international pariah is being created.

From the time she assumed the 1919 mandate over Palestine until the very eve of Israel's independence on May 15, 1948, Britain pursued a policy of foiling the development of a Jewish State. She continues to this date to put forth policies that challenge Israel's very existence. Since 1973, Britain and the rest of Western Europe have pursued a policy of politically delegitimatizing the State of Israel.

Of all the nations in the world, Britain should have the best understanding of the Middle East, since she had the greatest influence and the longest presence there of any Western nation. The existence of Arab national movements and power were figments of British imagination. It was Britain's "Lawrence of Arabia" who created the Arab myths that have come to plague the Free World. British leaders, possibly because of their vast experience and long-time presence in the Middle East, seem to be guided in their attitudes toward Israel by a combination of anti-Semitism and a need to punish Israel. They cannot forget their perception that it was the establishment of the State of Israel that began the swift decline of the great British Empire, relegating her from a global to a regional power.

Since 1973, many key Western policymakers have viewed their nations' relationships with the State of Israel as an embarrassment. They have behaved as if their continued support of Israel, regardless of the level, assists in dividing the Arab world. Their perception of the nature of the conflict between Israel and the Arab nations precludes a joint effort by the Middle East and the West in a concerted drive to contain the Soviet influence and presence in the region.

The Soviet Union, however, viewed Israel's existence as a stabilizing force that acted as an impediment to the Arab revolutionary forces—forces that the Soviet Union supported in an effort to radicalize the Middle East. To the Soviet Union, the destruction of Israel would have strengthened these Arab revolutionary movements sufficiently to bring about the collapse of the present Arab ruling elite. This would have established the kind of atmosphere the Soviets could succeed in influencing. However, the Soviet defeat in Afghanistan and with Gorbachev's new internal and external tactical thinking, Israel's survival now plays an important role in the Soviet ability to influence events in the area.

CHINA AND ISRAEL

Mainland China views Israel and her role in the Middle East from an entirely different perspective. Unlike the Soviet Union, China is not now in conflict with the Western European nations or with the United States. Unlike Western Europe and the United States, China does not have any short- or medium-range interests in the oil or wealth of the Middle East, since she has vast known oil reserves of her own that she is in the process of developing. To China, what makes Israel the most valuable power in the Middle East is that she *is* the only force blocking the Soviet Union from undermining and establishing control over the existing Arab elite. Israel's military presence has reduced the threat of direct invasion of the Arab elite regimes by the Soviet Union or by the radical Arab countries. To China, only the military presence of Israel and Pakistan block her own total encirclement by the Soviet Union and, therefore, her access to the shores of the Mediterranean, the Persian Gulf, and the Indian Ocean. From the perspective of China, Israel's presence in the Middle East greatly contributes to her security since it virtually eliminates Soviet influence in the region.

Now, the West, with the exception of Britain, has reached the same conclusion as China about Israel's essential contribution to blocking increased Soviet influence in the Middle East. The Lebanon debacle (the failure of the multinational force in 1983 and 1984 to stabilize that country) and the present decreased role of Middle East oil have served as eye openers for the West.

Based on the present state of Israel's relations with the West and on China's understanding of the need for Israel's military presence, the PROC can become an important friend of Israel.

As we approach the twenty-first century, this Chinese-Israeli relationship could help Israel withstand an onslaught to erode her political position in the area vis-à-vis the Arab world.

At first glance, a relationship between these two countries seems absurd. It is quite apparent, however, that mainland China and Israel share a number of mutual interests, even though, by rational speculation, a comparison of the two countries produces many differences. China is the world's largest nation, containing 1 billion people and encompassing millions of square miles of territory. The State of Israel is one of the world's smallest nations, with less than 4 million Jews and a territory that is measured in just thousands of square miles. Mainland China is totalitarian elite (completely authoritarian) with an economy strictly controlled by Marxist principles (which are now being modified to include a modicum of entrepreneurships and incentives for workers). Israel is a freewheeling democratic state with an economy that combines Milton Friedman economic principles and labor-owned management.

The type of relationship that might develop between these two nations makes sense only when the magnitude of their individual national problems is analyzed. Israel, a nation in almost political isolation, suffers what appears to be insoluble economic problems. These problems have been exaggerated by an uncontrolled arms race, the costs incurred by Israel's Sinai evacuation—a result of the Camp David Accords of 1979, and the subsequent step-function price increase in oil.

Although Israel lacks essential natural resources, she has made great strides in her agricultural and technoindustrial development. Science and technology, particularly as applied to the development of military weapon systems, mushroomed during the past forty years—a period in which six wars have been waged successfully against larger armies equipped with vast quantities of Soviet weapon systems.

Israel's export growth in agriculture, light industry, and advanced-technology weapon systems is exceeded by very few other nations in the world. The achievement of this record growth has required much improvisation and ingenuity. What Israel lacked in capital, communications, water resources (i.e., rain), arable land, natural resources, and accessible markets, she compensated for with a remarkable degree of resourcefulness.

China, by contrast, while rich in energy and natural resources, is decades behind Israel in the application of modern technology to the fields of agriculture, light industry, and advanced-technology weapon systems. As an example of China's backward military development, in 1979, she invaded Vietnam and suffered a humiliating military defeat because she fought that war with the same equipment and tactics she had utilized in Korea twenty-five years earlier. In the war against Vietnam, China lost 30,000 men and 150 jet fighters in only a few days, suffering a stunning setback at the hands of a small, backward nation. The Vietnamese, however, had already acquired decades of fighting experience in their war against France, then the United States, which culminated in the U.S. evacuation.

Chairman Mao Ze-dong (a/k/a Mao Tse-tung) believed that in all future wars China would overcome any enemy by utilizing masses of men and materials. China's experience in Vietnam (plus the experience of Israel's enemies in her last few wars) have proven Mao's concept to be fallacious. As a result of China's Vietnam experience in 1979, her political power in Southeast Asia eroded. Five years earlier, when the United States retreated from Vietnam, U.S. influence in the area also perceptibly diminished (resulting in a power vacuum that the Soviet Union sought to fill).

Not only did China's political power erode in the eyes of other nations of Southeast Asia, but the Chinese people lost face and were humbled. Their perception of their own power underwent a radical change. This situation created pressure within China's ruling circles to redress that wrong and re-establish China as the leading power in the region. To do this, China will have to engage and defeat Vietnam in a future war. This will be necessary in order to establish Chinese supremacy beyond any doubt. In addition, China must also punish Vietnam for her harsh and cruel treatment of the ethnic Chinese residing within her borders—most of the "boat people" were of Chinese origin.

But to achieve this, China must equip her armed forces with modern weapon systems. In addition, she must prepare for a possible future conflict with the Soviet Union, which maintains a huge army along her border with China. Tanks with 105 millimeter guns appeared in Peking on the anniversary of the Chinese Revolution in the summer of 1984. To all Western observers, it appeared that those guns were of Israeli origin. At that time, there was a spate of speculative, unsupported articles in the Western press purporting a massive Israel-China arms deal.

China must expand her industry, especially in the field of electronics and computers—areas in which Israel possesses much expertise. The modernization of her agriculture to increase both the quantity and the variety of food production is high on China's priority list. The achievement of this goal requires the introduction of advanced irrigational techniques as well as the economical application of chemical fertilizers. Israel uses the most modern agricultural methods in the world and is second only to the United States in overall agricultural productivity. An Israeli entrepreneur admitted being involved in the planning of the modernization of China's agriculture.

In order to implement any future modernization program, the Chinese must utilize huge doses of improvisation and innovation, since they lack modern communications and infrastructure. Because of her own unique experience, Israel is probably the only nation in the world that can meet some of China's requirements in exactly the way they are needed.

The Chinese have learned hard lessons from the cultural revolution and have now embarked upon a course that encourages motivation through incentives. A class system is evolving and a disparity in rewards is being established. Their Marxist purity is undergoing the kind of change that took place within Russia in the 1930s and 1940s. There is now a great striving for education. With only the best students being admitted to the great university in Peking, there is an enrollment in the millions.

Today, the Israeli economy requires an infusion of work (new markets) to expand military and domestic industries. Likewise, Israel is in need of natural resources (raw materials). China's energy resources—oil and coal—and other natural resources could be exchanged for Israel's manufactured goods, know-how, and turnkey mass production facilities. This could form a natural, logical synergism between these two diverse nations.

The nations of the West have pursued economic and political relations with all nations and societies in order to expand their economic and political power. Even though Israel's long-term strategic interests are with the free democratic nations, she must seek economic relations with other nations, including mainland China, in her quest for political survival.

While the logic of this analysis is sound, fulfillment requires China to behave in a rational manner to solve her fundamental problems. Historically, nations behave to support their own best interests. Unfortunately, how they define these interests are not always logical or rational.

A Chinese-Israeli economic relationship, in whatever form or shape, would be good for both nations. It would strengthen Israel and, therefore, would ultimately help to improve her relations with the Western world. At the same time, China would achieve her goal of modernization, without which she will not be able to withstand the growing Soviet influence over Southeast Asia and without which she will not be able to establish herself as the major power in that region.

As the world enters the twenty-first century, it is highly probable that mainland China and Israel will have strong economic ties and, as a result, subsequent political relationships.

Part Four

ISRAEL'S MILITARY DEVELOPMENT: IMPACT ON GLOBAL INTERESTS IN THE MIDDLE EAST

Israel's Military Development: Impact on Global Interest in the Middle East

Overview

The political disunity and weakness in government that have been the hallmark of Israeli politics since the 1973 Yom Kippur War have in no way hampered Israel's phenomenal military development. Since the establishment of the State in 1948, Israel has always been faced with the threat of war from a combination of enemies—all of whom are determined to wipe her off the map. This ongoing economic, political, and military war between Israel and the Arab nations is one that appears not to have any solution.

Peace between Israel and the Arab nations—other than Egypt—has not been possible because the leaders of those nations make as a precondition the settlement of the legitimate rights of the Arab Palestinian "people." But a settlement of the conflict between the Arab Palestinians and Israel requires a dialogue between those Palestinians and Israel. Since there is no peace between Israel and the other Arab nations, however, the Palestinians dare not make any deal that might aggravate the very Arab nations from which they draw their political support. This is a real "Catch-22." The essence of the problem lies in the fact that the Arab-Moslem world is not prepared to accept any non-Arab-Moslem nation on lands that they have staked out to be Arab lands. This is why Christian Lebanon was crushed, why no Kurdish state has evolved, and why no Druse, Copt, or other national independent group has developed. All the Arab nations are united on one point beyond their hatred for the State of Israel—the total opposition to the development of any non-Arab, non-Moslem entity in the Middle East.

Israel's ability to defend herself over the past four decades has grown dramatically. The national commitment for military preparedness is unmatched any place in the world. Over the past four decades, the people of Israel have allocated enormous resources in money and people to the problem of defense.

The development of Israel's defense industries has been nothing short of phenomenal. Today, Israel has the capability of absorbing the latest in technology and applying it toward the development of tactical weapon systems with unique performance characteristics. This will provide an edge in any future war, since the capability for the element of surprise can mean the difference in any battle. Israel is militarily stronger today than ever before, and the level of stability in the area is determined by that strength.

Israel's special relationship with the United States continues to grow stronger in proportion to the growth of Israel's military strength. The close of the Reagan administration was marked by the recognition of Israel as a strategic ally with all the status and benefits that accrue to a North Atlantic Treaty Organization (NATO) nation.

The history of modern Israel—pre-state and post-state—has been that the Arab-Israeli struggle has flared into active war every decade: starting with the bloody riots of 1929, 1936, and 1939; the 1948 War of Independence; the 1956 100-hour Sinai Campaign; the June 1967 Six-Day War; the 1969 to 1970 Canal War; the 1973 Yom Kippur War; the 1982 Peace for Galilee War; and, now, in 1988, an *Intifada* or uprising, which resembles the riots of 1929 and the 1930s, is taking place.

Although throughout the rest of the world wars are winding down and the ability to wage them successfully is becoming increasingly more costly and difficult, in the Middle East the possibility and probability of violence and war have not been minimized—not even by those same factors that have been effective elsewhere. The Middle East is the only region in the world in which there is too much hatred by too many people of too many other people, coupled with too much money available to buy too many weapons from too many sources with too much interest in an area where there are too many differences. This is not a good profile for peace.

The prospects for a Middle East devoid of any military conflict over the next twenty years is not good. From Israel's perspective, she can only avoid war if her enemies believe that fighting such a war would be, for them, too costly to wage. But one thing is certain: as new technologies develop, Israel's scientists and engineers who are working in the military industries will be there to apply them to developing new tactical weapon systems that will enable Israel to cope with any challenge that may arise.

Impact of Technology on the Philosophy of War

HISTORICAL REVIEW

Throughout the ages, the evolution of weapons and the by-products of the new developments have been the major determinants of the outcome of war. It has been the modernization of weapons and the application of accompanying new tactics and strategies that have determined who would be the victor. It has not been enough for countries to possess modern weapons if tactics and strategies remained outdated; the victor has always been the one who had the strategies and tactics that matched the new weapons.

Hyskos, for example, some 4,000 years ago, conquered Egypt by introducing chariots upon which two people rode instead of one. The second party, not hampered with steering the chariot, was free to shoot arrows. Hannibal, through the use of the naturally armored elephant that rendered the Roman slings and arrows ineffectual, conquered the great Roman Empire some 2,000 years ago.

More recently, during World War II, it was only Germany who had mastered the appropriate strategies and tactics for air and ground warfare in order to neutralize and by-pass the great French supertrench, the Maginot Line. In 1939, both sides had enormous numbers of troops along with sizable air forces and many tanks. In fact, France actually had more tanks than Germany, but they were dispersed over vast areas of territory while the Germans concentrated their tank forces toward one objective. It was the German tactical innovations of dive bombing and low flight air support for their massive concentration of tanks which allowed them to break through and by-pass the "impenetrable" barricade known as the Maginot Line. History shows, then, that innovative tactics and strategies have rendered the once great advantages of troop strength and sheer masses of armaments virtually ineffectual.

There was a time, too, when it was possible for a large nation to conduct warfare without mobilizing the entire industrial base. Once the technology changed, however, it was no longer possible to mobilize *only* the armed forces—as it was before World War I. For example, prior to the Napoleonic wars, ground battles were fought hand to hand with swords and small personal arms, therefore utilizing only limited-sized forces and only highly trained professionals. Mass production of musket-type rifles (1796 to 1818), however, provided Napoleon the opportunity to mobilize a huge illiterate, nonprofessional army because it took only weeks to train a soldier to use a rifle, whereas to use swords, training had taken years. Later—in 1871, the Germans retaliated with the next major innovation as the Prussian military giant, Bizmarck, introduced the cannon to modern warfare.

For the sake of overview, the significant innovations introduced during the major conflicts of the late nineteenth and twentieth centuries are identified.

The Sino-Japanese War

The Sino-Japanese War in 1895 saw the introduction of a very simple tactic by the Japanese—the use of trenches. Hundreds of thousands of marching Russian troops were slaughtered by Japanese soldiers waiting in trenches. The Japanese were also among the first to introduce the machine gun in a major war. Prior to that, the Gatling gun had been used by the U.S. Army against the Indians during the post-Civil War period and was a determining factor in the defeat of the Indians.

World War I

During World War I (1914 to 1918), both sides fought in trenches. The deadly force of the machine gun and mortar exacerbated an already deadly stalemate. Millions died in that war. A whole generation of male youth from Germany, France, Russia, and England were wiped out. This war necessitated the invention of the tank, airplane, and mustard gas, which became essential for breaking the stalemate. The tank was invented as a tool to save downed pilots who fell near Dunkirk. The first tank was, basically, an automobile fitted with armor plating from an armor chimney factory. Tanks and planes were used sparingly by the end of the war.

World War II (1939 to 1945)

It took 100 to 200 years to apply the theoretical breakthroughs in electronics and nuclear science that had been uncovered during the nineteenth century. There were three major areas of innovation during the great war: the massive use of tanks and airplanes; the introduction of radio, radar, and electronic communication; and, in the final stages of the war, the introduction of jet aircraft, surface-to-air missiles (SAMs), ballistic missiles, cruising missiles, precision-guided munitions (PGMs), and the atomic bomb.

Because of the explosion of military technology during World War II, the entire industrial and manpower base of a nation had to be mobilized for war to satisfy the need for the vast quantities of complex equipment that were being consumed by the nation-states and their war machines. By the close of the war, nations had learned how to produce technological weapons in huge quantities—10,000 planes a month, tens of thousands of tanks, massive quantities of vacuum tubes. There became a shortage of aluminum for consumer goods because of its extensive application as chaff to fool radar.

The major beneficent effect of the development of all this war machinery was the infectious spread of technological know-how throughout society. As a result of World War II and the technologies that were discovered and introduced during that period, the post-World War II era saw the broad societal usage of the telegram, computers, photography, and consumer electronics.

The Korean War

During the Korean War (1950 to 1953), all the existing technologies that had been developed during World War II were applied. While the role of jet aircraft was expanded, communications returned to the extensive use of the telephone rather than the radio because of the terrain. The Korean War ended in a stalemate of static trench warfare. No innovation was presented that could break the stalemate.

The Vietnam War

The Vietnam War (1963 to 1973) saw the first massive use of SAMs, which exposed aircraft to serious limitations in their missions and made them highly vulnerable. There was massive use of helicopters for many purposes, especially as gunships and transports. Also during the Vietnam War, the use of electronic warfare, primarily against missiles, was introduced.

The United States had to mobilize tremendous logistic efforts to fight a primitive peasant army that lacked modern weapons. The Vietnam War showed that a highly motivated, unsophisticated army utilizing simple weapons could overcome a most sophisticated force. It exhibited the vulnerability of complex weapon systems to simple tactics and weapons and the limitations of a great power with an unmotivated army in fighting a small idealistic force.

The Six-Day War

The Israeli-Arab Six-Day War in June 1967 showed that by a combination of the proper tactics (air force and electronic warfare), an entire army and air force could be decimated in a few hours. This war demonstrated, for the first time, that the attrition rate of aircraft and tanks could actually exceed the production rates of those weapon systems by the major powers.

The War of Attrition

The War of Attrition (1968 to 1970) between Israel and Egypt took place at the Suez Canal. This war witnessed the first introduction of massive combinations of various types of SAMs—SA-2 high altitude (several kinds), SA-3 low altitude, and SA-7 shoulder fired—against jet aircraft. It was the first clear sign that, without neutralizing the SAMs, the beginning of the end of close air support had arrived. The use of aircraft in the role of flying artillery was being challenged. This was the first time, also, that electronic warfare was being used on a massive scale.

The Yom Kippur War

The 1973 Yom Kippur War saw the first extensive use of electronic intelligence—including satellites and surveillance aircraft—*during* warfare. Massive numbers of antitank missiles—PGMs—were utilized to destroy entire tank forces within days; in particular, the U.S.-made Maverick was used extensively by Israel against Egyptian and Syrian tanks and exhibited a high hit ratio. This was the first war in which air-to-air missiles were used extensively with great effect in air-to-air combat—over 400 Syrian and Egyptian aircraft were shot down.

During this war, Egypt introduced long-range air-to-surface missiles, employing the Soviet Kelp, while Syria introduced the Soviet Frog, a surface-to-surface missile. The introduction and extensive use of Soviet infrared night-fighting equipment by the Egyptians and Syrians gave the Arabs an advantage in conducting night-time warfare.

The decisive factor in the war became Israel's extremely well-organized air-to-air battle with the Command Control Communications and Intelligence (C-3I) system in conjunction with highly skilled, trained pilots. If it was indeed employed, this was probably the first application of real-time C-3I in control of the battle. It appears to be the case.

As a result of the Yom Kippur War, several lessons were—or should have been—learned.

- The use of low- and medium-altitude SAMs (SA-2, SA-3, SA-6, SA-7, SUZ-23) can render close air support for ground troops ineffective. Israel's air force was denied its traditional role of providing close ground support by the presence of SAMs.
- The massive use of antitank missiles (PGMs) can virtually eliminate entire tank forces quickly.
- The use of infrared night-fighting equipment allows the extension of active combat to night hours; that is, fighting can take place twenty-four hours per day.
- The vulnerability of a surface navy became apparent when more than thirteen Arab ships were sunk in combat by Israeli sea-skimmer, surface-to-surface missiles. This lesson was obvious to all who fought in that war, but, apparently, not to other nations of the world.

There were almost as many new technology weapons and weapon systems introduced during the three-week Yom Kippur War as there were during World War II, which lasted six years. During that three-week period, over 500 airplanes and 5,000 tanks were destroyed—at that time, fifteen years of U.S. tank production, one year of Soviet tank production, and almost two years of U.S. plane production. And the amount of missiles and ammunition expended was more than either the United States or the Soviets produced in one year at that time.

The huge attrition rate of aircraft, missiles, tanks, and ammunition during the 1973 Yom Kippur War amplified the first sign of the 1967 Six-Day War that huge quantities of equipment that took months or years for either major power to produce could be expended in a matter of days. It became obvious that irreplaceable battlefield equipment had to be manned by highly trained and competent personnel in order to obtain its maximum utilization, and, even more significant, that large and small nations alike could operate in a modern warfare environment for only a limited time—measured in weeks, not in months, and, certainly, not in years.

The Yom Kippur War became the model war for modern conventional high-technology warfare. The essential need for real-time supply information was another important lesson learned by those engaged in the war but, again, apparently not by other nations of the world.

Soviet Invasion of Afghanistan

When the Soviet Union invaded Afghanistan in 1980, a highly organized and mechanized modern army—equipped with sophisticated weapon systems—was sent to fight against illiterate, ill-equipped, religiously motivated Islamic Fundamentalists operating in small units on horses in the mountains. The Soviets—without motivation—went to fight an enemy with the wrong tactical equipment. They had to replace their entire force with Moslems from the Soviet Union after their elite "Russian" (non-Moslem) soldiers collapsed in battle.

The Soviets never anticipated the strength of the religious commitment of the Afghans nor did they realize the intensity of the Afghani motivation to resist. Now, eight years later, the Soviets are caught in their own Vietnam—they can't win and can't afford to lose. Their Afghan troops are deserting—so similar to what occurred in Vietnam. They are in the war forever, unless they are prepared to withdraw their army without achieving their goals.

The most significant development in technology from this war has been the massive use of helicopter warships. (They were originally used in Vietnam but not as extensively.) The Soviets, however, have suffered tremendous helicopter losses. The Afghan rebels received stinger missiles from the United States and Blowpipe radio beam-directed missiles from Great Britain. Since there is no defense against either of these deadly missiles, they brought down Soviet helicopters daily. Additionally, the Soviet SA-7 shoulder-fired SAM, either captured by the Afghan rebels or obtained by them from the Egyptians, has proven to be extremely effective against Soviet helicopters. Simple weapons such as a hand grenade attached to a balloon have also harassed the Soviet helicopters. The Soviet military as well as the total Soviet power structure have been unable to cope with this kind of warfare. The Soviet Union has learned that the only way to end this war is to leave Afghanistan just as the United States had to leave Vietnam.

The Iraqi assumption that destroying an army and bombing cities could bring down the government of a highly motivated, fanatical religious society proved to be totally incorrect. In September 1981, Iraq invaded Iran with a massive, sophisticated modern army but without either an adequate supply system or the support needed to maintain and resupply losses in battle sufficient to sustain a continuous forward thrust. The Iraqis planned for a two-week battle to achieve their political objectives, but seven warring years and one cease-fire later, they are no closer to those objectives than when they started.

Saddam Hussein made another error in judgment when he thought that the Iranian military—equipped with the most sophisticated U.S. weapon systems, such as F-14 fighter planes with Phoenix missiles, phantom war planes, Hydrofoil ships, M-60 tanks, and PGMs—would be incapable of fighting because of the extensive purging of the officer corps and the decimated command structure that remained. The entire Iranian army helped to operate and maintain Iranian forces in battle by applying innovative simplicity—by using sophisticated weapons in a simple mode. Hussein also erroneously believed that Iran's political fight with the United States would deny her access to U.S. spare parts.

Additionally, Hussein genuinely thought that the Arabs of Kurdistan would defect to the Iraqi side, along with the Sunni majority of Arabastan. He assumed that their common nationality would be a strong enough bond to gain their support. This was not the case. Hussein made a major blunder when he pummeled the population centers in Kurdistan and Arabastan with Iraqi missiles and bombs. That action assured the allegiance of those provinces to the ayatollah.

In his wildest imagination, Hussein never believed that the Ayatollah Khomeini would unleash his fire power against Iraq's oil installations, thereby forcing him to reciprocate with the destruction of Iran's economic installations. Hussein had $35 billion in the bank and $35 billion in yearly oil income. He had the largest Arab army on the Gulf, extensively equipped with the most sophisticated weapon systems. His military was equipped by the Soviets and courted by the Americans and French. Iraq was on the verge of joining the nuclear club, and Hussein was confident enough to say publicly that Tel Aviv must be totally annihilated. Until the spring of 1988, however, he hovered on the brink of defeat and internal collapse.

The Iraq-Iran War was the first arena for the extensive use of modern ballistic missiles—the Soviet Scud and Frog—against population centers. (It was done on a smaller scale in World War II when the Germans employed the crude V-I flying bomb and the V-2 ballistic missile against London.)

A lesson learned from the Iraq-Iran War is that a sophisticated weapon system, not operated as intended, can still be deadly even if used in a manner not anticipated. For example, the F-4 Phantom was flown by Iranians without the fire control radar and communications navigation. It was used only as a flying platform to unload iron bombs, employing a World War II strategy that made simple bombs effective deadly weapons when there were huge targets (such as oil installations) and good weather conditions.

Another lesson learned from this war is that if the objectives of modern, sophisticated, technological warfare are not met by the end of the first phase of a war, then the combatants enter a phase in which the battle deteriorates to a World War I style trench warfare. And under such circumstances, it is not the army with the most training and the most advanced weapon systems that will determine the outcome; rather, it is the army that can amass the greatest number of motivated men prepared, not to win, but to die.

Neither Iran nor Iraq has the capability to gather and analyze intelligence in real time in order to locate large concentrations of enemy forces and weapon systems. Each must have an elite force to accomplish these tasks. So yet another lesson learned from this war is that a warring nation must have proper intelligence capability to locate enemy-massed forces in real time, and then must concentrate nonatomic, mass-destruct weapons—like cluster bomb units (CBUs)—against them in order to kill and wound large numbers of people, demoralize and panic the balance, and eliminate the enemy's strike capability. Large numbers of wounded, groaning men can be more demoralizing than an equivalent number of dead ones.

The United States provided some intelligence—gathered from satellites—to the Iraqis, which helped them cope with Iran's massive human wave offensives. Iraq is the largest single importer of modern weapon systems, including the world's most advanced. Yet, until the spring of 1988, she was unable to destroy Iran's infrastructure (oil installations, power stations, radio and television stations) because she lacked the appropriate weapons, tactics, and human resources. The Iranians retaliated with simple missiles, unsophisticated weapons, and small boats, nibbling and eroding away Iraq's position. Simple mines in the Persian Gulf temporarily neutralized the protection of the entire U.S. fleet and exasperated the Arab world.

Saddam Hussein, unwittingly, consolidated the power of the ayatollah by permitting him the ability to exterminate all his opposition within Iran and rally his Shi'ite forces around a holy war to which there could be no negotiated end—only, possibly, a temporary cease-fire to recuperate from exhaustion and rebuild. This also unleashed Shi'ite minorities into political action throughout the entire Middle East. If the Shi'ites remain in power in Iran, an unconditional surrender can be the only terms for peace.

Saddam Hussein's war enabled the ayatollah to formulate his

long-term goals and give them credibility. It also split the Arab world into two fundamental camps that were diametrically opposed in this conflict. It put to bed any credible focus on the Arab-Palestinian issue as the fundamental problem in the Middle East. As long as the war actively continued, the West could not place its primary attention on the Palestinian problem but had to focus on the Persian Gulf and the Shi'ite problem. Even after the Iraqis abandoned Iranian territory, the war raged on because Iran would not accept a settlement. There was no end in sight for this war—everyone was in it to the death—until the United States sent her navy into the Gulf against Iran and until the new long-range missiles used by both sides against enemy population centers were also used by Iraq to destroy Iran's oil infrastructure, rendering her incapable of financing the war. Post-World War II experience—the Soviets in Afghanistan, the Iraqis in Iran, the Americans in Vietnam, and the Israelis in Lebanon—has demonstrated that it is necessary to know not only how to begin a war but how to end it as well.

The Falkland War

The Falkland War of 1982 between Argentina and Britain made it obvious that the British have not learned a lesson from any war since World War I. If Argentina had been a clever adversary with weapon systems at her disposal, she could have sunk the entire British fleet in the first few days of the war. The British, who for years had the world's greatest naval power, could not adapt the most modern, sophisticated technology applied in other wars to their naval structure.

Throughout history, many great nations have suffered glaring defeats because their military was tied to obsolete doctrines that didn't take into account the real significance of new weapon systems. No one was more guilty of this than the British. In short, they learned nothing from the Falkland War. Britain suffers from the inertia of an old, established infrastructure that relies on its laurels and, therefore, is resistant to the most rudimentary changes.

This is also true of many other Western nations and their navies. It is seen in their inability to recognize and react to the impact of the combination of low-cost accurate missiles and modern intelligence gathering, which makes billion dollar ships—such as the British Invincible—totally vulnerable and at the mercy of those missiles.

Today, the U.S. Navy is faced with an awesome problem—the continuing development of larger missiles with all aspect attack capability, longer range, and more effective warheads of higher degrees of accuracy. These missiles cost only $1 million at the most, yet they have the capability to destroy a $10 billion, fully equipped aircraft carrier. It is easy to draw the conclusion that large surface vessels like aircraft carriers are an outmoded way of doing battle. But can you imagine the upheaval of a total redirection from surface ships such as cruisers, destroyers, battleships, and aircraft carriers to small, fast, surface, and subsurface ships? What a problem it would be politically to implement such a plan, given the size of the U.S. Navy, the budget, and the economic effect on the industry developed and dependent upon the present naval tactics and strategy. The implementation of such a program would be literally impossible to achieve. In a smaller way, this was Britain's problem, and it was only after the Falkland War that she had a chance to rethink her whole naval strategy. It is most likely that the British will try to salvage their present naval aircraft and look for quick-fix solutions.

The Falkland War in 1982, the U.S. missile attack on the Libyan navy in the Bay of Sidra in 1986, and the Iraqi missile attack on the U.S. Stark in 1987 are excellent examples of the vulnerability of existing warships to modern missiles. When will Western nations draw the proper conclusion that today's navies are totally defenseless and modernize around small ships?

Today, the deployment of aircraft carriers in combat is based on the assumption of a three-layer defense:

- first, the EC-2 Hawkeye radar surveillance for long-range target acquisition of enemy ships, aircraft, and missiles followed by the use of the F-14 Tomcat warplane with Phoenix missiles to destroy those enemy targets;
- second, the missile cruiser modified with the AEGIS weapon system; and
- third, the AEGIS point defense system, which contains complete requisition for guarding and tracking multi-targets approaching the aircraft carrier itself.

If the three defenses work, all is well. If one missile gets through the three huge defense systems, however, then a one-half ton warhead disables the aircraft carrier.

Such technological advances as supersonic attack missiles with last minute final attack maneuvers and supersonic dash capability will render large aircraft carrier defense impossible. The two most serious problems facing both small and large nations in this regard are:

- adapting new tactics to operational new weapon systems and
- escaping the vested interests as reflected first by the military commanders, second by the industry, and third by the communities economically affected.

In 1938, a famous U.S. general couldn't understand the necessity for modernizing ground forces with the use of tanks. He felt that since horses had served well in battle for 300 years, they shouldn't be replaced. One year later, in 1939, German Panzer divisions, led by tanks, quickly slaughtered the elite Polish Cavalry. We must remember the famous trial of Billy Mitchell who was court-marshaled because he challenged fundamental navy doctrine by proposing the building of aircraft carriers. Today, over fifty years later, some admiral will probably have to be court-marshaled for proposing the scrapping of aircraft carriers, while demanding a navy built around small, fast, and highly maneuverable surface and subsurface ships, small aircraft carriers that carry only a few planes, and/or subsurface aircraft carriers. Present submarines, for example, are already 18,000 tons; and there is good reason to believe that they could be 30,000 tons and carry military aircraft. Even large commercial submarines are going to be built because of the vulnerability of tankers and surface transport ships.

The Peace for Galilee War

Israel's June 1982 incursion into Lebanon to destroy PLO bases and Syrian missile sites established in violation of an earlier agreement among Syria, Israel, and the United States marked the beginning of the Peace for Galilee War. The tactical military results of this conflict for Israel were outstanding as they relate to operations against the Syrian military. The Israeli air force shot down almost 100 Syrian advanced jet fighters in air-to-air combat without a single loss of an Israeli warplane. The Israeli air force also destroyed twenty Syrian missile sites each of which contained SA-2s, SA-3s, SA-6s, SA-8s, and SA-9 infrareds (designed to combat low-flying planes). All this, too, was achieved without the loss of a single Israeli warplane. And for the first time, T-72 tanks—armed with what was thought to be impregnable armor—were destroyed by the Israeli forces.

To achieve these results, the Israeli military made widespread use of weapon systems introduced in previous wars; however, extensive modifications made by the Israeli military industries provided extended capability and improved performance specifications. These weapons modifications plus the application of more advanced tactics to take advantage of the improved performance specifications enabled Israel to obtain outstanding battlefield results. Additionally during this war, Israel introduced improved air-to-air missiles, better tanks (the Merkava), more advanced electronic warfare systems, more extensive use of night vision equipment, and, for the first time in combat, C-3I—utilized by integrating real-time battlefield intelligence in coordination with reconnaissance remotely piloted vehicles (RPVs).

The lessons of this war served to reinforce what had been experienced in previous wars and known for decades—that tanks and armor cannot be used effectively in hilly regions (like Lebanon). The tank was invented for the flat lands of Europe and is applicable only where there are large areas of flat terrain.

ASSESSMENT OF THE PRESENT

At the end of his second term in the 1960s, Eisenhower warned us to beware of the industrial-military complex, but he never explained why. Today, the problem goes well beyond the industrial-military complex. Technology is moving so rapidly and in so many different applicable directions, that decision making, even unencumbered by outside influences, is extremely difficult. It is providing alternative solutions to existing military problems while simultaneously developing completely new military systems, which, if made operational, could dramatically effect modern warfare.

Never before in the history of mankind has changing technology affected warfare so quickly. Earlier, hundreds of years passed before technology dramatically changed the conduct of war. More recently, only fifty-year periods, then twenty-year periods, then ten-year periods were required. Today, only five-year periods are needed for modern technology to impact the conduct of war. The introduction of new weapon systems and the application of appropriate tactics is lagging—by as much as fifteen years—in the large nations. A small nation like Israel, however, can react faster and introduce new technologies much more quickly and thus revolutionize the battlefield. A good example is the RPV. But by the twenty-first century—only twelve years away—there could be a dramatic change in the application of technology such that only two or three years will be required for major developments to take place and, therefore, effect change in the battlefield. This means that a small nation like Israel could stay ahead of the superpowers and thus ahead of their Arab-client states that rely solely on imported weapon systems and tactics.

Over a 4,000-year history, only those nations that were flexible and made basic changes in their military structure—probably incorporating revolutionary weapons—succeeded on the battlefield. In the future, any nation that has the capability to be flexible enough to change basic military doctrine (which tends to be very rigid) will be able to take advantage of the revolutionary weapon systems that will most certainly be available by the turn of the twenty-first century. But those nations that cannot incorporate these new revolutionary weapon systems into their existing military tactics and strategies will lose wars very rapidly—perhaps in a period measured in hours instead of days.

The "superpowers" are the most vulnerable because of their massive investments of money, time, and prestige in the tried and true tactics. The Third World countries will continue to be victims of the superpowers who supply them with the most modern weapon systems based on obsolete tactics. The Arab nations, which are totally dependent upon either Soviet, U.S., or Western European weapon systems and tactics, will not be able to take advantage of the revolutionary changes in warfare.

Few nations are actually in the position to incorporate the revolutionary weapon systems that will derive from the advances in technology likely to take place by the twenty-first century in computers, microelectronics, sensors, new propulsion systems, and new guarding systems. It may be difficult to believe, but only five nations possess the ingredients required to revolutionize tactical conventional warfare within the next twenty years. These countries are South Africa, South Korea, Singapore, Israel, and, possibly, Taiwan. The necessary elements are:

- a viable, constant, ideological enemy posed for war in which the enemy is numerically much larger and compromise would jeopardize the nation's very existence (the exception to which is South Korea);
- a strong scientific base to incorporate ongoing technological changes into existing weapon systems; and
- a vital need to survive that will overcome the resistance of the military-industrial-economic complex to change—that is, their recalcitrance to manufacture and make operational new revolutionary weapon systems and to create the new organization and tactics required to obtain the maximum benefits of such new systems.

France, which is second only to the United States in military technology, suffers from rigidness in structure and the lack of a perceived immediate threat. Remember, it was the French who built the Maginot line. The other Western European nations are inextricably tied to NATO and the United States for their weapons development. Since the decision-making process within NATO is political as well as military and requires the approval of all the NATO nations, it is time consuming and tedious. The Eastern European nations who are supplied by the USSR and, therefore, militarily dependent upon her, inherit the built-in problems of a superpower, compounded by the high-technology gap between the East and the West. Sweden feels secure because of her long-term neutrality, while Switzerland's security derives from favorable defensive terrain and the absence of immediate threat.

Given all these considerations, Israel is best equipped to revolutionize warfare completely by the turn of the century. The lapse of time from conceptualizing a new weapon system to making it operational is much shorter for Israel than for most other countries. The number of new tactical weapon systems made public by Israel in 1987 proves the agility of the Israeli defense establishment in applying known technology to develop new weapon systems and make them operational. These include:

- stand-off, laser-guided bombs;

- Barak antimissile missiles;
- OFER infrared-guided bombs (primarily antitank);
- Arrow antiballistic missiles;
- the AWAC system in a modified Boeing 707; and
- the Phantom 2000 (a re-engined Phantom with new avionics and armament).

Israel will be forced to develop revolutionary weapon systems and suitable tactics because of a number of very serious factors. First, Israel's external threats challenge her very existence. Second, Israel's enemies outnumber her by tens of millions. They have huge financial resources and almost unlimited access to weapon systems from the East as well as from the West. Superficially, it's a grim situation, especially since much of the world tends to be unsympathetic to Israel's plight. This combination of factors forces Israel to continue to probe technology to seek new solutions to existing military problems.

Israel is small in land and population in relation to the Arab nations confronting her, individually or collectively. Relative to her size, she has exceedingly long borders with her neighboring Arab nations—borders void of natural obstacles to block enemy attack. Israel's long, narrow shape offers no land depth and, therefore, provides no room for error. She can't lose any territory in the initial stages of a war and still recover. Since Israel maintains a small standing army and requires seventy-two hours to mobilize her forces to full combat strength, it is her air force— always at full strength—that must defend the country during those first critical seventy-two hours. The Arab nations have access to relatively unlimited quantities of the most sophisticated and expensive weapon systems from both the East and the West. Therefore, Israel can never match quantitatively the combined Arab forces confronting her, and maintaining her security under the existing 5/6:1 ratio may be difficult in the future. The ever-increasing cost of modern weapon systems forces Israel to seek alternative solutions through application of modern high technology.

By seeking the most simplistic solutions to even the most complex military problem while utilizing the most advanced technology available, Israel exercises financial and temporal expedience. She is confronted by neither the expense nor the time required by the more fractional methods of military problem solving as practiced by advanced Western nations. Additionally, Israel is in a unique situation because the industrial managers who design and manufacture military weapon systems also serve as reservists in the military and actually use the equipment they build. Therefore, there is rapid cross-fertilization between the military's technical needs and the industrial solution.

Although most countries advance through agrarian, heavy industrial, technological, and service stages of economic growth, Israel never developed or invested in smokestack industries—for the most part because of their capital- and energy-intensive nature. Other deterrents to the development of heavy industry by Israel include her lack of natural resources, the absence of a population base sufficient to support such industry, the lack of natural trading partners, and the Arab economic boycott. Additionally, Israel's observations of the Western industrial developed societies indicated that smokestack industries would not remain growth industries. Because of high energy needs and the rising cost of energy, new methods to spur economic growth would be required.

It became apparent to Israel that to secure her future and encourage *aliyah* from the United States, Europe, and the USSR, it was essential to progress directly from an only agrarian economy to one that would be primarily based on technology. She realized that a technological and science-based economy is technology intensive and, therefore, requires a highly trained and skilled manpower pool supported by a well-developed scientific community. To this end, Israel established major universities in Haifa, Tel Aviv, Jerusalem, and Beir Sheva and a major advanced science center—the Weizman Institute—in Rohovot. In addition, close relations with the American-Jewish community—well trained in the industrially related areas of science and technology—have provided Israel a highly skilled manpower pool familiar with U.S. high technology and vastly experienced in U.S. high-technology industries.

Israel's industrial base consists of hundreds of small enterprises, many of which fall under large umbrella companies. Since a large number of these enterprises contribute to the development of high-technology weapon systems and since they provide the flexibility characteristic of small companies as opposed to the rigidity of large industrial complexes, the rapid change required to apply new technology to revolutionary new weapon systems is facilitated.

While Israel's technological and scientific community was rooted in pure science and established by German and American scientists who settled there, her industrial technological infrastructure grew to support a rapidly expanding military requirement for self-sufficiency. This created the Israeli military-industrial complex.

A series of wars and other military confrontations in which the technologists themselves participated provided first-hand experience not diluted by a third-party bureaucracy with all its vested interests. This process has continued since the establishment of the State.

The growth of the Israeli military-industrial complex has been stimulated greatly by three events:

- the fear of a French-Arab political orientation—in 1963;
- the French arms embargo against Israel—in 1967; and
- the twofold realization that the United States—Israel's only arms supplier—could not provide the weapon systems required to accommodate Israel's unique needs to offset massive U.S. arms shipments to moderate Arab nations still at war with Israel.

Today, the massive incentive for greater weapon systems production and, therefore, the highest degree of weapons independence for Israel stems from:

- the need to develop unique warning weapons capable of neutralizing both U.S. and Soviet weapon systems utilized by the Arab nations;
- the need to facilitate the immigration of Soviet and Western Jewry—many of whom are technicians, scientists, and engineers—by providing employment in their fields within the required proper technological infrastructure;
- the need for high-technological advances that are fundamental to successful military programs;
- the preoccupation of the United States with her Strategic Defense Initiative (SDI)—Star Wars—and strategic parity in nuclear weapons, along with her lack of commitment to the development of short-range tactical conventional weapons (the area of Israel's greatest concern), which forces Israel to seek unique home-grown solutions;

- the recent concern of NATO about tactical nonnuclear weapons and its Arab political orientation, which makes available to the Arab nations whatever is available to NATO; and
- the hope that Israel's prior achievements in developing and manufacturing military weapon systems will enable her, by the turn of the century, to develop, manufacture, and make operational a number of original weapon systems—one or more of which may possibly revolutionize warfare and provide Israel with military hegemony over the area and, possibly, with the basis for increased exports to nations with similar problems.

Israel, with the world's sixteenth largest scientific community and the world's largest number of scientists per capita, provides a natural scientific infrastructure to support and encourage the growth of an economy, including the military-industrial complex, based on high technology. This military industry provides approximately 50 percent of Israel's dollar value military needs and 25 percent of the nation's industrial exports—$1.2 billion of the $5 billion in 1983.

THE TWENTY-FIRST CENTURY

By the twenty-first century, Israel must develop a credible strategic deterrent against mass destruction weapons (nuclear or other) delivered by any one or combination of her Middle East neighbors, including Iran. She must have available both defensive and offensive strategic deterrents:

- defensive to provide the ability to intercept and destroy enemy mass destruct weapons before they reach vital targets within Israel; and
- offensive as a means of delivery of similar weapons to any hostile neighbor.

Although an agreement should be reached not to introduce these weapons into the area, Israel must have the capability to do so quickly, if necessary.

Since no nation, including the United States, will provide Israel with the means to achieve this twofold goal, she must develop this capability by herself. Israel's destruction of Iraq's nuclear reactor signals the fact that she doesn't as yet have a credible deterrent. The announcement of the 1,450 km (1,000 mile) capability of the Jericho II—a ballistic missile for which there is no known defense—puts every Arab country and some major sites of the Soviet Union (e.g., Odessa and huge Soviet naval installations) within its range and, therefore, neutralizes the kind of threat Bulganin made against Israel in 1956. Now the Soviet Union will find it much more difficult to intimidate Israel by the threat of direct Soviet military intervention (similar to France's *Force de Frappe*).

The experience gained from the long Iraq-Iran War has shown that when sophisticated weapon systems run out, the warring nations are reduced to trench warfare, with masses of men fighting with simple weapons. Israel's relatively small population places her at a terrible disadvantage, when compared to her neighbors with their magnitude of manpower from societies where human life has little value. Sadat said he was ready to sacrifice 1 million men to destroy Israel, and Khomeini said that for every Shia male it's an honor and duty to die (not to fight) for Islam with a stated goal of freeing Jerusalem from the Jews.

The Arab-Israeli problem will face Israel for many decades. It is an ideological conflict with no negotiable solution in sight; yet, there may be minor settlements along the way. The Arab world is continually being prepared by its leaders for the ultimate destruction of Israel.

The Arabs can be tempted to utilize two-stage tactics:
• first, the mutual destruction of modern weapon systems that cannot be replaced rapidly and in sufficient numbers to sustain modern warfare and,
• second, the utilization of their large manpower resources to drain Israel and inflict unbearable losses even at the cost of tenfold losses on their side.

The only logical conclusion is that Israel must develop, produce, and field (make operational) two classes of weapon systems. Effective weapon systems using high technology to neutralize the enemy's sophisticated weapons must be created on the basis of a large force multiplier. Although the technology must be cost effective, the major factor must not be cost or quantity but, rather, the force multiplier effectiveness. In addition, nonnuclear mass destruct weapons must be mass produced inexpensively. They must be simple to use and coupled with real-time intelligence in order to counter the enemy's second stage attack—often based on utilizing a mass of manpower without regard for losses.

New types of laser-guided SAMs—like the ADATS (air defense antitank system) developed jointly by the Swiss and Americans—provide a threat to aircraft and tanks against which there is no known defense. These are laser-guided missiles with optical tracking that can operate day and night within a range of 8 km. This makes low-flying aircraft totally vulnerable. Because of the vulnerability of attack aircraft, heavy installations such as bunkers will be destroyed by aircraft 40 to 50 km from target-firing, standoff PGMs or glide bombs with pinpoint accuracy.

Weapon Systems for the Twenty-First Century

By the turn of the century, there will be a major decline in the role of manned aircraft in the close ground support role. This is due to the proliferation of shoulder-fired SAMs utilizing electro-optical guidance systems, which any soldier can be trained to operate readily. And their low cost makes mass distribution feasible. These shoulder-fired SAMs make the use of low-flying aircraft in the ground support role against enemy troop positions costly and almost impossible. Countermeasures against this type of weapon are not yet available; in fact, no practical approach to resolution has even been conceived. The problem is the huge quantity of these missiles that can be fired at one plane by ordinary foot soldiers; it makes it statistically impossible for a plane to defend against such an attack. In 1983, within a two-month period of minor ground support roles, four attack jets were downed by these SA-7 missiles—two American in Lebanon, one Israeli in Lebanon, and one French in Chad. Jet attack fighters cost between $10 and $25 million each, while the shoulder-fired SAM costs between $10 and $40 thousand each. (The former is the cost of a SA-7, and the latter is the cost of a French MISTRAL missile.) This makes the SAM an extremely cost-effective weapon system.

A real challenge, then, faces military strategists and planners in the future. There is a decreasing cost trend for missiles manufactured in larger quantities, while airplane costs will continue to rise, making the cost ratio of missile-to-plane even more unfavorable. When the cost of training a pilot, which takes three years, is taken into account, the cost ratio becomes totally intolerable. The continuing development of radar-controlled guns—such as the Russian ZU-23/4, which is a mobile system, and the French GIPARD, which has increased fire power—will further terrorize the attack aircraft.

The most devastating threat to attack aircraft comes from the combined use of shoulder-fired missiles and mobile radar-controlled guns—called SHORAD by the United States. Their use has forced tactical attack aircraft to adopt new tactics. To avoid the effects of these combined weapons, the aircraft must approach at medium altitude, dive on to the target, and then shoot right up again, thus minimizing exposure to that fire. Those tactics, however, are now threatened by recently developed mobile shoot and move missiles that are deadly against jet aircraft flying at medium altitudes.

In addition, stand-off weapons have been developed and their further refinement will continue. The new problem created by the use of these stand-off weapons—target acquisition and identification from extended distances—will be solved by synthetic aperture radar (SAR) systems—all-weather, long-range reconnaissance systems mounted on an aircraft.

The only long-term solution to the restoration of attack aircraft in their traditional role of close ground support, as of now, is to destroy the medium altitude SAMs by means other than aircraft before bringing in the attack planes. However, the continuous upgrading of the shoot and move SAMs makes this task somewhat elusive. To cope with this difficulty, an air force must chase and destroy these mobile missile systems and divert them from the attack mission. This is an unacceptable focus of attention and, certainly, not cost effective.

The primary role of the tactical air force—battlefield close air support—will no longer be feasible or cost effective at the turn of the century. This role must be returned to the ground forces to implement by themselves; however, totally new revolutionary weapon systems must be developed for the ground forces for that purpose. These new weapon systems must combine the use of remote-controlled vehicles (loitering weapons) with real-time target acquisition systems. These unmanned vehicles (RPVs) should have sensors combined with artificial intelligence. Such attack weapons, however, must be sufficiently low in cost for the ground defenses to be able to use them in large numbers since it is not feasible to fire large numbers of relatively expensive missiles at a very inexpensive RPV.

The effect of RPVs on battlefield conditions can be devastating. Five hundred such unmanned vehicles hovering over a battlefield are equivalent in cost to one attack fighter but are much less vulnerable to destruction. At the same time, they are capable of terrorizing an area and destroying hundreds of targets such as tanks. As a real force multiplier to defend against, RPVs will require a whole new generation of defenses at a huge cost. This loitering weapon (RPV) becomes a simple, low-cost deadly weapon system, triggering the need for the enemy to spend huge sums of money and time and requiring a complete change in military doctrine.

The same unmanned vehicles (RPVs) can be adapted to destroy extensive mine fields and/or achieve rapid dispersement of mines. They also afford an alternative technique for bringing real-time battlefield recognition and intelligence down to the battalion level. By the turn of the century, Israel must develop and make operational a host of RPVs to replace attack aircraft or find another method to deal with the SAM missile threat, thus revolutionizing battlefield conditions.

Israel:
The Only Middle East Military Ally
of the United States

Since the conclusion of the Vietnam War, there has been a steady decay in the tactical conventional military forces of the Western nations. This is in spite of the vast increase in U.S. military spending by Carter in his last year and Reagan during his time as president. However, Israel's phenomenal development during this period has made her one of the leading tactical conventional military powers in the Western world—a power which, in terms of Middle East presence, is second only to that of the Soviet Union.

Obviously, England, France, Japan, Germany, and the United States also have the potential to become great tactical military powers. To fulfill that potential, however, would require a major leadership decision as well as the national will for its implementation. That could take years. Yet, Israel can already field, within seventy-two hours, an integrated tactical military force of considerable size. Modern tactics, advanced technological operation of equipment, and C-3I, as we shall see later, are already "givens" in the IDF.

Although the United States could create a viable tactical military potential sooner than her allies, the problem then becomes the ability to deploy those forces in the Middle East. Even though enormous efforts have been expended toward this goal, the conventional fighting capability of the U.S. armed forces has, unfortunately, deteriorated. The Lebanon debacle, where scores of U.S. Marines lost their lives, is only one of many small-scale indicators of this fact. Another was the aborted effort to rescue the U.S. hostages in Iran during Carter's administration and, still another, the less-than-adequate performance of U.S. forces in the Grenada campaign during Reagan's presidency. The present and future problem for the United States is twofold: she must improve radically both the fighting capability of her armed forces and her ability to deploy them.

The decay of U.S. conventional forces can be traced to the nation's post-Vietnam War mood. The draft was replaced by an all-volunteer army. The size of the tactical force was reduced, as was the spending on tactical weapon systems. Spiraling oil prices contributed to the prevailing mood, which produced opposition to increased military spending, since a reduction in government services was essential. Even though there were dramatic increases in military spending during the Reagan administration, these revenues focused primarily on strategic forces and SDI, while the establishment of a serious tactical conventional capability was neglected. At the same time, however, the Soviet Union has increased her spending on new operational tactical weapon systems, while expanding her conventional forces.

The lack of U.S. national will was only enhanced by both the Ford and Carter administrations' changes in political perception. They adopted a policy that ruled out the use of force to achieve political objectives. They propounded the theory that the world had undergone a fundamental change, claiming that the Vietnam and Yom Kippur Wars had proven that military power could no longer be used to achieve political goals. Instead, political power would be attained through the appropriate application of economic force. The establishment of a new world order, as envisioned by a consensus of U.S. foreign policy experts, would be achieved through the clever application of economic power (thus believed the "Pollyannas"). They argued that future Soviet expansion would be contained through a creative application of economic incentives and deterrents—sell, lend, or grant the Soviets the food and technology they might gain through aggression, thus diminishing the spoils a war might yield.

As a result, during the Ford/Carter/early Reagan period of military de-emphasis, Saudi Arabia—an oil-rich sheikdom ruled by a family of several thousand—became a world power. By the new rules of the post-Yom Kippur War power game, this half illiterate, feudal, sixteenth century tribal state—bereft of any

Western concept of human life, human values, or human dignity; with slave trade in the tens of thousands; and with no hope of achieving plausible military power for decades to come—was anointed "superpower." This was the result of successive U.S. administrations that viewed the world as they would have liked it to be, instead of viewing the reality of the world as it existed and would exist for a number of years to come. Only the decline in oil prices and the failure of U.S. policy in Lebanon caused the political clout of Saudi Arabia to be viewed in the proper perspective.

Since the Yom Kippur War, successive Israeli governments have borrowed and spent a large proportion of their national resources on military modernization and preparedness. Israel has been spending a higher percentage of her GNP on military hardware than any other nation on the globe. Her present high level of military spending has been determined by a Middle East arms race precipitated in the main by the political rivalries of the superpowers, as well as the West's need for the recycling of petrodollars.

TACTICAL CONVENTIONAL MILITARY POWER REDEFINED

The rapid pace of technological developments necessitates a redefinition of tactical conventional military power. In order to avoid erroneous conclusions, a fresh approach to the subject is necessary—an approach that reveals major weaknesses in what have been accepted as conventional methods of defining tactical military power.

Basically, tactical military power contains four elements, three of which can be quantified: military industrial power, national will to manufacture tactical military systems, and operational tactical C-3I. The fourth element, the quality of the military personnel, has been extremely difficult to measure; nevertheless, its importance cannot be neglected or minimized. The first three elements and their requirements are outlined below.

Military Industrial Power

- There must exist a scientific base dedicated to basic research that is strong enough to achieve fundamental breakthroughs in basic technology. Only three nations in the world now

meet this criterion. In rank order they are: the United States, the USSR, and France (which established its scientific base under Charles De Gaulle).
- There must be an ability to apply basic known technology to weapon systems. Today, only seven nations have this capability. In rank order they are: the USSR, the United States, France, Israel, England, Sweden, and Italy.

The National Will to Manufacture Tactical Military Systems

- A nation must have the functional knowledge to define correctly the operational military systems that need to be developed. This is critical since more than half of the problem lies in determining the correct operational specifications and defining the requirements. There are four nations that meet this standard. In rank order they are: the USSR, the United States, Israel, and France (a poor fourth).
- The national will must be present to develop, manufacture, and then make operational the tactical military systems before technological obsolescence occurs. A failure to gain operational experience on existing weapon systems before obsolescence compromises the ability to define adequately the next generation military system. The qualifying nations in rank order are: the USSR, the United States (in limited areas), Israel, France, England (in limited areas), and Germany (in limited areas).

Operation Tactical Level Command and Control Communications with Intelligence (C-3I)

C-3I requires a method of providing the military command with the capability to control and monitor completely, and in real time, all aspects of the operations of each military unit. Only the three nations identified below have this capability today.
- The USSR has built an extremely sophisticated C-3I through the utilization of unsophisticated equipment coupled to a tremendous organization in electronic warfare that reaches down to the lowest level unit.
- Israel has built a complex C-3I by combining sophisticated and unsophisticated equipment with very large numbers of computers.

- The United States has a sophisticated C-3I in her air force and navy but none in her army.

An analysis of overall tactical military power applying the three quantifiable elements (military-industrial power, national will to build tactical military systems, and C-3I), but *disregarding* the fourth element (the quality of military personnel), glaringly indicates that, today, the USSR is the world's greatest tactical military power. The United States, though second to the USSR, is far behind. Israel is the world's third greatest (and only other) tactical military power. A fourth does not exist on any continent.

When the analysis is applied strictly to the Middle East, U.S. tactical military power is almost nonexistent. U.S. tactical forces are spread thinly throughout the world but are absent from the Middle East, and the United States lacks the ability to move her existing tactical forces to that region. It would take years to develop the means even if a decision were made to do so. Therefore, in the Middle East today, and for years to come, Israel's tactical military power will grow stronger and remain unchallenged—as her new weapon systems become operational and as she expands her C-3I. Right now, for instance, Israel is developing new tactical weapon systems—on her own—that are yet to be known by the West. This creates the advantage of secrecy of new discoveries, since weapons developed in the West are most certainly going to be known to the Soviets.

The Soviet intervention in the Horn of Africa and subsequent invasion of Afghanistan have dimmed America's perception of her own economic power and, consequently, her influence on political events. By these military moves, the Soviets have indicated that they will conform to the new power rules established by the West only when it suits them. They have also demonstrated that they will continue to utilize conventional tactical military power as a means to extend their political influence.

As a consequence of the changing perception of military power, the Israeli role in the Middle East must be analyzed from a different point of view. Three major events that happened in the Middle East forced the United States and the West to reconsider their views—the Iraq-Iran War, the bombing of Iraq's nuclear facility, and the Lebanon War.

THE IRAQ-IRAN WAR

In September 1980, Saddam Hussein, "the ruthless butcher of Baghdad," rallied his army and his people to fight "to the death" as he launched the invasion of Iran for which he had prepared for over a year. The plan required a decisive military victory—with all military objectives to be taken within five to six days. The objectives were: control over the Shatt Al-Arab waterway, occupation of the three islands at the entrance to the Strait of Hormuz, and the annexation of the oil-rich Khuzistan province—the area settled by Iranian-Sunni Arabs.

Hundreds of foreign correspondents, mostly from Western Europe, were attached to the carnival-like invasion of Iran. Glowing reports of victory appeared daily in such prestigious London newspapers as the *Guardian,* the *Observer,* the *Financial Times,* and the *Daily Telegraph,* which competed each day for the most sensational headlines in reporting stunning Iraqi military victories. The fall of the strategic cities of Abadan, Khorramshahr, Ahwaz, and Dezfil were described in detail by British journalists. They printed eyewitness accounts of the mighty Iraqi army's crushing defeat of the ragtag Iranian forces who, by the end of the first week of fighting, were reported to be in complete disarray. Television camera crews supplied BBC TV with daily film coverage providing a visual display of the wonders of Iraq's heroic forces, which was then duly broadcasted to the British people.

After the first week of the war, the headlines of a London Sunday paper read, "I Witnessed the Fall of Khorramshahr." This front-page lead article was written by that paper's ace foreign correspondent. By the close of the second week, Iraq had reported the conquest of the six major cities controlling the Shatt Al-Arab waterway, as well as the imminent fall of Susangard, the vital city in Khuzistan province. Today, eight years after the war began, there is a cease-fire. During this entire period, the Iraqi forces never captured a single Iranian city, although they conquered and controlled large chunks of desolate and unpopulated territory. They were unable to achieve a single, declared military objective.

The ambitious Saddam Hussein sought, through war, to establish Iraq as the preponderant military power in the Persian Gulf. At the same time, he hoped that Iraq would replace Egypt as the political power of the Arab world. Hussein assumed that Iran would be a pushover because of her disarrayed armed forces and no known source of military supply (for almost two years). Hussein anticipated that his attack—along with the Iranian internal problems among the ethnic, linguistic, and non-Shi'ite communities—would tip Iran into physical disintegration. Paramount in Hussein's expectations was control over the oil-rich Khuzistan province, which Iraq has always referred to as Arabastan. He assumed that the Arab inhabitants would seek to abandon Iranian rule to become part of Iraq, bringing with them control over Iran's oil wealth.

Hussein spent the better part of a year preparing his army for battle, while also accumulating a vast arsenal of weapons and supplies. He made a number of visits to Arab capitals, establishing his political position vis-à-vis the Arab world. He appears to have obtained tacit approval, if not outright political support, for his projected military venture from Jordan, Saudi Arabia, and the Arab Gulf states. The conservative Arab leaders supported Hussein's forthcoming folly under the assumption that an Iraqi victory was a certainty. The problem that faced them was not the outcome of the war but its political aftermath.

The war quickly deteriorated to the level of partisan fighting. The Iraqi army was trained and organized for mobile offensive war. Until the spring of 1988, however, it was stationed in fixed defensive positions subjected to the daily cruelty of guerrilla fighting by a crazed enemy that was defending its homeland. The fanatic Shi'ite-Moslem revolutionaries were trained as guerrilla fighters against an enemy whose positions were fixed, open, and known. These Iranian guerrilla fighters entered into a state of euphoria as they achieved small individual victories in their vendetta against the Iraqi occupying force. That this took a serious toll on the morale of the Iraqi army can be supported in part by Saddam Hussein's public plea to the women of Iraq, exhorting them not to sleep with any soldier known to have deserted from battle. After more than seven years of fighting, there was a tip in the scales of the war, in Iraq's favor, because of the destruction of Iran's oil infrastructure and, therefore, her inability to pay for the existing war.

A review of eight years of combat reveals some important military lessons. First, a small backward nation such as Iraq,

284 / God, Allah, and the Great Land Grab

which has built a large modern army and equipped it with the most modern, high-technology weapon systems, cannot fight an intensive war for any extended period of time. Three to four weeks appears to be the limit of intensive operation before the long "supply train" breaks down. Equipment repair and maintenance, with all the associated logistic problems, then dominate the command structure.

Second, a nation like Iraq, which does not possess a technological infrastructure, cannot plan and operate one of the basic ingredients of modern warfare—C-3I. (As a result, the Iraqi military does not have access to a complete air defense system.)

Third, the lack of morale and motivation can deprive a country like Iraq of required quick success, even given the element of surprise and a vastly superior military force. Iraq failed to achieve her military objectives despite a quantitatively and qualitatively superior military force because her army was not prepared to sustain the casualties required to capture and control the population centers. The fact that these cities were being defended by fanatic forces, poorly trained and poorly supplied but determined to die rather than surrender, only made the task more dangerous. Due to insufficient morale and motivation, the Iraqis were able to use their equipment only to destroy, not to conquer.

Fourth, modern equipment not properly applied loses its effectiveness and can handicap an army. Iraq deployed the latest Russian tank, the T-72, when she invaded Iran. This tank proved in battle to be impervious to Western anti-armor weapons; yet, it was ultimately not a useful fighting weapon on Iran's terrain.

During the fifth, sixth, and seventh years of the war, the Iranians used their numerical superiority by mounting massive frontal assaults. They suffered astounding losses of manpower, but they did not desist from the fight. As a result, the war deteriorated into a stalemate similar to the trench warfare of World War I.

By the eighth year, the Iraqis had acquired enough strategic firepower to destroy Iran's oil infrastructure and her ability to export enough oil to be able to finance the war. In that year, the United States sent her fleet into the Persian Gulf because she thought the war was tipping against Iraq; she attacked Iranian infrastructure and used her force against Iran. By the end of the eighth year, Iran was suing for some sort of cease-fire in order to retrench and rebuild her oil exports to finance a future war.

The political implications of this war are most significant. Iraq's failure to achieve a decisive military victory was perceived by the Shi'ites throughout the Gulf area as an Iranian victory and emboldened them. The Shi'ites form a very significant minority in Saudi Arabia and the Gulf states, as well as the majority within Iraq itself, where the perception of an Iranian victory began to take hold.

Recent Shi'ite disturbances within the Iraqi army have been a cause of much alarm within the Iraqi command. Shi'ite revolt within Iraq against the Hussein regime could spread throughout the Gulf area where the ayatollah's Iranian-Shi'ite Moslems have been actively fomenting unrest for the past few years. In Saudi Arabia, for example, the 300,000 Shi'ite Moslems are concentrated in the oil-producing areas and comprise most of the work force. A Shi'ite uprising in the region would have far-reaching effects.

The extensive damage to the Iraqi oil fields and installations, which was completely unanticipated, disrupted oil shipments from Iraq. This situation diminished Iraq's political leverage among the nations in Africa and the Indian Ocean on whom she had exerted great political pressure—pressure to deny both the USSR and the United States their bases and pressure to adhere to a nonaligned, anti-Israel policy. As long as the fighting continued, there was a distinct possibility of one or more of the neighboring states entering into or expanding their support role, thus widening the scope of the confrontation. Thus, the war has had a deeply unsettling effect on Middle East stability.

In the long term, the consequences of the war will be even more lasting. The hatred left within Iran by Iraq's brutal and senseless use of Scud and Frog surface-to-surface missiles against Iranian population centers, which caused many thousands of civilian casualties, will keep the embers of revenge glowing for years. The intensified bombing retaliations of the Iranians and the "war of the cities" during the sixth year of the war has caused the deepening of the profound hatred between the two peoples. The use of poison gas by Iraq against both civilian and military targets has further embittered the Iranians. The divisive effect upon the many Arab states (which have been split in their support for the warring parties) cannot help but sow seeds for future conflict within the region, even though both Iran and Iraq became too crippled and preoccupied to expand the scope of their military activities and entered into a cease-fire.

Saddam Hussein has fashioned his career tactic and strategy after the late Egyptian dictator, Gamal Abdel Nasser. Hussein decided to adopt Nasser's game of playing off the two super-powers. This was earlier exemplified in a preinvasion speech in which he said, "We must understand the way in which the Soviets think; we must learn how to deal with international politics without . . . submitting to them and becoming enmeshed in their game of ignoring them . . ." He added, "We believe there are certain factors which have not been exploited to bolster the Arab nation to confront the enemy, to increase the international importance of the Arabs, and to act from stronger positions in influencing the trends of international affairs, whether in relation to the United States, the Soviet Union, or any other power."

Hussein's intention to emulate Nasser was reflected not only in his speeches but also in his deeds. The invasion of Iran was only part of a "grand plan" to attain unchallenged dominance of the Persian Gulf and, ultimately, leadership of the Arab world. Just prior to the invasion of Iran, it appeared as if Hussein was on the verge of receiving U.S. political support from Zbigniew Brzezinski, the former national security council advisor. The Carter administration seemed to be toying with the idea of supporting Iraq as the new strong nation in the Persian Gulf, if she, in return, would loosen her ties with Moscow. Hussein's effort to play the superpowers against each other was in contrast to that of Sadat, whose game plan called for forming an alliance between Egypt and the West, as one means of limiting Western support for Israel.

That there were those within the U.S. government prior to the invasion who considered closer relations with Iraq and who supported Hussein in achieving his original goals is reprehensible; the fact that there is still strong support for this position today is almost unbelievable. Hussein's philosophy is based not only on his aim to destroy Israel but also on his plan to continue military conflict within the region to achieve Arab unity.

Hussein's lust for war has been a dominant theme throughout his speeches. Excerpts from an interview given several years ago to an Egyptian journalist clearly reveals this:

"The Arabs are brought together at this stage by conditions of war rather than by conditions of peace. . . . Our divisive regional characteristics reveal themselves more in the circumstances of peace than in the circumstances of war. . . . The regional characteristics which prevent serious participation in the preparation for confrontation are more pronounced under the circumstances of peace than under the circumstances of war. . . . We should keep up the atmosphere of war to strengthen our political approach and enable ourselves to exploit any suitable opportunity which offers itself. . . . To maintain an atmosphere of war and prepare its requisites will enable us to enter any war successfully at the time of our choosing. . . . Militancy must not be absent from politics. This is the control point of our policy for the confrontation with the Zionist enemy. . . . The main approach for the achievement of the phased aims is to recover one piece of territory after another and at the same time to maintain the atmosphere of war with continuing political action."

A positive development since Hussein's invasion of Iran was the change in U.S. presidents from Carter to Reagan and the resultant shift in emphasis of policy from one dominated by the Arab-Israeli dispute to one more recognizant of the Arab threat to the security of the Persian Gulf. After eight years of war, Western security is not threatened predominantly by the collapse of either or both of the leaders of Iraq and Iran but rather by the effect such a collapse would have on their Arab neighbors because of the possibility of internal uprisings. Rebellions within states such as Saudi Arabia and the Gulf sheikdoms would surely test the predisposition of those societies to continue to supply the oil needed by the West—at the prices and in the quantities required.

The "visionary" leadership of Saddam Hussein was emboldened by the exhilarating sight of the massive array of new weapon systems Iraq acquired from the Soviet Union and from some greedy Western nations who were led by the self-righteous French. Hussein guided his nation into a holy war against the Shi'ite fanatics of Iran who, through their penchant for making political mischief, had become politically isolated from all world forums. Hussein was encouraged by biased estimates of the effect of the collapse within Iran's once "mighty" military establishment. Executions and desertions, which decimated the ranks of Iran's armed forces and obliged Iran to abandon her advanced technology weapon systems, served to increase Hussein's expectations of achieving a victory as great as Israel's in her Six-Day War. Hussein contemplated a speedy military operation of limited objectives designed for minimum battle casualties and little collateral damage to the civilian and industrial infrastructures.

Saddam Hussein's blunder was his inability to weigh the benefits of victory against the costs of failure. He did not understand the full significance of Iran's race backward from the twentieth century to a feudal sixteenth century society—one that spurned material wealth for an ascetic spiritual life that glorified death as a religious duty. Hussein did not fully comprehend the implications of Khomeini's destruction of Iran's budding modern economy and his voluntary drastic cutback in oil production. The ayatollah's initial escalation of the war through effective bombing and shelling of Iraq's multibillion dollar oil infrastructure shocked and horrified Iraq's unsuspecting leader. Hussein's response in kind turned a very logically planned, limited military operation against a weak and disunited Iran into a mindless, illogical, costly war with no predictable end in sight other than the existing cease-fire.

In retrospect, one can see that, in his search for power, Iraq's Saddam Hussein entered into a battle to fulfill a grand mission in pursuit of what was thought to be a clearly defined national interest—like President Johnson in Vietnam and Brezhnev in Afghanistan. All three leaders entered a war extremely confident they would achieve a clear-cut victory over military forces that, in their best estimates, were vastly inferior. Although the Soviets did not learn from the United States' sad experience in Vietnam, Hussein gained nothing from either of the superpowers' previous miscalculations.

Hussein forgot that in the 1960s the United States, the world's mightiest superpower, was not capable of defeating North Vietnam, a small agrarian society of peasants. That war ended after ten bloody years with the total collapse of the U.S. effort, and at a cost to the U.S. economy of hundreds of billions of dollars and well in excess of 100,000 U.S. casualties—a higher price than the U.S. public was prepared to pay. The televised sight of helicopters hurriedly evacuating the last U.S. personnel from the roof of the embassy in Saigon as hordes of Vietcong enveloped the embassy compound has remained fixed on the U.S. psyche and has since then haunted U.S. national will.

Just as victory eluded the U.S. superpower because she could neither bomb the North Vietnamese into submission nor destroy their morale by constantly threatening their meager physical existence, victory—after eight grueling years—still eludes the Iraqis. The uncompromising national will and spiritual strength of the Iranians enabled them to sustain immense losses and endure incredible physical deprivation.

The North Vietnamese, like the Iranians, were prepared to lose everything to win, while the United States—the world's greatest industrial, economic, and military power—did not have the national will to allow the war to interfere with the customary niceties of daily civilian life. U.S. forces were pitted against a ruthless, self-sacrificing enemy prepared to lose all save the hope of achieving its national goals. U.S. military doctrine dictated that large, highly organized tactical units equipped with expensive, highly technical, sophisticated weapon systems be used in Vietnam. These were clearly not designed for the tactical requirements of subtropical jungle warfare. The U.S. conventional military forces faced very small Vietnamese tactical units—to the point of individual adversaries—utilizing rudimentary low-cost, anti-personnel weapons designed to maim and demoralize their victims. The United States was militarily ill-prepared to fight a war in Vietnam—a fact not realized, or not admitted, by the U.S. military. Simultaneously, the determined political will of the North Vietnamese was never understood by the Johnson administration. The Vietnam War was an example of total miscalculation at all levels. The costs in time, manpower, and money necessary to achieve the military goal, plus the serious miscalculation on how to achieve that goal, were never understood by either the civilian or military authorities.

Other nations should have learned their lessons about failure from the U.S. defeat in the jungles of Vietnam in 1975; however, this has not been the case. What neither Iraq nor the Soviet Union learned from the U.S.-Vietnam experience is that a nation with much to lose, but not prepared to lose it, should not take on an apparently weak adversary prepared to lose the very little that it has.

As a result of the Iraq-Iran War, the ancient feud between the

Shi'ites and Sunnis was brought to the surface, and it became apparent to the rest of the world that the remedy for all Middle East problems did not lie only in settlement of the Arab-Israeli conflict and resolution to the Palestinian problem. In fact, in this unstable region, Israel—with her Western values, her democratic institutions, and her military power—stands out as the single stabilizing factor. The ineptitude of the Iraqi forces throughout the eight-year Iraq-Iran War is a vivid contrast to the capability of Israeli forces in their June 1981 destruction of Iraq's nuclear facilities—a striking example of true military virtuosity. The lessons of this event cannot be separated from all other Middle East events and should be analyzed.

U.S.-Middle East policy following the Yom Kippur War was based on erroneous assumptions—most of which were shattered by a few 2,000-pound, precision-guided bombs that, with uncanny accuracy, struck the dome of and destroyed Iraq's nuclear reactor. While the United States was Israel's only external source for advanced technology weapon systems, by providing weapons to the Arab nations as well, she also set the pace for the brisk Middle East arms race and helped to make it the most dangerous and volatile region in the world. Each successive U.S. administration has led the Arab leaders to believe that U.S. political leverage was sufficient to control Israel's use of military power. Each Israeli government has behaved in a manner that supported this U.S. thesis—except for minor transgressions for which Israel had been soundly condemned in public forums.

Israel's destruction of Iraq's nuclear reactor has forced nations with interests in the Middle East, including the United States, to re-examine their political attitudes and tactics toward Israel, to reassess Israel's military role in the area, and to note Israel's ability to take independent political and military action. Successive U.S. administrations since the 1973 Yom Kippur War have publicly referred to Israel as a strategic asset with shared strategic interest; however, only in the final years of the Reagan administration—several years following the 1981 destruction of Iraq's nuclear reactor—was Israel elevated to the position of strategic ally, thereby requiring coordination between the United States and Israel on strategic planning for the area. Reagan's move was motivated by the U.S.-Lebanon debacle in

1983 and the subsequent Arab terrorist threats to U.S. global interests between 1984 and 1986.

ISRAEL'S MILITARY STRATEGY AND EXPANSION

Since the Yom Kippur War in 1973, Israel has had to re-structure her military forces. During this period, vast amounts of high-technology weapon systems have been acquired from the United States and a significant portion of Israel's GNP has been invested in expanding and modernizing her indigenous military industries. The entire nation has supported the expanded military establishment. There is consensus regarding the size and mission of the military and all sectors of the society participate in the provision of manpower for the world's only highly trained citizen's army.

Additionally, Israel has proved to be flexible in her nego-tiations for peace and stability in the Middle East. President Sadat discovered that by signing a peace treaty, he could retrieve every inch of land lost in 1967. As a bonus, he also received large-scale financial assistance from the United States and massive quantities of U.S. military hardware, which could be used to westernize and rebuild his military forces that were decimated during the 1973 War.

Prior to the fall of the shah of Iran, U.S. strategy for the defense of the Persian Gulf was based on a surrogate military force provided by the shah. The Iranian revolution left a dangerous military vacuum in the West's defense of the Persian Gulf. Saddam Hussein, the "Butcher of Baghdad," attempted to establish military hegemony over the Persian Gulf. A cross between Stalin and Nasser—with the killer instincts of Hitler— Hussein's lust for power increased with the price of oil. Iraq's expanding oil income provided him with the means to purchase weapon systems from the Soviet Union, England, and France and to build the largest military force in the area. Prior to Iraq's disastrous invasion of Iran, Brzezinski attempted to lay the foundation for the establishment of Iraq as the new U.S. military surrogate in the Gulf. Israel was not considered for this role as it would not have been acceptable to the Arabs.

The United States chose to ignore publicly the dangers of the French-German-Italian role in providing Iraq with the capability to produce nuclear weapons and to become, therefore, a nuclear power. The U.S. inhibition to apply public pressure was based on Iraq's potential value to the West, not only as a major oil supplier but as a defender of vital Western interests in the Persian Gulf. Israel was unable, politically, to convince the Western nations of the gravity with which she viewed Iraq's possession of this nuclear capability.

The Western world's focus of criticism of the Arab world has been on the behavior of Qaddafi and Libya and not on Hussein and Iraq. There is an almost universal Western consensus that Libya is a radical state. This is fortified by Libya's creation of a vast storage facility for warehousing weapons, which makes her a major staging area for the Soviet Union.

In contrast, Hussein's Nasser-style overtures to the West inhibited Western criticism of his violent anti-Israel pronouncements and his radical style. His brutal invasion of Iran, his use of Scud and Frog missiles against civilian targets, and his use of poison gas in combat went uncriticized in the Western capitals of the world until the last year of the Reagan administration when the United States publicly criticized Iraq for her use of poison gas. Saddam Hussein also introduced the indiscriminate use of chemical warfare without so much as a peep from the West. This dangerous and illegal means of warfare has now been legitimated because of the West's reluctance to censure.

Both Iran and Iraq attacked ships in the Gulf outside of their territorial waters; this, too, spread little alarm and, certainly, prompted no complaint from any Western power until—again during the last year of the Reagan administration—the United States entered the Gulf to oppose *Iranian* activity. As of August 1987, 350 tankers had been attacked by Iraqi and Iranian planes (60 percent by Iraq). It appears that their goal was *not* to sink the ships and destroy the environment but to harass the shipping.

ISRAEL'S MILITARY INITIATIVE

Israel's surgical-like destruction of Iraq's nuclear facility on June 7, 1981 shocked the entire world and forced all nations to take stock of the long-term political implications. The Arabs, the Americans, the Europeans, and the Soviets were startled by the following realizations.

• Israel is capable of making an unpredicted, independent

political decision, while utilizing military means in a manner not believed possible.

- Israel can absorb and adapt the most technologically advanced weapon systems to perform tasks believed to be beyond that equipment's capabilities and outside its design specifications.
- Israel has developed tactics utilizing the combination of air power and heavy PGMs to obtain the equivalent of a nuclear deterrent.
- Israel has the capability—through the pre-emptive destruction of valuable, vulnerable targets—to render her enemy incapable of waging war, without inflicting civilian casualties and collateral damage on her enemy.
- Israel's growing industrial and technological infrastructure, combined with the rapid pace of growth in weapon systems technology, will continue to improve her military strength relative to that of her Arab neighbors.

While these observations are of concern to the nations of, and with interests in, the Middle East, there are a number of specific political conclusions that any nation must draw for herself based on her perceptive global interests and alignments. In establishing the political implications of any international activity—including this Israeli military action—the following basic axioms must be assumed.

- Nations do not base decisions on morality or ethical considerations. They tend to be hypocritical in the public justification of their policies.
- Nations have neither permanent friends nor permanent enemies, only permanent interests.
- National materialism and national greed tend to dictate and mold behavior.
- Nations are judged primarily by their power as measured in either economic or military terms.

Impact on the Soviet Union

The Israeli air strike against Iraq required a 2,400 km round trip flight. There is no indication that this is the limit of Israel's strike capability utilizing the techniques developed for this raid; therefore, the Soviet Union cannot rule out an Israeli military capability against Soviet staging-controlled areas in Bulgaria,

Hungary, and Rumania or, for that matter, on Soviet soil itself—
in places like Odessa.

The elaborate Soviet air defense system, which protected the
Iraqi billion-dollar-plus nuclear facility, proved to be inadequate
against Israeli tactics; therefore, Soviet assistance can no longer
be perceived by the Arabs as a foolproof guarantee against
extremely vulnerable and valuable targets. The Soviet staging
area in Libya is within the 1,200 km range proven to be accessible to Israeli air power. Since it was designed to be defended
against an almost nonexistent Egyptian air power, the Soviets did
not install command and control communications or conceal
the targets in underground storage. The Libyan staging area
is presently extremely vulnerable to Israel's military power.
Similarly, Soviet bases and staging areas in Somalia and South
Yemen are now vulnerable to demonstrated Israeli deterrent
power.

Israel's attack on the PLO headquarters in Tunis—almost
1,800 km from Israel—utilizing air refueling techniques proves
just how far Israel's strategic reach can go. The development of
the Jericho II ballistic missile, with an ultimate range of 1,000
miles, adds yet another dimension to Israel's strategic reach.

The Soviet Union must assess Israeli intentions and reactions
to any future Soviet political incursions within the region. To
achieve this accurately would require the establishment of a
direct line of communication with Israel. Diplomatic relations
between these two nations now appear to be inevitable.

Impact on the United States

The Israeli attack on Iraq's nuclear reactor convinced the
United States to implement a meaningful strategic relationship with Israel. Without engaging in strategic coordination
with Israel, the United States faces the possibility of future
unpredictable acts that could destabilize the Middle East, such
as the 1982 Peace for Galilee War.

Since Israel has proven that great military achievements can
be made through the use of extremely small forces, U.S. political
leverage over Israeli policy, with the threat of an arms embargo,
has been rendered ineffective on a short-term basis. Israel now
has the capability of planning and executing pre-emptive

strikes without detection; the need for mobilization has been diminished.

The impotence of the Arab states, especially that of Saudi Arabia as demonstrated in the Lebanon war, has accelerated a reorientation of the U.S. outlook toward Israel and has forced the United States to a new level of awareness and realization regarding certain Israeli capabilities. Politically, Israel maintains a real rapid deployment force (RDF) in the Middle East. In fact, Israel's is the only one. This condition will prevail for years. Israel is not only the predominant military power in the region, including the Persian Gulf, but she has a strategic conventional power that approximates the effectivity of nuclear power. Israel's strategic reach is sufficient to allow her to dominate the Persian Gulf.

Additionally, the United States now realizes that the Iranian revolution, which brought Shi'ite-Islamic fundamentalism into power there and unleashed similar forces throughout the region—primarily in Lebanon, Bahrain, Kuwait, and Saudi Arabia, is not a transient phenomena. Rather, it is one with which the region will have to cope for years to come.

Military Implications

The military implications of the Israeli raid on the Iraqi nuclear reactor are profound and will have revolutionary effects on future military budgets, as well as on the development of weapon systems throughout the world. They include the following:

- Tactical, conventional PGMs will offer an effective alternative to low-yield nuclear devices which, for political reasons, nations, until now, have been reluctant to utilize.
- Military acupuncture will be achieved by a swift, decisive pre-emptive surgical blow that could destroy key, vital domestic installations such as power, water, and communications, as well as central military command and control communications, while causing sparse casualties among the civilian population.
- Small, specialized units will be developed and manned by intelligent, highly trained, and educated personnel organized to wage a short, devastating war.

- Wars will be short and measured in days or weeks—not months or years. The outcome will be most affected by PGMs, area weapons, and C-3I. Only nations with a technological base will have the capability of absorbing the fast pace of technological change that will take place.
- A small nation can be a limited deterrent against a large power.
- Arms embargoes by great powers against small nations will have reduced effectiveness, since preventive wars can be waged, if necessary, by small, highly trained forces.
- Existing air defense systems are not foolproof. One airplane carrying up to nine tons of precision-guided munitions can effect devastating destruction upon a number of vital targets. Almost all existing defensive hardware is obsolete. This will force the design and development of a new generation of air defense systems.
- The newly established strategic coordination between the United States and Israel is an inevitable consequence of the events that have taken place in the Middle East in recent years.

The future for most of the Middle East looks bleak. The Middle East is and will continue to suffer from ethnic and religious turmoil. The only island of democratic stability and technological progress in the whole region is Israel. By the year 2000, Israel will become both the fortress and the base for the West in the region.

Israel—Weapon Systems Self-Sufficiency

Since the establishment of the state of Israel in 1948, a source of continuing debate within the country's ruling circles has been the need to become self-sufficient in weapons development. This debate has been spawned and strengthened by Israel's history of dependence on foreign military supplies. At crucial moments, during times of impending or ongoing war, this dependency—the most serious weakness in Israel's defense system—has made Israel extremely vulnerable to external political pressures.

Many events have occurred in the past to instill in Israel a sense of necessity to establish an independent arms industry:

- In 1948, President Truman simultaneously recognized the newly created State of Israel and initiated an arms embargo against the fledgling nation—after the invasion of Israel by her neighboring Arab nations;
- In 1956, the Eisenhower-Dulles team decided to force Israeli withdrawal from Sinai, without preconditions, while sustaining the U.S. arms embargo against Israel—a decision made despite the massive Soviet resupply of weapon systems to Egypt;
- In 1967, President Charles De Gaulle applied a French arms embargo one week prior to the June 1967 Six-Day War at the height of Israel's crisis with Egypt;
- In 1973, during the Yom Kippur War, the Nixon-Kissinger team delayed the resupplying of the Israeli military during the most critical hours of the war;

- In 1977, President Carter made his first two presidential foreign policy decisions—to withhold the sale of both CBU-72 concussion bombs and the forward-looking infrared (FLIR) night vision system to Israel; and
- In 1981 and 1982, President Reagan, in response to Israel's destruction of the Iraqi nuclear reactor and the Peace for Galilee War, postponed shipment to Israel of F-15 and F-16 fighter planes and some other select weapon systems, including CBU artillery shells.

While, prior to 1976, it was certainly no secret that Israel had been denied approval by the United States for technology transfers in many areas, this fact had not received broad press coverage. However, in December 1976, Clarence Robinson wrote in *Aviation Week,* "In an early December meeting between the State and Defense Departments, methods were discussed to increase control of the export of U.S. technology to Israel." Included with this statement was an extensive and detailed list of Israel's recent requests that had been denied.

As a result of the various disengagement (political) agreements, the United States embarked upon a massive resupply of weapon systems at the conclusion of the Yom Kippur War that allowed Israel to rebuild her military with the most modern weapons systems then available (see Table III). This created, for the first time in almost four decades, a condition in which Israel's military forces possessed weapons substantially more advanced in technology than those of the Arabs.

TABLE III
A Partial List of New Weapon Systems Delivered or Promised to Israel as a Result of the Yom Kippur War

F-15 Eagle fighter planes
Lance, 70-mile surface-to-surface missiles
Maverick, electro-optional weapon systems
Laser-guided bombs
Harpoon, 100-mile sea-to-sea missile
Electronic countermeasure systems
Reconnaissance and signal intercept equipment
Walleye television-guided glide bombs
Tow wire-guided antitank missiles
Dragon hand-held antitank missiles
Redeye passive infrared homing antiaircraft missiles

Shrike passive radar homing air-to-surface missiles
Vulcan/Chaparral antiaircraft guns
Military helicopters, including Cobra attack helicopters
Antiradiation missiles
F-16 fighter planes
E-2C airborne early warning stations

However, in the years that followed the Yom Kippur War, it became apparent that U.S. military and economic aid to Israel was not intended for building an independent military/industrial infrastructure within Israel; nor was the aid intended to rehabilitate Israel's war-struck economy as the Marshall Plan had aided Western Europe and Japan after World War II. Rather, the decisions on U.S. weapons sales to Israel were based primarily on U.S. foreign policy interests; namely, to counteract the large quantity of military hardware and advanced technology that the Soviets were supplying to the Arabs based on their belief that (1) a sufficient quantity of weapons can compensate for lack of quality and (2) defensive weapons deployed in sufficient quantities become offensive. For example, the massive SAM system deployed in the 1973 war created a protective umbrella for the invading Egyptian and Syrian armies. The significance of both of these components was best illustrated during the Yom Kippur War and, also, in the resupply of the Syrian military after the 1982 Lebanon War.

THE ROLE OF SCIENCE AND TECHNOLOGY IN MEASURING A NATION'S POWER

A nation's size can no longer be measured just in terms of land mass, population, and natural resources. Recent history has shown that new dimensions have been added to the measurement of a country's strategic depth. Scientific effort, technological achievement, and industrial development must also be added to a nation's inventory of assets when attempting to assess its strength. Even though the 1973 step-function increase in Arab political and economic power served to intensify the Arab claim that time is on the side of the Arabs, it has since become obvious that time is only on the side of those nations that utilize it to keep pace with the scientific and technological infrastructure.

During the past forty years, few nations of the world—large or small—have paralleled Israel's record growth and achievements in this area. There is every reason to believe that knowledge and technological progress will multiply at an even faster pace in the next forty years; thus, an accelerating technology will play an even more important role in national development in the future than it has in the past. Israel, due to the propensity of the Jewish people toward science and engineering, has been able to absorb and keep pace with technological growth and is now in an even better position for the next forty years than she has been at any time in the past.

None of the twenty-one Arab nations, individually or collectively, has equaled Israel's accomplishments. In fact, in the area of science and technology, time has been unkind to the Arab nations; and there are no indications that they will be able to respond to the growing pace of technology in the future. The Arabs, unlike the people of Israel, have found military technology to be advancing more rapidly than their social structure. Integrating and absorbing such advancements into their national development has been difficult.

Since her establishment, however, Israel has been developing an independent military/industrial complex without diminishing the pace of her general economic development. Throughout modern history, except in the case of postwar Japan, it has been this development of a military/industrial complex that has been the catalyst for a nation's economic industrial development. All indications are that Israel will not be an exception.

WORLDWIDE WEAPONS DEVELOPMENT— HISTORY AND THE PRESENT

Historically, weapons technology has advanced at a slow and measured pace. There have been extensive periods when little or no improvement has taken place in the technology affecting weapons designs. The application of new technology to the design of weapons has usually resulted in only minor improvements of existing weapons rather than a major breakthrough from the past. Primarily, until the early 1970s, development in conventional (nonnuclear) armaments were extensions of technologies developed during World War II. The resultant weapon and delivery systems thus became more complex, more expensive, and more sophisticated, but they did not yield either a significant improvement in military effectiveness or a fundamental change in the conduct of war.

During the 1970s, however, the scientific and technological explosion had revolutionary effects on weapon design, development, and production. A new class of conventional weapons became operational—weapons that constituted a real break with the past. These weapons fall into four basic categories:

1. PGMs;
2. tactical cruise missiles;
3. area weapons; and
4. loitering weapons—RPVs.

Precision-Guided Munitions (PGMs)

PGMs are weapons that are terminally guided to their targets. Their introduction brought weapons technology to the threshold of a real revolution in conventional warfare. They are relatively simple to design, produce, and use. There is a substantial demand for these weapons, and their sale to all nations has been difficult to restrict.

American and Russian first-generation PGMs were used in Vietnam; they were also used in the Middle East during the Yom Kippur War. Typical of a first-generation PGM is the U.S. Tow wire-guided antitank missile, which can be vehicular mounted or launched from a helicopter. This missile proved to be a devastating tank killer in actual combat during the Yom Kippur War. The U.S. Dragon missile, a portable hand-held version, was developed from experience Israel obtained during the Yom Kippur War. Families of first-generation, air-to-air, air-to-ground, ground-to-air, and anti-ship skimmer missiles were developed, became operational, and found their way into use during the later stages of the Vietnam War, the Yom Kippur War, and the 1982 Israeli Peace for Galilee War in Lebanon.

The famous Maverick, Walleye, and Shrike air-to-ground missiles will soon be made obsolete by a whole new series of standoff missiles that will have a greater range, improved accuracy, and more explosive power. Within the next twenty years, second-, third-, and fourth-generation PGMs will have become operational. They will be portable, vehicular, and air-launched antitank missiles that will no longer be wire guided but will use electro-optics, laser, and/or infrared homing techniques for improved accuracies. They will also be larger, utilizing greater explosive capacities for longer range and better penetration of thicker armor plate.

An extremely important addition to the arsenal of PGMs that should be operational before the turn of the century is the loitering weapon system. This new class of weapon systems consists of harassment RPVs and loitering cruise missiles; both can hover for hours over a prescribed area and lock into the target. These will be relatively inexpensive and will be mass produced.

Tactical Cruise Missiles

Modern cruise missiles, like PGMs, are weapons that are terminally guided to their targets. The development of a series of cruise missiles equipped with precision guidance will dramatically expand the tactical battlefield potential of the nations that acquire them. The cruise missile is an excellent example of the kind of weapon system that small nations with advanced weapon system and subsystem technology (but not necessarily self-sufficiency in components or basic materials) can and, in time, will develop independently, with sufficient investment. Tactical cruise missiles will complement the second-generation PGMs that are becoming operational.

The forerunner to the cruise missile was the German V-1 of World War II—a crude, unsophisticated flying bomb with limited range, speed, accuracy, and flight stability. Later and more recent developments in data storage and retrieval, sensor technologies, integrated microcircuits, and materials science applied to weapons development has created the basis for a true revolution in weapons design and in the conduct of future conventional wars.

The recently developed U.S. cruise missiles deployed by NATO in Europe since 1986 have terrified the Soviets. These new cruise missiles make completely obsolete a Soviet air defense system based on an elaborate network of interlocking SAMs designed with overlapping capabilities. These SAMs have created an almost impregnable electromagnetic "wall" around major Soviet targets and protect them from all existing types of aircraft. The cost to the Soviets to develop and produce this wall must be measured in the hundreds of billions of dollars; some published estimates are as high as $.5 trillion. Its obsolescence would be a tremendous blow to the Soviet economy.

The cruise missile, which can fly great distances at altitudes below radar detection, can hit targets with pinpoint accuracy and render the SAM shield impotent. The relatively low cost of manufacturing cruise missiles has changed the whole concept of future weapon systems development. This weapon, coupled with the development of a whole new generation of short-range, tactical PGMs, puts the economic sacrifice required of the Soviets into serious question. Their prior and present investments for massive production of weapon systems are now on the verge of being rendered totally useless. The deployment of this family of weapon systems also places a very finite time limit to the past shortsighted U.S.-Middle East diplomacy—a policy of political leverage through control over Israel's source of weapons for defense.

Area Weapons

The third new type of awesome weapon, the area weapon, is a result of development in conventional technologies and has become important during the 1980s. Unlike PGMs, which are being developed for pinpoint accuracy, area weapons are designed for use against dispersed targets. They fall into three basic categories:

1. cluster bombs—developed as an antipersonnel weapon and designed for use against large concentrations of troops;
2. air-scatterable mines—developed for use against large concentrations of tanks and armored vehicles; and
3. bomblets with terminal guidance—designed for a high degree of accuracy.

The deployment of such weapons by the United States in Vietnam caused outcries in Congress, raising questions of the morality of their use. Yet, they are still an integral part of the planning for tactical conventional warfare by the United States and NATO. Like PGMs, area weapons are relatively simple to design, produce, and use. There is also a substantial demand for area weapons, and their sales to other nations has also been difficult to restrict.

Within the next twenty years, advanced design area weapons will be a significant portion of the arsenals of modern armies and their role too important to be discarded. Tactical wars will be designed to be fought quickly with the outcome to be determined in a matter of days, not years, months, or weeks. Therefore, these weapons will not be ignored or cast aside because of moral considerations, since the alternative could be construed to require a nuclear response, which must always be unthinkable.

The development of PGMs, tactical cruise missiles, and area weapons has been made possible by a series of technological developments in areas including microcomputers; terminal guidance; terrain radars; and infrared, electro-optical, and laser guidance techniques, coupled with greater advances in explosive technologies. The results will be missiles with greater penetration of fortified targets and greater accuracy; in addition, they will be fired from substantially greater distances. In future tactical wars, the use of these three weapon systems will be consumed in combat. Their application will, most probably, accelerate the pace and ferocity of warfare.

Loitering Weapons—RPVs

Loitering weapons, like remotely controlled, pilotless planes commonly referred to as drones, became popular after the IDF had used them in the Peace for Galilee operation in 1982. They have several advantages. Their cost is minimal compared to expensive reconnaissance aircraft. They burn much less fuel, are lightweight, have a very quiet engine, and can be maneuvered at a speed that no pilot could bear. Additionally, with regard to personnel, ground controllers are cheaper to train than pilots. RPV engine heat is so minimal that missiles equipped with infrared sensors cannot lock into them. They are difficult to see at low altitudes and are virtually impossible to spot at higher ones. Most importantly, if an RPV is shot down, not only has the financial loss been minimized, but there has also been no loss of life.

There is no doubt that a host of loitering weapons will be developed to perform specific military missions such as reconnaissance, surveillance, target acquisition, and bombing. They will carry television cameras, lasers, and infrared sensors that will allow for day and night surveillance.

The bombing ability of loitering weapons has incredible military implications. Loitering weapons, with the proper sensors, will be developed against such diverse targets as tanks, armored personnel carriers, radar installations, airfields, power stations, naval targets, and command and control installations. This ability to carry on an offensive attack by remote control could be the decisive factor in future confrontations.

THE EFFECT OF TECHNOLOGY ON TANK WARFARE

Modern-day tank warfare is reaching a stage similar to that of the foot soldier in World War I. It is one huge mass against another. There is a race underfoot to see who can create the thickest armor plate, the longest cannon, and the biggest engine. Tanks now weigh a massive sixty tons.

Yet, shells have been developed that can easily pierce the thickest, most advanced armor. Now, the question is whether a hundred-ton tank with the same maneuverability of its sixty-ton predecessor is feasible to build and deploy. The tank of World War II cost only $50,000; today's tank costs $2.5 million each. Compare this exorbitant price with the cost of an extremely accurate shell from a modern fire-control system—only $500 to $1,000. It means, then, that whoever gets the first $500 shell fired wins the duel between the tanks and has succeeded in destroying $2.5 million worth of hardware in the process.

Tank defense becomes further complicated with the invention of PGMs that have stand-off capability from helicopters or from ground vehicles. These would not require line of sight, would utilize a sting approach with an arc path, and could zero in on the most vulnerable part of the tank—the capula. These missiles would have a fifteen- to twenty-mile capability from the ground and a five- to seven-mile capability from a helicopter.

As of now, tanks must move with ground-to-air support protection. If the protection is neutralized, the tanks are sitting ducks for helicopters. Even with functioning ground-to-air support, there is no protection for the tank yet known against the ground-to-ground missiles. Area weapons such as rapid fire rockets, which are fired from the ground and concentrate on saturating a finite area, will be the modern-day tank's nightmare. This new, relatively inexpensive technology renders the concentrated massive use of tanks in a small area totally ineffective. The days of the massive tank invasion are numbered.

With the rapid translation of these technological developments into the realpolitik of the arms industry, it becomes painfully clear that, in a high-tech war, the victorious army will not be the one with the greatest number of tanks. Neither will it be the one with the most antitank missiles. Rather, it will be the one with the most modern PGM capacity, which consists of an assortment of mortars, artillery, ground-to-ground missiles, air-to-ground missiles, and other weapons that are portable and can be hand held.

What is most significant about these new developments is the realization that the nation that is most wealthy, has the greatest resources of manpower, or has the largest productive capacity will not be the one most likely to survive. The survivor will most certainly be the one with the greatest technological capability for solving the problems presented by the latest generation of PGMs. The tactical land strength of a nation will not be decided by the type and number of tanks possessed but by the various ways it has for the inexpensive wholesale destruction of any other tank force.

ISRAEL'S MILITARY-INDUSTRIAL COMPLEX MEETS THE FUTURE

Israel, as noted before, has had the capability and the technological infrastructure to design and produce the most sophisticated weapon systems. Because Israel also has had financial and time pressures and has been shackled by an often laborious decision-making process, the Kfir, Merkava, and missile boat projects were all embarked upon with certain fears: that they would be obsolete before production was complete, that they might not perform with reliability, and that they might be hampered with maintenance and logistic problems. It was also a concern that the provision of local documentation and the training of personnel might prove to be problematic.

All these projects, however, have been declared unequivocal successes. And the confidence these brazen experiments have inspired, coupled with a flurry of scientifically oriented R & D activity, has already encouraged the industry to move ahead in anticipation of the next generation of devices necessary for

Middle Eastern warfare. This innovative ability will allow Israel to be a front runner in the definition of the future requirements of weapon platforms.

One must realize that Israel has the most experience when it comes to the employment of her entire military machine. She has the inside knowledge about the performance of most of the weapon systems used in the world. She can test these systems practically and determine what modifications are necessary for improving the performance of the equipment. Israel's civilian technologists and heads of R & D are now doing their reserve duty in high level calibration and maintenance depots where they are training staff and advisers. They are not only available for their month of reserve duty but are also on call during their normal work hours.

The sad fact that Israel has had so many wars in her brief history also allows her to use the battlefield as a laboratory for determining future needs and solving the problems of existing equipment. Even in peace time, equipment is being tested. For example, Ariel Sharon employed night vision equipment on land and air to spot the infiltration of illegal settlers into the Yamit area. All kinds of updated surveillance devices were used to track down recalcitrant settlers.

Israel is not manufacturing additional tanks, boats, or planes but is, instead, upgrading existing ones. She is developing the next generation of weapon platforms while improving the technological abilities of personnel. She has begun to use advanced microprocessor technology as well as small and medium sized computers to control maintenance and inventory even down to the smallest individual field units.

Israel is almost completely self-sufficient in the production of supercomponents such as serial electronic components, memory units, and amplifier chain transmitters. Since the Yom Kippur War, she has developed greatly in critical fields such as microwaves, electron tubes, precision resistors, capacitors, transformers, power supplies, gyroscopes, and mechanical parts (such as pumps and motors).

In the field of materials, Israel has developed tremendous capability in the area of basic material evaluation centers and has become adept in working with exotic metals, ceramics, and compound materials. She is already a forerunner in the development of critically required materials for military systems. Today, Israel is dependent on the United States for critical materials only where there is no other source. The ability to evaluate and check source supplies provides Israel the possibility of opening other markets in the world.

The United States is still developing cumbersome complex systems that could bankrupt the budgets of many small nations. Israel must develop more streamlined weapon systems that are much more suited to her needs. As Israel's arms industries export more, they become less dependent on the United States. When nations perceive that their defense needs are more similar to Israel's, they will see Israel as the home address for their defense needs.

Tactical Antiballistic Defenses

As a result of the intensive research in Israel and the United States for SDI, a limited tactical antiballistic defense system will be developed. This system will be used, primarily, to protect key strategic installations such as airfields, utility stations, depots, etc. A defense system of this kind will neutralize the threat from ballistic missiles aimed at key targets or, perhaps in the future, even at population centers. It is indeed possible that a limited system of this nature could be developed and deployed within twenty years.

MIDDLE EAST ARMS RACE—THE FACTS

A report published by the 1980s Project Council on Foreign Relations entitled "Controlling Future Arms Trade," in which Zbigniew Brzezinski is listed as a member of the Committee on Studies of the Board of Directors, makes the following disturbing points:

- The technical trends in evidence in the late 1970s clearly suggest that arms transfers will become increasingly difficult to control in the 1980s.
- The oil-producing nations will continue to account for a substantial portion of the world's arms purchases. The pre-eminence of petroleum-financed arms orders is obvious and, by any calculation, Middle East demand is destined to remain predominant through the 1980s. With enormous oil-

based buying power currently unchecked, it can legitimately be considered the key region with regard to future arms transfers.

- From 1975 to 1980, Saudi Arabia spent $30 billion for military purposes. She will spend tens of billions of dollars in the 1980s to build up her weapon inventories. Since she has less than 4 million indigenous people and a high rate of illiteracy, it is likely that a new corps of white-collar mercenaries serving in Saudi Arabia will emerge in the 1980s.
- Deliveries made to the Middle East in the last few years are such that groups of Arab countries of this region can deploy 2,300 combat aircraft and 10,500 armored vehicles (at a time when there are only 3,000 planes and 12,250 armored vehicles in all of Western Europe).
- Rather than any prospects of either disarmament or arms control in the Middle East, evidence shows that, in the 1980s, the area will be allowed to purchase sufficient arms to enter into a condition of weapons saturation.
- The major asymmetries in manpower existing between Israel and the Arab states require Israel to move toward more fire-intensive systems to achieve a greater firepower per man.
- Modern technology is advancing at a lightning pace, and even weapons of moderate sophistication tend to become outdated before they wear out.
- The United States sells to Israel's enemies equipment that was in great part developed with Israeli know-how.
- The establishment of the weapons industry in Israel and the subsequent development of a weapons export business are in good part a result of U.S. past policies. During her first fifteen years of existence, Israel was unable to buy any U.S. weapons. It wasn't until after her twentieth birthday that she was able to buy weaponry of real consequence. At the same time, the Arabs had many sources of supply. This situation necessitated the development of an independent Israeli weapons industry.
- The post-Yom Kippur War step-function increase in the level of the arms race in the Middle East, to which the United States has been a main contributor, has caused Israel to turn to export. The foreign currency earned provides cash for an

economy not yet able to absorb this new high level of military spending.

This report was published in 1979. Time has proven the estimates made on this report extremely accurate. Now there is reason to believe that these trends will not continue until the turn of the century because of the drop in oil prices, the decreased value of the dollar, and the financing of the Iraq-Iran War by the Gulf states. While the dramatic drop in oil revenue of the Arab states has not yet slowed down the pace of the Middle East arms race, there is every indication that it will. The United States is now the major supplier of arms to Egypt—based on loans and grants—relieving Saudi Arabia of the financial burden. There are sufficient financial reserves within the Arab world, as well as sufficient incentives by the world powers, to maintain an arms flow, but not necessarily a race as existed in the 1980s. Given the trends in weapons development and in the political condition in the area, Israel will be forced to continue to develop her own independent military industry.

THE ISRAELI MILITARY INDUSTRY

The Development

The present state of Israel's military industry is best understood by a series of events that took place in the history of its development.

- The British mandate policy allowed the Arabs to possess arms but denied the Jewish settlers the same means for self-defense. This policy forced the Jews to establish and maintain a modest weapons industry—underground shops manufactured crude handguns, submachine guns, light mortars, and limited quantities of small caliber ammunition.
- The embargo on Western arms during the War of Independence forced Ben-Gurion to allocate precious resources to lay the foundation for a major permanent Israeli weapons industry.
- The massive Soviet-Egyptian arms deal of 1955 intro duced the latest in Soviet weapons to the Middle East. Israel's inability to purchase comparable weapons from any source—between the War of Independence and 1955—

forced her to make a weapons deal with France and England and led to the 1956 Sinai Campaign.

- The forced evacuation of Sinai in 1957 and the continued U.S. arms embargo created the "French Connection." At that time, Ben-Gurion and Shimon Peres, then deputy minister of defense and Israel's recent prime minister, decided to establish nuclear technology—the foundation for Israel's missile development—along with a military electronics industry.

- Charles De Gaulle's embargo of the prepaid fifty Mirage V planes and Saar missile boats (Cherbourg) set the stage for Israel's entry into major weapon systems manufacturing. The Kfir fighter plane, Reshef missile boat, Gabriel sea-to-sea missile, Shafrir air-to-air missile, Jericho surface-to-surface missile, and a major basic electronics industry are some of the more dramatic developments that evolved from Israel's investment of money and technology—developments directly attributable to Israel's reaction to De Gaulle's decision.

- The Soviet Union's massive supply of tanks to the Arabs—prior to, during, and after the October 1973 Yom Kippur War—along with the unprecedented deception by the entire British government on sales of the Chieftan tank to the Israeli military forced Israel to develop the Merkava, her own tank. After England enticed Israel to help design and test the prototype Chieftan tank, she reneged on selling these tanks to Israel and instead sold them to the Arabs. This took place despite the assurances to the contrary by the highest levels of the British government to equivalent levels of the Israeli government. It was only after these assurances were made that Israel agreed to provide Britain with combat-developed design information, engineering assistance, and test evaluation of the first Chieftan tank. This was just another episode in a long history of British duplicity and animosity in dealing with the Jews during the thirty-year Palestinian mandate, as well as the years since Israel's establishment.

- Kissinger's unfulfilled promise to provide Israel with Pershing missiles, as part of the 1975 disengagement agreement, as well as Carter's unfavorable arms decisions, fanned a new debate within the Israeli government's military-industrial circles about providing the investments required to attain the next level of self-sufficiency in defense.

Based on these more recent dealings with the U.S. administrations, a fundamental decision was made to embark upon design and production of an Israeli combat jet fighter for the 1990s, rather than to purchase the most modern U.S. fighter— the all-weather F-18; thus, the Lavi aircraft was born. This decision was affected by the events of the first three years of the Reagan administration. A number of presidential decisions, which were unfavorable to Israel, jeopardized the smooth flow of U.S. weapon systems to Israel. Reagan placed embargoes on various weapon systems and delayed shipment of previously contracted F-15 and F-16 jet combat aircraft. The Lavi project was scrapped in January 1988 primarily because the attack role for this plane had been reduced to its use with stand-off weapons against hardened military targets rather than as direct ground support. Therefore, the number of planes required by the Israeli air force dropped from 300 to 60 planes—not enough to justify the high cost of Lavi production in lieu of purchasing the most advanced F-16C from the United States.

Israel's military industry became not only a developer and producer of major and minor weapon systems, but also an exporter, starting with $320 million worth of exports in 1976. By 1983, military sales reached $1.2 billion. By the turn of the twenty-first century, military exports should be a multibillion dollar business for Israel. But Israel most probably will have to import major weapon systems (such as air superiority and first-line aircraft) as well as components and materials.

The Present and the Future

Over the years, Israel's military industry has developed the basic capabilities for designing, developing, and manufacturing sophisticated tanks, fighter planes (including engines), ships, missiles (including the inertial platform), many types of guns, small arms, munitions, a sophisticated military electronics infrastructure, and precision metal-working and fabrication facilities. (See Table IV for a partial list of military products produced by Israel.) While the existence of these products is common knowledge, it must be assumed that there are, also, other products in various states of development, as well as products that have not yet been made public.

TABLE IV
Partial List of Military Products Produced by Israel

Missiles
Air-to-Air
- Shafrir I, II, and III—infrared missiles guided by proportional navigation designed with special proximity fuse
- Python—a dog-fight missile used effectively in the Lebanon War

Sea-to-Sea
- Gabriel II—a 24-mile skimmer missile

Surface-to-Surface
- Jericho I—a 200-mile tactical land missile
- Jericho II—a 1000-mile strategic ballistic missile
- Barak—an antimissile missile
- Arrow—an antiballistic missile

Boats

- Dabur—a 65-foot, twin-screw, diesel-powered patrol boat
- Reshef—a 180-foot, 450-ton missile boat equipped with Israeli-built radar, communications, electronic countermeasures, missiles, and weapon systems

Armored Vehicles

- RBY—a multipurpose, light armored reconnaissance vehicle
- Merkava—a 58-ton battle tank proven in the Lebanon War to be superior to the new USSR T-72 tank
- Sherman tank (U.S.)—rebuilt with a 155-mm Israeli gun, creating a mobile artillery piece
- T-54/55 and T-62 (USSR)—tanks rebuilt with a new engine and a 105-mm Israeli gun
- Centurion tank (Britain)—rebuilt with 105-mm Israeli gun
- Patton M-60 tank (U.S.)—significantly modified

Guns

- Light, medium, and heavy mortars
- Galil 5.56 assault rifle
- UZI 9-mm submachine gun
- Light machine guns
- 105-mm and 155-mm tank guns
- 106-mm recoil-less gun
- 30-mm aircraft cannon
- 82-mm air-to-ground rocket system
- 240-mm artillery rocket system

Aircraft

- Kfir—a mach 2.2 plus fighter plane
- Arava—a STOL short-range transport plane
- Westwind—a 1,124 to 2,500-mile range multipurpose jet plane
- Nesher—a Mirage V with French engines
- Lavi—a fly-by-wire, all-weather/night ground support fighter. (Was to be fully operational in the early 1990s, but production for operational use has been scrapped. Several Lavis will be flown for development of future aircraft.)
- F-4 Phantom (U.S.)—locally re-engined and modernized for all-weather, night, and strategic bombing, to be operational by the late 1980s
- Israel's modern AWACS system built into modified Boeing 707

Armaments

- A variety of bombs up to 750 pounds
- Rockets and artillery shells
- Ammunition of various types for small arms, mortars, tank and antitank guns, aircraft cannons, and antiaircraft guns
- PGMs of various types
- Various types of mines
- OFER infrared (IR) guided bombs—antitank
- Stand-off, laser-guided bombs

Electronic Systems and Subsystems

- Airborne, shipboard, and ground computer systems
- Multimode weapons delivery and navigation system
- Computerized tactical command and control system
- Communications shelter equipped with teletype, radio, and carrier equipment
- Multiplexers, UHF-FM radio terminals, and repeater sets
- Portable, vehicular, and airborne AM-FM transceivers
- Integrated communications and control system
- Divad—a computer for the artillery designed for use at the battery level
- High-powered RF amplifiers and VHF amplifiers
- Airborne radar for Kfir—all Israeli designed
- Radar and communications for Reshef—all Israeli designed
- Electronic warfare equipment
- Electro-optical systems for night vision and target tracking

Nuclear Weapons

- As exposed by the Vananu Affair

To speak of a total independence and self-sufficiency in weaponry requires more than an impressive list of products. It requires three distinct levels of capability, and each level requires its own distinct design, development, and production:

1. total weapon systems (i.e., the fighter plane);
2. subsystems (i.e., jet engines); and
3. components and basic materials (i.e., high-temperature, plasticized metals used in engine construction).

Satisfying the first two levels—total weapon systems and subsystems self-sufficiency—is within the capability of a technologically advanced nation such as Israel. The accomplishments of the Israeli industrial-military complex indicates that self-sufficiency in the area of defining and developing total weapon systems and then producing quantities of them is achievable. Additionally, much has been achieved toward self-sufficiency in the area of subsystems—the basic modules or building blocks that constitute the total system. One good example is the Israeli-made Reshef missile boat that contains Israeli-made subsystems (including the Gabriel missile; radar, communications, and electronic countermeasure equipment; and weapon systems).

Total self-sufficiency in the area of components and basic materials technology is achievable only by nations that possess both advanced industrial technologies and a population in excess of 80 to 100 million to produce all the components required. The United States, Russia, Japan, and China now have, or will have, the ultimate means to achieve this kind of self-sufficiency. A joint effort by some combination of European countries, including England, Germany, and/or France, could also achieve ultimate weaponry self-sufficiency. If these countries had the collective national will, they could achieve independence. With commercial access to components and basic materials in the open markets of the Western world (the United States in particular) within the next ten to twenty years, Israel will have both the technological base and the incentive to become self-sufficient in weapon systems and subsystems, as well as in some critical components and basic materials.

As Israel continues the process of adopting new technologies, a new generation of innovative tactical weapon systems will be developed. Within the next ten to twenty years, these new systems will be unique, designed to be adapted to practical battlefield conditions, and very affordable to small nations. As U.S. weapon systems become more and more complex, prohibitively expensive, and in need of U.S. logistic support, Third World countries will, by sheer necessity, look for other sources to satisfy their requirements in tactical, conventional weapon systems. By the year 2000, Israel will be a major supplier to the Third World. This will be done with U.S. consent and will counteract Soviet influence propagated by arms deals to the Third World. It can be achieved through selling weapon systems proven in battle against Soviet arms. There is every indication that Israel will be the leader of the Western world in the development and production of conventional tactical weapon systems within the next ten to twenty years. However, given the pace of the Middle East arms race, there is very little reason to believe that Israel will be economically self-sufficient within that period of time.

SUMMARY

From its very inception, the basis of Israel's military planning has been that no foreign troops would be available for her defense. The great distances for travel and the time required for a decision-making process makes help from friendly countries impractical. The pace of modern warfare has heightened to the point where help could not arrive in time to determine the course of battle. Middle East wars move too rapidly, and the course of battle is determined in a matter of hours or days, not in weeks or months. In addition, given the post-Yom Kippur War dimension of Arab political and economic power, it is conceivable that weapon supplies would not be available to Israel from foreign sources during a future crisis.

Israel has continually found her political independence and freedom of action limited by her dependence on weapon shipments from external foreign sources. Major political concessions have been made because of her lack of self-sufficiency in weapons development and production.

For the nation of Israel actually to broaden the base of her military-industrial infrastructure before the twenty-first century, she must have the availability of financial investments and sufficient allocation of resources for R & D. In addition, the time required for Israel to achieve self-sufficiency in weapons development and production is subject to a number of factors, not the least of which is national will. However, with the appropriate resources, the task of achieving these capabilities could be accomplished not within decades but, rather, within years.

An indigenous defense industry is of great strategic value to Israel. The ability to design, develop, and produce advanced weapon systems locally can add to Israel's total military capability and become a measure of her total strength. With sufficient financial investment, Israel's industrial capacity will grow enough to support both the development and the production levels required to become self-sufficient in weapon production within the next twenty years.

With this autonomy comes the secrecy of end-item design necessary for proper national security and a higher degree of political independence. In addition, the dimension of secrecy gained, which cannot be attained when purchasing weapons from foreign sources, greatly enhances Israel's ability to keep the Arabs from gauging accurately the total tactical strength of Israel's armed forces.

Impact of Weapon Sales on the Middle East

Never has it been the case—throughout the history of warfare—that a nation entered into conflict without having provided, itself, for its own basic weapons needs. Those weapons and tactics, then, were often supplemented by outside forces either after a protracted effort or for expansion into peripheral areas. Vietnam was an excellent example of a nation provided with tremendous logistical and financial support, while the basic level of technological weapons and tactics were still totally developed locally. Today, however, the world sees for the first time whole military complexes being exported to any nation who is willing to pay.

The means and methods of waging war have never before in history been imported from the outside on the scale that now exists throughout the world. The primary recipients of this change have been the Arab nations—with Pakistan and India to a lesser degree since each has a somewhat advanced local weapons manufacturing capability. The Arab nations have received relatively unlimited quantities and types of the most advanced operational weapon systems from both the West (primarily, England, France, and the United States) and from the East (primarily, Czechoslovakia and the Soviet Union). These Arab nations, however, have no history of weapons development or production and lack an industrial and technical infrastructure. This reality forces them to absorb not only the weapon systems and their tactics but also the know-how for the maintenance and logistics of these systems. This presents them with a dilemma since they totally lack the required organization, training, and support mechanisms.

The most serious difficulty is that in the development of tactical weapon systems the total operational capability is really understood only by the developing military-industrial complex and either cannot be transferred or will not be transferred for political reasons. Therefore, the Arab nations—while having the finances to purchase or acquire the most advanced tactical weapon systems—lack the means of absorbing these systems and utilizing them to their full capacity. There is no reason to conclude that this difficulty will cease to exist. Even with the oil wealth some Arab nations have accumulated since 1973, in general, the Arab nations are no closer to providing the basic means or methods of fighting a war than they were then. They are not producing the scientists, engineers, technicians, or industries necessary for the development of weapon systems any more advanced than those used in the trench warfare of World War I.

In the Iraq-Iran War, for example, each side started with the most advanced (for the time) imported high-technology weapon systems and the tactics with which to utilize them. Within two weeks that war deteriorated to a World War I style trench war in which the quantity, quality, and stamina of the men who were ready to sacrifice their lives would determine the results. And, just as in World War I, a chemical weapon system—that had, in fact, been banned unanimously by the "family of nations" as a result of that war—was indiscriminately employed by one nation against the other. This measure was taken by Iraq in order to neutralize the larger, superior human force of Iran and their pertinacity to die for Allah.

There are a number of observations that have emerged as a result of the phenomena of the export of high-technology weapon systems and tactics to underdeveloped societies that are neither agrarian, industrial, technological, or service societies but, rather, are more appropriately classified as feudal. The source of wealth of the importing nations comes only from the exploitation and export of oil or some other natural mineral resource found in the area—an accident of nature requiring no cleverness or skill on the part of the possessing society.

Until now, no nation has been able to import a military

organization and its military war machinery and successfully exploit that advantage to win a war. There is no reason to believe that the Arab world will change that. Even if the Arab nations acquire the next generation of high-technology weapon systems, it is unlikely they will fare better than they have in the past, whether the adversary be Israel; other Arab nations; or Turkey, Iran, or Pakistan. The only exceptional situation would be their acquisition and use of rudimentary mass destruct weapon systems such as poison gas, chemicals, and/or nuclear weapons.

Should one or more of the Arab nations acquire mass destruct weapons, they would put them to "good" use. Iraq is an interesting case in point. In June 1981, Israel destroyed Iraq's imported capability for building nuclear weapons on the assumption that Saddam Hussein would not be influenced by world public opinion and would not, therefore, desist from the use of nuclear weapons against Israel. His indiscriminate use of gas against Iranian troops brings to focus an essential point in understanding the effect of high technology on feudal nations that are provided with the means to wage ultramodern warfare. The result is that these feudal societies, with their questionable attitudes toward human life and the dignity of man but without the moral and ethical values that evolve with the process of industrial and technological development, have been given the ability to destroy a nation within days. (Interestingly enough, the Soviet Union has always been reluctant to export nuclear technology. Her refusal to provide China with such technology was one of the causes of the political break between them.)

Due to the arms sales policies of both the West and the East, it is inevitable that one or more Arab nation will acquire mass destruct weapon systems—either nuclear and/or gas and chemical. Because it may not be possible for Israel to wage a preventive strike every time an Arab nation acquires nuclear or chemical capability, she must acquire, between now and the twenty-first century, real-time—to the minute—intelligence to be able to respond before one or more of her Arab neighbors can utilize such weapons. Awareness by the Arab nations that Israel possesses such capability in itself becomes a deterrent against their use.

In time, the Arabs will acquire, as Pakistan has, the rudimentary means to manufacture mass destruct weapons. Israel's utilization of reconnaissance satellites, whose very existence may act as a deterrent, will be mandatory by the twenty-first century to establish real-time intelligence in order to provide pre-emptive strike capability.

Military history proves that there has been no correlation among intellect, culture, and morality in that the most intellectually, culturally—and, therefore, economically and industrially—advanced nations have, since the beginning of time, behaved mercilessly in their conduct of war. Only since the culmination of World War II have the advanced society of nations, in general, seriously attempted to avoid participating in war as a means of resolving political dispute. There has been an assumption, however, that regional struggles between and among societies more intellectually and culturally primitive were generally solved by territorial compromise and public opinion, since the means of waging war was not present. The infusion of high-technology weapon systems into such non-Western, feudal-type nations can lead to a mentality of megalomania and, therefore, make their region precariously explosive. Such is the primary case in the Middle East.

Iran is a case in point. With her transnational aspirations and imperialistic exportation of the religious revolution, she has rejected the concept of the integrity of the borders of nation-states and has created a very dangerous ideological struggle for which there can be no negotiated solution—only ultimate victory or defeat. She has given rise to the struggle within Islam not only between Shi'ite Fundamentalists and Sunni Fundamentalists, but between Islamic religious fundamentalism and Islamic secularism as practiced by those Islamic nations—Ba'athist Syria and Iraq, for example—that have not imposed Islamic Sharia law as national law. The major struggle in the region is a triangular one among Islamic secularism, Sunni-Islamic fundamentalism, and Shi'ite fundamentalism.

Such inter- and intra-Arab disputes have been considered by others—benignly ignorant of the realities—to be resolvable through negotiation and/or compromise. Since the 1967 Six-Day War, so, too, has the Arab-Israeli conflict fallaciously been considered soluble under the rubric of U.N. resolutions (that is, if we are to believe the political jargon of the communications media and the world of politicians).

The basic problem is that the powers outside the region still attempt to promote peace by territorial negotiation in a juridical fashion in an area where the trend is toward religious-political fanaticism without a compromise solution other than unconditional surrender. Possession of mass weapons in the hands of these religious Islamic fanatics whose historical record is one of mass slaughter—even of their own—will make wanton massacre in the region inevitable. It has been taking place for many hundreds of years. The difference is that now these forces have available from outside sources the means to reek havoc, destruction, and slaughter on a grand scale. The world's arms suppliers are becoming "merchants of death." The fundamental problem is that there is no reason to believe that arms sales will be reduced and every reason to assume that the number of nations supplying arms into the region will increase, thus further enhancing the danger of serious confrontations.

ISRAEL'S ARMS PROCUREMENT AND MANUFACTURING

On May 15, 1948, at the time of the establishment of the State of Israel, she had a relatively minor arms manufacturing capability—small quantities of submachine guns, rudimentary grenades, and mortars. All military procurement was from World War II stockpiles purchased on the surplus market. There were no government-sanctioned sales to Israel, except from Czechoslovakia. With one stroke of the pen, President Harry Truman recognized the State of Israel, and with the other, he placed an embargo on arms sales to the fledgling state as did every other Western nation. The Arab states that invaded Israel were able to purchase the weapons they required to wage war from many sources and in types and quantities that they could absorb. It was this prejudicial act by the United States and her Western Allies that provided the impetus to establish a weapons industry.

Israel's first official arms supplier, in 1949, was Czechoslovakia. For cash, they sold Mussenschmidt fighter planes and assorted armaments. This provided Israel with a balance to Egypt's British-supplied armed forces.

The first official major Western weapons supplier was France in 1956. She sold Israel tanks, aircraft, and radars. Prior to that, the small propeller air force, as well as armaments, tanks, etc., were purchased (subcontracted) by Israel through third-party arrangements. The 1955 Soviet-arranged arms deal between Egypt and Czechoslovakia created an extremely serious arms imbalance, because, at that time, Israel had no source of arms supplies for the air force, army, or navy.

At the outset of the 1956 Sinai Campaign, which was a preventive war to stop Egypt from absorbing the massive acquisition of arms, Israel had only France as her supplier of weapon systems. By that time, the local weapons industry was manufacturing various types of ammunition, refitting and modernizing old tanks, manufacturing mortars, and making major overhauls of its military aircraft.

Between 1956 and 1967, France was the major arms supplier for the modernization of the Israeli military, then threatened by Egypt and Syria who were receiving massive arms supplies from Eastern Europe. In 1962, President Kennedy agreed to the first official sale of military systems to Israel. The Hawk SAM batteries (antiaircraft) and some radar equipment were sold. Additionally, obsolete transport helicopters were purchased from Germany. In the late 1960s, Britain offered to sell the Chieftan tank. Israel tested the tank and made modifications for its optimal use in the Middle East; and all pertinent data was reported to Britain. In the standard British tradition of doing business with Israel, they canceled the agreement to sell Israel these tanks and sold them to the Arabs instead—another chapter in the British devious, double-dealing in the Middle East and a worthy appendix to their infamous "White Paper" policy.

At the time of the 1967 war, Israel had only France as her primary arms supplier for missile boats, tanks, artillery, radar, and jet aircraft. At that time, the local industry provided service and support for all military equipment in Israel's possession. By the 1967 war, Israel's local industry was heavily into electronic applications for warfare.

Then came the great military victory coupled with the famous Charles De Gaulle embargo and the unilateral abrogation of all previous weapons agreements. For example, fifty Mirage V fighter aircraft and a number of missile boats—all of which had been paid for—were placed under the embargo. This single act by the President of France provided a tremendous impetus for Israel to make a huge investment in manpower and money to create her own aircraft, missile boat, and missile industries. Israel's Nesher jet, Reshef missile boat, and Gabriel missile all should have been named the Charles De Gaulle.

After the 1967 war, the United States placed a total embargo on all requests for new weapons and all spare parts for Hawk radars—even down to nuts and bolts. This embargo lasted several months. Then, after she lifted the embargo, the United States became the single major weapons supplier to all branches of Israel's military. The first major weapon systems provided were the Skyhawk fighter, then the Phantom aircraft, along with electronic warfare equipment, Patton tanks, M-60 tanks, and various types of artillery.

From 1967 to 1973, the United States was responsible for modernizing all branches of Israel's armed forces with the largest flow in quantity and types of armaments after the Egyptian-Soviet violation of the August 1970 cease-fire at the Suez Canal. However, all arms purchases from the United States were subject to tremendous political pressures (for and against), required presidential intervention in all cases, and were always held as a threat or whip to obtain political concessions for Israel's Arab enemy.

All arms deals with the United States have been schizophrenic in character and political in nature with culmination always in doubt. All U.S. administrations since President Johnson have used public pronouncements, as well as leaks to the press, to threaten Israel and punish her. This has created, within Israel's military establishment and government, an atmosphere of extreme insecurity about future availability of new equipment and spare parts to keep existing equipment operational.

Also between 1967 and 1973, there was a tremendous surge in the development and manufacture of Israeli original weapon systems. By the outset of the Yom Kippur War, the Nesher was flying; the Gabriel I missile was operational and sinking Egyptian and Syrian ships; the Reshef missile boat was sailing and was equipped with the Gabriel; and the Shafrir missile was shooting down Egyptian and Syrian planes fired from the Nesher. Artillery, mortars, and armaments of original Israeli design as well as Israeli-modified Centurion, Patton, and Sherman tanks fought the tank battles in the Sinai and the Golan Heights. The Yom Kippur War provided a major testing ground for Israel's military industry. The results proved to local politicians and military personnel that the investment in human and material resources had paid off. And, motivated by the British double-dealing on the Chieftan tank sale, the ground work was laid for the development of the Merkava tank.

During this same period, Britain, France, and the United States carefully limited weapon sales to the moderate Arab states—with each sale painstakingly calculated for what was thought to be a delicate balance. In those days, Iran was the major recipient of U.S. weapon sales.

The 1973 Yom Kippur War changed the whole pattern of Western weapons sales in the Middle East. A policy of selected weapon systems sales based on military-political considerations and an effort to control the military offensive capabilities of the moderate Arab states was replaced with a policy of selling unlimited quantities of the most modern operational weapons to any Arab country that could pay for it. The decision to sell or not to sell became an economic one—not a political one. Neither Israel's welfare nor her sensitivities were taken into consideration.

The post-1973 Yom Kippur War period was one of massive, hectic, frenzied arms shipments that totaled—over a ten-year period—between $150 to $200 billion. The West sold to the "good" (moderate) Arabs, as well as to the "bad" (radical) Arabs. The United States sold only to the good Arabs. The Soviet Union also sold to the good Arabs but mostly to the bad Arabs. The net result was chaos with respect to gaining political leverage in the area—based on arms sales. The West never threatened or applied an arms embargo on the Arabs, but, until the present time, Israel has been under constant embargo or threat of embargo since the State's independence. Every U.S. president since Harry Truman has either threatened or imposed an arms embargo. (The latest—in 1982 following the Lebanon incursion—was placed by President Reagan on F-16 and F-15 fighters despite signed contracts.)

During the period 1973 to 1982, the United States sold Israel major weapon systems, including the F-15 and F-16 jet aircraft, M-60 tanks, armored personnel carriers, and various types of long-range mobile artillery. There were also sales of a number of missile systems including the Dragon shoulder-fired antitank missile, as well as the Maverick, Walleye, Tow, Lance, and Harpoon missiles. Additionally, large stocks of munitions and supplies were sold.

The unprecedented scale of the oil-embargo-induced arms race forced Israel to expand dramatically her total military capability in size, scope, and quantity. Israel's nuclear capability forced the United States to honor her needs in order to keep her from introducing nuclear weapons into the area. This was the case because Israel could no longer meet her defense needs by tactical nonnuclear weapon systems.

The period between 1973 and 1982—until the Peace for Galilee War—saw great accomplishments by the Israeli military industries:

- The Kfir fighter, which was designed and developed in Israel, was produced and became operational.
- The Merkava tank, totally Israeli designed, went into production and became operational.
- A variety of electronic systems for communications, radar, and electronic warfare—including computers for the navy, air force, and army—were designed, developed, produced, and became operational.
- Kinetic artillery shells, developed in Israel, were produced and became operational.
- Scout RPVs for reconnaissance purposes were designed, developed, produced, and became operational.
- A new generation of air-to-air dogfight missiles (the Phantom) was developed and became operational.
- A variety of munitions were developed, produced, and became operational.

This period saw Israel become an exporter of military supplies and weapon systems worth the phenomenal sum of $1.2 billion by 1982.

During this post-1982 Peace for Galilee era, Israel has signed no new major weapon systems purchase with the United States. This is not because the United States is unwilling, but because Israel is now entering into an era when she will no longer require the purchase of major U.S. tactical weapon systems. She will, however, require massive U.S. financing to produce locally developed weapon systems.

A multitude of military projects have been started as a result of the Peace for Galilee War:

- the Lavi advanced fighter;
- the modification and modernization of Israel's fleet of F-4 Phantoms to extend their life to the end of the century;
- the development of a new generation of various types of PGMs, including long-range, stand-off PGMs;
- the introduction and production of an advanced designed Merkava tank;
- the expansion of the microelectronic capability of several major integrated circuit manufacturing facilities;
- the introduction of the first reconnaissance RPV providing immediate visual intelligence;
- the development of the Jericho II ballistic missile;
- the development of Israel's AWACS;
- the development of the Borak antimissile missile (for the navy);
- the development of an air refueling tanker in the Boeing 707; and
- the development of the Arrow antiballistic missile.

Since the establishment of the State of Israel, U.S. relations with Israel have been at arms' length. Over the years, however, as the United States has gained experience in the region, the arm has been growing shorter. On the surface, it would appear that Israel has become more and more dependent upon the United States— not only for weapon systems, etc., but also for more basic forms of economic support. One might assume that dependency on the United States is now so great Israel will be forced to dance to any U.S. tune. Superficially, it would seem that the United States, the great superpower, now totally dominates Israel.

The real reason for the closer relationship between the United States and Israel is that a strong interdependency between both nations has developed. The United States has finally come to understand, or at least behaves as if she understands, that the fundamental major problem in the Middle East is not the Arab-Israeli dispute or the Palestinian issue. She also must have come to appreciate the significance of the emerging Islamic-Fundamentalist forces, which cross national borders and are transnational in nature. The problem facing the United States and the Western world is how to contain or suppress these growing forces and thus maintain the national integrity of the existing nations in the area.

Previously, the U.S. approach to peace in the region was to attempt to moderate or seek political solutions to what were viewed as boundary disputes. What the Iraq-Iran War has proven is that Islamic fundamentalism has goals that cannot be negotiated away. The basic goal becomes the creation of a massive area of Shi'ite-dominated societies. To achieve this will require creation of revolutions in the entire Middle East, including North Africa, Europe, and Pakistan. Revolution and instability are the goals—not mediation and negotiation. Religious fanaticism, not political compromise, dominates the political process. The area is becoming polarized, and transnational lines have been drawn between three ideological forces: Sunni Fundamentalists, Shi'ite Fundamentalists, and Moslem non-*Sharia* Nationalists.

Since most existing nations in the Middle East, except for Egypt, Israel, and the North African states, are governed by minority governments, these nations are extremely vulnerable to revolution and internal turmoil. They are integrated and supported by small numbers of religious fanatics—externally controlled—who join forces with other opposition elements. The struggle in the Middle East is one of an ideological "holy war." The traditional method of negotiation is not applicable now to the Middle East.

The other problem recognized by the United States is that it cannot project military power by maintaining permanent military presence in the area. The U.S. forces in Lebanon only highlighted the fact that the United States lacks the will to sustain casualties and will probably seek to avoid sending ground troops into the area for any future conflict. She hasn't even been able to defend her own embassies from local terrorists. The U.S. use of aircraft carriers for projection of power has not been successful in the Middle East and can only, at best, have limited political effects.

Despite the problems, it is a bipartisan conclusion that the United States must maintain political influence in the region, which is believed to be critical to her interests. The Middle East is of vital strategic importance—with or without the oil of the area—because it is the crossroads between three continents and controls the shipping and air routes from Europe to Asia. Additionally, it is critical for the containment of Russian aspirations to dominate Turkey and reach India and Asia.

It can be assumed that as long as the Soviet Union and the United States remain adversaries, the United States will consider the Middle East to be of vital strategic importance and seek methods of projecting political influence into the region. As long as the United States requires political influence and projection into the area, she will have to support the sustenance of the existing national orders—whether they are friendly or unfriendly (moderate or radical) dictatorships, monarchies, or autocratic disparate regimes.

The other point to be noted is that U.S. policy has been and is based on trying either to eliminate or contain Soviet presence in the Middle East. The only stable democratic society in the Middle East with values shared by the United States is Israel. She has proven over the years to be the dominant military force in the region and has also been forced by Soviet policy to be anti-Soviet. Israel becomes a deterrent against any direct or indirect Soviet intervention in regional conflicts.

The United States decided to place in Israel—in the Negev—the Voice of America programs and to beam them at the Soviet Union. That required a U.S. investment of over $250 million. At one time, she could have placed it in Cypress, but the Cypriot-Turkish war there made it impossible, and no Arab nation would allow it, including Saudi Arabia.

Israel's military power has been and is a stabilizing influence over the maintenance of orderly arrangements between the nations of the region. For example, if Israel were unstable, Syria would have conquered Jordan and Lebanon years ago, thus threatening Saudi Arabia. Israel provides the only stable logistic base for a U.S. military presence in the region. She has a technological infrastructure for maintenance of the most advanced U.S. weapon systems including the F-15, the F-16, cargo planes, and sophisticated electronics. Additionally, Israel's medical facilities are on a par with those of the United States.

The present Shi'ite threat to all Sunni regimes makes an

alliance between Israel and the United States more palatable than the nation-state conflict. For the United States to provide a military alternative to Israel by her own means would require more than ten carrier groups, and the cost certainly would exceed what it currently costs in aid to Israel. In addition, the United States would have to engender the national will to do so as well as conjure up a political consensus within the United States.

The rise to power of Shi'ite fundamentalism and the political awakening among the Shi'ite masses represent a trend that will continue to grow. It is a religious reaction to the secularism of some Islamic states as practiced by Egypt's Nasser, Iran's shah, and Iraq's Saddam Hussein. This religious group is vehemently anti-West as well as anti-East. Neither the Soviet Union nor the United States will be able to come to terms with Shi'ite-Islamic fundamentalism, and the presence and interests of both are threatened. The existing leaders of the secular states in the area will tend toward exhibiting greater religious fervor within their nations because Shi'ite-Islamic fundamentalism has aroused a counterforce—violent anti-secularism among a growing Sunni-Islamic-Fundamentalist movement. This is a problem that had been faced by President Reagan and must be addressed by subsequent Republican and Democratic presidents; therefore, U.S. relationships with Israel will grow even closer as Israel becomes more stable economically and stronger militarily.

This, more than anything else, is why the United States will do what is possible to assist Israel not only in maintaining a modern powerful military but in achieving economic stability as well. Conditions within the Middle East necessitate the continued shortening of the arms' length relationship between the two nations and establishment of strategic cooperation within the area. The United States must find the means to strengthen Israel's economy by helping Israel to help herself while simultaneously serving overall U.S. interests.

Since 1974, the United States has become the world's largest exporter of military weapon systems, and the trend for the balance of the 1980s and 1990s is in the direction of further expansion of weapon sales—not only for political reasons but also because of strong economic considerations. Whether or not the pursuit of this policy is considered humane seems to be of no concern to the people of the United States, and it appears to be acceptable across the vast spectrum of political thinking within the nation. Except for a small, not so vocal, leftist minority, it is a policy that has gone unchallenged. President Carter, in his first years, attempted to alter the trend of arms exports on humanistic grounds, but by the end of his presidency, he yielded to the considerations of the national interest.

The problem in pursuing a policy of supplying military weapon systems to all countries in the world where political influence or money is the consideration is that the recipient nation usually demands weapons that either have been combat proven or are operational with U.S. forces. The U.S. weapons development philosophy, at least on major weapon systems development, has been to anticipate usage any place on the globe—on the highest mountains and the lowest plains—and under whatever extreme conditions prevail: desert heat, Artic cold, sand storms, blizzards, etc. This increases significantly not only the cost, but also its complexity and, thus, its maintenance requirements. The recipient nation, therefore, must have extremely sophisticated maintenance and logistic facilities, which none of the Third World countries possess. In the case of Iran and Saudi Arabia—both of whom have purchased tens of billions of dollars of the most sophisticated U.S. military systems—the answer was (1) the hiring of thousands of American technicians to maintain the equipment and (2) the importing of turnkey maintenance bases. This is beyond the economic reach of most Third World countries.

The U.S. weapon system development program is primarily aimed for use by NATO and the defense of Western Europe. The weapons are designed to be used in technologically intensive, high-density threat areas such as Eastern Europe, Syria, and the Chinese-Russian border.

U.S. tactical weapons development is based on the U.S. perception of how a war will start and how it will be conducted, which may not be the perception or actual conditions that exist in the case of every Third World country. Perfect examples of this situation were the development of the F-111E, a stand-off jamming airborne system that cost in excess of $100 million, and the F-4E Wild Weasel, also a standoff platform for locating and destroying SAMs. In both cases, they were too expensive and too complex for Third World nations to operate and maintain; they were really designed for operation in Europe. Additionally, the HARM antiradiation missiles cost $350,000 each and are extremely sophisticated.

Many Third World countries are faced with the need for high technology in weapons but low density in quantities. The type of weapon system required to address this problem must be low in cost and simple in design, operation, and maintenance—most probably a completely different type of weapon system than the United States would send. It isn't clever to send a $350,000 missile, or even a $100,000 missile, to destroy $50,000 targets. If there are a few expensive targets, they can be destroyed by low-cost conventional means. The vast majority of Third World countries are dollar poor and are forced to make weapon systems purchases by barter arrangements, which U.S. companies don't find desirable. The problem of Third World poverty will most probably be as acute at the turn of the century as it is today; the lack of technological infrastructure works against their improving their economic lot.

The problem facing the U.S. government is that, if the Western nations cannot meet the weapon systems needs of the Third World countries, those nations will look to the Soviets to fulfill their requirements. An alternative solution for the United States would be to allow Israel to supply the weapon system needs of some of these countries. As time progresses, Israel will have varied types of tactical weapon systems designed for limited regional conflicts. Such weapon systems tend to be simpler to maintain and operate, as well as less costly, and they can readily serve the requirements of many of the nations in the less developed world. Since she is not an importer, Israel is prepared to barter. This arrangement would prevent the problem of the Third World countries going to the Soviet Union, would help stabilize Israel's grave economic problems, and, because Israel imports U.S. subsystems, would provide export for U.S. industry.

For example, the Kfir jet fighter utilizes the GEJ-79 engine, which is manufactured in Israel with materials bought from General Electric. Israel's sale of weapon systems to Third World nations serves U.S. strategic needs and enables Israel to support an extremely expensive weapons development program thrust upon her by the pace of the arms race established by the superpowers' (U.S.S.R.-U.S.) arms policies. Contrary to past U.S. policy, it no longer serves U.S. national interests to keep Israel economically weak due to the new and more severe threats to the stability of the Middle East. It is, and will continue to be, in the best interest of the United States to establish Israel as a supplier of weapon systems to those nations the United States wants supplied but can't or won't for geopolitical reasons—just as Czechoslovakia serves that role for the Soviet Union.

Over the next decade, Israel must conform to the basic approach to military preparedness as philosophized by the Romans 2,000 years ago. Their motto was: *Ci Vi Pacum Parn Bellum*—If you want peace, prepare for war.

Israel will enter the twenty-first century in a continual process of preparing for war. There is a high probability that this will spread out the frequency of confrontation; minimize the number of adversaries at one time; and reduce the scale, scope, and length of any specific confrontation. However, given the dynamics of the Middle East arms race, the ideological nature of the grievances, the interests of the superpowers, and the multidimensional scope of the adversaries, there is a low probability that Israel will be able to avoid military confrontation in the next ten to twenty years and almost zero probability that confrontations between other Middle East nations won't take place. As it enters the twenty-first century, the Middle East will undoubtedly be an area of high risk and violence.

Israel's Rapid Deployment
Force (RDF)

The amazing situation exists that within seventy-two hours the State of Israel can mobilize the Free World's largest, most powerful, and, undoubtedly, the most effective RDF. The Israeli armed forces have achieved this real military power through a combination of factors. The acquisition, deployment, and integration of the most advanced technological weapon systems available from importation and local production have contributed to this unique phenomenon. The primary element, however, has been the ability to enlist the most qualified manpower that society can provide. An extremely high level of national purpose has enabled the nation to support a state of military modernity and competence unparalleled any other place on the globe.

The modern State of Israel is history's most powerful small nation—a status achieved out of sheer necessity based on sensitivity to the external perils to her society and exasperation by her inability to obtain equal status in world forums. The manpower composition of the Israeli armed forces—drawn from every stratum of society—has provided the competence to absorb and deploy the proliferating advanced-technology tactical weapon systems more rapidly and more proficiently than any other military force on the globe, including those of the two superpowers—the Soviet Union and the United States.

The Syrian missile crisis and Israel's surgical-like destruction of Iraq's nuclear reactor have placed into focus the rapid and dramatic changes taking place in modern warfare. The technological developments since World War II, particularly in the past fifteen years since the Yom Kippur War, have altered the nature of warfare drastically. However, societies—and their politicians—who are arming with advanced-technology weapon systems do not behave as if this fact is understood.

There exists today a little recognized phenomenon facing every army in the world that is equipped with modern weapon systems. It is that intense battle conditions can be sustained for a relatively short period of time, while utilizing the tactics developed to employ these super sophisticated armaments. Future wars will be measured in days—possibly weeks—but not longer. No nation has acquired the industrial capacity, the resources, the "supply train," or the maintenance capability to feed combat forces with the high volume of missiles, ammunition, spare parts, and replacement weapon systems needed to maintain a modern war machine. The enormous rates of consumption developed in present-day modern combat cannot be sustained for long periods.

Unconsciously, the military is entering into a technological trap. The "god" of technology demands the development of more and more sophisticated multifunction weapons, which are then designed and produced in quantity. But these weapons cannot be operated and maintained by the common soldiers who are conscripted by the random mobilization of the masses. The military now requires access to a group of highly trained and intellectual individuals just to sustain this modern war machine. Weapons become more complex and their multipurpose design necessitates the need for more trained people to maintain them. Consequently, most of these weapons are stored for future use.

The trap is obvious: the people needed to maintain and operate these weapons require an extremely long time for training. Complexity dictates that support logistics can no longer be developed until the war machinery starts running. This circle is insidious—during a war, there may not be sufficient time to train the specialists and to develop the logistical support. While unused weapons are stored, people cannot be trained. Time is needed to train the people; yet, support logistics cannot be developed before the war begins. Given this condition, future wars will have to be fought by a relatively small group of highly trained professionals operating sophisticated weapons.

It is impossible to combine untrained and uneducated masses with technologically intensive war machines and still utilize the weapon systems for the tactics for which they were designed; however, unconsciously, the Western armies are following this course. There is not one army in all the major Western democracies based on conscription. The U.S Army, the largest, is based on volunteers. The United States is finding it difficult to maintain existing equipment because her enlistees do not come from the intellectually elite sectors of the society. This problem will become even more critical during a period necessitating the expansion of the armed forces. Determining who will maintain and operate the stockpiled equipment looms as one of the most serious problems facing military planners. Present military strategists are still planning in World War II terms—mass conscription and the use of masses of equipment—while technology has passed the generals by. They have not yet established whether the society can or will provide the quality and quantity of people needed to operate the enormously complex equipment being built and stored. Future wars will not provide the time necessary to train the masses of people.

Armies of the future will have to be organized around an elite force that is equipped with new, highly accurate, single-purpose weapons, mass produced and not requiring the large-scale complex logistical systems now so necessary. Technological solutions to this system complexity now exist to achieve this. In the field of electronics, particularly, there have been recent developments in the areas of microprocessors and very large-scale integrated circuits, combined with the use of new types of sensors. Utilizing such technology, the less skilled would be able to operate the newly designed single-function weapon systems. If there were a true understanding of the problem, along with a consensus by both military and industrial strategists, a real change in weaponry could be implemented well before the end of the century. At present, there appear to be only a few lonely voices in the wilderness proposing such developments.

Israel can never hope to match the Arab nations in quantities of equipment or in the numbers of men that she can place into combat. A continuing cynical approach to weapon systems' sales has been pursued by the Western European merchants of death. This, combined with the rivalry for favor from the Arab nations competitively pursued by the two superpowers, forces Israel to plan for a region saturated with the latest high-technology weapon systems. The terms of Middle East peace perceived by a sanctimonious Western world, coupled with an Arab society of nations beset by ongoing violence and political instability, will only exacerbate the problem instead of easing it.

Israel learned some very practical lessons during the opening days of the Yom Kippur War:

- The use of massive quantities of men and weapons can more than compensate for superior quality in weapons and manpower.
- Israel cannot afford, either economically or politically, to absorb again a first strike, but must be prepared to take preventive measures to discourage or disable her enemy from mounting war.
- Israel must continue the utilization of modern technology to develop in parallel relatively simple single-purpose devices and weapon systems. The enhancement of existing U.S.-supplied weapon systems should allow Israel to maintain military superiority.

During the Syrian missile crisis, Israel proved the value of low-cost, single-purpose systems in executing a single task. Inexpensive RPVs replaced manned aircraft to perform battlefield surveillance of Syrian movement and fortifications in Lebanon. This saved the lives of irreplaceable pilots and preserved aircraft that cost from $6 to $20 million each. The use of this low-cost alternative weapon system opened vast new horizons in the field of air defense suppression. Western military planners have been plagued since the Yom Kippur War when the problem of the Soviets' investment in SAM systems became apparent.

The application of advanced technology to the development of weapon systems and modern warfare meshes well with the scientifically and industrially based Israeli society. This condition will exist so long as Israel possesses the national will to invest in her defense and is prepared to take independent action.

In time, the Arab states should develop serious doubts about the military value of modern armaments. Sophisticated weapon systems are highly capital intensive and require an advanced industrial base for repair, maintenance, and operation. The Arab shortage of skilled industrial manpower will magnify the impairment of their military efficiency; however, Arab vanity, inter-Arab rivalry, Arab fantasy, and Western greed all will continue to impede their ability to draw the proper conclusion.

If present trends persist, the cost of defense will continue to rise astronomically. The expanding complexity of weapon systems, combined with inflation, will challenge the ability of all nations to defend themselves through the maintenance of totally balanced high-technology forces. In the next decade, neither Israel nor the Arab nations will be able to maintain both quantity and quality in their forces. The Arabs who can afford to purchase massive quantities of modern weapons have the problem of providing trainable manpower. Israel, on the other hand, faces the financial burden of maintaining the quantities of the modern weapon systems that she can hardly afford to purchase.

Israel's strategic planners will be faced with very undesirable alternatives. The least costly to the society, in terms of manpower and money, will be to destroy the Arab war-making capability as rapidly and with as few casualties as possible as each threat arises. Undoubtedly, this will not be acceptable to Western leaders who seek to impose a one-sided morality on Israel and allude to some legalistic international rules of acceptable behavior. However, the alternatives to Israel and the Jewish people are too gruesome to even entertain. While such a policy cannot be pursued indefinitely, there are not many options at the present time. Peace on Arab terms may be good for some but not for Israel and the Jewish people.

Until the Western society of nations pursues politics that recognize the permanent status of the Jewish state in the Middle East and the Arab societies truly appreciate this Western commitment, only then is peace possible for Israel. But until that time, the Middle East region will be similar to that of Europe and Southeast Asia where a permanent condition of armed truce was characterized by short periods of military activity. For Israel to hope for more is certainly noble—to plan for less is suicidal. In a very real sense, the West can be the beneficiary of Israel's military power.

Israel's ability to combine high technology with the development of unique tactical systems will assure her superiority over any combination of Arab armies. Uniqueness in weapon systems in itself is an advantage because it has the element of surprise. A purchased system is not a surprise. By the end of this century, Israel will develop and produce most of her tactical systems. There is a strong possibility that even the United States will use them. As a consequence, the Israeli armed forces will be the world's first most advanced tactical force.

Impact of Technology on Israel Over the Next Twenty Years

AREAS OF IMPACT AND THE EFFECT ON THE NATION

Because Israel will still be in conflict over the next twenty years, she will be required to continue to apply advanced technology techniques to develop, manufacture, and make operational all of her required military weapon systems, except for some major systems such as aircraft and SAMs. For Israel, the only other source of tactical weapon systems is the United States. And by the very nature of U.S. tactical weapon systems development, she would not produce or develop the type of weapon systems most applicable to Israel's tactical needs. Because of her physical isolation—surrounded by two oceans—and her policy of mutually assured destruction (MAD) with the Soviets, the United States does not foresee herself engaged in a ground tactical war. Therefore, she is not preparing weapons and tactics to conduct such a war as Israel would be required to fight. For the United States, preparing for nonnuclear tactical warfare is only a matter of policy decision; for Israel, it is a matter of survival.

The development of the most advanced tactical weapon systems is a requirement for Israel in order to maintain the confidentiality of her arsenal and inventory of weapon systems. This will provide Israel with an element of surprise, while depriving the Arabs of like weapon systems, since their only source is either the Soviets or the West. No Arab nation will develop the capability of producing similar high-technology weapons during the next twenty years.

Until now, Israel has been developing weapon systems to kill masses of soldiers. But over the next two decades, she must develop weapon systems that destroy weapons that are intended to destroy masses of people. Because of vital security requirements, Israel is forced to maintain the highest level of technology and keep up to date with the most advanced technological developments. Continued growth in weapon systems exports, therefore, is anticipated because no other nation in the world will be producing weapon systems similar to Israel's.

Europe's lack of combat experience since World War II and its post-war reliance on the United States for military know-how has created a predicament that encourages close military cooperation with Israel in the form of joint projects. For such ventures, Israel will provide the definition (specifications) and combat experience, while Europe will provide some unique technology and components as well as scale of production for unit cost amortization. Both will share in the capital cost of development.

Israel will also be obtaining advanced technology from the United States. Her unique situation as the only Western-oriented ally of the United States in the Middle East provides her with a unique opportunity to have access to U.S. high technology. Israel's involvement in the SDI program will provide her with that much needed technology. One ongoing project, for example, is the weapon system called Arrow—a tactical antiballistic missile defense system against short- and medium-range ballistic missiles such as those acquired by Syria from the Soviet Union. Being the sixteenth largest scientific community in the world, with a per capita scientific activity on par with that of the United States, provides Israel with the infrastructure and the means to absorb and apply this technology to solve problems indigenous to Israel.

History has shown that unless major investments are made in the military sector, significant societal technological developments don't occur; and unless large investments are made in military preparedness, creative improvements in consumer products don't take place. Major advances in transportation, communications, and computer technology, for example, were the result of military investment. Advances in the development of the airplane, automobile, telephone, telecommunications, radio, television, major medications against bacterial infections, synthetic fibers, and all synthetic materials were catapulted by the need to fulfill military requirements. Sadly enough, if there weren't any major wars between major powers, the world we live in today would be more like the world of the seventeenth century.

Technology—financed by vast military budgets—has been growing at an accelerating pace. Even Israel's nearly miraculous agricultural development takes a back seat to the military. Israel's unique situation requires her to continue spending in the area of weapon systems development and production way out of proportion to the size of her population. This emphasis on military technology will provide the nation with sufficient know-how which, when transferred and applied to the civilian sector, will give the society new means to achieve economic independence.

In 1988, Israel exported approximately $1.3 billion worth of military-oriented products. Local consumption of the military industry for the same year was between $2 and $2.5 billion. Military export can only expand as local consumption increases. In 1988, Israel provided approximately 50 percent of her own military requirements. (If military aircraft—F-16 and helicopters—and submarines are excluded, Israel produced almost 90 percent of her military requirements.) During the next two decades, she will not be able to increase the overall percentage substantially, because she will have to continue to import major military aircraft, specialized systems, and exotic components. Military exports will increase, but they cannot be the major component in Israel's export figures.

Although military exports could grow over the next twenty years, it would not solve Israel's balance of trade problem. However, the transfer of technologies used within the military industries to the civilian sector will enable Israel to develop a new generation of advanced-technology products, unique and proprietary, and enable her to establish new export markets. The development of civilian industrial products utilizing sensors, computers, material technologies, and control systems will provide Israel with commodities for export way beyond what the military industries can supply.

For example, today, Israel's agricultural exports are equivalent to those of the military industries. Through the application of modern technology, Israel's agricultural industry will continue to develop at a rapid pace. New products will be created and productivity of existing products will be increased, enabling Israel to maintain her position as one of the world's leading agricultural societies.

The need to increase agricultural exports to be competitive with the most advanced nations of the world forces Israel to apply the most advanced technologies, including genetic engineering and robotics, to solve problems such as the shortage of water, the limitations in quantity and quality of land, the shifts in available markets, and the need to enter new markets (through the creation of new varieties of products). Because of her limitations in water and land for expansion, Israel must increase her output—as measured in dollars per dunam—if her agricultural export is to grow.

To achieve agricultural export expansion, or even keep pace with the anticipated growth in military exports, there must be a transfer of technologies from the military, in conjunction with the application of genetic engineering, to solve the problems that now exist within Israel's agricultural sector. Aside from the incredible advances in irrigation and genetic engineering, Israeli scientists have embarked on the creation of a self-fertilizing plant that would render whole chemical fertilizing industries obsolete. Bioengineering applied to Israel's agricultural sector can create enormous new industries—the products of which are still in the imaginations of scientists.

Israel's military expertise can easily be translated into scientific breakthroughs in the field of medicine as well. The use of advanced sensors and sophisticated electronics, combined with genetic engineering, will make Israel a forerunner in the field of medical technology.

And so, too, will Israel's military knowledge facilitate growth in computer science industries. Legions of highly capable experts in computer science are available in all sectors of the Israeli society. The Haifa Technion has an enviable standard of excellence and quality that is on par with any major university in the world. A traditional Talmudic education is a fertile ground for software specialists from the religious sector of the population; the logic required for deciphering ancient medieval texts is easily transferred to computer programming. In Israel, most computer programmers "cut their teeth" in the defense industry before they transfer to the private sector. High-technology industries have been favorites of small, cooperative farming settlements, and they represent one of the most popular "cottage" industries on these settlements. Once again, the greatest resource for these industries is the people themselves. This industry will continue to grow in Israel as more markets appear.

Israel has always been a leader in the development of solar energy, and because of her practical concerns, she continues to develop more sophisticated systems that are applicable to a variety of climatic conditions. As alternative forms of energy become more of an issue, this industry will also thrive as a result of the transfer of military technical know-how.

Over the next twenty years, the growth in standard of living and the security of Israel are both tied to the continuing application of advanced technology to all sectors of Israel's economy. There is every reason to believe that during the next twenty years Israel will benefit much more than her Arab neighbors as new technologies are developed throughout the world.

Prospects for Arab-Israeli Peace

THE CAMP DAVID PEACE AGREEMENT: A MODEL OR ANTI-MODEL FOR FUTURE ARAB-ISRAELI TREATIES?

As Israel enters the twenty-first century, there may arise a number of "opportunities" for peace with one or more of her Arab neighbors. Whether the opportunity will be one that is real or just perceived will most probably be determined by the needs and national interests of Israel's "friends"—the nations of the West, led by the United States. Israel will then have to evaluate the results of the Camp David Accords, which were signed with Egypt in 1979, and determine whether those results are relevant enough to be used as a model for future agreements. This evaluation will be drawn from Israel's historical experience with the Accords.

The Camp David Accords were based on the fundamental principle of relinquishing a tangible for an intangible—a piece of territory for a piece of peace. Israel's contribution to the Accords—relinquishing Sinai—was irreversible without war; Egypt's contribution—good will—was not. Egypt's "good will" would, however, be tested by time.

Before Camp David

The Camp David Accords of 1979 materialized because of the international environment—specifically, conditions within the United States, Israel, and Egypt and the strategic positions of their leaders. On the eve of the Camp David summit, Prime Minister Menachem Begin was the master of his house and approached the negotiations with great self-confidence; however, this was true neither of Carter nor Sadat.

The United States and Carter

Carter was in deep trouble domestically; his public approval rating had dipped below Nixon's all-time low. An unpublished Harris poll taken two weeks after the Saudi Arabian-Egyptian military jet deal (which the Carter administration rammed through Congress) revealed that Carter's approval rating fell from 75 percent at the time of his election to an unbelievable .10 percent (1:1,000).

Carter's popularity within the Jewish population was even worse. During the eighteen-month period following his 1976 election, an unprecedented erosion in Jewish support had taken place. Since the Jewish voters had provided Carter with his margin of victory in four states (with almost 100 electoral votes) and had supplied the majority of his national campaign funds, this erosion spelled trouble. Carter could not have defeated Ford without Jewish support; therefore, a total loss of that support dimmed his hopes for a 1980 re-election. Carter required a major foreign policy achievement to bolster his sagging leadership prior to the 1978 congressional elections.

Egypt and Sadat

Sadat's political quagmire was even worse than Carter's. Sadat had failed in his quest to achieve Egypt's national goals through an alliance with the Soviet Union, and in the summer of 1972, he expelled the Russian advisers stationed in Egypt. This, coupled with the debilitating $12 billion indebtedness to the Soviet Union, was sufficient motivation for Sadat to seek new alliances. He embarked upon the long road toward economic, military, and political alignment with the West.

Sadat's launching of the Yom Kippur War of October 6, 1973 succeeded in seriously weakening Israel's economy, created great strains in U.S.-Israeli relations, and further isolated Israel from the Western community of nations; however, Egyptian losses were far from insignificant. Not only did the Egyptian military suffer a devastating defeat, but the performance of the Egyptian economy after the Yom Kippur War was dismal—an extremely significant factor in Sadat's calculation of the need for a peace treaty with Israel.

Egypt required more than a massive infusion of money into her economy; a major restructuring of her burgeoning bureaucratic system was needed. Despite increased loans, grants, financial windfalls, and a unilateral abrogation of payments of principal and interest on previous loans from the Soviet Union, Egypt's economic performance worsened each successive year following the Yom Kippur War. Also, during those post-war years, much unrest existed within the society exemplified by attempts made on Sadat's life. One year after the devastating food riots in Cairo and Alexandria, which very nearly brought down the Sadat government, Sadat was forced to seek emergency financial aid from the oil-rich Arab nations and became a political captive of Saudi Arabia.

The handful of sheiks who ruled over Saudi Arabia and the oil-rich Gulf states dispensed economic aid to Sadat sparingly and with short political strings attached. The wealth of the oil sheikdoms had increased dramatically as a result of the rise in the price of oil made possible by Sadat's initiation of the Yom Kippur War. However, their generosity was not commensurate with their new-found wealth nor with the Egyptian sacrifices. Certainly, the economic assistance that they provided did not match Egypt's basic economic requirements. The reopening of the Suez Canal, the return of the Abu Rodeis oil fields, and the U.S. grants-in-aid—all of which were the economic benefits that resulted from the Yom Kippur War—were not nearly sufficient to provide Sadat with the economic independence he sought and needed to maintain political leadership within the Arab world. Billions of dollars were required from Saudi Arabia just to cover Sadat's foreign arms purchases and to keep his poverty-stricken masses sufficiently fed in order to prevent rioting.

Egypt moved from a position of Soviet dominance to one of Saudi Arabian subservience. Egypt had been replaced by Saudi Arabia as the perceived protector of Arab interests in the forum of the Western seats of power. Saudi Arabia had achieved this dominant position despite the fact that her ruling class numbered less than 2,000 people. Her massive oil reserves had given Saudi

Arabia political power totally disproportionate to the size of her population, her technological-scientific-industrial base, or her military strength.

Sadat attempted to regain the dominant position in the Arab world by his appeal to the United States in 1977 to pressure Israel to accept a comprehensive settlement. Such a settlement would have left Israel sufficiently weakened—politically and strategically—to ensure her future destruction. Sadat needed peace with Israel desperately, but he also required that any progress toward peace and normal relations had to be linked to the aspiration toward the resolution of the "problem" of a Palestinian homeland. Before signing a separate peace with Israel, Sadat insisted on U.S. political and economic compensation. That these tactics for achieving his long-term strategy were certainly his intention has been well documented.

Sadat's need for an instant peace also involved his view of the speed with which the Soviet Union had been gaining ground in the Middle East at the time. The USSR's five-pronged approach—the growing unrest in Iran and the threat to the shah's throne, the Communist takeovers in Afghanistan and South Yemen, the success of Soviet support of Ethiopia in her defeat of Somalia in the Ogaden Desert, and the massive stockpiling of Soviet military supplies in Libya—presented threats that Sadat could not ignore.

At the time, the greatest challenge to Sadat was the possible resolution of the Eritrean and Djibouti secessionist movement in Ethiopia's favor. This would have increased dramatically the very grave risk of an Ethiopian Russian-backed move to support materially the national political aspirations of the large black minority that inhabited southern Sudan. This non-Moslem, black population had been subjugated politically by the Arab Moslems of northern Sudan. Egypt and Sudan not only share the Nile River, but 90 percent of the Egyptian people live on its banks and/or depend upon it for survival. No Egyptian government could tolerate an unfriendly or unstable nation to its south. As long as there was not peace with Israel, Sadat had to keep his army massed at the Suez Canal. This inhibited him from providing future military support of the Sudan on his southern border.

Sadat could neither support Sudan militarily nor deal with his biggest nemesis—the oil-rich Colonel Qaddafi of Libya on his western border. At that time, Libya's $12 billion oil revenue was highly coveted by Sadat. Libya's alignment with Algeria and their Soviet connection also posed a grave threat to an Egypt whose army was tied down at the Suez. Libya's Colonel Qaddafi and his Soviet friends had every reason to be concerned for an Egyptian-Israeli peace not only enhanced the possibility of an Egyptian takeover of the Libyan oil fields but made it a distinct probability.

Sadat could not have made many fundamental concessions to Begin if he were not preoccupied by problems such as these— greater than Israel's long-term survival or concern for his short-term position within the Arab world. Sadat's timetable was delayed due to the ferocity and complexity of the 1976 Lebanese civil war. That war placed Syria in control of the PLO, an organization which had been a political invention of Gamal Abdel Nasser and a key to Sadat's master plan to destroy the State of Israel and become leader of the Arab nations. When Syrian domination of the PLO became evident, Sadat decided to abandon support of the PLO—in contradiction to the wishes of Saudi Arabia and the rest of the Arab world.

Another setback for Sadat was the defeat of the Ford-Kissinger administration in the 1976 election. Much of Sadat's initial success and progress toward obtaining his strategic aims had been achieved through the results of the brutal pressures placed upon Israel by the Ford-Kissinger team. Subsequently, Sadat had indicated, on a number of occasions, that the election of Carter was a blow to his perception of the orderly process required for achieving his strategic goals.

The basic Middle East policies of the Carter administration, along with its fundamental support and orientation toward the Egyptian and Saudi Arabian positions, did not differ from those of the Ford administration. However, Carter's ineptness and incompetence in the implementation of those policies served to frustrate Sadat, forcing him to alter his tactics in pursuit of his strategic plan for the area.

Begin's rise to power in May 1977 only served to magnify the problems created by the Brzezinski-Carter duo. From the day Carter assumed power until the Camp David summit, his administration's blind determination to achieve an overall comprehensive settlement, which would satisfy the Saudi Arabian perception of pax Middle East, was pursued with great vigor and determination. Unfortunately, it was also pursued with little skill.

The Negotiations

The aims and actual results of the Camp David Accords for the three parties involved were quite different. Given the realities of the Middle East and the parties' perceptions of their national interests during the process, each of the three leaders sought to revise his commitments and seek further clarification along with new concessions from the other two.

For Israel, the problem was most serious because national survival was at stake. From the standpoint of real tangible concessions for peace, Israel's contribution—the total return of the Sinai—was undoubtedly the greatest, not only because it could be measured but, also, because it was reversible only by war. For the United States, the problem was a question of what degree of influence she would have in the region. For Egypt, the problem was the nature of her future role within Israel and in the rest of the Arab world.

Both Carter and Sadat conceded on the issue of a separate Israeli-Egyptian peace treaty unlinked to progress on all other outstanding Arab-Israeli issues. This concession, unlike Israel's, was not only *not* measurable but could easily be abrogated at any time in the future without any serious or visible repercussions. In fact, soon after the Camp David Accords, Carter, followed by Sadat, attempted to link Israel's relinquishing of Sinai with progress on issues concerning Judea, Samaria, and Gaza. This was an abrogation of the documents, as well as of their intent. This shift was hardly noticed by the unsophisticated in the public arena.

With a view toward the long-term interest of modern Egypt— to be the leader of a united Arab world as repeatedly defined by Nasser and Sadat dating back to the Egyptian Officers' Revolution in 1952—and her record of past violations of treaties, accords, and agreements, there was every reason to believe that, in time, the Camp David Accords would also be violated. The value of any long-term, written commitment to

Israel made by the United States was also questionable, since the past record of U.S. commitments to Israel had not been very good. Therefore, the future value of a U.S.-Egyptian written commitment to Israel certainly had to be questioned seriously.

Israel's feeling of distrust was supported by the public testimony of both Henry Kissinger and James Ball given before the Senate Foreign Relations Committee on the then pending Panama Canal Treaty. Their testimony stressed the fact that no nation, including the United States, would honor previously signed agreements or treaties at a time when they were no longer perceived to serve that country's best interest. Both Kissinger and Ball attempted to assure the senators that any treaty returning the Canal would most undoubtedly be unilaterally abrogated by the United States if, in the future, it was perceived to serve her best interests. Begin and his advisers were certainly aware of this U.S. position, as well as similar behaviors by the rest of the Western community of nations.

After Camp David

The signing of the Camp David Accords had a major impact on the perceptions of the people of Israel, the United States, and the European nations.

Israel and Begin

Immediately after Camp David, Begin faced serious political problems both at home and abroad. Domestically, it became necessary for Begin to convince the people of Israel, and their duly elected political representatives, that the Camp David Accords would yield more than just continued U.S. economic and military support. Begin, also, had to convince his people that relinquishing the Sinai would enhance Israel's long-term interests in Judea, Samaria, Gaza, Jerusalem, and the Golan Heights and not compromise those interests. The fact is that Carter and Sadat did, eventually, agree to sign agreements that isolated the return of the Sinai from the problem of the ultimate status of Judea, Samaria, Gaza, Jerusalem, and the Golan Heights.

Diplomatically, he had the difficult challenge of finalizing the terms of the peace treaty with both Carter and Sadat, within the framework of the Camp David Accords, so that Israel could withstand a shift in both Carter's and Sadat's commitments. Begin required solid domestic support in order to stand firm against any abrogation, not only of the spirit of Camp David but also of the actual terms of the documents. This was necessary because neither Carter nor Sadat were satisfied with the terms or the implications of the documents.

The United States and Carter

The events following the Camp David Accords tended to support those who had been critical of Carter's lack of preparation for the peace talks. However, the Accords did achieve the much sought after boost in Carter's domestic popularity—the primary goal set for Camp David by Gerald Rafshoon, Carter's senior adviser in charge of public relations. Whether or not it would bring peace any closer than traditional foreign policy techniques was highly questionable. Carter had a desperate need to achieve a quick agreement, not just a framework for future negotiations.

A sagging popularity with the U.S. public and deadlocks with Congress over critical legislation forced Carter to increase the expectation level of what had to be achieved at Camp David. Nixon and Ford had been guilty of such tactics; then, it was Carter's turn to use U.S. leverage on Israel for domestic political gain, even if it meant jeopardizing the long-term security of Israel and her ability to negotiate a meaningful settlement that could pass the test of time. The world was witness again to a U.S. president who risked achieving peace in the Middle East in order to bolster his position with the electorate and divert attention from serious domestic problems.

As a result of the Camp David Accords, Carter achieved worldwide acclaim and notoriety through the clever use of pizzazz, fanfare, and public relations gimmickry. Along with that instant diplomatic success came the much-needed increase in his domestic popularity.

European Perception

The European perception of the Israeli-Egyptian peace was totally different from that of the United States. For the Europeans, the never-ending struggle in the Middle East could be linked to a three-ring circus. The Arab-Israeli confrontation was one small ring; the European involvement in the events taking place was another small ring; but the struggle within the twenty-three-nation Arab community, coupled with the competitive involvement of the United States and the Soviet Union in Arab affairs, was the very large center ring—the main show. To the Europeans, this was the ring on which to focus. This was where the future would be determined, not only for Europe but for the future of all Western civilization. The Carter administration's two-year total preoccupation with the Arab-Israeli "small ring side show" left Europe amazed, dismayed, and seriously questioning the ability of the United States to cope with the more serious problems of that region. This U.S. preoccupation with Egypt and Israel left all of Western Europe troubled and deeply concerned.

The Risks and Rewards

The agreement created risks for both Egypt and Israel, but, of course, there were also rewards.

For Egypt

The rewards for Egypt were apparent. The return of the Sinai, with its strategic and economic importance, would have been sufficient to justify the treaty, but the establishment of closer political, military, and economic ties with the United States was a very significant by-product for Sadat. In fact, because of it, Egypt is in the process of rebuilding her military, utilizing Western weapon systems and tactical military doctrines.

Egypt's preoccupation with peace with Israel discouraged Iraq, Jordan, and Syria from pursuing policies that could have led to war against Israel. Egypt's absence from the confrontation status had left the balance of the Arab world without a credible or viable military option. But this binding contractual peace between Egypt and Israel was to be contingent only upon the issues covering the Sinai; it was not linked to achievements on the other outstanding intractable issues between Israel and her Arab neighbors. By having agreed to this form of settlement, Sadat had isolated himself from the rest of the Arab world.

For Israel

Neither simple to define nor easy to comprehend were the real gains for Israel from Egypt. Undoubtedly, Begin thought they existed. Begin, Dayan, and Weizmann, the architects of the pact, apparently felt that the Accords would yield significant long-term benefits for Israel, even though the perceived rewards were somewhat difficult to quantify and would only become apparent in time. This explains Begin's need to exaggerate the significance of each positive step taken toward normalization of relations with Egypt—no matter how slight. A perfect example was Begin's historic trip to Cairo. Sadat didn't want him there; he wasn't welcome. The United States believed the trip to be ill-timed. Yet, Begin rightfully insisted on making the visit. His reception had been described as correct but cool.

The Camp David Accords resulted in an arms agreement between Israel and the United States. This agreement provided Israel with the means to maintain and expand her regional military superiority. The modern weapon systems supplied by the United States provided Israel with access to new advanced technologies that enhanced her burgeoning local military industries and took her many years beyond what she would have achieved if that agreement had not been signed. In addition, the agreement made provision for Israeli manufacturers to qualify for the sale of their military products in the United States. The United States, also, relaxed the restriction on the export of Israeli-made military hardware to Third World nations, thus accelerating the growth of Israeli military exports.

The black African nations broke relations with Israel during the Yom Kippur War in the unfulfilled expectation that they would receive preferential treatment from the Arab oil-producing states. While it did take a few years, the Camp David Accords eventually created a politically opportune condition for most of the black African states to return their ambassadors to and restore diplomatic relations with Israel. And Israel is in the process of restoring, overtly and covertly, relations with most of the other African nations.

The peace treaty with Egypt did enable Israel to accomplish several things; one was to deal freely with the PLO in Lebanon. In the Peace for Galilee War of June 1982, Israel permanently destroyed the PLO military power base in Lebanon and derailed its political potency for many years. The peace treaty, also, enabled the Israeli government to create an irreversible trend of political facts within Judea and Samaria. It provided Israel with the political climate and time to initiate and carry out extensive Jewish settlement in Judea and Samaria, thus laying the foundation for future expansion of the Jewish population in those territories.

A Retrospect

Looking back after the period of the 1979 peace treaty with Egypt, a number of conclusions can be drawn and a number of lessons have been learned.

In the Middle East, nothing is forever. It is the one area of the world where more written agreements have been signed and broken than in any other region. While the Accords have been kept, the spirit of the agreement has not. The portion that dealt with normalization of trade, tourism, cultural ties, and the cessation of vilifying propaganda has not been honored by Egypt. After the Egyptian ambassador to Israel was recalled, the relationship between Egypt and Israel became what can best be described as a "cold peace." Even with the recent return of the Egyptian ambassador to Israel, the relationship between the two countries remains a cold peace.

Given the political environment that existed at that time, Israel had to make a deal with Egypt that could serve as a prototype for the future. Israel had little choice but to enter into the Camp David Accords, since the Accords provided her government with an opportunity to test the intentions of one Arab government (Egypt) in order to determine whether such an agreement with any Arab government was possible. Additionally, by entering into the Accords, the Israeli government could reassure the people of Israel and world Jewry that Israel was prepared to give peace a chance, even if it meant taking serious risks to realize that "opportunity."

It soon became evident, however, that the Israeli negotiating team, headed by Begin, Dayan, and Weizmann, had made an unsatisfactory agreement. The Accords proved, once again, that entering into a treaty with an autocratic regime meant entering into an agreement not with a nation or a people, but with one man. In this case, it was Sadat. The assassination of Sadat by Islamic Fundamentalists decreased the probability that any Arab ruler could enter into a future peace treaty with Israel unless, of course, the political climate within the world of Arab nations changed dramatically. Therefore, it was not surprising that once Israel returned all of Sinai, it didn't take long for Mubarak—Sadat's successor—to renege on the agreement by undoing most elements of the normalization process.

It is now obvious that it will not be possible for Israel to use the Camp David Accords as a model for any future peace treaties with other Arab nations. Tangibles, such as territory, in return for a signed agreement, which required the good faith of Arab signatories for the fulfillment of the agreement, can no longer be used as the basis for a peace treaty. Any further agreement with an Arab nation will have to be based on tangibles for tangibles and be self-enforcing. Nor will it be possible for the ruler of Jordan or of Syria to use the Camp David Accords—a treaty of land for peace—as the basis for any future peace treaties with Israel, because no Arab ruler could accept less than Sadat—that is, every inch of land—and no Israeli ruler will ever return every inch of land acquired in 1967 either in Judea and Samaria or on the Golan.

THE MIDDLE EAST BY THE TWENTY-FIRST CENTURY

Given the world as it appears today, it is doubtful that by the year 2000 any Arab nation or group of nations will see formal peace with Israel as being in their national interest. However, there is every reason to believe that Egypt and Israel will have coincident interests for about another five to ten years.

By the mid-1990s, the Egyptian military should feel confident about having fully integrated their Western arms. Once the military develops a perception of confidence, there may arise an Egyptian ruler who will again seek to tie his fortunes to the great

Arab-Moslem cause. At that time, the loss of Sharm El Sheik and the Rafiah settlements' strategic and tactical value will become immensely significant.

During the intervening period, Israel will continue to expand her technological and industrial base; find ways to increase her Jewish population; develop relevant, low-cost, modern tactical weapon systems; and, above all, strengthen her economy. Only in these ways can Israel hope to attain sufficient strength to be able to make independent political decisions—decisions that may run totally counter to the wishes of the leaders of the Free World, regardless of how righteous and just Israel's case may be. Because of Israel's size and strategic location, she will always be dependent on maintaining close economic, political, and military ties with nations of the Free World. But, as history has already shown, as Israel grows stronger, an interdependency will develop with the Western nations that will provide her with political options not previously available.

Most likely, the status of Judea and Samaria will be reconciled as part of Israel, and Jordan will be Palestine—both are inevitable. The Arab population of Judea and Samaria will either emigrate to Palestine (Jordan) or remain and enjoy limited autonomy. Ultimately, the United States will accept this *fait accompli* as the interdependence between herself and Israel. This, too, is inevitable due to the unreliable nature of the Arab states and their inability to stabilize the region, make peace among themselves, and cope with an honest peace with Israel.

As was the case during the Yom Kippur War, Israel will not be able to rely on Western Europe for political, economic, or military support in any future confrontation with the Arab nations. Israel's survival as a nation is essential to the Western European community of nations, but G-d forbid that those nations should ever be needed to assist Israel during a crisis when her survival is in doubt. Western Europe has looked to the United States to assure Israel's existence; yet, it has pursued policies of narrow self-interest that tend to undermine U.S. efforts in support of Israel. Europe was not prepared to support one of the results of the Sadat-Begin treaty—the normalization of Egyptian-Israeli relations.

As the twenty-first century approaches, Europe will probably not support any political arrangement Israel might make with an

Arab state, if that agreement is opposed by any radical Arab nation. Europe is putting its economic house in order and, most probably, as it enters the twenty-first century, will be a power to be reckoned with. Recently, its industrial base has begun to keep pace with the technological developments of the Pacific Basin and the United States. This will make Europe economically less dependent on trade with the Soviet Union and better able to maintain a totally independent political position from the United States—in contrast to almost total dependency during the post-World War II era.

While the prospect of Israel's entering into formal peace treaties with her Arab neighbors is not good, the absence of war will be based more upon the Arab perception of Israel's military and economic power and the quality of Israel's relationship with the United States than on the signing of an agreement.

Epilogue

Peace in the Middle East? Certainly, it would make the world feel less precarious. Yet true peace would require normal relations between Israel and her neighbors, not to mention among those neighbors themselves. Peace in the Middle East will occur only when there is peace on earth. Peace will come when the two global superpowers decide not to placate the countries involved with promises of billions of dollars of weapon systems. Peace will come when these superpowers decide not to intervene in the affairs of the region. And, after those improbabilities have occurred, the nations of Western Europe, in spite of their precarious economies, would have to follow suit. All this is very unlikely given the economic scruples of the West and the geopolitical designs of the East.

Once the superpowers agree—and Western Europe also agrees—to leave the Middle East alone, there still remains the need for the Arab nations to cooperate with each other. In a region that has seen so many blood baths in the last millennium and has been so erroneously and arbitrarily carved up into nations by its Western "protectors," it is difficult to imagine that every nation in the region will ". . . beat their swords into plowshares . . ." in the near or even distant future.

Even if these miracles were to happen, there would still need to be a strong middle class in each Arab country that would support a democratic government. Such a government would have to be secular in nature since fundamental Islam does not allow any foreigner to rule over land on Islamic soil—not Jew,

Christian, Kurd, Armenian, Druse, or Persian. If these governments were accountable to this educated middle class, then internal issues would be more important than military adventures. For this to occur would require a reversal in the trend toward transnational Islamic fundamentalism—both among the Shi'ite and Sunni—which has developed over the last decade. This change would allow for a more moderate view of Islam to take hold and might temper the zeal that is so much a part of the imperial designs these regimes have on each other. However, if we are to be realistic, there is nowhere from which this moderate perspective can emerge—not the military, not the government bureaucracy, not the universities, and not the *mosques*. And if the intellectuals are leading the Fundamentalist revolutions, then where is one to turn for this moderately considered view? From the *mullahs?*

Since the outside powers will not be able to control the behavior of the Arab nations between and among themselves, from Israel's perspective, one can only hope for a situation of "no war and no peace." To insure this possibility, the following steps must be taken:

- First, there can never be military parity between Israel and her enemies. It must always be obvious that Israel has clear military superiority.
- Second, Israel must assure that, should there be another conflict, the aggressor will know that no conquered land will be returned in the interest of some mythical diplomatic solution called "peace." This time Israel would maintain the most important spoils—land. This is the only real deterrent to aggressive behavior in the Middle East—the realization by Arab leadership that they have something tangible to lose which is not easily expendable. This would require the political support of the United States.
- Third, Israel must receive the economic support necessary for her to develop her own resources both technologically and militarily. The most important dimension of this state-of-affairs would be that the United States make it unequivocally clear that she is indeed a strategic ally of Israel in the full sense and spirit of the word. This would be in the interest of both Israel and the United States, since Israel will continue to be the singular, most powerful deterrent to active

Soviet maliciousness in Middle East affairs and will continue to maintain the precarious stability of that troubled region.

Although these steps are the most plausible, there are very real obstacles to their implementation given the U.S. record concerning Middle East diplomacy. It is difficult to imagine that the muddled, ambiguous signals so often given to Israel will cease, and that strong, clear, decisive statements will be their replacement. The Middle East will remain in turmoil for the foreseeable future and it is we—the citizens of the world—who will endure the consequences.

The possibility for the creation of a Jewish state was always viewed—by Jew and non-Jew alike—with much skepticism. In 1948, when the deferred dream was realized and Israel had, already, survived her first war, people declared that a "miracle" had occurred. Forty years and six wars later, the State of Israel continues to thrive. Are supernatural words such as "miraculous" the only explanation for this reality?

Certainly, there continues to be a perilous dimension to the life of Israel. It seems she will always be besieged by threat of conflict or worthless treaties. The West's version of peace offers no relief for this beleaguered country. Yet, why should we be so flippant as to declare that it is only the miraculous that can explain the enigma of Israel's existence?

It is easy to understand the trepidation one feels when Israel's ability to enter into the twenty-first century is discussed. After all, twenty-one Arab nations yearn for her destruction, which would seem to imply a bleak future—Israel is out-manned, out-gunned, and out-spent on every front quantitatively.

If we were to play the numbers game, such realities would cloud my vision of a future for Israel so contrary to the prevailing wisdom that I can almost hear the critics' ridicule. Yet, there are numbers, and there are realities. The problem is getting at the facts that count, and when people see clearly, it is easy to realize that Israel's existence is not based on anything so elusive and ephemeral as a miracle. In fact, there is no room for miracles in Israel's future.

Israel has prepared herself for the future. Her persistence in the removal of obstacles thrown her way by friend and foe alike is no more miraculous than the magician's trick of pulling a "rabbit out of a hat." It's all a matter of technique. The only magic is the insufferable amount of effort, energy, and perseverance it takes to master her craft. Israel's magic is the result of years of preparation, undaunted purpose, and unswerving tenacity, and a continuing dedication to national purpose.

So as she approaches the twenty-first century, Israel has prepared herself and has demonstrated that she is a nation willing to sacrifice in order to insure her survival. It is only when we become intimate with the self-determination and character of the Israeli people that we truly understand the facts of Israeli development as opposed to the history and development of her Arab neighbors. It is only then that we can draw the inevitable and astounding conclusions which I have enumerated in this volume.

If this book were to be digested fully, it would be clear to the reader that Israel shall not only survive well into the twenty-first century, but she will thrive as the major force in the Middle East. The reasons for this have been documented herein. The fact that is indeed irrefutable is that Israel has no other recourse but greatness. She cannot afford to lose one war. Unlike her Arab neighbors who cannot be pummeled into oblivion, one loss for Israel is the end of Israel.

When trying to assess the future, the truth is the key to understanding. It may make perfect political sense for the United States to overlook Arab shortcomings, but it makes absolutely no sense at all to ignore harsh realities when trying to project the future in the coming decades. Once the turbulent character and history of the Arab world is understood more completely and there is a more complete knowledge of its tyrannies, inequities, and discriminations—even within its own society—then a clearer vision of the twenty-first century will begin to emerge.

In these pages I have attempted to destroy the myth that "peace at any price" is in the interest of Israel, because time is on the side of the Arabs. If the issue is time, then she who takes advantage of these precious moments is the one who will endure. Quite simply, a new world is upon us. The smokestack industries of the past are gone—no more empires will be built on steel and oil. Technology is the new frontier, and only the powers that can absorb new technologies such as computers, microelectronics, bioengineering, and robotics will prosper. Israel has the necessary scientific infrastructure to insure her bright future. The

Arabs, for reasons already described in meticulous detail, are hopelessly behind and will be lost in this new reality.

Israel is ready for the future; the Arabs are not. My assessment is based on the role that technological infrastructure will play in the growth of a nation. Japan and the United States have the infrastructure. England, France, Germany, and Italy are rapidly developing it. The Soviet Union may never have it and neither will the Arabs. Israel, however, does, and it is this fact that will insure her place of power in the twenty-first century.

Bibliography

Allon, Yigal. *Shield of David: The Story of Israel's Armed Forces.* New York: Random House, 1970.

———. *My Father's House.* New York: W. W. Norton & Company, Inc., 1976.

Altman, Sima, et al, eds. *Pioneers from America—75 Years of Hehalutz, 1905-1980.* Tel Aviv: Bogrei Hehalutz America, 1981.

Arnoni, M. S. *Rights and Wrongs in the Arab-Israeli Conflict.* Passaic, NJ: The Minority of One Press, 1968.

Bar-Siman-Tov, Yaacov. *A Case-Study of Limited Local War: The Israeli-Egyptian War of Attrition, 1969-1970.* New York: Columbia University Press, 1980.

Barnaby, Frank. *The Automated Battlefield.* New York: The Free Press, 1986.

Becker, Jillian. *The PLO: The Rise and Fall of the Palestine Liberation Organization.* London: Weidenfeld and Nicolson, 1984.

Bell, J. Bowyer. *The Long War: Israel and the Arabs Since 1946.* Englewood Cliffs: Prentice-Hall, Inc., 1969.

Ben-Gurion, David. *Israel: A Personal History.* Tel Aviv: American Israel Publishing Co., Ltd., 1972.

Berler, Alexander. *New Towns in Israel.* Jerusalem: Israel Universities Press, 1970.

Bethell, Nicholas. *The Palestine Triangle: The Struggle for the*

Holy Land, 1935-1948. New York: G. P. Putnam's Sons, 1979.

Binder, Leonard, ed. *The Study of the Middle East: Research and Scholarship in the Humanities and the Social Studies.* New York: John Wiley & Sons, 1976.

Bolitho, Hector. *The Angry Neighbours.* London: Arthur Barker Ltd., 1957.

Bondy, Ruth, et al, eds. *Mission Survival.* New York: Sabra Books, 1968.

Brown, L. Carl. *International Politics and the Middle East: Old Rules, Dangerous Game.* London: I. B. Tauris & Co., Ltd., 1984.

Burdett, Winston. *Encounter with the Middle East: An Intimate Report on What Lies Behind the Arab-Israeli Conflict.* New York: Atheneum, 1969.

Carlson, John Ray. *Cairo to Damascus.* New York: Alfred A. Knopf, Inc., 1951.

Carter, Jimmy. *The Blood of Abraham.* Boston: Houghton Mifflin Company, 1985.

Collins, Larry, and Dominique Lapierre. *O Jerusalem!* New York: Simon and Schuster, 1972.

Corson, William R., and Robert T. Crowley. *The New KGB: Engine of Soviet Power.* New York: William Morrow and Company, Inc., 1985.

Cottrell, Alvin J., ed. *The Persian Gulf States: A General Survey.* Baltimore: The Johns Hopkins University Press, 1980.

Davis, Moshe, ed. *The Yom Kippur War: Israel and the Jewish People.* New York: Arno Press, 1974.

Dietl, Wilheim. *Holy War.* New York: MacMillan Publishing Co., 1983.

Dodd, C. H., and Mary Sales. *Israel and the Arab World.* London: Routledge & Kegan Paul, 1970.

Doran, Charles F. *Myth, Oil, and Politics.* New York: The Free Press, 1977.

Dov, Joseph. *The Faithful City: The Siege of Jerusalem, 1948.* New York: Simon and Schuster, 1960.

Dupree, Louis. *Afghanistan.* Princeton: Princeton University Press, 1980.

Dupuy, Trevor N. *Elusive Victory: The Arab-Israeli Wars, 1947-1974.* New York: Harper & Row, 1978.

Eban, Abba. *The New Diplomacy: International Affairs in the Modern Age.* New York: Random House, 1983.

Elazar, Daniel J. *Community and Polity: The Organizational Dynamics of American Jewry.* Philadelphia: The Jewish Publication Society of America, 1976.

Emerson, Steven. *The American House of Saud: The Secret Petrodollar Connection.* New York: Franklin Watts, 1985.

Evenari, Michael, et al. *The Negev: The Challenge of a Desert.* Cambridge: Harvard University Press, 1971.

Farago, Ladislas. *Palestine at the Crossroads.* New York: G. P. Putnam's Sons, 1937.

Farwell, Byron. *Prisoners of the Mahdi.* New York: Harper & Row, 1967.

Frischwasser-Ra'anan, H. F. *Frontiers of a Nation.* London: The Batchworth Press, 1955.

Gervasi, Frank. *Thunder Over the Mediterranean.* New York: David McKay Co., Inc., 1975.

Gervasi, Tom. *The Myth of Soviet Military Supremacy.* New York: Harper & Row, 1986.

Gibbons, Scott. *The Conspirators.* London: Howard Baker, 1967.

Glubb, Sir John Bagot. *A Soldier With the Arabs.* New York: Harper & Brothers, 1957.

Golan, Galia. *Yom Kippur and After: The Soviet Union and the Middle East Crisis.* Cambridge: Cambridge University Press, 1977.

Grose, Peter. *Israel in the Mind of America.* New York: Alfred A. Knopf, 1983.

Harkabi, Y. *Arab Attitudes to Israel.* Jerusalem: Israel Universities Press, 1972.

Harkabi, Yehoshafat. *Arab Strategies and Israel's Response.* New York: The Free Press, 1977.

Harkavy, Robert E., and Stephanie G. Neuman. *The Lessons of Recent Wars in the Third World. Volume 1, Approaches and Case Studies.* Lexington, MA: Lexington Books, D. C. Heath and Company, 1985.

_____. *The Lessons of Recent Wars in the Third World. Volume*

2, Comparative Dimensions. Lexington, MA: Lexington Books, D. C. Heath and Company, 1987.

Hart, Harold H. *Yom Kippur Plus 100 Days: The Human Side of the War and Its Aftermath, as Shown Through the Columns of The Jerusalem Post.* New York: Hart Publishing Company, Inc., 1974.

Hatem, M. Abdel-Kader. *Information and the Arab Cause.* London: Longman Group Ltd., 1974.

Hauer, Jr., Christian E. *Crisis & Conscience in the Middle East.* Chicago: Quadrangle Books, 1970.

Heikal, Mohamed *Nasser: The Cairo Documents.* London: The New English Library Ltd., 1972.

————. *The Road to Ramadan.* London: William Collins Sons & Co. Ltd., 1975.

————. *The Return of the Ayatollah: The Iranian Revolution from Mossadeq to Khomeini.* London: Andre Deutsch Limited, 1981.

Helms, Cristine Moss. *The Cohesion of Saudi Arabia.* London: Croom Helm, 1981.

Herzog, Chaim. *The Arab-Israeli Wars: War and Peace in the Middle East.* London: Arms and Armour Press, 1982.

Hiro, Dilip. *Iran Under the Ayatollahs.* London: Routledge & Kegan Paul, 1985.

Hirst, David, and Irene Beeson. *Sadat.* London: Faber and Faber Limited, 1981.

Hobday, Peter. *Saudi Arabia Today: An Introduction to the Richest Oil Power.* London: The Macmillan Press Ltd., 1978.

Hoffman, Gail. *The Land and People of Israel.* Philadelphia: J. B. Lippincott Company, 1950.

Hoffmitz, Laible. *The Other Side of Israel.* Tel Aviv: Nateev, 1978.

Holden, David, and Richard Johns. *The House of Saud.* London: Sidgwick and Jackson, 1981.

Horowitz, David. *State in the Making.* New York: Alfred A. Knopf, 1953.

Howe, Irving, and Carl Gershman, eds. *Israel, the Arabs, and the Middle East.* New York: Quadrangle Books, 1972.

Hudson, Michael C. *Arab Politics: The Search for Legitimacy.* New Haven: Yale University Press, 1977.

Hurewitz, J. C. *Middle East Politics: The Military Dimension.* London: Pall Mall Press, 1969.

Hutchison, Commander E. H. *Violent Truce: A Military Observer Looks at the Arab-Israeli Conflict, 1951-1955.* New York: The Devin-Adair Company, 1958.

Jacobs, Dan. *The Brutality of Nations.* New York: Alfred A. Knopf, 1987.

Katz, Samuel. *Days of Fire: The Secret Story of the Making of Israel.* Jerusalem: Steimatzky's Agency Ltd., 1968.

_____. *Battleground: Fact and Fantasy in Palestine.* London: W. H. Allen, 1973.

Kelly, J. B. *Arabia, the Gulf and the West.* London: Weidenfeld and Nicolson, 1980.

Kimche, Jon. *The Second Arab Awakening.* London: Thames and Hudson, 1970.

_____. *There Could Have Been Peace.* New York: The Dial Press, 1973.

Kollek, Teddy, and Amos Kollek. *For Jerusalem.* New York: Random House, 1978.

Kurzman, Dan. *Genesis 1948: The First Arab-Israeli War.* New York: The World Publishing Company, 1970.

Lacey, Robert. *The Kingdom.* London: Hutchinson & Co. Ltd., 1981.

Laqueur, Walter. *The Road to Jerusalem: The Origins of the Arab-Israeli Conflict, 1967.* New York: The Macmillan Company, 1968.

_____. *The Struggle for the Middle East: The Soviet Union in the Mediterranean, 1958-1968.* New York: The Macmillan Company, 1969.

Longregg, Stephen Hemsley. *Oil in the Middle East.* 3d ed. London: Oxford University Press, 1968.

Male, Beverley. *Revolutionary Afghanistan.* London: Croom Helm, 1982.

Manuel, Frank E. *The Realities of American-Palestine Relations.* Washington, D.C.: Public Affairs Press, 1949.

Mardor, Munya M. *Haganah.* New York: The New American Library, Inc., 1957.

Meinertzhagen, Colonel Richard. *Middle East Diary, 1917-1956.* New York: Thomas Yoseloff, 1960.

Merlin, Samuel. *The Search for Peace in the Middle East.* New York: Thomas Yoseloff, 1968.

Miller, Aaron David. *Search for Security: Saudi Arabian Oil and American Foreign Policy, 1939-1949.* Chapel Hill: The University of North Carolina Press, 1980.

Moore, John Norton, ed. *The Arab-Israeli Conflict: Readings and Documents.* Princeton: Princeton University Press, 1977.

Morris, Yaakov. *Masters of the Desert: 6000 Years in the Negev.* New York: G. P. Putnam's Sons, 1961.

Mosley, Leonard. *Power Play: The Tumultous World of Middle East Oil, 1890-1973.* London: Widenfeld and Nicolson, 1973.

Naff, Thomas, ed. *The Middle East Challenge, 1980-1985.* Carbondale, IL: Southern Illinois University Press, 1981.

O'Ballance, Edgar. *No Victor, No Vanquished: The Yom Kippur War.* San Rafael, CA: Presidio Press, 1978.

O'Neill, Gerard K. *The Technology Edge: Opportunities for America in World Competition.* New York: Simon and Schuster, 1983.

Payne, Keith B. *Strategic Defense: "Star Wars" in Perspective.* Lanham, MD: Hamilton Press, 1986.

Powell, Ivor. *Disillusion by the Nile.* London: Solstice Productions, 1967.

Rabinovich, Itamar, and Haim Shaked, eds. *From June to October: The Middle East between 1967 and 1973.* New Brunswick, NJ: Transaction, Inc., 1978.

Ramazani, R. K. *Revolutionary Iran: Challenge and Response in the Middle East.* Baltimore: The Johns Hopkins University Press, 1986.

Robertson, Terence. *Crisis: The Inside Story of the Suez Conspiracy.* New York: Atheneum, 1965.

Robinson, Donald, ed. *Under Fire: Israel's 20-Year Struggle for Survival.* New York: W. W. Norton & Company, Inc., 1968.

Rose, Herbert H. *The Life and Thought of A. D. Gordon.* New York: Bloch Publishing Company, 1964.

Sachar, Howard M. *Europe Leaves the Middle East, 1936-1954.* New York: Alfred A. Knopf, 1972.

————. *Egypt & Israel.* New York: Richard Marek Publishers, 1981.

Safran, Nadav. *The United States and Israel.* Cambridge: Cambridge University Press, 1963.

————. *Saudi Arabia: The Ceaseless Quest for Security.* Cambridge: The Belknap Press of Harvard University Press, 1985.

Sampson, Anthony. *The Seven Sisters: The Great Oil Companies & the World They Made.* New York: The Viking Press, Inc., 1975.

Samuel, Maurice. *Prince of the Ghetto.* Philadelphia: The Jewish Publication Society of America, 1948.

Sayigh, Yusif A. *The Economies of the Arab World: Development Since 1945.* London: Croom Helm, 1978.

Schechtman, Joseph B. *On Wings of Eagles.* New York: Thomas Yoseloff, 1961.

Schoenbrun, David, et al. *The New Israelis.* New York: Atheneum, 1973.

Segal, Ronald. *Whose Jerusalem? The Conflicts of Israel.* London: Jonathan Cape Ltd., 1973.

Shamir, Moshe. *With His Own Hands.* Jerusalem: Israel Universities Press, 1970.

Sherrill, Robert. *The Oil Follies of 1970-1980: How the Petroleum Industry Stole the Show (And Much More Besides).* Garden City, N.Y.: Anchor Press/Double Day, 1983.

Sinai, Anne, and Allen Pollack, eds. *The Hashemite Kingdom of Jordan and the West Bank.* New York: American Academic Association for Peace in the Middle East, April 1977.

Slater, Leonard. *The Pledge.* New York: Simon and Schuster, 1970.

Spiegel, Steven L., ed. *At Issue: Politics in the World Arena.* 2nd ed. New York: St. Martin's Press, 1977.

Spiegel, Steven L. *The Other Arab-Israeli Conflict: Making America's Middle East Policy, from Truman to Reagan.* Chicago: The University of Chicago Press, 1985.

Spiro, Melford E. *Children of the Kibbutz.* Cambridge: Harvard University Press, 1958.

Syrkin, Marie. *The State of the Jews.* Washington, D.C.: Herzl Press, 1980.

Teller, Judd L. *The Kremlin, the Jews, and the Middle East.* New York: Thomas Yoseloff, Inc., 1957.

Teveth, Shabtai. *Moshe Dayan: The Soldier, the Man, the Legend.* Jerusalem: Steimatzky's Agency and Weidenfeld and Nicolson, 1972.

Thomas, Lowell. *With Lawrence in Arabia.* 18th ed. London: Hutchinson & Co., Ltd.

Tuchman, Barbara W. *Bible and Sword: England and Palestine from the Bronze Age to Balfour.* New York: Funk & Wagnalls, 1956.

Van Paassen, Pierre. *Jerusalem Calling!* New York: Dial Press, Inc., 1950.

Velie, Lester. *Countdown in the Holy Land.* New York: Funk & Wagnalls, 1969.

Warburg, James P. *Crosscurrents in the Middle East.* New York: Atheneum, 1968.

Waterbury, John, and Ragaei El Mallakh. *The Middle East in the Coming Decade: From Wellhead to Well-Being?* New York: McGraw-Hill Book Company, 1978.

Weizman, Ezer. *The Battle for Peace.* New York: Bantam Books, March 1981.

Wilson, Evan M. *Jerusalem, Key to Peace.* Washington, D.C.: The Middle East Institute, 1970.

Wyman, David S. *The Abandonment of the Jews: America and the Holocaust, 1941-1945.* New York: Pantheon Books, 1984.

Ziring, Lawrence. *The Middle East Political Dictionary.* Santa Barbara, CA: ABC-Clio, Inc., 1984.

Index

al-Abbas, Abu, 38, 39
Abbasyd Empire, 78, 91, 162
Abboud, Gen. Ibrahim, 103-104
'Abd Al 'Aziz al-Saud (Ibn Saud), 112-
    114, 134
Abd Al-Rahim Ahmad, 38
Abdullah (King of Transjordan), 48, 85-
    86
Abdullah (Prince of Saudi Arabia), 125
Abu Dhabi, 150-152
Aden, South Yemen, 172-175
    Jewish community of, 20
AEGIS system, 264
Afghanistan War, 220-222, 259-260
Agriculture of Israel, 246, 343
Aircraft
    Israeli-produced, 312, 314
    missiles against, 274-276
Aircraft carriers, obsolescence of, 264-
    265
Ajman, 150
Al-. *See substantive part of Arabic
    names, eg* (al-)Khalid
Al Bu Sa'id Dynasty, 158-159
Al Thani Clan in Qatar, 154-156
Alawi of Syria, 79-82
    Lebanon involvement of, 76
    Sunni slaughter by, 194
Algeria
    future of, 179
    history of, 176-178
    Jewish community of, 22-23
    as Morocco enemy, 182-183
    present status of, 178-179
Ali, Mohammed (Egypt), 59
    Arabian conquest by, 110-111

Saud family defeat by, 109-110
Amman, Jordan, as banking center, 88
Ansari, Sheikh Daoud, 29
Anti-Semitism. *See* Persecution of Jews
Antiballistic defenses, tactical, 308
Arab(s)
    civil disobedience by (*Intifada*), 48-49
    definition of
        literal, 10
        in tenth century, 11
    Egyptian conquest by (642 A.D.), 59
    immigration to Palestine
        during British Mandate, 15-18,
            206-207
        during nineteenth century, 12
        during Ottoman Empire, 13-14
    intolerance of non-Arabs by, 251-252
Arab-Israeli War (1948), 59
Arab League
    nations comprising, 53
    origin of, 29
    PLO recognition by, 42
Arab Liberation Front, 38-39
Arab nations. *See also specific nation*
    common characteristics of, 53-55
    demographics of, 54
    disagreements among, 54-57
    governments in, 53
    Iranian relations of, 55-56
    middle classes of, 359-360
    oil resources of, 55-56
    sense of history in, 54
    unemployment in, 54
    weapons sales to, 231-232, 299, 318-
        320, 325
    Western placation of, 242-244

Arab Summit (1985), 181
Arabia. *See also* Saudi Arabia
  Baghdad caliphate of, 10-11
  conversion to Judaism in, 8
  Jewish presence in, 8-9
  Palestinian conquest of, 10-11
  Umayyad caliphate of, 10
Arabian American Oil Company, 113
Arafat, Yasir. *See also* Palestinian
    Liberation Organization
  as *Fatah* leader, 35-37
  on Palestine boundary, 48
  United Nations appearance of, 45
ARAMCO (Arabian American Oil
    Company), 113
Area weapons, 303-304
'Arif, Abd al-Salem, 92
Armaments, Israeli-produced, 314
Arrow weapon system, 341
al-Assad, Hafiz (Syria), 43, 79-81
Assad, Rifat, 194
Aswan, Arabia, Jewish settlement at, 8
al'-Attas, Haydar Abu Bakr, 174

Baaka Valley, Lebanon, history of, 69
Ba'ath Party
  in Iraq, 81, 92-96
  in Syria, 37-38, 78-82
Bab el Mandeb, Strait of, 171, 174-175
Babylonia, 91
Bahrain
  future of, 148-149
  history of, 146-147
  present status of, 147-148
al-Bakr, Ahmad Hasan, 92
Ball, James, on treaty violation, 351
Barbary pirates, 177
Bedouins, Palestinian conquest by, 10-
    11
Begin, Menachem
  Cairo trip of, 354
  Camp David Accords and, 346, 349,
    351-352, 355
Beirut, Lebanon, 71, 75-76
Ben-Gurion, David, Jewish weapons
    industry and, 311
Berbers
  in Algeria, 176-177
  in Libya, 98 in Morocco, 181
Biluim, 14
Bizmarck, cannon introduced by, 255
Black June, 39
Black September, 39-40, 44
Blood libel of 1840, 24
Boats, Israeli-produced, 313

Bomblets with terminal guidance, 303-
    304
Bourguiba, Habib, 184-186
Brezhnev, Leonid, 232
Britain
  Falkland War and, 263-265
  Jewish refugees and, 206-209
  Libyan occupation by, 98
  Middle East involvement of
    in Egypt, 59
  future of, 211
  history of, 205-211
  in Israel, 243
  in Kuwait, 162-163
  present Israeli relations, 210-211
  Suez Canal withdrawal, 60
  in United Arab Emirates, 150
British Mandate, 85, 206-209, 220, 243
  Chieftain tank incident in, 311, 323
  immigration during, 15-18
  Jewish weapons industry beginning
    in, 310
  Palestine division in, 14-15
Brzezinski, Zbigniew, on Middle East
    arms race, 308-310
Bulganin, Nikolay, Israel relations with,
    231
Bulgaria, Munich massacre and, 44-45
Bundism in pre-revolutionary Soviet
    Union, 233

C-3I (Command Control
    Communications and Intelligence
    system), 258, 266, 280-281
Cambodia, extermination in, 229
Camp David Accords, 345-356
  basis of, 345
  conditions before, 345-350
    Carter situation and, 346
    Sadat situation and, 346-350
  European perception of, 353
  impact of
    on Begin, 351-352
    on Carter, 352
    on Israel, 351-352
  long-term results of, 355-356
  negotiations of, 350-351
  potential for violation of, 350-351
  rewards/risks of, 353-355
Carter, Pres. Jimmy
  Camp David Accords and, 346, 350,
    352
  Iran and, 191
  Israeli arms limitations by, 298
  Middle East policies of, 349-350

post-Vietnam War policy on use of
    force, 278
potential Iraq support by, 286
Sadat perception of, 349
on weapons and war, 204
weapons limitations by, 331
Carthage, 184
Chad, Libyan interest in, 99-100, 102
Chazan (Mapam Party head), 232
Chemical weapons in Iraq-Iran War,
    292, 320
Chieftain tank, British deception and,
    311, 323
China, People's Republic of
    as Israel ally, 240-241
    Israel relations with, 244-248
    military capability of, 246-247
    present status of, 245-246
    Vietnam invasion of, 246
Christians
    in Lebanon, 69-71, 75-76
    in Sudan, 104-105
Churchill, Winston, on Palestinian
    immigration, 18
Cluster bombs, 262, 303-304
Command Control Communications
    and Intelligence system (C-3I),
    258, 266, 280-281
Communications, electronic, wartime
    use of, 256
Communism
    as competitor of Zionism, 235
    Palestinian organizations for, 37-40
    Soviet Jews involved in, 233-234
Computer science in Israel, 343-344
"Controlling Future Arms Trade," 308-
    310
Cosmopolit, Jews as, 234
Cruise missiles, 302-303
Crusades
    German participation in, 213
    Jerusalem population decimation in,
    11
Cuba, African involvement of, 222
Cyrenaica, 97-98
Czechoslovakia
    anit-Semitism in, 234
    Israeli weapons purchases from, 231,
    322

Damascus, Syria, blood libel of (1840),
    24
Damour, Lebanon, PLO violence in, 42
Daoud, Abu, Munich massacre and, 44-
    45

Dariya, emirate of, 108, 110
De Gaulle, Charles
    Israel arms embargo of, 297, 311,
    323-324
    Israel policy of, 212
"Death of a Princess" film, 133
Debussman, Bernard, 44
Destour movement in Tunisia, 184
Dhimmi
    in Algeria, 22
    in Arabia, 9
    in Lebanon, 25
    in Libya, 25
    in Tunisia, 23
Dir el-Qamar, Lebanon, Jewish
    community destruction in, 25
Dispersion, Jewish population before, 8
Doctors' plot in Soviet Union (1953),
    229, 234-235
Druse
    in Lebanon, 25, 70-71, 75-76
    in Syria, 80
Dubai, 150-153

Eagles of the Palestinian Revolution, 39
Education in Israel, 270
Effendis
    anti-Jewish actions of, 13
    exploitation by, 13-14
Egypt
    Arab economic aid to, 347
    Camp David Accords and, 346-350,
    353-356
    future of, 65-68, 356
    history of, 58-63
    Jewish community of, 21-22
    North Yemen involvement of, 168
    present status of, 63-64
    Sudan relationship with, 103, 105-
    106
    Syrian merger with, 60, 78-79
    weapons purchases of, 231
Eichmann, Adolph, mufti of Jerusalem
    and, 29
Eisenhower, Pres. Dwight D.
    on industrial-military complex, 266
    Israeli arms embargo of, 297
    Sinai control and, 60
Electronic systems
    Israeli-produced, 314
    in weapons, training and, 336
Ethiopia, Libyan alliance with, 100

Fahd
    as government official, 116, 118, 121

as king, 125-126
Faisal (King of Iraq), 92
Faisal (King of Saudi Arabia)
    19th century, 110-111
    20th century, 115-118, 134
Falkland War, weapons used in, 263-
    265
Farouk, King, 59-60, 62
Fasht al-Dibal, conflict over, 147
Fatah, 37, 40
    Baghdad-based dissident of, 39
    cover for (Black September), 39-40,
        44
    creation of, 35-37
Fedayeen, 35-37
Fezzan, 97-98
Ford administration, post-Vietnam War
    policy on use of force, 278
France
    Algerian involvement of, 177-178
    arms embargo of, 297, 311
    intervention in Lebanon, 70-71
    Israel relations with, 212-213
    Israeli weapons purchases from, 322-
        324
    Libyan occupation by, 98
    Middle East involvement of, 211-213
    Morocco control by, 180
    Syrian involvement of, 78
    Tunisia control by, 184
    weapons of, 268
Frog missile, 258, 261
The Front of Palestinian National
    Struggle, 39
Fujira, 150

General Command of Popular Front for
    the Liberation of Palestine, 38-39
Germany. See also Nazism
    Holocaust in, 207-209, 214
    Israel relations with, 214-216
    Jewish immigration from, 16-17
    Middle East involvement of
        future of, 215-216
        history of, 213-215
    weapons of, World War II, 254-255
Ghalib, as Oman imam, 159
al-Ghashmi, Ahmad, 169
Ghoshe, Samir, 39
GIPARD missile, 275
Gorbachev, Mikhail, 225
    Jews' treatment under, 235
    problems facing, 237
"Green Book" by Qaddafi, 99
Gulf Cooperation Council, 123

Guns, Israeli-produced, 313

Habash, George, 38, 40, 82
Haddad, Dr. Wadi', 38, 40
Hadrian, Palestine named by, 84
Haifa Technion, 343
al-Hamdi, Ibrahim, 168-169
Hannibal, weapons of, 254
Hassan I (Morocco), 181
Hassan II (Morocco), 181-182
Hawadmeh, Nayef, 38, 40
Helicopters
    in Afghanistan War, 260
    in Vietnam War, 257
Himyar, Arabia, Jewish settlement at, 9
Hitler, Adolph. See also Nazism
    as Arab hero, 208
Holocaust, 207-209, 214
Al-Huayni family, as landowner, 12
Hussein (King of Jordan), 86, 92
    Fatah attack on, 40
Hussein, Saddam (Iraq), 92-95
    Iraq-Iran War and, 282-288
    war tactics of, 260-263, 320
    weapons purchases by, 291
    Western criticism of, 292
Al-Husseini (mufti of Jerusalem), 28-29,
    208
El-Husseini, Sheikh Yamin, 28
Hyksos, weapons of, 254

Ibadi sect of Islam, 158-159
Ibn Saud ('Abd Al 'Aziz al-Saud), 112-
    114, 134
Idris, King, 98
Immigration. See country or people eg,
    Israel; Jews; Palestine
Imperialism
    of Britain, 205
    of Soviet Union, 218-222
Industrial-military complex
    of Israel, 271, 306-308
    resistance to change, 266-268
Intelligence, military, 262
Intifada, 48-49
Iran
    dangers of, 321
    future of, 196-199
    history of, 187-191
    present status of, 191-196
    shah of
        Mohammed Reza Pahlavi, 135,
            138-139, 188, 190-191
        Shah Pahlavi (father of Reza), 188
    similarities to Soviet Union, 227-228

war with Iraq. *See* Iraq-Iran War
Iraq
  Ba'ath Party in, 81, 92-96
  future of, 95-96
  history of, 91-93
  Jewish community of, 20-21
  Jordan relations with, 88
  as nuclear power, 291-292
  nuclear reactor destruction in, 290,
    292-295
  present status of, 93-95
  Syrian relations of, 81
Iraq-Iran War, 56, 74, 81, 93-95, 282-
    290
  advantages to Iran, 193-194
  chemical warfare in, 292
  future of, 197-198
  guerrilla fighting in, 283
  hatred caused by, 285-286
  Hussein blunders in, 287-289, 292
  journalism during, 282
  Kuwait and, 165
  military lessons from, 283-284
  national will in, 289
  negotiation failure in, 328
  objectives of, 282-283
  Oman involvement in, 161
  political consequences of, 262-263
  political implications of, 285-287
  positive results of, 287
  preparation for, 283
  Saudi Arabia and, 123-126, 136
  weapons used in, 260-263, 273, 284,
    319-320
Islam. *See also* Shi'ites; Sunnis
  Arab history interwoven with, 54
  fundamentalist groups of. *See also*
    Wahhabiism
  anti-secularism of, 330
  fanaticism of, 328
  in Iran, 188-197
  in Kuwait, 165-166
  in Libya, 101-102
  Western misperception of, 242
  Khariji sect of, 158, 160
  in Lebanon, 69-71, 75
  mass conversion to, 11
  moderation in, as peace requirement,
    360
  origin of, 107-108
  religious centers of, 107-108
  in Soviet Union, 221
  struggles within, 321
Israel
  agriculture of, 236, 343

  arms agreement with United States,
    354
  black African nations break with,
    354-355
  as block to Soviet control of Middle
    East, 244
  British relations with, 210-211, 243
  Camp David Accords and, 350-351,
    354-356
  China relations with, 244-248
  civil disobedience in (*Intifada*), 48-49
  computer science in, 343-344
  as democracy model, 236
  economic conditions in, 245, 270-
    271, 360-361
  establishment of, 209
  exports of, 245
  Fatah raids on, 36
  France relations with, 212-213
  future of, 356-363
  Germany relations with, 214-216
  immigration from Arab lands, 19-27
  industrial base of, 270-271
  industrial-military complex of, 271,
    306-308
  Iraqi nuclear reactor destruction by,
    290, 292-295
  Khomeini view of, 194-195
  Lebanon involvement of, 71-73, 75-
    77
  medical technology developments in,
    343
  military industry of, 310-316
  military initiative of, 292-296
  military strategy of, 291-292
  oil politics and, 241-242
  PLO attacks on, 44-46
  rapid deployment force of, 295, 334-
    339
  reparations from Germany, 214
  Saudi Arabia policy toward, 131-132
  scientific infrastructure of, 272
  Soviet Union relations with
    future of, 236-239
    history of, 230-235
    present status of, 235-236
  as stabilizing influence, 329
  technology of, 299-300, 340-344
    education in, 270
  threats to, 269, 361-362
  Transjordan invasion of, 86
  United States arms deal with, 61
  United States relations with, 252,
    327-329
  wars of, 252. *See also specific war*

weapons of. *See under* Weapons
Yemeni Jews airlift to, 20
Italy, Libyan invasion of, 98

Jabril, Ahmed, 39-40
Jamahiriya in Libya, 100-101
Japan, weapons used in Sino-Japanese
　　War, 255
Jerusalem
　depopulation of, 11-12
　Grand *Mufti* of (Al-Husseini), 28-29,
　　208
　Jewish population of (19th century),
　　13
　name retained as, 7
Jews
　in Aden, 20
　in Algeria, 22-23
　ancient cities in Jordan, 87
　in Arabia, 8-9
　conflict with Arabs, origin of, 8-9
　in Egypt, 21-22
　immigration of
　　from Arab lands, 19-27
　　from Germany, 214
　　to Palestine
　　　during British Mandate, 15-18,
　　　　206-209
　　　during nineteenth century, 12-13
　　　during Ottoman Empire, 13-14
　in Iraq, 20-21
　in Lebanon, 25
　in Libya, 25-26
　Mohammed's treatment of, 9-10
　in Morocco, 22
　in Palestine, 7-8
　persecution of. *See* Persecution of
　　Jews
　in Saudi Arabia, 130-131
　in Soviet Union
　　current population, 221
　　post-revolution, 234-235
　　pre-revolution, 233-234
　　Stalin treatment of, 229, 234-235
　in Syria, 24
　in Tunisia, 23-24, 185
　in Yemen, 19-20, 168
John Paul II, Pope, attempted
　　assassination of, PLO involvement
　　in, 45
Jordan. *See also* Transjordan *Fatah*
　activity in, 36
　future of, 88-90
　history of, 84-86
　present status of, 86-88

Jordan River, as boundary, 85-86
Journalism
　in Iraq-Iran War, 282
　PLO interference with, 44
　Saudi Arabian interference with, 133
Judea
　future of, 357
　Jewish settlement in, 355
　name retained as, 7

Kajar Dynasty, 188
Karameh, battle of, 36
Kazakhstan, Moslem slaughter in, 221
Kelp missile, 258
Kennedy, Pres. John F., Israeli weapons
　　sales and, 323
Khaibar, Arabia, Jewish slaughter at, 9
Khalid, King of Saudi Arabia, 118-125
Al-Khalidi family, as landowner, 12
Khalifa Clan in Bahrain, 146-148
Khariji sect of Islam, 158, 160
El Khatib, Sheikh Alinur, 28
Khomeini, Ayatollah, 92-93
　goals of, 194-195
　Iran status after, 196-199
　regime of, 193-194
　rise to power, 188-189
　war tactics of, 261-263, 288
　world view of, 191
Khrushchev, Nikita, demilitarization by,
　　224
Khuzistan Arabs in Iran, 192
Kishinev program, 233
Kissinger, Henry
　missile order cancellation by, 311-312
　on treaty violation, 351
Kitchener, Gen. Horatio, 103
Korean War, weapons used in, 256-257
Kuwait
　future of, 166
　history of, 162-163
　present status of, 163-165

Landes, David, on Palestine desolation,
　　12
Lavi aircraft, 312
Lebanon
　French influence in, 211-212
　future of, 77
　history of, 69-74
　immigration to, 70
　Jewish community of, 25
　Peace for the Galilee War in, 46, 72-
　　74, 233, 265-266
　PLO activity in, 41-43

PLO exodus from, 46
present status of, 74-77
terrorist movement through, 45-46
Lenin, Vladimir, land reform program
  of, 223
Lewis, Anthony, on *Intifada*, 49
Libya
  Egypt relations with, 65-67
  future of, 102
  history of, 97-100
  Jewish community of, 25-26
  present status of, 100-102
  Tunisia unity agreement with, 185
  United States attack on, 99, 264
  vulnerability to Israeli air strikes, 294
  Western opinion of, 292
LISTEN electronic surveillance system,
  45
Loitering weapons (RPVs), 275-276,
  304-305
  advantages of, 337

MacDonald, Malcolm, on Jewish
  immigration to Palestine, 17
Maghreb, definition of, 177
Maimonides, Yemenite Jews and, 19
Manama, Bahrain, 147
El Manouri, Sheikh, 29
Manpower, as military resource, 281
Mao Ze-dong, on war tactics, 246
Mapam Party of Israel, 234
Maronite Christians in Lebanon, 69-70,
  76
Marxist organizations in Palestine, 37-40
Mecca
  Egyptian capture of, 109-110
  Grand Mosque seizure in, 121
  as religious center, 107-108
  tourist revenue in, 133
Medical technology developments in
  Israel, 343
Medina
  Egyptian capture of, 109-110
  Jewish settlement at, 8
  as religious center, 108
  tourist revenue in, 133
Mesopotamia, 91
Military industry of Israel
  development of, 310-312
  exports of, 342
  future of, 315-316
  present status of, 312-315
Military intelligence, need for, 262
Military resources. *See also* Industrial-
  military complex; Weapons

of Algeria, 79
of Bahrain, 148
of China, 246
of Egypt, 64
of Germany, 215
of Iran, 260-262
of Iraq, 260-263
of Israel, 251-253. *See also* Weapons,
  of Israel
of Jordan, 88
of Kuwait, 165
of Lebanon, 77
of Libya, 101
manpower as, 281
of Morocco, 82
of North Yemen, 70
of Oman, 161
of Qatar, 156
of Saudi Arabia, 136-141
of South Yemen, 74
of Soviet Union, 225-226
of Sudan, 105
of Syria, 81
of Tunisia, 86
of United Arab Emirates, 152
of United States, 277-278
Mines, air-scatterable, 303-304
Mishari, as Saudi leader, 110
Missiles
  in Afghanistan War, 260
  cruise, 302-303
  first use of, 256
  in Iraq-Iran War, 260-262
  Israeli-produced, 313
  laser-guided, 274
  against navy, 264-265
  precision-guided, 301-302
  in War of Attrition (1968-1970), 257
  in Yom Kippur War, 258-259
Mitchell, Billy, 265
Mitterand, Francois, Israel policy of,
  212-213
Mohammed, Prophet
  Islam establishment by, 108
  persecution of Jews by, 8-9
  Shi'ite theology and, 195
Morocco
  future of, 182-183
  history of, 180-181
  Jewish community of, 22
  Libyan alliance with, 100
  present status of, 181-182
Moslem religion. *See* Islam
Movement for the Liberation of
  Palestine, 35

Mubarak, Hosni, 62, 65, 356
Mubarak the Great (Kuwait), 162
Mufti of Jerusalem (Al Husseini), 28-29, 208
Muharraq, 147
Muhsin, Zuhayr, 37, 43
Munich massacre of Israeli athletes, 44
Muscat, 159-160
Mussolini, Benito, anti-Jewish actions in Libya, 26

Naguib, Mohammed, 60
Napoleonic wars, rifles used in, 255
Al-Nashashibi family, as landowner, 12
Nasser, Gamal Abdel, 59-60
    Hussein strategy fashioned after, 286
    Jewish persecution by, 21-22
    PLO creation by, 29-30, 35
    as Qaddafi influence, 99
    in Suez Canal War, 61
    weapons purchases of, 231
Navy, obsolescence of, 264-265
Nazism
    British involvement with, 207-209
    Egyptian sympathies with, 21-22
    Iraq influenced by, 21
    Middle East involvement of, 214
    mufti of Jerusalem and, 29, 208
    similarities to Khomeini regime, 194
    Syria influenced by, 24
Neo-Destour Party, 184
New Economic Policy of Lenin, 223
Nidhal, Abu, 39
al-Nimeiry, Gaafar, 104
Nixon, Pres. Richard M., Israeli arms supply delay by, 297
North Atlantic Treaty Organization
    Israel and, 252
    weapons availability from, 272
North Yemen
    future of, 170-171
    history of, 167-169
    present status of, 169-170
    Saudi Arabia involvement with, 122, 124
Nubia, 103
Nuclear reactor destruction in Iraq, 290, 292-295
Nuclear weapons in Israel, 326

Oil
    in Algeria, 179
    in Arab nations, 55-56
    in Bahrain, 146-148
    in China, 244

    in Iran, 192
    in Iraq, 93-95
        damage to installations, 285
    in Kuwait, 165
    in Libya, 98, 101-102
    politics of, 241-242
    in Qatar, 154, 156
    in Saudi Arabia, 113-115, 119, 122-123, 125-126, 133-136
    in South Yemen, 174
    in Sudan, 105-106
    in United Arab Emirates, 151-53
Oil crisis of 1973, 117-118, 134-135, 241-242
Oil crisis of 1979, 122
Olympic Games massacre of Israeli athletes, 44
Oman
    future of, 161
    history of, 158-160
    present status of, 160-161
    South Yemen war with, 173
Organization of Petroleum Exporting Countries (OPEC), 56, 125
Ottoman Empire, 216
    Algeria in, 177
    Egyptian rule by, 59
    immigration during, 13-14
Oujda Accords, 181

Pahlavi
    Mohammed Reza, 135, 137-138, 188, 190-191
    Shah, 188
Palestine. *See also* Transjordan
    administrative boundaries of, 6-7
    Arab conquest of, 10-11
    Byzantine occupation of, 8
    Crusader conquest of, 11
    division of (1922), 14-15
    future of, 357-358
    history of, 3-5, 84-86
    immigration to
        British control of, 206-209
        during British Mandate, 15-18
        during nineteenth century, 12-14
        during Ottoman Empire (1517-1917), 13-14
        restrictions on, 13-17
    Jewish dispersion from, 8
    Jewish presence in, 7-8
    Jewish refugees excluded from, 16-17
    multiethnic nature of, 11
    naming of, 6, 84
    occupation of, 6-7

population of
    in 637 to 1840, 11-12
    in 1800s, 11-12, 14
    in 1931, 15
    in 1945, 27
    in 1982, 27
religious center of, 8
Roman occupation of, 7-8
Syrian claim to, 7
Palestine Liberation Front, 38
Palestinian Liberation Organization
    Arab League recognition of, 42
    creation of, 29-35
    destruction of, 72
    Intifada and, 49
    Israeli attack on, 294
    as Jordan enemy, 88
    in Lebanon, 41-43, 46
    propaganda of, 44
    Soviet Union and, 45, 233, 238
    splinter groups of, 37-41
    statement of purpose of, 30-35
    Syrian control of, 349
    terrorism by, 44-46
Palestinian National Covenant, 30-35
Palestinian National Front, 39
Palestinian National Liberation
    Movement. See *Fatah*
Pamiat, as anti-Semitic organization,
    237
Pan-Arabism, 82
Peace
    outlook for, 356-358
    requirements for, 359-362
Peace for the Galilee War (1982), 46,
    72-74
    PLO destruction in, 355
    weapons used in, 233, 265-266
    weapons developments after, 326-327
Peoples Democratic Republic of
    Yemen. See South Yemen
Peres, Shimon, Jewish weapons industry
    and, 311
Persecution of Jews
    in Aden, 20
    in Algeria, 22-23
    by British, 206-209
    in Egypt, 21-22
    in Iraq, 20-21
    in Lebanon, 25
    in Libya, 25-26
    by Mohammed, 9-10
    in Morocco, 22
    by *mufti* of Jerusalem, 28-29, 208
    in Soviet Union, 233-235

in Syria, 24
in Tunisia, 23-24
in Yemen, 19-20
Persia, 187-188. *See also* Iran
Persian Gulf
    defense strategy for, 291
    mines in, 262
Personnel training for sophisticated
    weapons, 335-336
Pfeffer, Robert, 44
PGMs (precision-guided munitions),
    301-302
Philistines, Palestine name derived from,
    6
Pirates, Barbary, 177
PLO. *See* Palestinian Liberation
    Organization
Poland
    anti-Semitism in, 234
    power structure of, 227
Polisario, 178, 182
Popular Democratic Front for the
    Liberation of Palestine, 38
Popular Front for the Liberation of
    Oman, 159
Popular Front for the Liberation of
    Palestine, 37-38, 40
Popular Front for the Liberation of the
    Arabian Gulf, 159
Precision-guided munitions, 301-302
Project Council of Foreign Relations, on
    Middle East arms race, 308-310

Qabus ibn Sa'id, 159
Qaddafi, Mu'ammar, 99-102
    Jewish property confiscation by, 26
    popularity in Egypt, 64
    as Sadat nemesis, 349
Qassem, General, 92
Qatar
    Bahrain conflict with, 147
    future of, 156-157
    history of, 154-155
    present status of, 155-156

Rabat Conference of 1974, 42
Rahim, Sheikh Nusbi Aboul, 28
Railroads, German-built, 213
Rapid deployment force of Israel, 295,
    334-339
Ras al-Khaima, 150-151
Reagan administration
    Iraq-Iran War and, 287
    Israel policy of, 290-291

Israeli arms limitations by, 298, 325
Israeli weapons industry and, 312
Persian Gulf activity of, 292
al-Rishad family, 111-112
Robinson, Clarence, on technology
  transfer to Israel, 298
Roosevelt, Franklin D., on oil politics,
  241
RPVs (loitering weapons), 275-276,
  304-305, 337

al-Sabah Dynasty of Kuwait, 162-164
Sadat, Anwar, 60
  Begin Cairo trip and, 354
  Camp David Accords and, 346-350,
    352-354, 356
  Nazi sympathies of, 21-22
  socialism and, 62
  Soviet arms deal with, 61
  United States aid to, 291
Safavid Dynasty, 188
Said, Nuri, Jewish persecution by, 21
Sa'id ibn Taimur, 159
Al-Sa'iqa, 37-38
  cover for (Eagles of the Palestinian
    Revolution), 39
  in Lebanon, 42-43
Saleh, Ali-Abdullah, 169
al-Sallal, Abdullah, 168
SAM missiles
  effectiveness of, 275-277
  Soviet, 302-303
Samaria
  future of, 357
  Jewish settlement in, 355
San Remo Conference (1920), 14
Sanusi Brotherhood in Libya, 98
Saud family
  Egyptian conquest of, 109-110
  exile of (1891), 111
  Ibn Saud, 112-114, 134
  King Saud, 114-116, 134
  military expansion of, 109-110
  origin of, 108
  threats to, 141-142
Saudi Arabia
  development plans of, 119-120
  economic situation in, 133-136
  Egypt relations with, 65, 347
  external threats to, 140-141, 143-144
  foreign workers in, 120, 128, 139-140
  future of, 141-145
  history of, 107-127
  internal threats to, 139-140, 142
  middle class in, 121, 139, 142

military situation in, 136-141
political situation in, 129-133
present status of, 127-141
Qatar destiny and, 156
as "superpower," 278-279
Yemen involvement of, 168-169
Scud missile, 261
Shah of Iran
  father of Mohammed Reza, 188
  Mohammed Reza Pahlavi, 135, 137-
    138, 188, 190-191
Sharia law
  in Libya, 101
  in Saudi Arabia, 116, 130, 139
  in Sudan, 105
Sharjah, 150
Sheikdoms of United Arab Emirates,
  150-153
Shi'ites
  anti-secularism of, 330
  in Bahrain, 148-149
  civil disobedience promoted by, 49
  in Iran, 188-196
  in Iraq, 91, 94, 96, 196-197
  Iraq-Iran War and, 262, 285
  in Kuwait, 164-166
  in Lebanon, 70-71, 75-76
  organizational structure of, 188-189
  in Qatar, 155-156
  in Saudi Arabia, 128, 140
  Syrian support of, 81-82
  theology of, 195
  as threat to Soviet Union, 238
  in United Arab Emirates, 151, 153
  in Yemen, 20
  Zaydi sect, 168-171
Ships, vulnerability of, 264-265
SHORAD missile, 275
Shuquairy, Ahmed, 35, 48
Sib, Treaty of (1920), 159
Sidra, Gulf of, U.S.-Libyan
  confrontation in, 99, 264
Sinai, return to Egypt, 350-351, 353-
  354
Sinai Campaign (1956), 60
  British involvement in, 210
  Sino-Japanese War, weapons used in,
    255
Six-Day War (1967), 87
  Nasser role in, 61
  PLO and, 36-37
  Saudi Arabia policy after, 134
  Soviet Union influence in, 232
  weapons used in, 257
Slansky Trial, 234

382 / Index

Socialism
  in Libya, 101-102
  in Tunisia, 186
South Yemen
  future of, 175
  history of, 172-173
  Libyan alliance with, 100
  as North Yemen threat, 170-171,
    173-175
  present status of, 173-175
  Saudi Arabia involvement with, 122,
    124
Soviet Union
  Afghanistan invasion of, 220-222,
    259-260
  bureaucracy of, 224-226
  Chinese view of, 244
  Egypt arms deal with, 60-61
  imperialism of, 218-222
  internal purges in, 223, 228
  Israel relations with
    future of, 237-239
    history of, 231-235
    military capability and, 293-294
    present status of, 235-236
    support by, 243-244
  Jews in
    doctors' plot and, 229, 234-235
    post-revolutionary period, 234-235
    pre-revolutionary period, 233-234
  middle class in, 223
  Middle East involvement of, 229-230,
    348
  military buildup in, 224-226
  missile defense system of, 302-303
  political structure of, 223-229
  Saudi Arabia relations with, 124
  similarities to Iran, 227-228
  South Yemen influences of, 172-175
  technological gap in, 236-238
  terrorism support by, 45
  weapons of
    C-3I, 280
    inferiority of, 236
    sales to Arabs, 231-232, 299, 311,
      325
    Zionism in, 233-234
Spain, Algerian involvement of, 177
Spanish Sahara, disputes over, 181
Stalin, Joseph
  collective farms established by, 223
  imperialistic actions of, 219-220
  Jewish doctors' plot and, 229, 234-
    235
  Kazakhstan slaughter and, 221

purges of, 223, 228
  Jewish community, 234-235
  resettlement programs of, 228-229
Star Wars, 271
Stark, U.S.S., attack on, 264
Strategic Defense Initiative, 271
Submarines, advantages of, 265
Sudan
  Egypt relations with, 65, 67, 348
  future of, 105-106
  history of, 103-104
  present status of, 104-105
Suez Canal
  British control of, 205
  nationalization of, 60, 209-210
  Soviet Union military presence at,
    232
Suez Canal War (1968-1970), 61
Suleiman the Magnificent, 91-92
Sultan, Prince (Saudi Arabia), 125
Sunnis
  in Algeria, 178
  in Bahrain, 148
  in Egypt, 62-64, 66-67
  in Iraq, 94-96
  in Jordan, 87
  Khomeini opposition to, 194-195
  in Kuwait, 164
  in Lebanon, 71, 75-76
  in Libya, 101-102
  in North Yemen, 168-169
  in Qatar, 155
  in Saudi Arabia. See Wahhabiism
  in South Yemen, 173
  in Sudan, 104-105
  in Syria, 79-82
  in Turkey, 216
  in United Arab Emirates, 151, 153
Sweidan, Col. Ahmad, Fatah creation
  and, 35
Sykes-Picot Agreement, 211-212
Syria. See also Hussein, Saddam
  Fatah creation in, 35-37
  future status of, 81-83
  history of, 78-79
  immigration from, 15
  involvement in Lebanon, 75-77
  Jewish community of, 24
  Jordan relations with, 88
  military humiliation of (1982), 72-73
  present status of, 79-81
  in United Arab Republic, 60

Tactical antiballistic defenses, 308
Tactical cruise missiles, 302-303

Tactical military power, definition of, 279-281
Tanks
British deception and, 311, 323
first use of, 256
Israeli-produced, 313
vulnerability of, 305-306
Technology, impact on Israel, 340-344
Terrorism. *See also* Palestinian Liberation Organization
in journalism, 44
organizations for, 37-41
Saudi Arabian support of, 130-131
in Soviet Union, 223, 228
Soviet Union support of, 233
Theocracy
in Iran, 190-191, 227-228
in Soviet Union, atheism and, 227-228
Tlemcen, Algeria, Jewish persecution at, 23
Toolan, Sevn, 44
Tourism in Saudi Arabia, 133
Training for sophisticated weapons, 335-336
Transjordan. *See also* Jordan; Palestine
citizenship in, 48
establishment of, 14, 206
history of, 85-86
Treaty of Sib (1920), 159
Tripoli, as PLO base, 43
Tripolitania, 97-98
Trotsky, Leon, 234
Truman, Harry S., Israeli arms embargo of, 297, 322
Tunisia
future of, 186
history of, 184-186
Jewish community of, 23-24
PLO based in, 46, 185
Israeli air strike on, 294
Turkey, Middle East involvement of, 216-217. *See also* Ottoman Empire
Turki, as Saudi leader, 110

Ukraine, Jewish pogroms in, 233
Umayyad Dynasty, 78, 91
Umm al Qaiwain, 150
United Arab Emirates
future of, 153
history of, 150-151
present status of, 151-153
United Arab Republic, 60, 78-79
United Arab States, creation of, 60

United Nations, Arafat appearance before, 45
United States
Camp David Accords and, 346, 350, 352-353
Iran support by, 137
Iraq policy of, 291-292
Israel arms deal with, 61
Israel image influenced by, 243
Israel relations with, 252, 327-329
Israeli military capability and, 294-295
Lebanon intervention by, 71, 73-74
Libyan confrontation of, 99-100, 264
Middle East political influence of, 328-329
military resources of, 277-278
oil politics and, 241-242
Oman cooperation with, 161
Persian Gulf military presence of, 138
policy failures of, 242
Saudi Arabia relations with, 113, 117-118, 122-125, 132-133, 138
technology from, 341
weapons of
C-3I, 280
sales of, 298-299, 323-326, 330-331

Vanguards of the Popular Liberation War, 37-38
Vietnam, Chinese invasion of, 246
Vietnam War
United States failure in, 288-289
United States military resources after, 278
weapons used in, 257

al-Wahhabi, Prophet Mohammed ibn Abd, 108
Wahhabiism
decline of, 111
founding of, 108
militant brethren of, 113
present membership of, 128
principles of, 108-109
spread of, 109-110
Wanti-Tol, 40
War of Attrition (1968-1970), weapons used in, 257
Weapons
of Afghanistan War, 259-260
area, 303-304
arms race and, 308-310

development of, consumer benefits
   from, 341-342
evolution of, 254-267, 300-301
of Falkland War, 263-265
in feudal societies, 321
financial burden of, 338
force multiplier effectiveness of, 273
of France, 268
of Hannibal, 254
of Hyksos, 254
innovations in, 254-255
of Iraq-Iran War, 260-263, 273, 284,
   319-320
of Israel, 245, 277-279. *See also*
   specific war
C-3I, 280
critical materials for, 307-308
designed to destroy other weapons,
   341
electronic components for, 307
expansion of, 291-292
imported, 322-326
      from Czechoslovakia, 231
      from United States, 298-299
   independence in, 271-272
local consumption of, 342
manufacture of, 326-327
new developments in, 268-270
nuclear, 326
products list, 312-314
sales of, 312, 316, 342
      to Third World countries,
         332-333
   self-sufficiency in
      levels of, 315
      military industry in, 306-308,
         310-316
      reasons for, 297-299, 322-324
      technology and, 299-300
   spending for, 279
   technologic changes in, 267-269
   for twenty-first century, 272-276
of Korean War, 256-257
loitering, 275-276, 304-305, 337
against massed troops, 273-274
national will and, 280
new types of, 301-305
nuclear, 320, 326
obsolescence of, 265
of Peace for Galilee War, 265-266
personnel needed for, 335-336
present-day, 266-272
in rapid deployment force, 334-339
research on, 306-308

sales of
   after Yom Kippur War, 325-326
   to Arabs, 318-320
scientific base for, 279-280
self-sufficiency in, 315. *See also*
   Weapons, of Israel, self-sufficiency
   in
of Sino-Japanese War, 255
of Six-Day War, 257
sophisticated
   simple application of, 260-262
   for Third World countries,
      331-332
tactical, definition of, 279-281
training requirements for, 335-336
of twenty-first century, 272-276
of United States, 280, 298-299, 323-
   326, 330-331
of Vietnam War, 257
of War of Attrition (1968-1970), 257
of World War I, 255-256
of World War II, 254-256
of Yom Kippur War, 258-259, 324-
   325
Weizmann, General Chaim, 210
West Bank
   PLO murders in, 46
   Rabat Conference and, 42
   Transjordan takeover of, 86
White Paper of 1939, 16-17, 208-209
World War I, weapons used in, 255-
   256
World War II
   Jewish refugees in, 16-17, 207-209
   Libyan battles of, 98
   Libyan Jews fate in, 25-26
   Saudi Arabia neutrality in, 113
   weapons used in, 256

Yamani, Oil Minister, 125-126
Yemen. *See also* North Yemen; South
   Yemen
   Egyptian fighting in, 60-61
   Jewish community of, 19-20
   in United Arab States, 60
Yom Kippur War (1973), 61-62
   black African nations break with
      Israel after, 354-355
   Egyptian losses in, 346-347
   lessons learned from, 337
   oil embargo after, 134-135
   Soviet Union weapons in, 232
   weapons deals after, 298-299, 325-
      326

weapons used in, 258-259, 324-325

Zaydi sect of Islam, 168-171
Zionism
British policy toward, 206-208
as competitor of Communism, 235

German attitude toward, 214
in Soviet Union, pre-revolutionary,
233-234
Soviet Union policy toward, 230-232
Zoroastrianism, 187-188